AI-Driven Digital Twin and Industry 4.0

This book presents the role of AI-Driven Digital Twin in the Industry 4.0 ecosystem by focusing on Smart Manufacturing, sustainable development, and many other applications. It also discusses different case studies and presents an in-depth understanding of the benefits and limitations of using AI and Digital Twin for industrial developments.

AI-Driven Digital Twin and Industry 4.0: A Conceptual Framework with Applications introduces the role of Digital Twin in Smart Manufacturing and focuses on the Digital Twin framework throughout. It provides a summary of the various AI applications in the Industry 4.0 environment and emphasizes the role of advanced computational and communication technologies. The book offers demonstrative examples of AI-Driven Digital Twin in various application domains and includes AI techniques used to analyze the environmental impact of industrial operations along with examples. The book reviews the major challenges in the deployment of AI-Driven Digital Twin in the Industry 4.0 ecosystem and presents an understanding of how AI is used in the designing of Digital Twin for various applications. The book also enables familiarity with various industrial applications of computational and communication technologies and summarizes the ongoing research and innovations in the areas of AI, Digital Twin, and Smart Manufacturing while also tracking the various research challenges along with future advances.

This reference book is a must-read and is very beneficial to students, researchers, academicians, industry experts, and professionals working in related fields.

Intelligent Manufacturing and Industrial Engineering

Series Editor: Ahmed A. Elngar, Beni-Suef University, Egypt
Mohamed Elhoseny, Mansoura University, Egypt

Machine Learning Adoption in Blockchain-Based Intelligent Manufacturing
Edited by Om Prakash Jena, Sabyasachi Pramanik and Ahmed A. Elngar

Integration of AI-Based Manufacturing and Industrial Engineering Systems with the Internet of Things
Edited by Pankaj Bhambri, Sita Rani, Valentina E. Balas and Ahmed A. Elngar

AI-Driven Digital Twin and Industry 4.0: A Conceptual Framework with Applications
Edited by Sita Rani, Pankaj Bhambri, Sachin Kumar, Piyush Kumar Pareek and Ahmed A. Elngar

Technology Innovation Pillars for Industry 4.0: Challenges, Improvements, and Case Studies
Edited by Ahmed A. Elngar, N. Thillaiarasu, T. Saravanan and Valentina Emilia Balas

For more information about this series, please visit: https://www.routledge.com/Mathematical-Engineering-Manufacturing-and-Management-Sciences/book-series/CRCIMIE

AI-Driven Digital Twin and Industry 4.0

A Conceptual Framework with Applications

Edited by
Sita Rani
Pankaj Bhambri
Sachin Kumar
Piyush Kumar Pareek
Ahmed A. Elngar

CRC Press
Taylor & Francis Group
Boca Raton London New York

CRC Press is an imprint of the
Taylor & Francis Group, an **informa** business

Designed cover image: Shutterstock – Photon photo

First edition published 2024
by CRC Press
2385 NW Executive Center Drive, Suite 320, Boca Raton FL 33431

and by CRC Press
4 Park Square, Milton Park, Abingdon, Oxon, OX14 4RN

CRC Press is an imprint of Taylor & Francis Group, LLC

© 2024 selection and editorial matter, Sita Rani, Pankaj Bhambri, Sachin Kumar, Piyush Kumar Pareek, and Ahmed A. Elngar; individual chapters, the contributors

ISBN: 978-1-032-49473-9 (hbk)
ISBN: 978-1-032-49783-9 (pbk)
ISBN: 978-1-003-39541-6 (ebk)

DOI: 10.1201/9781003395416

Typeset in Times
by MPS Limited, Dehradun

Contents

Chapter 4   Digital Twin Technology: A Review 49

Ambika Nagaraj

Chapter 14 Environmental Impacts of Industrial Processes in Industry 4.0
Ecosystem: Artificial Intelligence Approach 221

*Pankaj Bhambri, Sita Rani, Inderjit Singh Dhanoa,
and Tien Anh Tran*

Chapter 15 Digital Twin for Sustainable Industrial Development 241

Rachna Rana and Pankaj Bhambri

B. N. Chandrashekhar, H. A. Sanjay, and V. Geetha

Shilpa Mayannavar and Uday Wali

Preface

Welcome to the academic book titled AI-Driven Digital Twin and Industry 4.0: A Conceptual Framework with Applications. This literary work delves into the revolutionary convergence of artificial intelligence (AI), digital twins, and Industry 4.0, providing a detailed examination of the theoretical underpinnings and practical implementations within this swiftly advancing domain.

As we transition into the era of Industry 4.0, which is distinguished by the incorporation of digital technology into manufacturing and industrial operations, the necessity for inventive resolutions becomes progressively apparent. The core of this transition is centered upon the notion of a digital twin, which refers to a virtual replication of a physical system or process. This digital twin is augmented and supplemented with real-time data and capabilities powered by AI. The integration of AI with digital twin technologies holds the potential to significantly transform various industries, encompassing manufacturing, healthcare, energy, and transportation. The objective of this book is to offer readers a coherent and organized conceptual framework that facilitates their understanding of the key ideas, processes, and strategies that form the foundation of this revolution.

The target audience of this book encompasses a broad spectrum, ranging from scholars and learners to practitioners and experts in the fields of research, education, engineering, and industry. The book aims to provide comprehensive insights into the interplay between AI, digital twins, and the Fourth Industrial Revolution, also known as Industry 4.0.

We would like to extend our sincere appreciation to the multitude of persons and organizations that have made invaluable contributions to the production of this book. The proficiency, assistance, and commitment provided by the individuals involved have been of immense use in actualizing this project.

About the Editors

Dr. Sita Rani is a faculty member in the Department of Computer Science and Engineering at Guru Nanak Dev Engineering College, Ludhiana. She earned her PhD in Computer Science and Engineering from I.K. Gujral Punjab Technical University, Kapurthala, Punjab in 2018. She has also completed a post graduate certificate program in Data Science and Machine Learning at the Indian Institute of Technology, Roorkee in 2023. She completed her postdoc at the Big Data Mining and Machine Learning Lab, South Ural State University, Russia, in August 2023. She has more than 20 years of teaching experience. She is an active member of ISTE, IEEE, and IAEngg. She is the receiver of ISTE Section Best Teacher Award – 2020, and International Young Scientist Award – 2021. She has contributed to various research activities while publishing articles in renowned SCI and Scopus journals and conference proceedings. She has published seven international patents and authored, edited and coedited seven books. Dr. Rani has delivered many expert talks in A.I.C.T.E. sponsored faculty development programs and key note talks at many national and international conferences. She has also organized many international conferences during her 20 years of teaching experience. She is a member of the editorial boards and reviewer of many international journals of repute. She is also the vice president of SME and MSME (UT Council), Women Indian Chamber of Commerce and Industry (WICCI) for the last three years. Her research interests include Parallel and Distributed Computing, Data Science, Machine Learning, Internet of Things (IoT), and Smart Healthcare.

Dr. Pankaj Bhambri is affiliated with the Department of Information Technology at Guru Nanak Dev Engineering College in Ludhiana. Additionally, he fulfills the role of the Convener for his Departmental Board of Studies. He possesses nearly two decades of teaching experience. He is an active member of IE India, ISTE New Delhi, IIIE Navi Mumbai, IETE New Delhi and CSI Mumbai. He has contributed to the various research activities while publishing articles in the renowned SCIE and Scopus journals and conference proceedings. He has also published several international patents. Dr. Bhambri has garnered extensive experience in the realm of academic publishing, having served as an editor and author for a multitude of books in collaboration with esteemed publishing houses such as CRC Press, Elsevier, Scrivener, and Bentham Science. Dr. Bhambri has been honored with several prestigious accolades, including the ISTE Best Teacher Award in 2023 and 2022, the I2OR National Award in 2020, the Green ThinkerZ Top 100 International Distinguished Educators award in 2020, the I2OR Outstanding Educator Award in

2019, the SAA Distinguished Alumni Award in 2012, the CIPS Rashtriya Rattan Award in 2008, the LCHC Best Teacher Award in 2007, and numerous other commendations from various government and non-profit organizations. He has provided guidance and oversight for numerous research projects and dissertations at the postgraduate and PhD levels. He successfully organized a diverse range of educational programmes, securing financial backing from esteemed institutions such as the AICTE, the TEQIP, among others. Dr. Bhambri's areas of interest encompass machine learning, bioinformatics, wireless sensor networks, and network security.

Dr. Sachin Kumar is a professor and leading researcher in the laboratory of Big Data and Machine Learning at South Ural State University (National Research University), Chelyabinsk, Russia. He earned his PhD in Data Mining at IIT Roorkee, India, in 2017 under an MHRD fellowship. He then worked as a postdoctoral fellow at National University of Science and Technology, MISiS, Moscow, Russia, where he received the young scientist award of 4.2 million Russian rubles. Besides, he is a visiting professor at National University of Science and Technology, MISiS, Moscow Russia and West Kazakhstan State University, Uralsk. He has around 15 years of Academics, Research and Administrative experience. He has also worked in several government funded research projects as PI/CoPI. Dr. Sachin has delivered various talks at international conferences as a keynote speaker. He was also a session chair, technical program committee member at several conferences. He is also the member of the PhD dissertation council at South Ural State University and Chelyabinsk State University, Russia. He also delivered expert talks in various AICTE sponsored Faculty Development Programs at various Institutes in India. He is a member of editorial/ reviewer committee of various reputed journals including IEEE, Springer, and Elsevier. His major research interests fall within Artificial Intelligence for Smart Healthcare, Smart Transportation, and Smart Industries.

Dr. Piyush Kumar Pareek has an interest in continuous learning and teaching. He completed his BE, MTech, PhD, Post Doc (Post-Doctoral fellowship at Instituto Federal do Ceará, Public university in Limoeiro do Norte, Brazil) in the field of Computer Science Engineering. He is a registered patent agent, Govt of India and has 12+ years of teaching experience. Dr. Pareek has published 80+ research articles in Scopus indexed journals/conferences. He has also published 10+ textbooks and has 50+ industrial designs registered at the Indian Patent Office. He has 25+ international patents granted, filed and published 50+ Indian utility patents, and is now guiding PhD scholars at Visvesvaraya Technological University, Belagavi. He has awarded six PhD students at VTU and is a senior member in IEEE and MIE. Dr. Pareek is a reviewer for international refereed journals as well and serves the National Crime Control Board (NGO) as assistant director in Social Service Cell Bengaluru North.

Dr. Ahmed A. Elngar is an associate professor and head of the Computer Science Department at the Faculty of Computers and Artificial Intelligence, Beni-Suef University, Egypt. Dr. Elngar is also an associate professor of Computer Science at the College of Computer Information Technology and the American University in the Emirates, United Arab Emirates. Dr. Elngar is also adjunct professor at the School of Technology, Woxsen University, India. He is the founder and head of the Scientific Innovation Research Group (SIRG) and a Director of the Technological and Informatics Studies Center (TISC), Faculty of Computers and Artificial Intelligence, Beni-Suef University. Dr. Elngar has more than 106 scientific research papers published in prestigious international journals and over 25 books covering such diverse topics as data mining, intelligent systems, social networks, and the smart environment. Dr. Elngar is a collaborative researcher and a member of the Egyptian Mathematical Society (EMS) and the International Rough Set Society (IRSS). His other research areas include the Internet of Things (IoT), network security, intrusion detection, Machine Learning, data mining, Artificial Intelligence, Big Data, authentication, cryptology, healthcare systems, and automation systems. He is an editor and reviewer of many international journals around the world. He has won several awards, including the "Young Researcher in Computer Science Engineering," from Global Outreach Education Summit and Awards 2019, on 31 January 2019 in Delhi, India. He has also been awarded the "Best Young Researcher Award (Male) (Below 40 years)," Global Education and Corporate Leadership Awards (GECL–2018).

Contributors

Sundaravadivazhagan Balasubramanian
University of Technology and Applied Sciences
Al Mussanah, Oman

Pankaj Bhambri
Guru Nanak Dev Engineering College Ludhiana
Punjab, India

Ashima Bhatnagar Bhatia
Vivekananda Institute of Professional Studies-TC
New Delhi, India

Dileep Reddy Bolla
NITTE Meenakshi Institute of Technology Bangalore
Karnataka, India

Latha C.A.
RV Institute of Technology and Management Bangalore
Karnataka, India

B.N. Chandrashekhar
BMS Institute of Technology and Management, Bangalore
Karnataka, India

Inderjit Singh Dhanoa
Guru Nanak Dev Engineering College, Ludhiana
Punjab, India

Elakkiya Elango
Government Arts College for Women, Sivaganga
Tamilnadu, India

V. Geetha
Reva University, Bangalore
Karnataka, India

Aman Kataria
Amity University, Noida
Uttar Pradesh, India

Jaskiran Kaur
Guru Nanak Dev Engineering College Ludhiana
Punjab, India

Alex Khang
Global Research Institute of Technology and Engineering
Fort Raleigh City,
North Carolina, USA

Suresh Kumar
Geeta University, Panipat
Haryana, India

B.A. Manjunatha
NITTE Meenakshi Institute of Technology, Bangalore
Karnataka, India

Shilpa Mayannavar
The University of Sydney
Sydney, Australia

Venugopal Reddy Modhugu
Oracle Cloud Infrastructure
Fairfax, Virginia, USA

Ambika Nagaraj
St. Francis College, Bangalore
Karnataka, India

Ramesh Naidu
NITTE Meenakshi Institute of
  Technology, Bangalore
Karnataka, India

Gnanasankaran Natarajan
Thiagarajar College, Madurai
Tamilnadu, India

N.C. Naveen
JSS Academy of Technical Education,
  Bangalore
Karnataka, India

Piyush Kumar Pareek
NITTE Meenakshi Institute of
  Technology, Bangalore
Karnataka, India

Malini M. Patil
RV Institute of Technology and
  Management, Bangalore
Karnataka, India

K.R. Pradeep
BMS Institute of Technology and
  Management, Bangalore
Karnataka, India

Preethi Prerana
NITTE Meenakshi Institute of
  Technology, Bangalore
Karnataka, India

P. Priyanga
RNS Institute of Technology,
  Bangalore
Karnataka, India

Vikram Puri
Duy Tan University
Danang, Vietnam

Rachna Rana
Ludhiana Group of Colleges, Ludhiana
Punjab, India

Sita Rani
Guru Nanak Dev Engineering College,
  Ludhiana
Punjab, India

H.A. Sanjay
M.S. Ramaiah Institute of Technology,
  Bangalore
Karnataka, India

K. Aditya Shastry
NITTE Meenakshi Institute of
  Technology, Bangalore
Karnataka, India

Maninder Pal Singh
I.K. Gujral Punjab Technical
  University, Kapurthala
Punjab, India

Vijay Kumar Sinha
Chitkara University, Baddi
Himachal Pradesh, India

Sandhya Soman
GITAM (Deemed-to-be) University,
  Bangalore
Karnataka, India

Rashmi Soni
Dayananda Sagar Academy of
  Technology & Management,
  Bangalore
Karnataka, India

Tien Anh Tran
Seoul National University
Seoul, South Korea

Uday Wali
KLE Technological University,
    Hubballi
Karnataka, India

Pawan Whig
Vivekananda Institute of Professional
    Studies-TC
New Delhi, India

Nikhitha Yathiraju
University of Cumberlands
    Williamsburg, Kentucky, USA

1 Industry 4.0

Framework and Applications

Sita Rani and Pankaj Bhambri

1.1 INTRODUCTION

Industry 4.0, also known as the Fourth Industrial Revolution, describes the continual change of businesses as a result of the use of cutting-edge digital technologies (Kataria, Agrawal, Rani, Karar, & Chauhan, 2022). The convergence of cyber-physical systems (CPS), Internet of Things (IoT), cloud computing, artificial intelligence (AI), and big data analytics have made this possible, marking a significant shift in manufacturing and production processes (Bali, Bali, Gaur, Rani, & Kumar, 2023; Puri, Kataria, Solanki, & Rani, 2022). Industry 4.0 is based on the idea that fully automated, networked, and smart "smart factories" will revolutionize the manufacturing sector (Ghobakhloo, 2020). To improve industrial operations' productivity, efficiency, and adaptability, it makes use of cutting-edge technologies. Industry 4.0 facilitates effective interaction between all participants in the value chain by integrating digital and physical systems (Bai, Dallasega, Orzes, & Sarkis, 2020).

Key technologies driving Industry 4.0 include AI, which allows machines to learn, adapt, and perform tasks traditionally done by humans; big data analytics, which allows the collection and analysis of vast amounts of data to gain valuable insights and make informed decisions; cloud computing, which provides scalable computing power and storage capabilities; and the IoT, which connects physical devices and enables real-time data exchange (Chen et al., 2017).

The effects of Industry 4.0 will be seen for years to come. Manufacturing, logistics, healthcare, transportation, and energy are just some of the fields that stand to benefit greatly from its implementation (Bhambri & Gupta, 2005; Tanwar, Chhabra, Rattan, & Rani, 2022). Smart factories have the potential to streamline operations, boost quality assurance, and introduce mass customization (P. Kumar et al., 2022; Rani, Pareek, Kaur, Chauhan, & Bhambri, 2023). Supply chain integration improves operations, cuts costs, and paves the way for real-time inventory management. Telemedicine, remote monitoring, and individualized treatment are just a few examples of how Industry 4.0 might transform patient care (Kataria et al., 2022).

However, there are still things to think about and adjust in the face of Industry 4.0. Large sums must be spent on infrastructure, cybersecurity, and training new workers to successfully integrate cutting-edge technologies (P. Kumar et al., 2022). There are worries about data privacy, security, and the impact on jobs if specific jobs are automated or replaced by AI. Industry 4.0 can only reach its full potential if governments, firms, and individuals work together to create digital transformation strategies, encourage innovation, and facilitate a seamless transition. Investment in R&D, workforce development, and the creation of norms and standards that take into account ethical, legal, and social ramifications is essential (Contreras, Garcia, & Pastrana, 2017).

Industry 4.0 ushers in a new era of manufacturing and production enabled by ubiquitous connectivity and cutting-edge technologies. Successful adoption needs careful planning, collaboration, and adaptation to address the difficulties and opportunities it provides, but it has the potential to revolutionize sectors, boost productivity, and generate new opportunities (Bhambri et al., 2005).

1.2 CONCEPTUAL FRAMEWORK OF INDUSTRY 4.0

Industry 4.0's conceptual framework provides a theoretical platform for grasping the fundamentals of the Fourth Industrial Revolution (S. Kaur et al., 2022; Rani, Kataria, Kumar, & Tiwari, 2023). It includes many components that work together to determine how Industry 4.0 is implemented and what effects it has (S. Kaur et al., 2022).

The framework revolves around the idea of CPS, which refers to the fusion of analog and digital systems. Data gathering, analysis, and control in real time are the backbone of Industry 4.0, and CPS is the technology that makes it possible, as shown in Figure 1.1. It includes the IoT, sensors, robotics, and AI, all of which link physical items, gather data, and facilitate smart decision-making (Bhambri, Rani, Gupta, & Khang, 2022; Bilal, Kumari, & Rani, 2021). There are several other critical components around CPS that aid in the development of Industry 4.0 (D. Kaur, Singh, & Rani, 2023). One of these is big data analytics, which entails sifting through copious amounts of data for insights and using those findings to guide deliberation and action (Salkin, Oner, Ustundag, & Cevikcan, 2018). When it comes to processing and storing data, cloud computing plays a crucial role by providing scalable

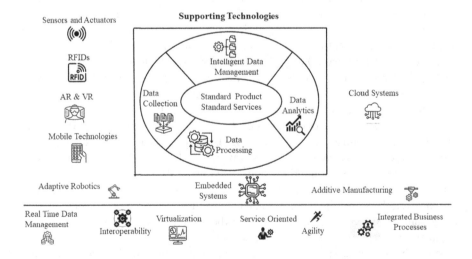

FIGURE 1.1 Industry 4.0: framework.

computing power and storage capacities (Rani, Kataria, & Chauhan, 2022b). The framework also includes consideration for horizontal and vertical integration. The term "vertical integration" is used to describe the close cooperation and coordination among all links in the value chain, from producers to buyers (Kataria, A., Agrawal, D., Rani, S., Karar, V., & Chauhan, M., 2022). Manufacturing, logistics, and marketing are just some of the internal business processes that benefit from horizontal integration (Bhambri & Bhandari, 2005).

The human element of Industry 4.0 is taken into account by the framework, which acknowledges the importance of having a trained and flexible staff. It stresses the need for workers to acquire new skills and retrain to take advantage of technological advancements (Saucedo-Martínez, Pérez-Lara, Marmolejo-Saucedo, Salais-Fierro, & Vasant, 2018). Industry 4.0 as a concept helps us see the big picture of what goes into the digital transformation of industries and how everything is connected (Kataria, Puri, Pareek, & Rani, 2023). It helps businesses and governments devise plans to take advantage of the potential and avoid the pitfalls of the Industry 4.0 era (Dhanalakshmi, Vijayaraghavan, Sivaraman, & Rani, 2022).

1.2.1 Key Principles

The concept of "Industry 4.0" refers to an overarching set of guidelines for the digitalization and networking of traditional economic sectors (Cañas, Mula, Díaz-Madroñero, & Campuzano-Bolarín, 2021). These guidelines are crucial for the efficient introduction of Industry 4.0 practices and methods. Some of the fundamental rules are as follows (Habib & Chimsom, 2019):

- **Interconnectivity.** The capacity of machines, devices, and systems to interact with one another and share data defines interconnectivity (Rani, Mishra, Kataria, Mallik, & Qin, 2023). The whole value chain may now communicate and share information without any hitches (Bhambri and Singh, 2005).
- **Information Transparency.** Manufacturing process information transparency refers to the availability of accurate and complete data in real time from a variety of sources (Kaur, D., Singh, B., & Rani, S., 2023). Stakeholders benefit from this openness because they can make better judgments and streamline processes (Singh et al., 2006).
- **Technical Assistance.** Assisting humans in their endeavors by employing cutting-edge technologies like AI, Machine Learning (ML), and robots is an example of technical help (Kumar, Rani, & Khangura, 2023). Help can come in many forms, from hands-on assistance in the factory to advice gleaned from data analysis and deliberation (Rani, Kumar, Kataria, & Min, 2023).
- **Decentralized Decision-Making.** Individual parts and systems are given decision-making authority, minimizing the requirement for top-down management. As a result, the manufacturing process can be more adaptable, agile, and responsive (Bhambri and Mangat, 2005).
- **Modularization.** Modularization refers to the practice of disassembling large, complex systems into smaller, reusable parts. This improves scalability and provides for adaptability to fluctuating needs.

- **Cybersecurity.** It refers to the practice of keeping digital assets safe from intrusion. Maintaining the trustworthiness of Industry 4.0 systems requires stringent cybersecurity precautions (Abrol et al., 2005).
- **Continuous Improvement.** Adopting a mindset that encourages constant growth and change. Data analytics and feedback loops are at the heart of Industry 4.0's commitment to continuous improvement (Kumar, R., Rani, S., & Khangura, S. S. (Eds.), 2023).

Through the use of these guidelines, traditional industries can be transformed into smart, linked ecosystems that can propel efficiency, productivity, and innovation in the age of Industry 4.0.

1.2.2 TECHNOLOGIES IN INDUSTRY 4.0

Integration of cutting-edge technologies with traditional industrial processes is a defining feature of the "Industry 4.0" paradigm. Increased efficiency, productivity, and adaptability are only a few of the outcomes of implementing these technologies across several business sectors (Bai et al., 2020). Some of the most important technologies in Industry 4.0 are discussed below:

- **CPS.** Integrating physical objects with digital technology to allow for real-time data interchange and automation, cyber-physical systems play a crucial role in Industry 4.0. Intelligent decision-making is facilitated by these systems, leading to increased productivity, efficiency, and connectivity in fields as varied as cutting-edge manufacturing, smart logistics, and driverless vehicles (Rani, Kataria, Chauhan, et al., 2022).
- **IoTs.** It is a key component of Industry 4.0 since it allows for the interconnection and automation of various devices, equipment, and sensors. Industrial operations may be monitored, controlled, and optimized in real time, leading to more output with less downtime (Kumar, Rani, & Awadh, 2022).
- **AI.** It is the capability of computers to mimic human intelligence. Algorithms trained by machine learning systems may sift through mountains of data in search of insights and opportunities for improvement. Automating difficult decision-making, improving quality control, and enabling predictive maintenance are all possible with AI-powered systems (Bhambri & Sharma, 2005).
- **Big Data Analytics.** Sensors, equipment, and production systems all contribute to Industry 4.0's massive data output, making it necessary to analyze this information. Data-driven decision-making, process optimization, and predictive maintenance are all made possible by the insights gleaned from this data thanks to the tools of big data analytics.
- **Robotics and Automation.** Industry 4.0's manufacturing processes have been completely transformed by robotics and automation technologies. Increased productivity, better product quality, and less human error are all possible thanks to the ability of robots to do repetitive operations with high precision and speed. Cobots are collaborative robots that improve

workplace safety and productivity by working in tandem with people (Goel & Gupta, 2020).

- **Additive Manufacturing.** It is also known as 3D printing and is a manufacturing technique that enables the production of three-dimensional things by superimposing successive layers of material according to computer-generated models. As a result, conventional production techniques are rendered unnecessary, and waste is cut down to manageable levels (Kataria, A., Puri, V., Pareek, P. K., & Rani, S., 2023, July).
- **Augmented Reality (AR)/Virtual Reality (VR).** Industry 4.0 makes use of augmented and virtual reality (AR/VR) technology to improve instruction, upkeep, and visualization (Tanwar, R., Chhabra, Y., Rattan, P., & Rani, S., 2022, September). AR uses digital information superimposed on the physical world to guide and teach workers in real time. VR generates photorealistic simulated settings, paving the way for online learning and distant teamwork (Machała, Chamier-Gliszczyński, & Królikowski, 2022).
- **Cybersecurity.** With Industry 4.0's emphasis on digitalization and connectivity, cyber security for factory networks and data is more important than ever (Rattan et al., 2005). Cybersecurity tools prevent hacking, data loss, and other malicious cyber activity. Encryption, authentication, and intrusion detection systems are just some of the methods used to keep the nation's backbone safe from harm (Rani, Kataria, & Chauhan, 2022a).
- **Cloud Computing.** It is a method of delivering scalable computing, storage, and service capabilities through the Internet rather than on-premises. It makes it easier for businesses to store data, analyze it, and work together in Industry 4.0. Data processing, remote monitoring, and global teamwork are all made possible by cloud-based platforms in real time.
- **Digital Twin.** A digital twin is an electronic copy of a real-world product, service, or system. To build a digital duplicate, it combines data from sensors in real time with simulation models. Reduced downtime and increased productivity are two of the many benefits that come from using digital twins for predictive maintenance, optimization, and simulation.
- **Blockchain.** It is a distributed ledger that may be used to securely record and verify transactions with a high level of anonymity. It is ideal for use in Industry 4.0 supply chain management, product verification, and IP protection due to its transparency, traceability, and immutability (Gupta & Bhambri, 2006).

Traditional industries are being transformed by these technologies, making them more nimble, efficient, and adaptable to the digital age (Singh et al., 2005). Manufacturing and industrial processes will undergo a dramatic transformation as a result of Industry 4.0, creating new opportunities for growth and development (Jain & Bhambri, 2005). By adopting these innovations, businesses may realize the full potential of Industry 4.0 and maintain competitiveness in the global economy of the future. Prominent Industry 4.0 technologies and their applications in various domains are summarized in Table 1.1.

TABLE 1.1

Industry 4.0 Technologies and Their Roles (Domain Wise)

Industry 4.0 Technology	Role in Manufacturing	Role in Healthcare	Role in Transportation	Role in Smart Cities
Internet of Things (IoT)	• Real-time monitoring of production processes • Predictive maintenance	• Remote patient monitoring and telemedicine • Data-driven treatment plans	• Smart logistics and routing for efficient transport • Connected vehicles and autonomous transportation	• Smart energy management and waste management • Public safety and security • Efficient urban planning
AI	• Quality control and defect detection • Predictive analytics for product optimization	• Medical image analysis and diagnosis • Personalized medicine and treatment recommendations	• Autonomous vehicle control • Smart traffic management • Predictive maintenance for transportation systems	• Predictive maintenance and anomaly detection • Environment monitoring and pollution control
Big Data Analytics	• Data-driven decision-making and optimization	• Health data analysis and population health insights	• Supply chain optimization • Demand forecasting	• Urban planning and development • Smart resource allocation
Robotics and Automation	• Automated assembly and material handling • Collaborative robots for human-robot interaction	• Robotic surgeries and rehabilitation • Patient care assistance	• Autonomous drones for delivery and surveillance • Smart warehouses	• Automated waste collection and recycling • Intelligent manufacturing and distribution systems
Additive Manufacturing	• Rapid prototyping and product development • On-demand spare parts and localized production	• Customized medical devices • Bioprinting of tissues	• 3D-printed spare parts	• On-demand infrastructure and construction
Cloud Computing	• Scalable data storage and preprocessing • Real-time collaboration	• Secure medical data sharing	• Connected vehicle data storage and processing • Real-time traffic data and analysis	• Centralized data management and analysis for smart services

Cybersecurity	• Protect critical manufacturing data • Prevents cyberattacks and data breaches	• Secure patient data and healthcare infrastructure	• Ensures secure vehicle communications and systems	• Secure smart city systems and networks
Augmented Reality	• Training and guidance for workers in manufacturing • Enhanced Product design and visualization	• Surgical planning and navigation • Remote patient care and training	• Maintenance and repair assistance for vehicles	• Navigation and location-based information services • Virtual tourism and experience
Virtual Reality	• Virtual product prototyping and testing • Immersive training for complex tasks	• Medical simulation and habitation	• Training for drivers and operators • Realistic driving simulators	• Urban planning and design visualization
Blockchain	• Smart contracts for automated transactions		• Blockchain-based identity verification	

1.3 APPLICATIONS OF INDUSTRY 4.0

The incorporation of cutting-edge technology such as the IoT, AI, big data, robotics, and more is at the heart of Industry 4.0, which is causing widespread disruption across many industries (Singh et al., 2004). This new paradigm has far-reaching consequences in many fields (Yadav et al., 2022). Several important industries and their potential benefits from adopting Industry 4.0 are discussed below:

- **Manufacturing and Production.** The introduction of Industry 4.0 technologies has resulted in dramatic changes throughout the manufacturing sector. To improve machine uptime and decrease the need for emergency repairs, smart factories use IoT sensors to track and record data in real time (Kothandaraman et al., 2022). Automating mundane operations using AI and ML-enabled robots boosts productivity, cuts down on mistakes, and raises the bar for quality control. With more adaptable production methods, businesses may more easily cater to the unique needs of their clientele through the use of customization (Gupta et al., 2007).
- **Supply Chain and Logistics.** Supply chain management has been optimized and made more efficient thanks to Industry 4.0. Goods may be tracked in real time thanks to the IoT sensors and gadgets that are built into them. Thanks to this improved oversight, management of both time and stock can be improved. AI and big data analytics allow businesses to anticipate shifts in consumer demand and quickly adjust operations (Bhambri et al., 2007).
- **Healthcare.** Telemedicine and other forms of remote patient monitoring have flourished as a result of Industry 4.0's implementations in the healthcare industry. Continuous health tracking is made possible by IoT devices, wearables, and connected medical equipment, which makes remote patient monitoring much simpler (P. Kumar et al., 2022; Rani, Kataria, et al., 2023). Algorithms powered by artificial intelligence examine massive volumes of patient data in search of trends that can aid in diagnosis. Care for patients, as well as the number of times they have to go to the hospital, benefit from this data-driven strategy (Bathla et al., 2007).
- **Agriculture.** Agriculture 4.0 is one example of how the Fourth Industrial Revolution has influenced formerly static industries. Information on soil quality, crop development, and weather patterns are all made available to farmers thanks to IoT devices, drones, and AI-powered analytics. By using this data-driven method, farmers may increase crop productivity while decreasing their footprint on the environment and wasting fewer resources, such as water and fertilizers. By having access to this data, farmers will be able to make more productive and long-lasting choices (Bhambri et al., 2008).
- **Energy and Utilities.** Industry 4.0 methods are used to enhance grid management and reduce energy waste in the energy industry. To better balance electricity supply and demand, smart grids use IoT sensors to track use in real time. As a result, there is less wasted energy and better energy

distribution. To further assure a steady and consistent energy supply, predictive maintenance of power plants and renewable energy sources is essential (Bhambri & Singh, 2008).

- **Transportation.** The transportation industry will be profoundly affected by Industry 4.0, especially with the advent of autonomous cars. AI algorithms and IoT sensors powering self-driving cars and trucks hold the promise of making transportation both safer and more efficient. Fleet management software optimizes itineraries and timetables to cut down on pollution and fuel costs. IoT-enabled traffic control solutions also help reduce congestion and boost mobility in congested urban areas.
- **Smart Cities.** The notion of "smart cities" centers on the adoption of Industry 4.0 solutions in urban planning and design. The city is filled with IoT devices and sensors that monitor things like traffic, air quality, trash management, and energy use. With this information, city planners may make choices that are more likely to result in better services, less damage to the environment, and a higher quality of life for residents (Dhanalakshmi et al., 2022; Rani et al., 2021).
- **Education.** Education is also affected by Industry 4.0, which drives new approaches to teaching and learning. Adaptive learning platforms driven by AI provide pupils with individualized curriculums that take into account their unique needs. Immersive educational experiences made possible by VR and AR technologies increase student engagement and participation. Data analytics also allows teachers to monitor student progress and zero in on problem areas (Chauhan & Rani, 2021).

In conclusion, Industry 4.0 is transforming many areas, creating new opportunities, and enhancing productivity, sustainability, and quality of life. Industries may prosper in the fast-paced, interconnected environment of the Fourth Industrial Revolution by adopting cutting-edge technologies and utilizing data-driven insights. To create a more innovative, connected, and affluent future in the face of these technologies' ongoing evolution, enterprises, governments, and individuals must exploit the potential given by Industry 4.0 while addressing the difficulties.

1.4 MAJOR CHALLENGES IN DEPLOYING INDUSTRY 4.0 APPLICATIONS

Many obstacles must be overcome before organizations and industries can fully take advantage of the opportunities presented by Industry 4.0 applications. The following significant hurdles must be examined and overcome for the successful implementation of Industry 4.0, despite its promise of enhanced efficiency, production, and innovation:

- **Cost of Investment.** Investing in the necessary infrastructure, hardware, software, and trained staff is usually necessary to implement Industry 4.0 technology. The entry price may be too high for many firms, especially for startups and Small and Medium Enterprises(SMEs). To maximize their return on investment, businesses must first build efficient plans for using these technologies (Bhambri et al., 2008).

- **Legacy System Integration.** It is possible that present manufacturing and industrial processes will not be able to make use of Industry 4.0 technologies since they rely on legacy systems and equipment. As a result, it is important to plan and allocate sufficient resources for the integration of new technologies with existing systems.

- **Data Privacy and Security.** Data gathering and analysis are crucial to many Industry 4.0 applications. Data privacy and security are at risk because of this deluge of information. Strong cybersecurity procedures are a must for companies to secure their customers' personal information from hackers and other cybercriminals.

- **Workforce Skill Set and Training.** A trained workforce that can operate, maintain, and debug complex systems is essential for the widespread implementation of Industry 4.0 technology. To guarantee that their personnel can make good use of emerging technologies, businesses should spend on training and upskilling.

- **Change Management.** Large-scale shifts in productivity, personnel composition, and management structure may result from adopting Industry 4.0. Employee and stakeholder resistance to change is a potential barrier to a smooth rollout. To overcome opposition and cultivate a culture of innovation and adaptation, effective change management tactics are required.

- **Interoperability and Standards.** There is a large variety of Industry 4.0 technologies and solutions on the market, which makes ensuring their compatibility difficult. Incompatibilities and difficulties in integrating multiple systems into one another might arise from a lack of common standards and protocols.

- **Connectivity and Infrastructure.** The success of Industry 4.0 applications is dependent on secure and stable network connections. The full potential of these technologies may be constrained by the lack of access to high-speed Internet and reliable communication infrastructure in some places or businesses (Bhambri et al., 2009).

- **Legal Compliance.** There are several potential privacy and safety regulations that could apply to the rollout of Industry 4.0 technologies. To avoid legal challenges and fines, it is essential to ensure compliance with these requirements.

- **Scalability and Complexity.** Many fields, including engineering, data science, and cybersecurity, will need to be involved in the development of effective solutions for Industry 4.0. Managing the complexity of these solutions as they are implemented throughout a company or industry may become more difficult as they are scaled up (Bhambri & Hans, 2010).

- **Environmental Impacts.** While enhanced productivity and decreased waste are possible outcomes of Industry 4.0, so are increased energy consumption and electronic waste due to the proliferation of linked devices and increased data processing. Industry 4.0's negative effects on the environment must be mitigated if it is to be adopted sustainably.

Overall, implementing Industry 4.0 applications has the potential to greatly boost business efficiency and competitiveness. Costs, data privacy, worker skills, legacy systems, and regulatory compliance are just some of the obstacles that organizations and sectors must face and overcome. Organizations can better position themselves for success in the rapidly developing digital age by proactively and strategically tackling these difficulties and thereby gaining access to the full benefits of Industry 4.0.

1.5 FUTURE RESEARCH DIRECTIONS

To fully realize their promise and address their current obstacles, future research in the deployment of Industry 4.0 applications will center on a few fundamental areas. Predictive maintenance, resource allocation, and production planning are all areas where smart factories might benefit greatly from AI and machine learning breakthroughs. To improve decision-making processes, researchers will look at new algorithms that will allow for dynamic optimization in real time.

Second, protecting the confidentiality of information in distributed industrial networks will be of paramount importance. To protect against cyber threats and attacks on critical infrastructure, cybersecurity measures must be continuously developed and enhanced (Bhambri & Hans, 2009).

Third, the integration of 5G and beyond-5G communication technologies will be crucial to provide dependable and ultra-low latency data transmission, allowing robots and human operators to work together in smart factories without any hitches.

Fourth, research into human-robot collaboration will be stepped up, with the end goal of establishing workplaces where machines and humans can work together safely and effectively, bringing out the best in each other.

Finally, sustainable practices will be highlighted, with an emphasis on fostering the growth of environmentally friendly technology and energy-efficient manufacturing processes to lessen the impact of Industry 4.0 on the natural environment.

To sum up, the main areas of focus for future studies of implementing Industry 4.0 applications are the utilization of cutting-edge technology, the guarantee of security, the encouragement of human-robot interaction, and the emphasis on sustainability.

1.6 CONCLUSIONS

Industry 4.0 describes the continual change of businesses as a result of the use of cutting-edge digital technologies. Key technologies driving Industry 4.0 include AI, big data analytics, cloud computing, IoT, CPS, etc. In this work, the authors have reviewed the role of different key technologies in the Industry 4.0 ecosystem. Various Industry 4.0 principles are also discussed in detail along with applications of Industry 4.0. The authors analyzed that the cost of installation, data security, change management, interoperability, etc., are major challenges in the deployment of Industry 4.0 applications. Major future research directions to overcome these challenges are also discussed in this work.

REFERENCES

Abrol, N., Shaifali, Rattan, M., & Bhambri, P. (2005). Implementation and performance evaluation of JPEG 2000 for medical images. In International Conference on Innovative Applications of Information Technology for Developing World.

Bai, C., Dallasega, P., Orzes, G., & Sarkis, J. (2020). Industry 4.0 technologies assessment: A sustainability perspective. *International Journal of Production Economics, 229*, 107776.

Bali, V., Bali, S., Gaur, D., Rani, S., & Kumar, R. (2023). Commercial-off-the shelf vendor selection: A multi-criteria decision-making approach using intuitionistic fuzzy sets and TOPSIS. *Operational Research in Engineering Sciences: Theory and Applications.*

Bathla, S., Jindal, C., & Bhambri, P. (2007, March). Impact of technology on societal living. In International Conference on Convergence and Competition (pp. 14).

Bhambri, P., & Bhandari, A. (2005, March). Different protocols for wireless security. Paper presented at the National Conference on Advancements in Modeling and Simulation, p. 8.

Bhambri, P., & Gupta, S. (2005, March). A survey & comparison of permutation possibility of fault tolerant multistage interconnection networks. Paper presented at the National Conference on Application of Mathematics in Engg. & Tech., p. 13.

Bhambri, P., & Hans, S. (2009). Direct non iterative solution based neural network for image compression. *PIMT Journal of Research, 2*(2), 64–67.

Bhambri, P., & Hans, S. (2010). Evaluation of integrated development environments for embedded system design. *Apeejay Journal of Management and Technology, 5*(2), 138–146.

Bhambri, P., & Mangat, A. S. (2005, March). Wireless security. Paper presented at the National Conference on Emerging Computing Technologies, pp. 155–161.

Bhambri, P., & Sharma, N. (2005, September). Priorities for sustainable civilization. Paper presented at the National Conference on Technical Education in Globalized Environment - Knowledge, Technology & The Teacher, p. 108.

Bhambri, P., & Singh, I. (2005, March). Electrical actuation systems. Paper presented at the National Conference on Application of Mathematics in Engg. & Tech., pp. 58–60.

Bhambri, P., & Singh, M. (2008). Image transport protocol for JPEG image over loss prone congested networks. *PIMT Journal of Research, 1*(1), 55–61.

Bhambri, P., & Singh, M. (2008). Direct non iterative solution based neural network for image compression. *PCTE Journal of Computer Sciences, 5*(2), 1–4.

Bhambri, P., Singh, I., & Gupta, S. (2005, March). Robotics systems. Paper presented at the National Conference on Emerging Computing Technologies, p. 27.

Bhambri, P., Singh, R., & Singh, J. (2007). Wireless security. In National Conference on Emerging Trends in Communication & IT (pp. 290).

Bhambri, P., Hans, S., & Singh, M. (2008, November). Bioinformatics - Friendship between bits & genes. In International Conference on Advanced Computing & Communication Technologies (pp. 62–65).

Bhambri, P., Hans, S., & Singh, M. (2009). Inharmonic signal synthesis & analysis. *Technia - International Journal of Computing Science and Communication Technologies, 1*(2), 199–201.

Bhambri, P., Rani, S., Gupta, G., & Khang, A. (2022). *Cloud and fog computing platforms for internet of things*: CRC Press.

Bilal, M., Kumari, B., & Rani, S. (2021). *An artificial intelligence supported E-commerce model to improve the export of Indian handloom and handicraft products in the World.* Paper presented at the Proceedings of the International Conference on Innovative Computing & Communication (ICICC).

Cañas, H., Mula, J., Díaz-Madroñero, M., & Campuzano-Bolarín, F. (2021). Implementing industry 4.0 principles. *Computers & Industrial Engineering, 158*, 107379.

Chauhan, M., & Rani, S. (2021). Covid-19: A revolution in the field of education in India. *Learning how to learn using multimedia*, 23–42.

Chen, B., Wan, J., Shu, L., Li, P., Mukherjee, M., & Yin, B. (2017). Smart factory of industry 4.0: Key technologies, application case, and challenges. *IEEE Access, 6,* 6505–6519.

Contreras, J. D., Garcia, J. I., & Pastrana, J. D. (2017). Developing of Industry 4.0 applications. *International Journal of Online Engineering, 13*(10), 1–17.

Dhanalakshmi, R., Vijayaraghavan, N., Sivaraman, A. K., & Rani, S. (2022). Epidemic awareness spreading in smart cities using the artificial neural network. In *AI-Centric Smart City Ecosystems* (pp. 187–207): CRC Press.

Ghobakhloo, M. (2020). Industry 4.0, digitization, and opportunities for sustainability. *Journal of Cleaner Production, 252,* 119869.

Goel, R., & Gupta, P. (2020). Robotics and Industry 4.0. *A Roadmap to Industry 4.0: Smart production, sharp business and sustainable development,* 157–169.

Gupta, S., & Bhambri, P. (2006). A Competitive market is pushing site search technology to new plateaus. In International Conference on Brand India: Issues, Challenges and Opportunities (pp. 34).

Gupta, S., Nischal, P., & Bhambri, P. (2007). Multimodal biometric: Enhancing security level of biometric system. In National Conference on Emerging Trends in Communication & IT (pp. 78–81).

Habib, M. K., & Chimsom, C. (2019). *Industry 4.0: Sustainability and design principles.* Paper presented at the 2019 20th International Conference on Research and Education in Mechatronics (REM).

Jain, V. K., & Bhambri, P. (2005). Fundamentals of Information Technology & Computer Programming.

Kataria, A., Agrawal, D., Rani, S., Karar, V., & Chauhan, M. (2022). Prediction of blood screening parameters for preliminary analysis using neural networks. In *Predictive modeling in biomedical data mining and analysis* (pp. 157–169): Elsevier.

Kataria, A., Puri, V., Pareek, P. K., & Rani, S. (2023). *Human activity classification using G-XGB.* Paper presented at the 2023 International Conference on Data Science and Network Security (ICDSNS).

Kaur, D., Singh, B., & Rani, S. (2023). Cyber security in the metaverse. In *Handbook of research on AI-based technologies and applications in the era of the metaverse* (pp. 418–435): IGI Global.

Kaur, S., Kumar, R., Kaur, R., Singh, S., Rani, S., & Kaur, A. (2022). Piezoelectric materials in sensors: Bibliometric and visualization analysis. *Materials Today: Proceedings.*

Kothandaraman, D., Manickam, M., Balasundaram, A., Pradeep, D., Arulmurugan, A., Sivaraman, A. K., & Balakrishna, R. (2022). Decentralized link failure prevention routing (DLFPR) algorithm for efficient internet of things. *Intelligent Automation and Soft Computing, 34*(1), 655–666.

Kumar, P., Banerjee, K., Singhal, N., Kumar, A., Rani, S., Kumar, R., & Lavinia, C. A. (2022). Verifiable, secure mobile agent migration in healthcare systems using a polynomial-based threshold secret sharing scheme with a Blowfish algorithm. *Sensors, 22*(22), 8620.

Kumar, R., Rani, S., & Awadh, M. A. (2022). Exploring the application sphere of the internet of things in Industry 4.0: A review, bibliometric and content analysis. *Sensors, 22*(11), 4276.

Kumar, R., Rani, S., & Khangura, S. S. (2023). *Machine Learning for Sustainable Manufacturing in Industry 4.0: Concept, Concerns and Applications*: CRC Press.

Machała, S., Chamier-Gliszczyński, N., & Królikowski, T. (2022). Application of AR/VR technology in Industry 4.0. *Procedia Computer Science, 207,* 2990–2998.

Puri, V., Kataria, A., Solanki, V. K., & Rani, S. (2022). *AI-based botnet attack classification and detection in IoT devices.* Paper presented at the 2022 IEEE International Conference on Machine Learning and Applied Network Technologies (ICMLANT).

Rani, S., Mishra, R. K., Usman, M., Kataria, A., Kumar, P., Bhambri, P., & Mishra, A. K. (2021). Amalgamation of advanced technologies for sustainable development of smart city environment: A review. *IEEE Access, 9*, 150060–150087.

Rani, S., Kataria, A., Chauhan, M., Rattan, P., Kumar, R., & Sivaraman, A. K. (2022). Security and privacy challenges in the deployment of cyber-physical systems in smart city applications: State-of-art work. *Materials Today: Proceedings, 62*, 4671–4676.

Rani, S., Kataria, A., & Chauhan, M. (2022a). Cyber security techniques, architectures, and design. In *Holistic Approach to Quantum Cryptography in Cyber Security* (pp. 41–66): CRC Press.

Rani, S., Kataria, A., & Chauhan, M. (2022b). Fog computing in industry 4.0: Applications and challenges—A research roadmap. *Energy conservation solutions for fog-edge computing paradigms*, 173–190.

Rani, S., Mishra, A. K., Kataria, A., Mallik, S., & Qin, H. (2023). Machine learning-based optimal crop selection system in smart agriculture. *Scientific Reports, 13*(1), 15997.

Rani, S., Kataria, A., Kumar, S., & Tiwari, P. (2023). Federated learning for secure IoMT-applications in smart healthcare systems: A comprehensive review. *Knowledge-based systems*, 110658.

Rani, S., Pareek, P. K., Kaur, J., Chauhan, M., & Bhambri, P. (2023). *Quantum machine learning in healthcare: Developments and challenges.* Paper presented at the 2023 IEEE International Conference on Integrated Circuits and Communication Systems (ICICACS).

Rani, S., Kumar, S., Kataria, A., & Min, H. (2023). SmartHealth: An intelligent framework to secure IoMT service applications using machine learning. *ICT Express.*

Rattan, M., Bhambri, P., & Shaifali. (2005, February). Information retrieval using soft computing techniques. Paper presented at the National Conference on Bio-informatics Computing, p. 7.

Salkin, C., Oner, M., Ustundag, A., & Cevikcan, E. (2018). A conceptual framework for Industry 4.0. *Industry 4.0: Managing the Digital Transformation*, 3–23.

Saucedo-Martínez, J. A., Pérez-Lara, M., Marmolejo-Saucedo, J. A., Salais-Fierro, T. E., & Vasant, P. (2018). Industry 4.0 framework for management and operations: A review. *Journal of Ambient Intelligence and Humanized Computing, 9*, 789–801.

Singh, P., Singh, M., & Bhambri, P. (2004, November). Interoperability: A problem of component reusability. Paper presented at the International Conference on Emerging Technologies in IT Industry, p. 60.

Singh, P., Singh, M., & Bhambri, P. (2005, January). Embedded systems. Paper presented at the Seminar on Embedded Systems, pp. 10–15.

Singh, P., Bhambri, P., & Sohal, A. K. (2006, January). Security in local networks. Paper presented at the National Conference on Future Trends in Information Technology.

Tanwar, R., Chhabra, Y., Rattan, P., & Rani, S. (2022). *Blockchain in IoT networks for precision agriculture.* Paper presented at the International Conference on Innovative Computing and Communications: Proceedings of ICICC 2022, Volume 2.

Yadav, V. S., Singh, A., Raut, R. D., Mangla, S. K., Luthra, S., & Kumar, A. (2022). Exploring the application of Industry 4.0 technologies in the agricultural food supply chain: A systematic literature review. *Computers & Industrial Engineering, 169*, 108304.

2 Artificial Intelligence Applications in Industry 4.0
Applications and Challenges

Latha C. A. and Malini M. Patil

2.1 PREAMBLE

If we consider history, the industrial revolution started somewhere in 1760 and lasted up till 1840. The invention of steam engines and the construction of railways initiated the whole process of the First Industrial Revolution. Then started the process of replacing the machines in the manufacturing of many products which were till then done by human beings. The First Industrial Revolution was followed by the Second Industrial Revolution, which started in the 19th century and lasted till the 20th century. The significant change in the Second Industrial Revolution was driven by electricity. This revolution resulted in mass production in the manufacturing sector which was very limited till then. The Third Industrial Revolution started in 1960. It was majorly due to the introduction of computers which revolutionized digital transactions. It was possible mainly due to the invention of semiconductor devices which are used in the mainframe computer, the personal computer, and most importantly the Internet (Singh et al., 2017).

The Fourth Industrial Revolution started in the 21st century. It was mainly proposed to uplift the German economy. It triggered the digital revolution. It resulted in the extensive use of the Internet, especially mobile Internet which is easily available and accessible to human kind. During this revolution sensors were invented. These sensors were available in low cost and reduced size and resulted in the most powerful mode of communication. The utmost usage of AI, Machine Learning, and also the cyber-physical system made Fourth Industrial Revolution a possibility and reality. In the Fourth Industrial Revolution, computers became more and more sophisticated and also integrated with other devices, making it a complete package for any purpose (Kumar et al., 2022). Industry 4.0 (I4.0) which is another name for the Fourth Industrial Revolution, was coined in Hannover fair in 2011. The Fourth Industrial Revolution resulted in smart connected machines which resulted in smart factories, nanotechnology, renewable energy, and most importantly the quantum computing. The scope of the innovations of the Fourth Industrial Revolution meet many of today's innovations like Alibaba, Amazon online

DOI: 10.1201/9781003395416-2

communications, online shopping, etc. The Fourth Industrial Revolution resulted in the smartphone which is being used by billions of people making our lives very easy. Google plans to launch autonomous driverless AI-based self-navigating cars. Such efforts are changing the industry both horizontally and vertically, changing its speed and scale drastically (Rani, Arya, and Kataria, 2022).

We can see a vast and systematic change in I4.0. It can be demonstrated with applications like Instagram, WhatsApp, Facebook, etc., which started with very minimal capital but brought enormous changes in society and are exponentially scaling business (Rani et al., 2023). The digital technologies are able to communicate with the Biological and Medical world too. They have enabled the Medical field to make swift and accurate diagnoses which are followed by treatment in a minimal amount of time and effort. If we combine the architecture of computational design in Material Engineering with synthetic biology and additive manufacturing, the products are very accurate, very small, and require less time to operate compared to the human intervention. They are all adaptable to any scenario irrespective of language, time zone, physical condition, geographical location, etc.

2.2 ARTIFICIAL INTELLIGENCE AND I4.0

In the context of the Fourth Industrial Revolution with extensive use of AI and Machine Learning, there are many applications worth mentioning such as discovering new drugs, self-driving car, sentimental analysis and prediction (Kataria et al., 2022). In all such cases, the drivers would be Megatrends classified into three categories: 1. Physical, 2. Digital, and 3. Biological. The physical Megatrends can be further categorized into four sub categories: 1. Autonomous vehicle, 2. 3D printer, 3. Advanced robotics, and 4. New materials. Autonomous vehicles, also called as driverless vehicles, can be drugs or drones also aircrafts and boats, covering vehicles of all media: Roadways, airways, and waterways.

Ricardo Silva Peres et al. (2020) mention that Industrial AI can be differentiated into the following five fields:

- Infrastructures: In terms of hardware and software requirements, real-time processing capabilities, ensuring industrial-grade reliability with high security and interconnectivity are very important.
- Data: Data should have large volume and high-velocity variety and should originate from various units, products, regimes, etc.
- Algorithms: It demands the combination of physical, digital and real-time knowledge. Highly complex algorithms are used for management, governance, and deployment.
- Decision making: In the industrial environment, accuracy and and efficiency expected are very high, along with the capability of handling unexpected situations.
- Objectives: Industrial AI addresses production objectives through a combination of factors such as waste reduction, improved quality, and operator performance.

2.3 APPLICATIONS AND RESPECTIVE CHALLENGES OF I4.0

3D printers help in transforming digital specifications into physical embodiments. This has a wide scope of applications starting from artificial human organs, wind turbines, building constructions, etc. Advanced robotics have redefined the definition of conventional robots and entered into almost all domains including domains inaccessible to humans (Kumar et al., 2022). It includes both software application as well as hardware orientedness. The scope includes chatting like a human being and serving in restaurant, agriculture, nursing, manufacturing, product delivery, etc. We are seeking innovative materials that are lighter, stronger, recyclable, and adaptive (Gupta, Rani, and pant, 2011).

In the digital field, IoT applications include Bitcoin, Uber model of transportation like carpooling and driverless vehicles, blockchain, RFID, various monitoring systems, etc. (Kataria and Puri, 2022). In Biological I4.0, some significant aspects are genetic sequencing, DNA writing, cell modification, and also genetic engineering (Bhambri et al., 2023).

The points which we are anticipating to bring radical changes in future are clothes or wearable devices that can be connected to the Internet. These devices are expected to help in the medical field, forensic domain, police, and investigations. It would also make Metaverse implementations easier. The metaverse idea which is still in its embryonic stage is expected to help in remote working, banking and finance, tourism, entertainment, private digital spaces, health care, new age education, gaming and E-sports, heavy metal industry and manufacturing, social media, and the list goes on.

To make all these happen, unlimited and free cloud storage is very much essential. As almost every device is going to be connected through IoT, we need almost 1 trillion sensors that are connected to the Internet (Bhambri et al., 2022).

In spite of several advantages, the digitization of the industries has to face many challenges. Some of these challenges mention are the availability and accessibility of data storage, data security, high-speed connectivity among the systems, and data protection. Achieving all these without compromising on any single issue is itself a big challenge. For example, some of the existing AI models do have security threats. If we think there is a strong relationship between Big Data and AI to process both in an integrated way, again it induces a lot of changes. These are very challenging demands, as it not only requires the investment but recurring maintenance, and its repercussion on the environment and human beings has to be considered (Rachna et al., 2022).

I4.0 proposes inclusion of the characteristics of the previous industrial revolutions in a very sustainable way. Sustainable industry provides energy efficiency, conservation of resource and less waste production. Thereby I4.0 provides a comprehensive I4.0 which incorporates globalization and emerging issues. Sustainability assessment in the manufacturing industry is considered as a base of modern industrialized society and also a milestone of the world economy. A strong manufacturing base stimulates other aspects of the economy of any country. The evaluation of sustainability assessment of manufacturing industry under I4.0 incorporates evaluation of various issues and performance metrics (Rani and Kaur, 2012).

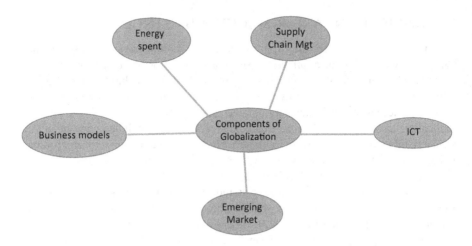

FIGURE 2.1 Globalization issues.

If we consider the globalization issues, shown in Figure 2.1, globalization is one of the main drivers of sustainable industries (Kothandaraman et al., 2022). Sustainability's impact on a production unit is one of the key prerequisites for Industry 4.0. Supply chain management is the second most critical issue in the manufacturing industry. It involves managing the many manufacturing phases and arranging them in a specific order to ensure the production of a high-quality product. The most crucial stage is deciding whether to outsource the raw material. Supply chain management is concerned with climate change, natural resource usage, and contaminations from production.

The next most important issue is Information and Communication Technology (ICT). ICT forms the main backbone of any industry especially in the modern-day digital world (Kataria, Ghosh and Karar, 2020). An enterprise can be considered zero communication in the absence of ICT as it help to share information among various stakeholders. Adjusting and getting acquainted to the ICT are some major issues in the adoption of the ICT. User unfriendliness, high usage of technical words, and various access control rights make adapting to ICT very difficult. The stakeholders should at least have computer knowledge to work and especially to use the ERP the company is following. Things become more complicated especially for the higher management and also the senior workforce of all categories of the company, as they feel it is very difficult to follow the ERP and its operations (Ritu et al., 2022).

The next issue to be considered is the energy quotient. It is preferred to have the least energy consumption in all sectors as we know that the lesser the energy consumption, the more are the economic and ecologic advantages. If you increase the price for the energy consumed, it affects the sustainability. Hence, it is advised to reduce energy consumption in non-renewable energy sources and encourage the company to increase the usage of renewable energy, which will have maximum positive effect on sustainability. The problem for the sectors where the usage of non-renewable energy sources is mandatory. Maybe a company cannot always go for the renewable energy sources in the technology used for the designed machines. Therefore, it is better for every industry to have a research centre which researches on options to reduce energy for the existing technology or machines. If it is difficult to have a research centre, then the company should go for a new technology or a set of machines which work on renewable energy sources. The vehicle manufacturing sector is a best example for this issue. Some automobile companies discovered the hybrid mode of fuel, some switched over to renewable energy sources like electricity or gasoline. It can be predicted that within ten years from now, almost all vehicles will be electric vehicles depending on non-renewable energy sources like petrol and diesel, which is an economic and ecological solution.

The selling market of the commodity also plays a major role in sustainability. Unlike the olden days, now there is a wide variety of markets available to market the products. The scope of the market ranges from a layout or an apartment to worldwide. Now with the help of social networking, it is to reach the restricted area confined to houses of an apartment or a layout or a township or a community group or an office personals. Reaching worldwide customers can obviously be done through online marketing. Therefore, depending on the scope of the commodity the vendor can choose any of these and can reach the customers, but the problem is to deal with customer limitations. The customer takes less time to reach from layout to global market. Hence, the vendor should be ready for scaling of customers in a short period. At the same time, if any mishap happens vendor should be also ready for downfall and recovery from the same. As the world has become very small, it's in finger tips for news to reach the world. The vendor has to be ready for both downfall and upscale. It is found that the emerging markets are more frequent in developing countries than the developed countries.

One of the issues that is to be considered which poses challenges for the AI implementation in I4.0 are technology. As already mentioned, technology is an important issue to be considered in sustainability. The more advanced the technology one has adopted, the higher will be the quality of the products, and the lower will be the cost of the product. It also reduces the manufacturing time. Hence, it is advised to convert the traditional manufacturing system to the automatic system, which introduces more flexibility and agility in the manufacturing process.

The next concern is government regulation. This is a problem in developing countries or underdeveloped countries wherein most of the regulations of the government are not updated to comply with I4.0 standards. This might be with respect to human resource policies, the technologies adopted, security especially cyber security, forensic science that would be required during the process. It can also be with respect to advertising policies, environmental policies, energy consumption policies, health and safety policies and privacy policies. Each of the above-listed issues has further rules and regulations to be framed in accordance with I4.0. Compared to all listed issues of industry that is Industry 1.0, 2.0 and 3.0, in I4.0 people expect the flexibility, mobility and friendly regulations with respect to employability regulations. Government has to redefine the emission and contaminations limit as this is the high time to take measures to reduce the global warming. All governments have to make strict regulations in spite of strong opposition from bureaucracy and capitalism, so that we give a livable world to the future generations, else there will be no one living in the next generations. Some of the other domains where the government regulations with respect to I4.0 need to concentrate on are, wages or salary of human resource, benefits like insurance and retirement plans, proper working environment, compliance with time zones if in different time zones, expatriate issues, maintaining equal opportunities and recognition of employees. The government regulation is first and foremost for the implementation of I4.0. Hence, it becomes a major hindrance to adapt I4.0, if even if we comply with all other issues. It is the government regulations that make people aware about the possibilities and the pros and cons to implement I4.0.

Similarly if you consider advertisement regulations, they have to focus on protecting customers' needs, honesty and ethical concern about the product, information regulations and transparency in manufacturing and also distribution.

If you consider environmental issue, it has to maintain clear air, minimum usage of water, soil and almost zero chemical effect in soil and river. The industries should also make an attempt to bring down the carbon print.

Population growth and the quality of the living becomes a major issue to be considered in the implementation of I4.0 because the population actually decides the status of the country whether it is developed or emerging. The population of a country affects the growth of the industry, the food supply, the economics of a country, politics of a country, and usage of various resources, the location of the industry, where it is to be established or extended. As per the UN report in the developed countries, the population growth has been reduced. Similarly in emerging and developing countries, it has increased. We can view the population growth in both pessimistic way and also optimistically. Population growth consumes most of the economic share in maintaining safety, schools, hospitals, and universities. But at the same time, the population growth increases the human resources which in turn increases the trade and commerce. Even though we have positive effects of population growth, it is advised to have a control population growth (Gupta and Rani, 2013).

The next challenge to be considered is economic crisis. This has become most common in the modern-day industrialization. Because modern-day industries have no boundaries (Kaur, Kaur, and Rani, 2015). Hence, they have to cater to all types of government policies, currencies, and HR policies. Economic crisis leads to recession and depression. In spite of the increasing opportunities in various sectors of employment, it is observed there is an exponential increase in the employment, reduction in suitable available opportunities, huge number of companies going under bankruptcy, volatile currency. Therefore, there is a need of joint brainstorming of industrialists, economist, and stakeholders who can do an analysis and forecast this recession so that measures can be taken to avoid recession which leads to depression. The company's top management also need to analyze the balance sheet and the stock market to speculate about its growth and take enough precaution not to become bankrupt. Although it is very difficult task to forecast in industry, a collaborative study by economists, bureaucrats policy makers can help to an extent in overcoming such situations. The natural disasters and natural calamities is an exceptional case to forecast in spite of advanced technologies. To deal such situations, a caution or corpus fund has to be maintained in all manufacturing sectors.

Consumption of natural resources is one of the important challenges to be considered in economic sustainability. Natural resources are one of the main resources of revenue factor in developing countries and also one of the major sources of social and political conflicts. Some of them are mining, gas extraction, demography ships, oil extraction, etc. There are two types of energy resources, renewable and non-renewable. Renewable energy is naturally available for example solar, air, water, and wind which can be generated easily and abundantly. Non-renewable energy resources are also naturally available but cannot be recycled and hence has to be used with caution, e.g., coal, diesel, and petrol.

2.4   LEAN PRODUCTION SYSTEM

To address all these challenges, one answer, as mentioned in Dutton, would be the Lean Production system which is originally a Japanese concept. Some of the Japanese companies are widely using it and showing positive results. It is basically finishing the product inventories by eliminating waste from the process. It mainly focuses on customers' needs and users' requirements. Lean production is based on two criteria: 1. Jidoka, which says when there is a problem, stop production and stop producing defective products. 2. Just-in-time, which says each stage produces what is needed by the next stage in a continuous flow of process. We can categorize generated wastes into seven types. These are: excessive and unnecessary movements of people for materials or data, some duration of inactivity among the people waiting for material or data, doing more work on a product than required for customer values, producing more products earlier to the customer requirement, defective products or paper works, unnecessary cost spent on raw materials processing, unnecessary movement of people which adds no value to the whole process. All these seven types of logical and physical wastes can be minimized and attempt has to be made to add value to resources or the process in the manufacturing. In the lean approach, the elimination of waste in various stages provides the best quality at the lowest cost and in shortest time. However, this can be achieved only when we implement it in a full manufacturing system that means all four main areas have to be concentrated: business requirements, operation improvement, performance governance, and people management.

Another way of establishing I4.0 is through the smart and connected approach. It concentrates on connecting the physical objects that share data among themselves, so that resource efficiency and productivity are increased. There are various ways of getting connected in a smarter way. Embedded systems, cloud computing, IoT, and various sensors are the ways through which units can be connected. Using this approach of smart and connected products, we can deliver at a faster rate, make better use of the product and reduce ecological impact.

In I4.0, creating value and business models also requires a significant change to the value added. A businessman model includes the market, the services, and innovations. If we consider the market, it has to be faster in correlating to the fast world, very simple catering to all walks of life, transparent and error free. The business model has to take measures to prevent the customer from migrating from one vendor to another. It also should avoid changing the cost frequently. It should try to build trust among the customers and distributors.

The main thing in I4.0 is manufacturing factories themselves have to be made smarter, so that, they address the evolution of technology, the highly competitive market with high amount of production in minimum timeline reducing risk of failure. The benefits of running smart factories are that they reduce the cost of production, efficiency is increased, the quality of the product is improved, the safety of the working environment is improved, and one can predict and analyze the market for the products very easily. Smart factory is a combination of smart machines, smart engineering, smart devices and smart technology, incorporating smart methodology of manufacturing with innovation. By smart machines we mean that each machine should communicate with other machines, other devices and human beings in an efficient and friendly way. To incorporate all this things everything has to undergo a major transformation which might bring a lot of disturbance in the beginning by both machines and human beings to adapt to the new environment (Kataria et al., 2020).

Some of the technologies that support the smart factory are big data, cloud computing, AI, machine learning, deep learning, smart grid, etc. Cloud computing enables high performance computing. It also provides easy access of designing the software and tools, and it makes the analysis of data very easy. Data storage and computing also become very efficient. At the same time, big data generates knowledge, it improves the value stream, and it helps in identifying key performance indicators. One more important technology that is to be used in smart factories is augmented reality; even though the technology is in its infant state, it allows us to operate instruments remotely providing the precision. It also provides safety in radioactive zones.

2.5 CONCLUSION

I4.0 aims to address not only technical and manufacturing issues but also addresses all the issues related to the industry in a holistic way. It may be HR policy, Enterprise Resource Planning (ERP), marketing, ecological effects, sustainability, etc. It is a 180 degree switch from traditional Industry standards, which needs redefinition of many things. As it involves a change in almost all domains, big or small, it creates a sort of disturbance till it is completely implemented and adapted. Hence, the biggest challenge is human adaptation to the new environment.

I4.0 is catering to all types of applications, not only manufacturing but also service-based products, not only hardware but also software products. In this stage, where metaverse is getting ready for delivery, things might take a lot of unexpected turns and expectations. So, I4.0 should be flexible, scalable and adaptable which is itself a big challenge in implementing I4.0.

REFERENCES

Bhambri, P., Singh, M., Dhanoa, I. S., & Kumar, M. (2022). Deployment of ROBOT for HVAC duct and disaster management. *Oriental Journal of Computer Science and Technology*, *15*, 1–8.

Bhambri, P., Singh, S., Sangwan, S., Devi, J., & Jain, S. (2023). Plants recognition using leaf image pattern analysis. *Journal of Survey in Fisheries Sciences*, *10*(2S), 3863–3871. Green Wave Publishing of Canada.

Gupta, O., Rani, S., & Pant, D. C. (2011). Impact of parallel computing on bioinformatics algorithms. In *Proceedings 5th IEEE International Conference on Advanced Computing and Communication Technologies* (pp. 206–209).

Gupta, O. P., & Rani, S. (2013). Accelerating molecular sequence analysis using distributed computing environment. *International Journal of Scientific & Engineering Research–IJSER*, *4*(10), 262–265.

https://www.analyticsvidhya.com/blog/2022/08/top-10-metaverse-uses-cases-and-applications/

https://onlinecourses.nptel.ac.in/noc23_cs52/preview Dutton, T. An Overview of National AI Strategies. http://www.jaist.ac.jp/~{}bao/AI/OtherAIstrategies/An%20Overview%20of%20National%20AI%20Strategies%20%E2%80%93%20Politics%20+%20AI%20%E2%80%93%20Medium.pdf.

Kataria, A., & Puri, V. (2022). AI-and IoT-based hybrid model for air quality prediction in a smart city with network assistance. *IET Networks*, *11*(6), 221–233.

Kataria, A., Ghosh, S., & Karar, V. (2020). Data prediction of electromagnetic head tracking using self healing neural model for head-mounted display. *Science and Technology*, *23*(4), 354–367.

Kataria, A., Ghosh, S., Karar, V., Gupta, T., Srinivasan, K., & Hu, Y. C. (2020). Improved diver communication system by combining optical and electromagnetic trackers. *Sensors*, *20*(18), 5084.

Kataria, A., Agrawal, D., Rani, S., Karar, V., & Chauhan, M. (2022). Prediction of blood screening parameters for preliminary analysis using neural networks. In *Predictive Modeling in Biomedical Data Mining and Analysis* (pp. 157–169). Academic Press.

Kaur, G., Kaur, R., & Rani, S. (2015). Cloud computing—A new trend in IT era. *International Journal of Scientific and Technology Management*, *1*(3), 1–6.

Kothandaraman, D., Manickam, M., Balasundaram, A., Pradeep, D., Arulmurugan, A., Sivaraman, A. K., & Balakrishna, R. (2022). Decentralized link failure prevention routing (DLFPR) algorithm for efficient internet of things. *Intelligent Automation and Soft Computing*, *34*(1), 655–666.

Kumar, J., Saini, S. S., Agrawal, D., Kataria, A., & Karar, V. (2022, December). Effect of complexity and frequency of projected symbology of head-up display while flying in low visibility. In *2022 IEEE International Conference on Machine Learning and Applied Network Technologies (ICMLANT)* (pp. 1–4). IEEE.

Lee, J., Davari, H., Singh, J., & Pandhare, V. (2018, October). Industrial artificial intelligence for industry 4.0-based manufacturing systems. *Manufacturing Letters*, *18*, 20–23.

Peres, R. S., Jia, X. et al. (2020). Industrial artificial intelligence in Industry 4.0—Systematic review, challenges and outlook. *IEEE Access*, December 18. DOI 10.1109/ACCESS.2020.3042874

Rachna, Bhambri, P., & Chhabra, Y. (2022). Deployment of distributed clustering approach in WSNs and IoTs. In *Cloud and Fog Computing Platforms for Internet of Things* (pp. 85–98). Chapman and Hall/CRC.

Rani, S., & Kaur, S. (2012). Cluster analysis method for multiple sequence alignment. *International Journal of Computer Applications*, *43*(14), 19–25.

Rani, S., Arya, V., & Kataria, A. (2022). Dynamic pricing-based e-commerce model for the produce of organic farming in India: A research roadmap with main advertence to vegetables. In *Proceedings of Data Analytics and Management: ICDAM 2021, Volume 2* (pp. 327–336). Springer Singapore.

Rani, S., Kataria, A., Kumar, S., & Tiwari, P. (2023). Federated learning for secure IoMT-applications in smart healthcare systems: A comprehensive review. *Knowledge-based systems*, 110658.

Ritu & Bhambri, P. (2022). A CAD system for software effort estimation. Paper presented at the International Conference on Technological Advancements in Computational Sciences, 140–146. IEEE. DOI: 10.1109/ICTACS56270.2022.9988123.

Singh, P., Gupta, O. P., & Saini, S. (2017). A brief research study of wireless sensor network. *Advances in Computational Sciences and Technology, 10*(5), 733–739.

3 Role of Artificial Intelligence in Industry 4.0
Applications and Challenges

Elakkiya Elango, Gnanasankaran Natarajan,
Sundaravadivazhagan Balasubramanian, and
Sandhya Soman

3.1 INTRODUCTION

Today, as the idea of linked and intelligent manufacturing gains hold, it can be challenging to compete in the Industry 4.0 world if we are not at the forefront of innovation. Various experts and investors have been predicting as a result of the IIoT's increasing economic significance on a global scale as to whether the industry is about to see a technological revolution. However, there is undeniable evidence, from data and projections, that the idea of smart production has so far permeated corporate awareness [1]. As per IDC, providing the present compound annual growth rate of 12.6 percentage points is maintained, global investment just on Internet of Things likely exceeds $840 billion in 2020.

There is no denying that a sizeable chunk of these kind of investment will have to go toward incorporating IoT into other businesses, especially manufacturing. But beyond just predictions and numbers, there are many more signs that perhaps the Industrial Internet of Things concept is gathering steam across practically all business sectors. By providing the security of preventative maintenance, the insight of big data analytics, and the dependability of machine-to-machine communication, IIoT has already shown that it is the key to production. To put it another way, the IIoT revolution has already begun. Figure 3.1 explains how smart factory 4.0 is interconnected by the smart world through Smart Products, Smart Mobility, Smart Manufacturing, Smart Buildings, Smart Logistics, Machine Learning, Smart Services, and Smart Retail.

3.2 BUILDING BLOCKS OF INDUSTRY 4.0

Small to half capital goods organizations, as well as textile, pharmaceutical, leather, and auto manufacturers, used to make up the majority of India's manufacturing sector. These industries have moved approaching Industry 3.0 during the past few

DOI: 10.1201/9781003395416-3

FIGURE 3.1 Smart applications of Industry 4.0.

decades in an effort to increase the efficiency of existing manufacturing processes by utilizing robotics and automation. The Indian sector is currently advancing faster and more rapidly toward Industry 4.0 than American and European businesses in order to speed up company choices via excellent big data which may actually help to boost performance and eliminate potential mistakes.

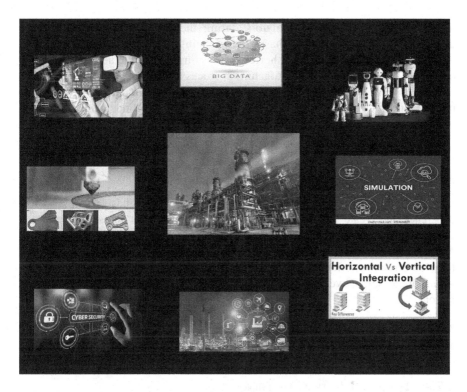

FIGURE 3.2 Top nine technologies that drive Industry 4.0.

Figure 3.2 outlines the Top 9 technologies supporting Industry 4.0, such as the internet of things, augmented reality, cloud computing, cyber security, and 3D printers [2,3]. Such aid in addressing a few of Industry 2.0's shortcomings, including its low-cost workforce and inadequate planning. Let's focus upon that nine Industry 4.0 modernization trends and advancements which, by uniting numerous units within one refined, computerized, and integrated process, can actually greatly boost the competitiveness of our organization.

3.2.1 Autonomous Robots

Flexibility and cooperation are the two key properties used to describe autonomous robots. Modern robotics has shown to be a highly effective approach to boost the effectiveness and caliber of the production process. Because autonomous robots can collaborate with humans and other machines through learning and interaction, they are being deployed by industries around the world to replace production lines and mechanical arms.

3.2.2 Simulation

Digital reproductions of actual machines, objects, and people can be created with the use of simulation technology. A product's machine settings can be tested and adjusted using simulators during the product discovery, material development, and production phases before being used in the real world. This will help keep quality high, shorten setup times for the actual machining operation, and help reduce manufacturing process failures. To deliver the next-best output, it is critical to be using real-time data as efficiently as possible in production lines. The creation of increased physical goods and its prompt release to the marketplace are made possible by quick and continuous evaluation of the 3D model.

3.2.3 SYSTEM INTEGRATION

It is both horizontal and vertical methods that allows a business to promote coherence and create links between their numerous divisions and services.

3.2.3.1 Horizontal Integration

Enables communication and information sharing about products and manufacturing processes between many parties, a single piece of hardware, or a whole factory.

3.2.3.2 Vertical Integration

Through assimilation, it gives the supply chain system control.

3.2.4 INDUSTRIAL INTERNET OF THINGS

IIoT focuses on developing intelligent factories, increasing productivity, and integrating machines. In high-demand industries, IIoT incorporates necessary hardware and precise sensors, including location-aware technologies, producing enormous volumes of data. People, analytics, and smart robots come together in the communication-based environmental for the industrial sector (production, distribution network surveillance, and monitoring systems) to speed up the collection, analysis, exchange, and tracking of important information.

3.2.5 CYBER SECURITY

Greater connectivity is required by Industry 4.0 technologies; therefore, safe-guarding vital industrial systems and production processes against cyber-attacks is essential. Businesses utilize cyber security to shield their systems, networks, and data against online attacks.

3.2.6 CLOUD

The company's different sites and verticals will exchange more data as Industry 3.0 speeds up manufacturing. Thanks to the cloud, everyone may utilize apps and save data online. By adopting machine data and functionality using Industry 4.0 cloud technologies, organizations may still work with both internal and external stakeholders to implement the best data-driven decisions.

3.2.7 ADDITIVE MANUFACTURING

Businesses use 3D printing and additive manufacturing to create prototypes of different product parts. Industries are using this technology extensively to create specialized products with a range of cost and production advantages.

3.2.8 AUGMENTED REALITY

We might give a person access to real-time data via the use of augmented reality eyewear, portable devices, and other items, which could make generating decisions easier and increase their ability to carry out tasks. The right knowledge may be acquired at the right time with the aid of AR technology, giving these people the freedom to act and think for themselves.

3.2.9 BIG DATA ANALYTICS

It could be one of the greatest crucial pillars of Industry 4.0. Big data analytics allows for the collection and thorough analysis of data from numerous sources. Data analysis makes it quick and simple to identify patterns, correlation, and developments which can drastically lower production problems and improve the production of higher quality products. Big data analytics can be applied to find and analyze huge and diverse amounts of information gathered through enterprise and customer relationship management systems, industrial systems and equipment and other sources that are essential for our business's speedy and quite well decision-making.

3.3 INDUSTRY 4.0 BASED ON ARTIFICIAL INTELLIGENCE

Industry 4.0 must get ready for networked factories that are deeply integrated with the design phase, production process, and quality management into something like a smart engine that uses AI to deliver useful insights. Businesses must create a system which takes into account the entire production process since Industry 4.0 requires collaboration throughout the entire supply chain cycle. Asset control, supply chain management, and resource planning are currently the three primary industries embracing AI, ML, and IoT. By merging such tools, it is possible to increase stock utilization, supply chain transparency, and inventory tracking accuracy. ML techniques such as algorithms, machine intelligence-driven procedures, and quality improvement can enhance preventive modeling [4]. AI may be used to quickly carry out efficient time tracking of operational loads just on production line that contributes to production scheduling efficiency. Production, preventive action, and asset burdens can all be increased by producers by merging ML with total equipment efficacy.

The core elements of Industry 4.0, which seems based on AI for such Internet of Things (IoT), must satisfy the manufacturing sector's requirements for improved productivity, the capacity to handle batches of up to 1, as well as the requirement for omni. These requirements, in the opinion of Siemens and with permission, can be grouped into four main categories: flexibility, connection, mobility, and digital twin. Several characteristics that relate to such fundamental elements describe smart factories: Personal and professional networks comprising base stations and real-time operational planning are necessary for a modern production system that really can adapt to processes that are changing. Production can be optimized by self-organization, such as through Cyber-Physical Production Systems. To monitor elements and outcomes, especially those that can be predicted ahead, and also to meticulously plan the launch of a new asset, product, or line, the entire process and all of its component parts must be Digital Twin.

The concept of "AI on Need" helps complicated AI systems meet those differing needs. In complicated systems, AI building blocks for detecting, comprehending, and acting collaborate effectively. Below are a few examples of how AI technology can be used for Industry 4.0 features.

3.3.1 Mass Customization Using Semantic Service Matching

* Additional Semantic AI Technologies and Descriptive Product Memories again for Digital Twin
* AR/MR/DR for Employee Assistance
* Program Recognition and Machine Learning
* Deep Learning and Active Sensor Fusion in Online Quality Control
* BDI (belief-desire-intention), Ontology Merging for Plug & Create
* GPU-based Anytime AI Planning Techniques for Real-time Line Balancing
* Deep Learning for Process Outlier Detection Multi-Agent Planning

3.3.2 Why Industry 4.0 Seems to Need AI as a Foundational Component?

Industry 4.0 depends on a wide range of innovations, like analytics, IoT, 3D printing, manufacturing techniques, robotics/cobotics, and additive manufacturing. In a smart factory, each element of manufacturing is monitored or controlled by sophisticated instrumentation, and there is an abundance of extremely detailed data on everything from the quality of the ingredients to millisecond-level device status updates.

In the majority of Industry 4.0's technology advancements, artificial intelligence - which includes deep learning and both generating and discriminatory AI - can produce valuable solutions. The usefulness of AI typically comes from increasing the threshold for automation by giving software human-like levels of comprehension. This lessens the number of locations that workers inside the production process must assess data and make decisions, which (when done correctly) both lowers costs and boosts productivity [5]. Robot activities can be guided by machine-speed understanding, for instance, by slowing, speeding up, or changing their behavior to deal with differences in raw material quality or in the speed of other process steps.

Despite automating in manufacturing lines, AI still has a wide range of applications in this kind of setting. In the beginning, it can help with the creation of digital twins, another method for accelerating product design lifecycles. Second, AI systems support the use of industrial IoT (IIoT) infrastructure, for instance, by filtering activity data to identify and anticipate future production issues utilizing sensor data. By spotting previously unnoticed trends in production and consumption data and utilizing that information to recommend design or process modifications, AI can also help with manufacturing data analysis.

3.4 INDUSTRIAL AI IoT (ARTIFICIAL INTELLIGENCE & IoT IN INDUSTRY 4.0)

At the forefront of upending an industrial ecosystem are AI and IoT. Businesses are already making investments in these popular technologies to obtain a competitive advantage and increase productivity.

3.4.1 THE CHALLENGES OF AI IoT's TERMINATOR

The absorption and handling of enormous amounts of data via edge devices is currently the most significant problem that IoT systems confront, second only to security concerns. The processing skills of artificial intelligence are currently being investigated in order to manage, analyze, and derive relevant insights from this data [6]. Artificial intelligence is used to create machines and technologies smarter and more intelligent on various levels as shown in Figure 3.3.

- *Assisted Intelligence:* At this level, AI makes it possible to identify hazards and gives businesses the capacity to anticipate or predict breakdown. Real-time machine monitoring enables them to prevent downtime and boost overall productivity.
- *Augmented Intelligence: However,* at this stage, AI enables devices to make determinations on their own and notify users of possible concerns or impediments.
- *Autonomous Intelligence:* During this level of intelligence, robots are capable of acting independently. They get new talents, which significantly contributes to raising the industry's production rates.

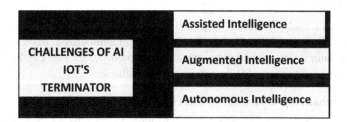

FIGURE 3.3 Challenges of AI-IoT's terminator.

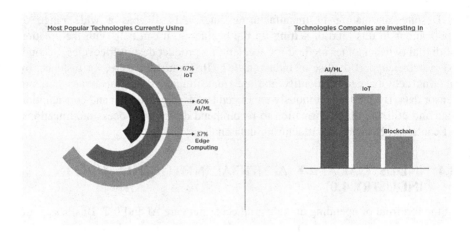

FIGURE 3.4 Recent tech trend survey by SADA System, IoT, and AI.

Source: https://www.clariontech.com/blog/ai-and-iot-blended-what-it-is-and-why-it-matters

3.4.2 Rising Interest in IOT and AI

Numerous businesses have already integrated AI and IOT into their practices and products. IOT and AI were currently a most extensively used technology, per a new Tech Trends study by SADA System. It was additionally found that businesses are making significant investments in AI and IOT as the leading technologies to improve efficiency and offer them a competitive edge. The data is displayed in Figure 3.4.

Executives in the C-suite start to reimagine their companies through digitizing conversations and communications, according to the IBM Global C-suite Study program. The results of an IBM Institute survey of C-suite executives revealed that 19% of those surveyed (classified as Reinventions, high performers) are particularly interested in the advantages of augmenting IoT with AI. The interview's response is represented in the following Figure 3.5.

Innovators and established businesses alike want AI technologies to maximize IoT's capabilities [7]. Leading IoT platform providers including Sales Force, Oracle, Microsoft, and Amazon have begun integrating AI technologies within various IoT applications.

3.4.3 Advantages of AI-Powered IoT

For businesses and customers, IoT artificial intelligence has a wide range of advantages, including preemptive intervention, individualized experiences, and intelligent automation. Among the most well-known benefits of combining these two emerging innovations for companies are as follows:

3.4.3.1 Enhancing Operational Effectiveness

IoT AI examines ongoing streams of data to identify patterns which are concealed by straight forward sensors. Machine learning and artificial intelligence are also

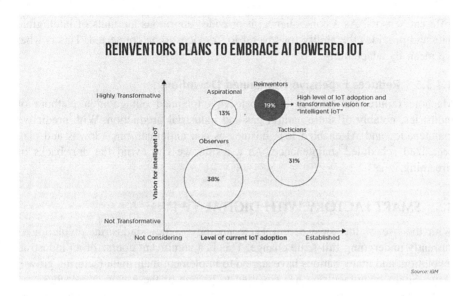

FIGURE 3.5   Reinventors' plans to embrace AI-powered IoT.

Source: https://www.clariontech.com/blog/ai-and-iot-blended-what-it-is-and-why-it-matters

capable of predicting operational conditions and identifying the variables that need to be altered for the best outcomes. As a result, intelligent IoT offers insight into which processes can be modified to streamline the process and which aspects are unnecessary and time-consuming.

3.4.3.2   More Effective Risk Control

Businesses may anticipate and understand a variety of threats and organize, enabling speedy response by merging AI with IoT. They can therefore gain more control over cash losses, safety regulations, and cyber threats.

3.4.3.3   Launching New and Improved Goods and Services

NLP (Natural Language Processing) is getting better at facilitating interpersonal interactions. IoT and AI unquestionably work well together to give businesses the capacity to analyze and evaluate data quickly in order to build new goods or improve existing ones. Innovators and established businesses alike want AI technologies for maximizing IoT's capabilities. Leading IoT platform providers including Salesforce, Oracle, Microsoft, Amazon, and Amazon have begun integrating AI technologies within various IoT applications.

3.4.3.4   Expand the IoT's Scalability

IoT devices range from pricey sensors to elevated PCs and mobile phones. However, the IoT environment that is typically employed consists of low-cost sensors that generate enormous amounts of data. An IoT ecosystem powered by AI assesses and highlights the data gathered by one device prior to delivering it to different sensors. As a consequence, it provides enormous amounts of intelligible data and provides the ability for several IoT devices to be connected. This is what we mean by adaptability.

3.4.3.5 Reduces Expensive Unplanned Downtime

Machine failure can lead to an expensive unplanned outage in a plethora of industries, notably offshore natural gas and industrial production. With predictive maintenance and AI-enabled IoT, businesses can anticipate breakdowns and plan organized scheduled maintenance. As a result, we can avoid the drawbacks of streaming.

3.5 SMART FACTORY WITH DIGITAL TWIN

With the use of the most recent IT technology, a new industrial revolution is currently undergoing full-scale change. This is a significant course of an industrial revolution, and many nations have started to implement their manufacturing growth plans. Smart manufacturing has emerged to be one of these new approaches as a crucial path for industrial growth and the industrial revolution. All nations in the world respect smart manufacturing. An automatic replica of a physical product, object, or services is called a "digital twin." It may be an automated replica of a larger thing, such as an entire city or a set of buildings, or a smaller object like a wind farm or a jet engine. By simulating processes, the digital twin technology can be utilized to collect data and make predictions about how they will function in the future.

3.5.1 SMART FACTORY

The term "Smart Manufacturing" (SM) refers to an Internet-connected machine-driven strategy to production chain monitoring. Automating processes and finding possibilities to boost production performance are the two main objectives of SM [8–10]. SM is one application of the Industrial Internet of Things (IIoT). In order to collect data just on functionality and performance state of industrial equipment, sensors are installed during installation. Previously, such information was typically only used to identify a gadget failure's cause when it had already happened and was stored locally for each individual device. By analyzing data streaming from devices in the entire facility or even across numerous factories, manufacturing engineers and data scientists can seek signs that specific parts may be temporarily out of service or unscheduled by predictive maintenance. Equipment unavailability can be averted.

3.5.2 DIGITAL TWIN

Digital twins are really a way to simulate the dynamical and physical components of an Internet of Things (IoT) device's operations as shown in Figure 3.6. It is more than just a map or a strategy. Not only an image, either. More often than not "virtual reality" goggles are involved [11]. The components and behaviors that determine

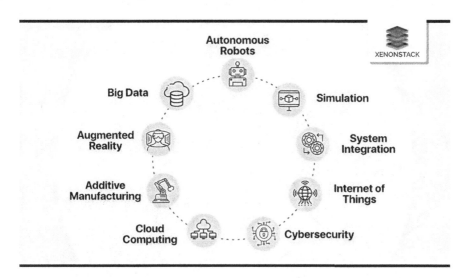

FIGURE 3.6   Digital twin in industry.

Source: https://www.xenonstack.com/insights/digital-twin-in-industry

how an IoT device behaves over the course of its life cycle are virtually represented. There are several items, including manufacturing floor operations, buildings, and jet engines. Digital twins are simply computer programs that collect data from the actual environment to create simulations that really can forecast how well a process or product will function. To enhance performance, these systems can incorporate software analytics, AI, and IoT.

These innovations are now a crucial component of the newest technologies to spur innovation and boost performance thanks to developments in machine learning and big data. Creating one, in essence, allows for the improvement of strategic technological trends, eliminates expensive failures of physical items, and makes use of predictive capabilities, services, advanced analytics, testing techniques, and surveillance.

3.5.3   How Does Industrial Use of Digital Twin Technology Work?

In order to construct a mathematical model that will imitate the genuine, applied data science is first used to examine the physics, mathematics, and transactional processes of a systems or material thing. Digital twin designers enable sensors to gather information from the real versions to provide input to virtual computer models [12]. This enables real-time simulation and imitation of exactly what is occurring inside the earlier design in the digital version, providing insights into efficiency and potential complications. Using different levels of information defining how precisely the model simulates the actual tangible version, digital twins can be as basic or complicated as required. The twin can also be utilized in conjunction with a prototype to get user input on the design or as a stand-alone prototype to simulate what will happen to the physical version when it is built.

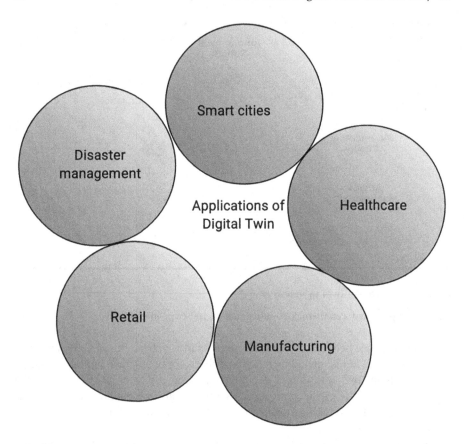

FIGURE 3.7   Applications of digital twin.

3.5.4 APPLICATIONS OF DIGITAL TWIN

In a wide range of uses and applications [13,14], digital twins are being deployed across numerous industries as shown in Figure 3.7.

3.5.4.1 Smart Cities

Digital twins are increasingly being utilized to assist cities in achieving greater societal, environmental, and economic sustainability. Innovation can aid in establishing priorities and offer answers to a number of common problems that face contemporary communities.

3.5.4.2 Healthcare

The medical field is using digital twins to reduce risk during surgery, educate surgeons, and donate organs, among other things. The system constantly monitors where the virus is and who might be at danger of exposure, as well as how patients move through the hospital.

3.5.4.3 Manufacturing

Digital twins can shorten queuing time while streamlining and increasing productivity in construction.

3.5.4.4 Retail

Using digital twins to simulate and improve the consumer experience is a trend in retailing that is distinct from industry and manufacturing.

3.5.4.5 Disaster Management

In light of the current negative impacts of climate change on the planet, digital twins can be used to build better intelligent infrastructures, monitor climate change, and develop emergency service strategies.

3.5.5 WHAT ADVANTAGES COME WITH USING A DIGITAL TWIN?

Utilizing digital twins has the following advantages [12,15]:

3.5.5.1 Remote Monitoring

In real-time is frequently highly challenging or even unattainable when trying to acquire a thorough picture of a massive physical system. But because digital twins are accessible from wherever, users may check on and manage the functioning of the system from a distance.

3.5.5.2 Expedited Risk Analysis and Production Time

With the help of digital twins, businesses may validate and test their goods before they are really used.

3.5.5.3 The Digital Twin Enables Engineers to Find Production Flaws

By correctly replicating the envisaged production chain, a product is developed prior going into production. Engineers can tamper with the network to examine its reaction, produce unforeseen changes, and select the best possible mitigation techniques. This function enhances risk analysis, speeds up the creation of new products, and boosts the dependability of the manufacturing process.

3.5.5.4 Improved Cooperation

Within the team technicians can concentrate more on team cooperation and operational effectiveness thanks to process mechanization and 24 × 7 accessibility to information system.

3.5.5.5 Predictive Maintenance

Businesses can evaluate data generated by the IoT technology in a digital twin system is to detect issues with the system before they arise. With the help of this tool, businesses may more precisely plan their preventative analysis, increase the productivity of their manufacturing lines, and lower upfront costs.

3.5.6 ARTIFICIAL INTELLIGENCE BOTS FOR THE INTERNET OF THINGS IN THE FUTURE

IoT (Internet of Things) and AI (Artificial Intelligence) are expected to modernize the planet in the upcoming years because they both make important contributions to cutting-edge technology that can change the world. IoT and AI may both produce intelligent machines that support decision-making processes and deliver data with little to no human input [16]. AI can evaluate and use the vast amounts of data generated by IIoT sensors and devices, and chat bots make it simple to obtain data. Additionally, as IIoT use grows, more data is generated by cutting-edge devices and sensors; managing the massive amounts of data generated by this requires digital twin and AI.

Governments and businesses are both concentrating on constructing smart cities utilizing new technologies. Hexagon, for instance, offers digital twins for cities that might aid in improved government planning. A digital terrain model, 3D building model, LiDAR point cloud, and HD images make up the new model. The business has produced 3D digital twins of the entire planet since the government will be able to monitor resources and predict risk with the aid of digital twins of cities. The construction of infrastructure initiatives for improved communication can also benefit from the use of this technology.

The patient care and healthcare industries are also gaining ground because of technologies like IoT, digital twins, and AI. For instance, a digital twin of a patient or organ can assist medical professionals in practicing complex procedures on mannequins rather than real people. Your business must be able to identify and respond in real-time in order to effectively utilize the power of digital twins. In order to avoid having any blind spots along the route, you also need a solid partner who can assist you with all facets of your marketing strategy. Innovative technologies can aid businesses in completing a variety of complex tasks, improving the implementation of corporate strategies. They can also aid in making better decisions in the volatile business climate.

3.6 SMART DECISION MAKING IN INDUSTRY 4.0

Industry 4.0 signifies the ongoing digitalization of industrial automation and processes, where IT and OT are seamlessly integrated to improve production and services. Operations technology (OT) refers to systems that carry out the real production/manufacturing job. On the other side, data or information is delivered, handled, analyzed, and stored using IT or information technology [17]. Through the use of technologies like IoT, intelligent systems, cloud technology, robotic systems, etc., Industry 4.0 unites these two. This gives users tremendous control and visibility over the production process as well as the activities that surround it. Industry 4.0 provides business and operational intelligence, which not only makes a factory smarter but also opens up the opportunity for quick decisions.

3.6.1 HOW TO IMPLEMENT INDUSTRY 4.0 INTO PRACTICE?

The first and most crucial step in implementing an Industry 4.0 solution is for a company to already possess Industry 3.0 in place as shown in Figure 3.8. A company

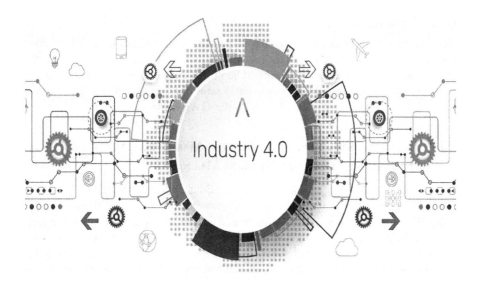

FIGURE 3.8 Smart Industry 4.0.

Source: https://www.nebeskie.com/blogs/Industry4.0.htm

cannot modernize without Industry 3.0 deployment. The following includes the most crucial areas on which you should focus while carrying out an E2E integration of I4.0 (Industry 4.0), presuming that it is already in position:

3.6.1.1 "IoT Stack"

Connecting OT to IT, IoT, or IIoT is essential. But you need an IoT stack in place for that to work seamlessly and reliably. There is no one right method to select or deploy a technology stack, but using a scalable, loosely linked design is the best option.

3.6.1.2 Stacks for Data Management or Analysis

Without data, nothing exists in the world. A low latency, high availability system must be built in the case of an Industry 4.0 solution to manage data processing and normalization. Additionally, it should be able to perform data analysis and, in some situations, machine learning.

3.6.1.3 Streams and Cloud-Based Storage

In order for the data set to really be valuable, it must be preserved. Cloud storage data can be used as a database in machine learning and data mining. For data distribution over APIs and IoT endpoints, a data streaming service is required.

3.6.1.4 User Interface

For the user to access the data, see reports, operate equipment, etc., this is necessary. Data visualization for business and operational intelligence should be possible with the UI.

3.6.1.5 Internet Safety

When deploying an Industry 4.0 solution, you shouldn't overlook one of the most important - and frequently forgotten - things. Without security, IT and OT integration is risky. A cyber-attack might be the outcome of solutions with exposed weaknesses. Encryption and compartmentalization are crucial. To make sure that your solution is secure, you can adhere to the OWASP top10.

3.6.2 INDUSTRY 4.0's IMPACTS ON BUSINESS MANAGERIAL ACTIVITIES, PARTICULARLY ON SMART DECISION MAKING

The leadership of a company makes the decisions necessary to run it. We might also state that decision-making and management are the same thing. I'm not going to get into the semantic distinctions between the definitions of a manager and a leader right now. The managing process is carried out by one or many more people in order to connect and synchronize the organizational activity, while the manager serves as the individual who determines the key decisions for the business's operation, based on the original study evaluation. Decision-making is one of the four responsibilities of management described above because planning, organization, management, and controlling all demand particular actions. I think that while thinking about managerial decision-making, one can start with the assertions given in reference [18]. It emphasized the importance of the manager's style allowing for the delegation of decision-making responsibility in relation to digitalization, among many other features. We wish to focus on the operational aspects of the envoy.

Identification of the data and processes influencing the business operations is the cornerstone of business decisions during the new industrial revolution. The information that the management needs in order to make a decision should first be articulated. Only very seldom does the existing evidence have an adequate structure, though. The accurate selection, sorting, and interpretation of the facts and information is a crucial part of the management's preparation for making important decisions.

Making decisions is a crucial component of management activity in the corporate world. On the basis of the information in the preceding sections, it can be concluded that digitalization is necessary for all decision-making in business operations that fall within Industry 4.0 [19,20]. Today, however, management is not solely responsible for making decisions because some of it can be delegated to others, specifically computers and other smart devices with algorithms. The discussion regarding the delegation of management's decision-making authority has intensified as a result of Industry 4.0, as it is no longer limited to humans. Not delegation itself, but the level of delegation is a topic of discussion all the time today. Only decisions that are predictable, easily significant, and later dependably revisable. Budgeting and distribution are best left to intelligent machines, robotics, and algorithms, but they can do the same with accuracy if they base their choices on defensible standards. This implies that management may designate the aforementioned tools to complete duties like predicting the amount of time required for a producing-servicing activity, figuring out how many machinery hours are required, distributing workers within the plant/factory/company, etc.

Several informational tools and digitalization solutions support management decision-making in the era of Industry 4.0. Data are available in far greater abundance than before. However, data redundancy, which seems to go on forever, only appears to make it tougher for management to make decisions [7]. All of that is achieved with the management's help in synthesizing a significantly larger amount of information utilizing significantly better productive and effective digitalization techniques compared to earlier. Industry 4.0 relies heavily on artificial intelligence because it allows managers to make computational decisions remotely. In this manner, the amount of time required for decision-making in production and production management can be decreased, increasing tool usage and efficiency.

The entire firm supply chain has been digitalized, which has made data processing and data structuring simpler. The autonomous development of infographics and reports, as well as the showing of its absolute values, are features that promote a greater knowledge of the production chain. As an outcome, they are capable of informing administration about the needed interventions. However, for sound decision-making, management must analyze the information produced and take into account more than just the automatically generated statements. Systems for organizing and analyzing product data and production-related characteristics provide effective decision-support for management within the Industry 4.0 framework.

Because all the information and features could be found during one place or might be obtainable in the processed stage, the time required of the decision-making process can be greatly reduced. According to Industry 4.0 [21], digitizing management decision-making can provide an uniform decision-making environment with all outcome, which is its major benefit. It is possible because a computer, a controller, or perhaps another smart gadget can offer the same data and information (even in the same environment). As a result, in this kind of situation, the manager who must make a decision is forced to do so it based solely on the information and facts that the technology has given him.

3.6.3 Industry 4.0: Increasing the Use of Data in Decision Making

Data is ubiquitous: Data becomes knowledge in the majority of companies (including the industrial sector), which in turn yields Intellectual Property (IP) and competitive advantage. In terms of business understanding, there is a lot to be done to distinguish usable or valuable data from non-value-added data.

With the proliferation of devices connected, large data, affordable storage options, data mining, and analytics technologies to visualize and explore (or "dig into") it to the desired extent of detail, there are many opportunities to harness data and turn it into value. However, the manufacturing domain has not yet caught up to the engineering and product development domain (upstream) in the drive to wealth generation (downstream). The Internet of Things (IoT) and Industry 4.0 frameworks are frequently "things" that relate to production process, typically after introduction of new products activities.

3.6.3.1 Information Supporting Various Choices at Various Product Lifecycle Stages

The questions that may result are mentioned below:

- How is data used differently in the manufacturing sector (downstream) compared to the engineering and product development sector (upstream)?
- Which decisions are made upstream and downstream, and in which domain are they more data-driven or intuitive?
- Are there any similarities or differences between data models, types, and structures, and if so, how are decisions made in the various fields?
- How much of the cascaded data is used downstream in the decision-making process, given that a lot of information goes from engineering and product development to manufacturing?
- Do decisions made downstream depend on information produced (or authored/mastered) upstream? How does data work?

3.6.3.2 Data-Driven Decisions Are Wise Ones

Since decisions are made by people, insights, rather than just statistics, information, and expertise, must guide them. Decisions are based on data, which may be retrieved at the appropriate time, in the appropriate format, and made available to the appropriate individuals. Information that individuals can rely on and understand.

- What potential changes to the decision-making process could Industry 4.0 bring? It will propel a concoction of:
- Better data infrastructure across activities and domains, including data stream feedback mechanisms and upstream data optimized for use downstream (e.g., design for manufacturing, and design for assembly).
- Stronger link between engineering and manufacturing thanks to data intelligence driven by decisions rather than by data.
- An understanding of "data effective judgments" as opposed to "data-aided decisions" - out of which structural modeling (and individuals) can better individuals by utilizing machine learning as well as, eventually, some form of artificial intelligence.

3.6.3.3 Extending from Explaining to Supporting Decision-Making

Business users and other relevant stakeholders can typically view "data," but due to various technical and procedural restrictions, which have repeatedly raised important issues in the manufacturing industry, they can hardly trust it. These worries result from a lack of data transparency and comprehension:

- Users should be able to identify the origin of data, as well as its dependencies and lifetime.
- Can they comprehend and effectively utilize its ever-increasing complexity?
- Can they rely on digital tools to manage and regulate it in addition to storing it?

- Can they foresee the appropriate level of flexibility to support the entire product realization cycle and therefore can they depend on lean production to build, adapt, and maintain it?
- Could people recognize the applicability and worth of the way it is provided to them?

Enterprise data appears to be becoming increasingly complicated in the background while still being user-friendly. Yet what do you accomplish with it? How is the fundamental information documented, maintained, and managed (or not)? How much knowledge of what robots are doing must users have in order for their decisions to be effective? Users may be able to search for and locate data traceability, but they may not be able to comprehend it or recognize its significance. Bureaucracy of processes and information won't be viable in the future. Prior to recently, most reasonable choices were irrational. Reliable data is required for smart judgments.

3.6.3.4   Intelligent Decision-Making

AI-driven optimization of supply chains software accentuates major decisions by recommending the optimum action to take based on cognitive forecasts [22]. The effectiveness of the whole supply chain might increase as a result. It also helps companies understand potential revenue, effort, and costs associated along a variety of scenarios. Furthermore, it keeps improving those suggestions as the conditions change as it acquires new knowledge over time.

3.7   INTELLIGENT AUTOMATION IN INDUSTRY 4.0

Intelligent automation (IA) is now the primary force behind digital transformation operations, assisting businesses in going digital smoothly. IA is built using robotic process automation (RPA) and artificial intelligence (AI), with RPA streamlining operations and reducing the amount of user interference and AI enabling extra perspective evaluation, outcome, and personnel planning (*see* Figure 3.9). The "Industrial Internet of Things" (IIoT) enables the interconnection, control, and monitoring of networking of devices, robots, automation, and cloud services in real-time (through "Cloud Monitoring"). They can accomplish all of this virtually, which minimizes the need for human interaction while improving output.

3.7.1   Automation's Role in Industry 4.0

Automated production should be deployed as a holistic solution that covers all of the firm's activities and enables knowledge to stream across all its components in order for its worth to be realized.

Industry 4.0 automation now places a greater emphasis on job margins of error reduction than just efficiency and profitability. It also offers greater flexibility and a considerable enhancement in the quality of the industrial processes [23]. Digital twins exercise virtual models that act as the foundation for smart decision-making

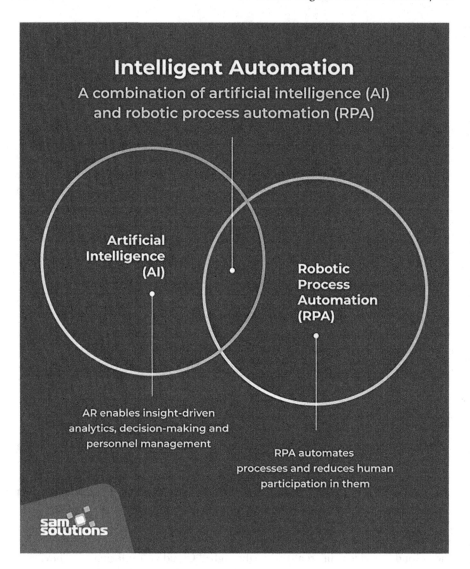

FIGURE 3.9   Intelligent automation.

Source: https://www.sam-solutions.com/blog/intelligent-automation/

throughout the lifecycle of the process. A smart manufacturing system could lower the margin of error in operations where it can reach up to 10% when the work is done by a human to as little as 0.00001%.

In Figure 3.9, IA is a general phrase that refers to a variety of tactics, methods, tools, and approaches that decrease the necessity for labor, boost services predictability and dependability, and cut costs. IA technologies that are enabled by guideline, patterned, and standardized data can help with the aforementioned workplace inadequacies:

- Massive price of labor
- Lack of workers and inefficiency
- Repetitious jobs that are resource and time-intensive
- Difficult to comprehend large amounts of intricate information
- Poorly made goods and services

3.7.2 Automation's Benefits in Industry 4.0

The following are the primary advantages of automation in Industry 4.0 [24] as shown in Figure 3.10:

3.7.2.1 Cost Effectiveness

Lowers labor expenses by automating parts of processes that don't need human judgment and utilizing human ingenuity to learn new abilities and perform tasks as needed. Technologies that use virtual or augmented reality can also expedite learning and improve efficient organizational frameworks.

3.7.2.2 Competitive Benefits

Procedures can be automated and standardized, rendering them reliable and ready to run continuously.

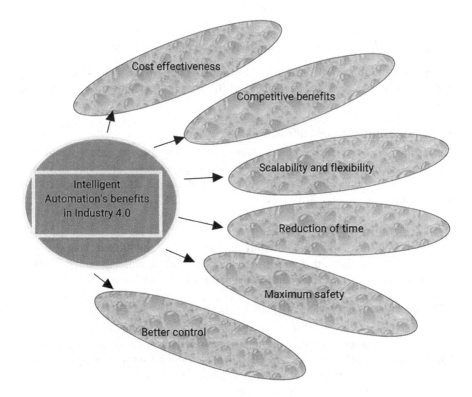

FIGURE 3.10 Intelligent automation's benefits in Industry 4.0.

3.7.2.3   Scalability and Flexibility

Human operators need training to add or change duties, whereas robots and gadgets can be precisely programmed in a short amount of time, which speeds up process execution and response time.

3.7.2.4   Reduction of Time

Fast turnaround durations for data. Data is derived from processes can be stored and managed extensively inside the automation systems.

3.7.2.5   Maximum Safety

The production line may assign robots and/or machines to risky jobs that put workers at risk. For equipment, components, people, and systems, enhanced comprehensive security measures can also be put in place. One of the key technologies to protect businesses' privacy is cyber security.

3.7.2.6   Better Control

Because these activities are monitored and documented, "Big Data" is produced. This is important information because it can be used to spot trends, enhance procedures, and make adjustments to stop future occurrences. Process optimization also makes "Insourcing" possible. This infrastructure centralization enhances data consistency and quality and enhances analytical capabilities.

3.7.3   Challenges with Intelligent Automation in Industry 4.0

Despite the enormous potential that automation 4.0 offers businesses [24,25], it is important to be aware of and evaluate the difficulties presented by this new business model.

3.7.3.1   Investment and Infrastructure

For businesses, adapting the current framework to the innovative one could be a significant challenge. Companies will need to engage significant sums of money and, frequently, obtain financing in order to purchase the necessary infrastructure and select the most areas of interest.

3.7.3.2   Strategic Plan

The transition involves time, a shift in perspective, intelligent analysis, and competence by continual that emphasizes adoption and capitalizing on the expenditure. It also depends on investments in technology and machinery.

3.7.3.3   Human Factor

Smart gadgets are no longer working tools; they have evolved into smart workers, and automating procedures are expected to result in the loss of billions of jobs in the future. Consequently, societies and big businesses should support ongoing training for employees to help them acquire appropriate digital skills that are compatible with this emerging sector of the economy.

3.8 CONCLUSION

This chapter elaborates in detail about Industry 4.0 coupled with Artificial Intelligence which is further integrated with intelligent decision making, smart automation in today's scenario of Industry 4.0 applications. The advancements and expanded enhancements in industry manufacturing and its modernized applications make the smart industries more productive and further it also presents more innovations and challenges in our smart world of technological advancements.

REFERENCES

[1] Deloitte Touche Tohmatsu Limited, commonly referred to as Deloitte, is an international professional services network headquartered in London, England.

[2] https://utthunga.com/blogs/9-technologies-which-form-the-building-blocks-for-industry-4-0/.

[3] Lee, J. (2015). Smart factory systems. *Informatik-Spektrum, 38.* 10.1007/s00287-015-0891-z.

[4] Javaid, M., et al. (2022). Artificial intelligence applications for Industry 4.0: A literature-based study. *Journal of Industrial Integration and Management, 7*(01), 83–111.

[5] Alao, B. B., and Gbolagade, O. L. (October 2019). An assessment of how Industry 4.0 technology is transforming audit landscape and business models. *International Journal of Academic Accounting, Finance & Management Research (IJAAFMR), 3*(10), 15–20, ISSN: 2643-976X.

[6] Stadnicka, D., S.ep, J., Amadio, R., Mazzei, D., Tyrovolas, et al. (2022). Industrial needs in the fields of Artificial Intelligence, Internet of Things and Edge Computing. *Sensors, 22,* 4501. 10.3390/s22124501.

[7] Nagy, J., Oláh, J., Erdei, E., Máté, D., and Popp, J. (2018). The role and impact of Industry 4.0 and the Internet of Things on the business strategy of the value chain—the case of Hungary. *Sustainability, 10,* 3491. 10.3390/su10103491.

[8] Vogel-Heuser, B., Bayrak, G., and Frank, U. (2011). Agenda CPS - scenario Smart Factory (Agenda CPS - Szenario smart factory). *Increased availability and transparent production,* pp. 6–21, Kassel.

[9] Lucke, D., Constantinescu, C., and Westkämper, E. (2008). Smart Factory—a step towards the next generation of manufacturing, in *Manufacturing systems and technologies for the new frontier,* Springer, pp. 115–118.

[10] Pires, F., Cachada, A., Barbosa, J., Moreira, A. P., and Leitão, P. (2019). Digital twin in Industry 4.0: Technologies, applications and challenges. 2019 IEEE 17th International Conference on Industrial Informatics (INDIN), Helsinki, Finland, pp. 721–726, doi: 10.1109/INDIN41052.2019.8972134.

[11] Wang, Z. (2020). Digital Twin Technology. 10.5772/intechopen.80974.

[12] Hinduja, H., Kekkar, S., Chourasia, S., and Chakrapani, H. (2020). Industry 4.0: Digital twin and its industrial applications. *RIET-IJSET International Journal of Science Engineering and Technology, 21,* 343–355.

[13] Hu, W., Lim, K. Y. H., and Cai, Y. (2022). Digital twin and Industry 4.0 enablers in building and construction: A survey. *Buildings, 12,* 2004. 10.3390/buildings12112004.

[14] Jiang, Y., Yin, S., Li, K., Luo, H., and Kaynak, O. (2021). Industrial applications of digital twins. *Philosophical Transactions of the Royal Society A: Mathematical, Physical and Engineering Sciences, 379,* 20200360. 10.1098/rsta.2020.0360.

[15] Mendonca, R., Lins, S., Bessa, I., Ayres, F., Landau, R., and Lucena Jr, V. (2022). Digital twin applications: A survey of recent advances and challenges. *Processes, 2022,* 744. 10.3390/pr10040744.

[16] Ghosh, A., and Chakraborty, D., and Law, A. (2018). Artificial Intelligence in Internet of Things. *CAAI Transactions on Intelligence Technology, 3.* 10.1049/trit. 2018.1008.

[17] Rosin, F., Forget, P., Lamouri, S., and Pellerin, R. (2021). Impact of Industry 4.0 on decision-making in an operational context. *Advances in Production Engineering & Management, 16,* 500–514. 10.14743/apem2021.4.416.

[18] Cianni, M., and Steckler, S. (2017). Transforming organizations to a digital world. *Human Resource Planning Society, 40*(2), 14–20.

[19] Porter, M. E., and Heppelmann, J. E. (2015). How smart, connected products are transforming companies. *Harvard Business Review, 93*(10), 96–114.

[20] Rosin, F., Forget, P., Lamouri, S., and Pellerin, R. (2022). Enhancing the decision-making process through Industry 4.0 technologies. *Sustainability, 14,* 461. 10.3390/su14010461

[21] Moeuf, A., Pellerin, R., Lamouri, S., Tamayo-Giraldo, S., and Barbaray, R. (2017). The industrial management of SMEs in the era of Industry 4.0. *International Journal of Production Research, 56*(3), 1118–1136. doi: 10.1080/00207543.2017.1372647.

[22] https://throughput.world/blog/ai-in-supply-chain-and-logistics/

[23] Tyagi, A. K., Fernandez, T. F., Mishra, S., and Kumari, S. (2021). Intelligent automation systems at the core of Industry 4.0. In: Abraham, A., Piuri, V., Gandhi, N., Siarry, P., Kaklauskas, A., and Madureira, A. (eds.) *Intelligent systems design and applications. ISDA 2020. Advances in intelligent systems and computing,* vol. 1351. Springer, Cham. 10.1007/978-3-030-71187-0_1.

[24] Vashist, A. (2022). Smart and Intelligent Automation for Industry 4.0 using Millimeter-Wave and Deep Reinforcement Learning. Thesis. Rochester Institute of Technology. Accessed from https://scholarworks.rit.edu/theses/11269.

[25] Coito, T., Viegas, J. L., Martins, M. S. E., Cunha, M. M., Figueiredo, J., Vieira, S. M., and Sousa, J. M. C. (2019). A novel framework for intelligent automation. *IFAC-PapersOnLine, 52*(13), 1825–1830, ISSN 2405-8963, https://doi.org/10.101 6/j.ifacol.2019.11.501.

4 Digital Twin Technology

A Review

Ambika Nagaraj

4.1 INTRODUCTION

Computerized Twin (Batty, 2018) is a digital picture of an existing object containing information about a stated thing, beginning in the field of item lifespan-sequence management. It comprises three parts, an essential item, a simulated portrayal of that item, the bi-guiding information associations that feed information from the biological to the representative example, and data and cycles from the simulated characterization to the material. The virtual spaces comprise several sub-spaces that empower explicit virtual tasks: demonstrating, testing, streamlining, and so forth.

The computerized twin (Chakraborty & Adhikari, 2021; Park, Woo, & Choi, 2020) refreshes with sensor information in close to ongoing. The sensor information expands with engineered information created from test systems, bringing actual authenticity at high spatiotemporal goals. The computerized twin doesn't just give real-time data for more educated navigation yet can likewise make expectations about how the resource will develop or act from here on out. It will be unclear from the actual help concerning appearance and conduct with the additional benefit of making future expectations. Figure 4.1 represents a block figure of the computer-oriented identical.

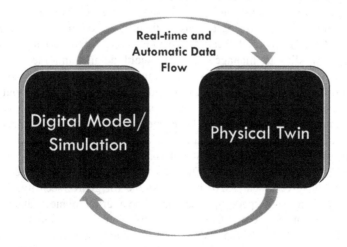

FIGURE 4.1 Block diagram of a digital twin (Singh et al., 2022).

DOI: 10.1201/9781003395416-4

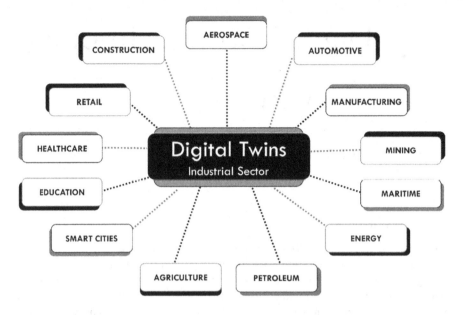

FIGURE 4.2 Applications of digital twins (Singh et al., 2022).

4.2 LITERATURE SURVEY

The section details the usage of the technology in various domains. Figure 4.2 represents applications of digital twins.

4.2.1 AEROSPACE

The virtual replica is a dynamic model incorporating biological samples, functional knowledge, and other details to their fullest potential. It is multi-disciplinary, multi-physics, and multiscale. It can achieve the mapping of bodily commodities in a digital area, thereby mirroring their whole life procedure. The virtual model can be constantly balanced and matched to the material commodity to manage real-time yield details and the bidirectional mapping between it and the physical item (Dhanalakshmi, R., Anand, J., Sivaraman, A. K., & Rani, S., 2022). The development of the computer-based replica is based on the modeling and simulation of systems. Numerous domestic and international studies have been carried out in aerospace system modeling and simulation. Various airplane approaches have been confirmed at tetrad stories of the segment representative.

AIRBUS Protection and Space Division of Airbus Gathering (Bécue, Maia, Feeken, Borchers, & Praça, 2020) is accountable for guard, security, correspondence, knowledge, and space applications. The martial plane industry unit of Airbus Defence and Space produces service carriers and combatant airliners, such as the A400M, C295, CN235, A330 MRTT, and Eurofighter Typhoon. The proposed use case seeks to incorporate Industrial IoT in Spain's Tablada, San

Pablo Sur, and CBC manufacturers for flexible management and system optimization. These AIRBUS D&S plants will soon see an industrial IoT deployment. After that, it will integrate factory assets like the rivet shaving apparatus (Roboshave), the manufacturing oven (Autoclave), and the progressive intellectual instruments control system (Gap Gun) into this IIoT Network. It will make it possible to monitor, control, and improve the resilience of remote processes close to real time (Bhambri et al., 2008). This Internet of Things (IoT) system will be used across three locations and encircle three kinds of fabricating investments. It will create a comprehensive virtual model of the system to facilitate secure network design, implementation, and procedure of this IIoT grid. Decision-making based on simulation, protection examination, testing and verification, process, and training will all be made possible by it. Intelligent wearable and environmental detectors will also make it possible to simulate human operator behavior, especially when handling a gap gun, a hand tool used to measure the quality of aeronautical parts. Using non-invasive sensing elements to backing Client and Commodity conduct statistics, it can also model user behavior on the IT tier by studying web gridlock and seed information. Figure 4.3 details the same.

The virtual element of the computerized twin framework (Liu et al., 2021) incorporates the attributes of natural imitation and adaptively gets comparable shape highlights and actual belongings. The digital twin model also possesses characteristics that change in response to the digital procedure. At long last, it can re-establish the item protests with high devotion from the parts of figure calculation, conduct, strategy, etc. The digital twin's reference model is derived by conducting an analogous analysis of the mimic process of the organisms above and the model-making procedure. The digital twin system uses the three dimensions of shapes,

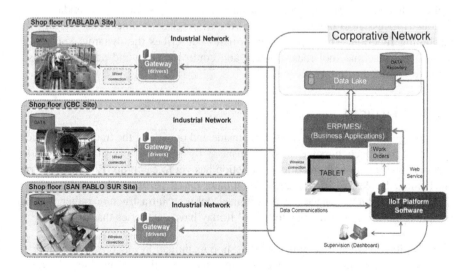

FIGURE 4.3 Architecture aerospace manufacturing use-case (Bécue, Maia, Feeken, Borchers, & Praça, 2020; Bécue, Maia, Feeken, Borchers, & Praça, 2020).

conduct, and text to make a computer-generated prototype (Chauhan, M., & Rani, S., 2021). The corporal item is then controlled through decision analysis using the virtual model. It emphasizes that the data prototypical of the corporeal object is created by the virtual entity from trio perspectives - geometry, behavior, and context (Bhambri & Singh, 2008). This reference model's virtual entity is highly self-adaptive. The concept of biological mimicry is combined with this study's virtual replica impersonator sample. By incorporating the metric information in the "*Model*-based definition" (MBD) and "Digital Transformation Maturity Model" (DTMM) model, it creates the in-process model, merges with the developed prototype, and combines data on manners and context. The DTMM's geometric details include the product's geometric information as designed and in-process geometric information, which reflects the product's shape changes during manufacturing. The operational condition of the creation, as mirrored by the material prototype in response to the external environment and stimulation and the fluctuating procedure of the product's biological tier, constitute the behavior information in the DTMM. The DTMM's context information comprises procedure preparation and precise machining operation surveillance data (Thapar & Bhambri, 2009).

Planning-relevant data from the machining process is combined with mathematical models and algorithms to determine process parameters in this system (Hänel et al., 2020). It must connect the production environment to various data sources to establish a virtual replica of the machining procedure. These data types come from multiple information repositories and can be divided into stationary and changing data types (Kothandaraman, D., Manickam, M., Balasundaram, A., Pradeep, D., Arulmurugan, A., Sivaraman, A. K., & Balakrishna, R., 2022). The relevant data are divided into five groups to make a computer-based procedure identical. These are examples of workpiece information, operation knowledge, technology details, digital info, and instrument details. These data serve as the data foundation for various process examples to choose the biological connections during the machining function. The approach information describes the dynamic knowledge cluster. All machine tool measurement and control signals and additional sensor data are included in the process data.

4.2.2 Healthcare

Technology for digital health exists both inside and outside of the traditional medical system. It has been pursued with enthusiasm by some sectors of the healthcare industry, but patient and practitioner adoption has yet to catch up (Rani, S., Kataria, A., Kumar, S., & Tiwari, P., 2023). Computer-based permitted isolated persistent nursing is becoming a necessity for clinical delivery infrastructure rather than an intriguing innovation or a "nice to have." It may have categories that overlap.

- Digital healthcare documents, workshop examination outcomes, drugstore information, fitness insurance lawsuits, and other details developed by an individual's dealings with the standard wellness design are all clinically developed data.

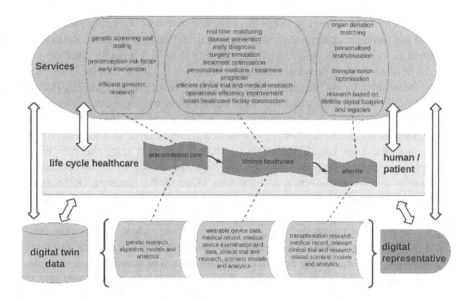

FIGURE 4.4   Digital twin model in healthcare (Hassani, Huang, & MacFeely, 2022).

- Saleable real-world fitness information is gathered by agendas aimed at inhabitants' healthiness administration that supplement conventional healthcare by providing targeted populations with wellness and disease management to increase risk pools.
- Data generated by consumer digital health devices are becoming increasingly sophisticated. An array of digital technologies that are commercially available and connections are now accessible to use in the maintenance and welfare of critical enduring residents and to breed information that is experimentally appropriate from non-scientific warehouses.
- People generate well-being-evocative information out of a combination of non-healthiness. These non-clinical data are not directly related to fitness but contemplate other routine components and can offer supplemental understandings of healthiness. Figure 4.4 illustrates digital twin model in healthcare.

The work (Kaul et al., 2022) is done in collaboration with a well-known tumor clinic in Australia. As a result, they have admission to doctors and pertinent information to help make digital twins and use them in healthcare to help make better patient decisions. It can use Artificial Intelligence (AI) algorithms to diagnose and predict cancer by considering various chance characteristics to decide the patient's survival and illness throughout its lifespan. Virtual replicas can help describe and incorporate this info into an individual's digital image while using AI procedures to diagnose tumors. Analytical information is used to determine if a patient has cancer, what kind of cancer it is, and how big it is. Information about potential outcomes, such as survival and recurrence, can be gained from predictive data. Prescient information is utilized to gauge and give data regarding the excellent result of the patient's malignant growth because of definitive treatment. Response to treatment is measured using treatment monitoring data, and outcome data are used to train new AI models or retrain existing ones.

The recommendation (Angulo, Gonzalez-Abril, Raya, & Ortega, 2020) introduces the invention of a virtual replica for individualized wellness regarding the behavior of this illness in an affected role, which is applied to the health field, specifically lung cancer. It promotes a renewed representative in which details are the essence, the most valuable acquisition, the asset it must spin, and the guiding principle for the solution of information systems thanks to advancements in information and communication technologies (Kumar, P., Banerjee, K., Singhal, N., Kumar, A., Rani, S., Kumar, R., & Lavinia, C. A., 2022). Anonymization is a method for determining and concealing susceptible knowledge in records, permitting its revelation without violating the liberties of individuals and organizations that it can reference to protect their data. It is used to reduce the dangers associated with receiving and massively calibrating private data. The training data serve as a seedbed, enabling the capture of information from authentic information and the generation of refreshed details with behavior comparable to the original. The term "medical knowledge" refers to the experience gained through learning, spotting signs and symptoms, weighing the risks, and finally coming up with a diagnosis and a treatment plan for each patient.

It is a digital twin healthcare framework (Liu, et al., 2019) for the cloud healthcare system (CloudDTH). In the cloud, it is a novel, general, and extendable structure for monitoring, analyzing, and forecasting a person's fitness characteristics. It employs wearable clinical instruments, for personal health management, particularly for seniors. External factors and DTH data primarily drive the system. The external driving force is the climate or pleasant procedure, which will impact patients' soundness and judgments, affecting the digital simulation and the cloud healthcare service platform's decision-making (Kataria, A., Puri, V., Pareek, P. K., & Rani, S., 2023, July). Basic item information, computerized article information, administration information, outer variables information, and their combination information are the leading interior impetuses of the framework. Actual situation details, environmental information, behavioral facts, and other details from a biological entity, digital object prototypical information, imitation statistics, assessment information, and other knowledge from the cloud healthcare service platform are all managed and analyzed by the DTH database.

The work (Zhang et al., 2020) is a brand-new deep neural model for capturing the risky code keywords' bidirectional context relationships. This type of parameter logic is captured using the word2vec CBOW example. Since the context in the corpus is used by the CBOW representative to generate the code vectors of the target code words, each corpus will have unique contexts for the mark regulation phrases. The study teaches the individual regulation embedding instances using nine open-source assignments and the SARD database to represent the source code better. Thanks to this setup, it captures the semantic information that the dataset's code stream is attempting to describe. The CBOW model is trained without supervision. It doesn't utilize weakness names and considers principal knowledge and portrayal at this phase. The whole token series vector represents the process's complete logic in the output code representation. The connection between the singular code pieces in a code succession might generate a weakness in the programming code.

4.2.3 Automobiles

The digital model and information about each actual plant asset make up the virtual replica, a digital representation of the presentation method. In the motorized enterprise, incorporating new automobiles into living display skills is progressively urgent. There are a variety of prototypes, including those with detonation machines, mixed and electric standards, and alternatives like sedans, coupes, and cabriolets that need to be incorporated into the current manufacturing scheme. The figure-in-white creation framework is a significant exchange for most car producers. This industry necessitates a great deal of experience gained over many years in the automotive industry. Here, the individual components are joined together downstream of the pressing plant. An automotive company's planners typically design the manufacturing facility. The details that can be divided into a production system are contained in the structure of the planning system. A production system's hierarchical structure is made up of a place, a zone, a cubicle, an element, and an apparatus segment. Organizers use a precise supply collection with numerous units to plan production systems. They locate the repositories geometrically as a yield structure based on the constructed facility. Figure 4.5 represents a digital twin system.

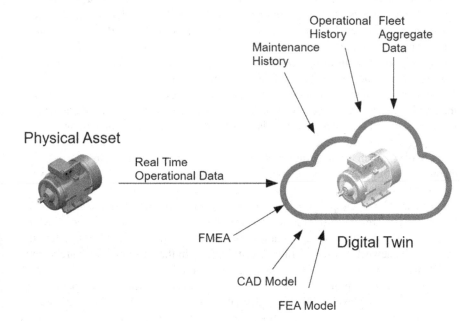

FIGURE 4.5 Digital twin system (Ibrahim, Rassōlkin, Vaimann, & Kallaste, 2022; Ibrahim, Rassōlkin, Vaimann, & Kallaste, 2022).

A digital twin uses the finest material instances, detectors, cavalcade records, and probabilistic simulations. It uses them at multiple scales and in various physics. It imitates the life of its physical counterpart. Working out mega-designs mirror designs, also known as incarnations, are digital representations of actual products, processes, or services (Rani, S., Arya, V., & Kataria, A., 2022). A virtual replica could be a digital copy of a real object like a wind farm, or jet engine, a bigger one like a building, or even a whole city. It can use them to repeat procedures to gather information to indicate how they will function, in addition to physical assets.

In this case study (Croatti, Gabellini, Montagna, & Ricci, 2020), a mediator-based digital twin digitalizes and supports the administration of severe traumas. There are two major stages to the trauma technique: the pre-clinical stage, in which the sick is seen by a doctor at the scene of the mishap to receive first aid and is taken to the infirmary trouble division. The operative step, in which the patient receives assistance from the hospital emergency department's trauma team, follows. Crisis recording is also necessary for a posteriori calculation when trauma surveillance is continuous. In this instance, the chief, or the medic in charge of the group, can consistently take an encyclopedic public gaze at the continuing trauma to make a more informed choice about saving the patient's life. A further essential requirement emerged after two years of system testing: the need for ongoing monitoring of the trauma's entire state, the involved sick, and the care unit, even during the pre-hospital phase.

Consequently, it re-planned the TraumaTracker system to employ an agent-based computer-based replica construction for both degrees. Rescue workers take charge of the patient's case during the PreH phase and determine whether the condition is an intense concussion; only in the latter case is the trauma team activated. The pre-hospital care process's digital counterpart is the PreH digital twin. It considers information provided by the primary division, the vehicle's GPS, and rescuers' intelligent devices used to create emergency forms when collecting real-time data. The most crucial point in its life cycle is the transition to the state at which rescue workers determine the severity of the ongoing trauma. The functioning stage of concussion administration begins when the crisis is identified as unembellished in the previous step. This digital twin starts before the patient arrives at the hospital for this case study. The concussion unit is cautioned to the incoming patient and begins gathering information directly from the accident scene. When the sick is brought to the trouble branch or the trauma team begins treating them, their internal state changes. All replicas are developed as a microservice that provides access to the digital twin's data and information via an ad-hoc RESTful API. It used Vert.x library and the Java programming language to create each microservice. The hospital's private cloud infrastructure hosts the digital twin microservices, which can only be accessed by applications operating in this context. It utilized the JaCaMo framework to create Multi-Agent Systems in the design of software agents, which were developed following the A&A meta-model.

It (Ahmadi-Assalemi et al., 2020) investigate precision healthcare's patient and healthcare system-level objectives. It enables scenario modeling established on actual information to construct a more well-organized sick gush through the crisis squad, decrease their visit, reduce resource need, and expand the number of ill ministers. The investigation emphasizes the creative usage of DES for the modeling and conclusion-making processes of the structure. A sectional prototype is connected to a procedure examination instrument that is fed with knowledge from the infirmary notification procedure and the prediction of the sick coming, which includes data from the GP system warnings, disaster signals, sick transmissions data, and utilization of other clinic benefits. The proposed DT-based modular framework used the MedPRO UML-based modeling framework to represent the model, and it used the ROCKWELL Arena 14.5 to implement it. It used observations, interviews with staff, and the hospital's information system to extract the variables. Various methods with predefined essential implementation gauges demonstrated the framework's viability. It utilized the FlexSim HealthCare 3D simulation and modeling tool in the model. The DT representative is based on a clinic sick gush, simulating various scenarios, such as real-time patient tracking from admission to discharge, allowing the ill to accept the suitable medicine, tools, or functional space at the proper period. In an assortment of diverse systems, it tested the methodology feasibility of the framework.

4.2.4 Retail

A product's life cycle begins with assembly, engineering, disbandment, deals, consumer utilization, ventures, and product expiration. As they advance through the generation cycle, these computer-based clones keep improving and elevating their product position. This continuous update commands the whole life pattern of an item which predicts and settles the issues well ahead of time. It can use data twins to improve data throughout their life cycles in retail. Digital twins allow all the information about a product's lifecycle to be kept digitally and used over the web. It includes discounts, product batches, new products on occasion, supply chains the product has traveled through, the location of the development at any given period, and the previous wrapping period. It will uncover new ways to enormous possibilities for retail applications.

The research (Lee & Lee, 2021) concentrates on 331 cold-chain freight of strawberries, raspberries, cucumbers, and eggplant from Spain to Switzerland. On the cold chain of four fruits from Spain to Switzerland, it looked at the temperature of the air. The natural outcomes are dispatched from Spain by a transporter in a chilled vehicle to a dispersion place in Switzerland and, after that, pushed by one more truck to a resident's retail area in Switzerland. We looked at two different datasets. Time-temperature data collected between the packhouse make up the first dataset. Between December 2019 and June 2020, during the import season, the second dataset was gathered. The purpose of acquiring this fact was to evaluate the entire cold chain and the cold chain at and after the DC (Tanwar, R., Chhabra, Y., Rattan, P., & Rani, S., 2022, September). It replicated the four fruits under investigation digitally. By receiving data on the temperature of the air from the sensor, it modeled a solitary berry connected to the real world. It simulated fruit conditions in the cold chain with a continuum Multiphysics model (Rani, S., Kataria, A., & Chauhan, M., 2022). It utilized 2D axisymmetric models. Resolving the energy conservation equation, it considered heat transmission and breathing warmth for temperature vehicle within the fruit. Figure 4.6 details the same (Kaur et al., 2012).

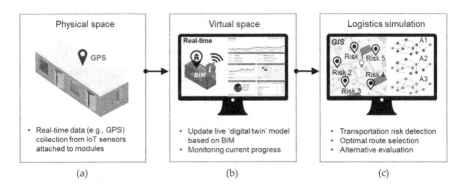

FIGURE 4.6 Digital twin framework for real-time logistics simulation in modular construction (Lee & Lee, 2021).

DTSC (Wang, Deng, Shen, Hu, & Qi, 2022) is a solution to the intelligent store chain. The physical reserve chain in a DTSC is connected to the digital store chain by clever detectors or online schemes that collect precise facts and details that allow the virtual stockpile chain to replicate the physical supply chain's stationary possessions and engaged enterprise operations. As a result, connectivity is established. The synchronized data result in agile, up-to-date simulated replication and optimization and chances to display, investigate, regulate, and enhance the stock chain. A DTSC actively participates in the whole commercial procedure during the stock chain. A DTSC's predictive analytics make the supply chain intelligent and permit conclusion-makers to scrutinize ahead rather than backward. It is a case study of JD.COM, the enormous dealer in China by income, using a DTSC medium to reconfigure the cache chain web during the COVID-19 crisis. Shipping and land transportation are two of the many modes of transportation that make up the transportation network. It uses multichannel models and digital and intelligent technologies, JD.COM plans and operates the supply chain from upstream to downstream.

During the 2019 growing period, the Citrusdal display location in the Western Cape, South Africa, was the location of the study (Onwude, et al., 2022), which was conducted on the "Valencia" orange. In five distinct orchards, two trees yielded five fruits per tree. An aggregate of 50 oranges was sampled. It gathered information on physicochemical properties. It checked the air temperature on the virus chain of oranges and transmission from TempTale®4. The information obtained pertains to 43 seasonal shipments from a packhouse in Durban, South Africa, to a dispersal base in Western Europe. These data provide naturalistic temperature information for the international freezing chain. The atmosphere detectors were placed half a palette high in the two rows of pallets from the entrance on the left flank of the receptacle.

4.2.5 SMART CITIES

The three-dimensional digital replicas of buildings, structures, and other connected material investments, as well as the information within and everywhere them, are created by digital twins. It could be an automatic model of a biological repository.

FIGURE 4.7 Graphical abstract (Dembski, Wössner, Letzgus, Ruddat, & Yamu, 2020).

It gathers statistics from detectors, strolls, and motorized IoT devices. It involves advanced examination, apparatus education, and AI to obtain real-time information about the implementation, process, or effectiveness of the physical asset. This innovation will become increasingly important in developing intelligent cities worldwide that address significant issues related to open well-being, security, and the environment. The city will not only be able to evaluate an endless number of anticipated future crises using the digital twin, but it will also be able to respond alone to complex weather events. Figure 4.7 represents a Graphical Abstract.

It (Ruohomäki, et al., 2018) made use of the modularity of the CityGML model. Using the thematic extension options for the CityGML model, the data generated by the mySMARTLife Helsinki project is being visualized and processed into spatial data at the building level. The HSY visual tools are usable alongside the 3D city model and work with the open data services. The Energy and Climate Atlas, the initial application built on top of that, used the CityGML model's modularity. Using the thematic extension options for the CityGML model, the data generated by the mySMARTLife Helsinki project is being visualized and processed into spatial data at the building level. The HSY visual tools are usable alongside the 3D city model and work with the open data services. The model will assist in evaluating various technological scenarios, including the technical potential for lowering the building stock's carbon dioxide emissions. The cost-impact methods for the most efficient measures have been outlined using the tool. Incorporating the digital platform's socioeconomic function into development projects is essential. Synchronous collaboration, collaborative work practices, and an institutional and cultural framework surround the platform's technical core. New opportunities and service concepts will emerge from co-creation with various stakeholders. The city functions will also include the venue and the city model. The SensorThings API is a comprehensive API for sensor connectivity developed by the Open Geospatial Consortium. In addition, they have worked for a considerable amount of time on data models for measurements and observations.

The work (Francisco, Mohammadi, & Taylor, 2020) used electricity data from smart meters to create daily building energy benchmarks. It is divided into strategic times to figure out how different they were from traditional final fuel benchmarking techniques and how this measurement can guide a power regime close to real time. It included busy times during the university time, vacant times during the school year, occupied times during the seasonal, unoccupied times during the summer, and highest temporary request times are all taken into consideration. It measures the temporal variation in construction vigor-efficiency notches within a municipal. The Georgia Institute of Technology grounds was chosen as the test bed. Headquarters, laboratories, entertainment, fitness, nutrition, retail, and classroom aptitudes make up university campuses' diverse and dynamic operations comparable to those of a minor city or municipality. The information extent of this examination covered building-level power utilization for 38 structures on the grounds. The findings demonstrated that building energy benchmarks for temporally sliced buildings differ from a building's overall standard. It indicates that a building's general criterion conceals periods during the day, week, or month when it performs too well or poorly. The temporally divided fuel benchmarks have the prospect of offering a model of formation efficiency that is more specific. A crucial step in incorporating clever measure examination with producing fuel benchmarking methods and carrying out more intelligent energy management across a large geographic scale of buildings is the generation of temporally sectioned power benchmarking standards from scholarly meter information datasets.

A conceptual model (Ford & Wolf, 2020) of an SCDT for disaster management is proposed and tested in the recommendation. It can mitigate two threats to SCDT development by concentrating product on catastrophe administration. It looked at 378 books. One hundred ninety-eight talked about how it could use them in a typical neighborhood or precinct strategy. The ward, framework method, application hierarchy, growth status, intelligent city description, digital twin description, and application to disaster management were all adequately assessed using 47 smart city, digital twin, or SCDT systems. The model comprises three main parts: intelligent city components, digital twin components, and components that are not part of the SCDT but have an effect on it either directly or through studies comprehended from the SCDT. Neighborhood Needs, its Features, and assignments understood from society replica prototype, and virtual Vision Instruments are the components that link the SCDT to the municipality and the tragedy. Information on community decision-making and its effects on the ward's capability to reply to the occurrence. Concerning capacity and timing, surveillance conclusions instantly influence the qualities and elements of the community. During and after a disaster, SCDT provides insights that fundamentally alter perspectives on the community.

4.2.6 MANUFACTURING

Since its inception, product lifecycle management has been influenced by the digital twin's active development in the engineering enterprise. It can implement the ever-developing characteristics of the virtual replica in various fresh manufacturing viewpoints, especially concerning the investment and the outcome. When corporeal possessions, like tools, are digitally characterized and associated based on how they work, the apparatus develops the stock chain's socket in the manufacturing industry. This intelligent computer-based depiction can send and accept information from all stages of linked manufacturing apparatus. There are additional advantages to using digital twins for a product, including the ability to control every aspect of the development's life revolution and any anomalies with the predesigned prototye.

- The industry's digital replica can assist in developing new supply chain models for efficient time management between locations of operation, such as workforce customization, spare part movement, and process rescheduling to increase efficiency (Garg & Bhambri, 2011).
- In the manufacturing sector, as well as in any other industry, maintenance plays a crucial role. A model that enables efficient handling of third-gathering sellers and buyers in terms of span, assessing, managing execution, eliminating product delivery potential, providing the best client assistance, and addressing guarantees can be created. There will be more business opportunities as a result of this (Singh et al., 2010).
- The devices, processes, and people immediately respond when these data interact. In this modern manufacturing environment, digital twins can result in a specialist technique replicating an effective judgment aid strategy that reacts positively to the environment. This intelligent professional method can propose a novel solution for immediately realigning human resources between units or altering assets' conduct. This instantaneous answer approach can boost the company's share value and address environmental factors like market demand and external parameters affecting supply and demand.
- Adjustment of the machines, transmission protocols, and data-allocation agents is necessary for fusion of myriad electronic gadgets connected to the web. This calibration does not exclude digital twins, which replicate the data-generating machinery and involve people, processes, and other processes.
- It is truly a work of art in boosting a company's performance, increasing its stock's market value, and establishing itself in the manufacturing sector. It demonstrates the necessity of providing a positive user experience by immediately incorporating employee feedback into processes and work practices.

The DTMC digital twin modeling process (Zhang, Zhou, He, Li, & Cheng, 2019) is first described. The digital twin robot's autonomous operation is then demonstrated using data and knowledge. The physical, virtual, and multidisciplinary simulation models make up the constructed digital twin robot. A publish-subscribe architecture connects these three components based on the announcement queuing telemetry conveyance messaging procedure. The physical model could automatically complete machining tasks. Using Modelica, the simulation model's four subcomponents - the route planning component, the electric unit, the robotic division, and the command segment - can carry out multidisciplinary simulations using real-time manufacturing data. It could use manufacturing data to comprehend the robot's performance, and then understanding is utilized to anticipate and stabilize its implementation. The virtual model could visualize the robot's motions following the place parameters published by the material or replica representative. A simulation model could use the following three steps to conduct multidisciplinary simulations. First, a point-to-point calculating strategy generates movement characteristics like curves, angular momentum, and angular pace for each axis of the robot from the real-time positions of the robot that the physical model perceives. Second, a control bus sends the motion parameters to the electric module, which is the enduring magnet servo engine unit. By employing a field-oriented authority strategy carried out by the control unit, the electric segment could produce suitable joint motor twisting, role, and pace to maintain the movements of the automatic team using these parameters. Figure 4.8 details the same.

The notion of a virtual replica shopfloor (DTS) is based on a digital twin. It is investigated (Tao & Zhang, 2017), and its four key elements - a material shopfloor, a digital shopfloor, a shopfloor assistance scheme, and shopfloor digital twin data - are discussed. The Physical Shopfloor comprises several real-world entities, like people, machines, and materials. Prototypes created in numerous measurements, such as geometry, physics, conduct, and management, make up the Simulated

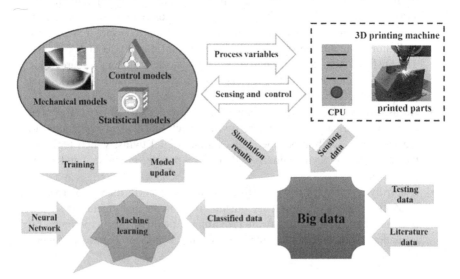

FIGURE 4.8 Logical representation of the digital twin for additive manufacturing (Zhang, et al., 2020).

Shopfloor (VS). The shopfloor digital twin data (SDTD) eliminates the information island because the data are integrated. Information on creation elements ought to be recovered continuously. The equipment can use wired or wireless sensors to acquire conditions such as engine pace, fuel consumption, and device attire. Tools with a heightened grade of automation can read these data from their entrenched units. Environmental sensors can detect modifications in the surroundings in reality, and RFID can be used to track materials throughout their lifecycle. It adapts to the various communication modes utilized by actuators in PS, and instructions from the co-operative system are sent to specialized permit segments for interaction and procedure transformation.

4.3 CHALLENGES

- **Cloud computing** - Users typically have access to cloud services (Devare, 2019; Nagaraj A., 2021; Kalyani & Collier, 2021) via the Internet, using standard protocols and communication mechanisms. Rejection of assistance, Man-In-The-Middle (MITM), overhearing, IP-spoofing, and masquerading attacks are among the challenges that the cloud faces in the same way that traditional IT solutions do. Secure Socket Layer (SSL), IPSec, cryptographic procedures, interruption discovery, anticipation schemes, and digital credentials are all solutions to these issues. Clients and scheme managers must be familiar that stockpile calibration techniques share calculation, warehouse, and grid framework storage, exposing them to risks from third parties. An attacker can use parallel privilege appreciation methods and exploit other organizations before the primary target with shared network components. Virtualization and storage are the cloud's two most essential components. With virtualization, it can share identical material warehouses with multiple system environments. The VM Monitor or hypervisor is the component in charge of managing the VMs and the allocated possessions, allowing the simultaneous operation of multiple operating systems. Each user's VM is separated, providing a digital operating scheme. Users need complete control over their data from cloud system providers, and some levels of management are only available to them on virtual machines. The way that clients do not have command over information having a place with the association results in critical outsider dangers like information breaks.
- **Internet-of-Things** - The Internet of Things (IoT) (Ambika N., 2019; Ambika N., 2019; Alshehri & Muhammad, 2020; Alshehri & Muhammad, 2020) is steadily expanding, and the medical industry is expected to adopt it more, leading to the developing of cutting-edge eHealth IoT devices (Ambika N., 2022; Nagaraj A., 2022) and embedded applications. The computational limitations posed by devices' low-speed processors, memory, and energy limitations make the Internet of Things (IoT) (Dian, Vahidnia, & Rahmati, 2020; L., He, & Li, 2014; Hassan, 2019) challenging for a secure healthcare networked environment. Scalability is challenging for IoT networks due to their high acquisition

rate and need for compatibility with established network protocols. Wireless protocols like Zigbee, WiFi, GSM, WiMax, 6LowPAN, 3 G/4 G, and soon 5 G networks connect medical devices. A challenge is that a cross-platform system must allow IoT devices to communicate with IP networks and integrate with established procedures. The ability to produce tamper-resistant packets is another crucial feature. DoS attacks that disrupt services, data breaches that compromise the privacy of patients, data tampering, and altering the behavior of sensing and delivering devices are all examples of attacks.

4.4 FUTURE SCOPE

DT technologies include the web of objects, the Manufacturing web of objects, manufactured smartness, big data, replication, and storage calibration. It has all been moving in a consistent direction. It is reasonable to assume that DT will continue to move in the same direction as these technologies. Humans must be considered when developing any DT because they are essential to any industry. DT technology has been utilized in manufacturing and aerospace, but agriculture, construction, automobiles, healthcare, and several other sectors are still in their infancy. Because DT MBSE can be utilized throughout the system's life cycle, it is anticipated that DT will become a central capability in manufacturing in the future. DT can assist MBSE in entering new markets like real estate, construction, and manufacturing. With advancements in predictive maintenance and analytics, General Electric anticipates that DT technology will be widely used in the automotive sector, from automobile proprietors to factories. Random investigations will be a thing of the past, and the car can schedule keeping arrangements on its own, making maintenance much more straightforward for car owners. Since they will already have all the relevant information about the vehicle at their disposal before the appointment, the industry of mechanics and service providers will be able to provide quicker and more effective solutions. In addition to managing customers, DT will assist the service department in more effective record and stock chain management.

4.5 CONCLUSION

In the past five years, there has been a significant surge in the number of publications, procedures, concepts, and anticipated benefits related to the digital twin. This growth has occurred in both academia and industry. The digital twin's fundamental idea was that a system would connect real-world objects to virtual ones, maximizing the benefits of both real-world and digital environments for the system. Information about a product is gathered, stored, analyzed, and learned for current and future developments. The web of objects, large datasets, multi-corporeal reproduction, Manufacturing 4.0, actual instruments and detectors, information administration, statistics calibration, and a push toward an information-driven and virtual industrial future are primarily responsible for this growth. This chapter summarizes some of works in certain domains.

REFERENCES

Ahmadi-Assalemi, G., Al-Khateeb, H., Maple, C., Epiphaniou, G., Alhaboby, Z. A., Alkaabi, S., & Alhaboby, D. (2020). Digital twins for precision healthcare. In *Cyber defence in the age of AI, Smart societies and augmented humanity* (pp. 133–158). Cham: Springer.

Alshehri, F., & Muhammad, G. (2020). A comprehensive survey of the Internet of Things (IoT) and AI-based smart healthcare. *IEEE Access, 9*, 3660–3678.

Ambika, N. (2019). Energy-perceptive authentication in virtual private networks using GPS data. In Z. Mahmood (ed.), *Security, privacy and trust in the IoT environment* (pp. 25–38). Springer Verlag.

Ambika, N. (2022). An augmented edge architecture for AI-IoT services deployment in the modern era. In *Handbook of research on technical, privacy, and security challenges in a modern world* (pp. 286–302). US: IGI Global.

Angulo, C., Gonzalez-Abril, L., Raya, C., & Ortega, J. A. (2020). A proposal to evolving towards digital twins in healthcare. *International Work-Conference on Bioinformatics and Biomedical Engineering* (pp. 418–426). Granada, Spain: Springer, Cham.

Batty, M. (2018). Digital twins. *Environment and Planning B: Urban analytics and city science, 45*(5), 817–820.

Bhambri, P., Hans, S., & Singh, M. (2008, November). Bioinformatics - Friendship between Bits & Genes. In *International Conference on Advanced Computing & Communication Technologies* (pp. 62–65).

Bhambri, P., & Singh, M. (2008). Biometrics: Face recognition using eigen faces. *Apeejay Journal of Management and Technology, 3*(2), 160–164.

Bécue, A., Maia, E., Feeken, L., Borchers, P., & Praça, I. (2020). A new concept of digital twin supporting optimization and resilience of factories of the future. *Applied Sciences, 10*(13), 4482.

Chakraborty, S., & Adhikari, S. (2021). Machine learning based digital twin for dynamical systems with multiple time-scales. *Computers & Structures, 243*, 106410.

Chauhan, M., & Rani, S. (2021). COVID-19: A revolution in the field of education in India. *Learning how to learn using multimedia*, 23–42.

Croatti, A., Gabellini, M., Montagna, S., & Ricci, A. (2020). On the integration of agents and digital twins in healthcare. *Journal of Medical Systems, 44*(9), 1–8.

Dembski, F., Wössner, U., Letzgus, M., Ruddat, M., & Yamu, C. (2020). Urban digital twins for smart cities and citizens: The case study of Herrenberg, Germany. *Sustainability, 12*, 2307.

Devare, M. H. (2019). Convergence of manufacturing cloud and industrial IoT. In G. Kecskemeti (ed.), *Applying integration techniques and methods in distributed systems and technologies* (pp. 49–78). US: IGI Global.

Dian, F. J., Vahidnia, R., & Rahmati, A. (2020). Wearables and the Internet of Things (IoT), applications, opportunities, and challenges: A survey. *IEEE Access, 8*, 69200–69211.

Dhanalakshmi, R., Anand, J., Sivaraman, A. K., & Rani, S. (2022). IoT-based water quality monitoring system using cloud for agriculture use. *Cloud and Fog Computing Platforms for Internet of Things, 28*(3), 1–14.

Ford, D. N., & Wolf, C. M. (2020). Smart cities with digital twin systems for disaster management. *Journal of Management in Engineering, 36*(4), 04020027.

Francisco, A., Mohammadi, N., & Taylor, J. E. (2020). Smart city digital twin-enabled energy management: Toward real-time urban building energy benchmarking. *Journal of Management in Engineering, 36*(2), 04019045-1 -04019045-11.

Garg, D., & Bhambri, P. (2011). A novel approach for fusion of multimodality medical images. *CiiT International Journal of Digital Image Processing, 3*(10), 576–580.

Hänel, A., Schnellhardt, T., Wenkler, E., Nestler, A., Brosius, A., Corinth, C., … Ihlenfeldt, S. (2020). The development of a digital twin for machining processes for the application in aerospace industry. *53rd CIRP Conference on Manufacturing Systems*, *93*, 1399–1404. Chicago, USA: Elsevier.

Hassan, W. H. (2019). Current research on Internet of Things (IoT) security: A survey. *Computer Networks*, *148*, 283–294.

Hassani, H., Huang, X., & MacFeely, S. (2022). Impactful digital twin in the healthcare revolution. *Big Data and Cognitive Computing*, *6*(3), 83.

Ibrahim, M., Rassõlkin, A., Vaimann, T., & Kallaste, A. (2022). Overview on digital twin for autonomous electrical vehicles propulsion drive system. *Sustainability*, *14*, 601.

Kalyani, Y., & Collier, R. (2021). A systematic survey on the role of cloud, fog, and edge computing combination in smart agriculture. *Sensors*, *21*, 5922.

Kaul, R., Ossai, C., Forkan, A. R., Jayaraman, P. P., Zelcer, J., Vaughan, S., & Wickramasinghe, N. (2022). The role of AI for developing digital twins in healthcare: The case of cancer care. *Wiley Interdisciplinary Reviews: Data Mining and Knowledge Discovery*, e1480.

Kaur, J., Bhambri, P., & Goyal, F. (2012). Phylogeny: Tree of life. Paper presented at the International Conference on Sports Biomechanics, Emerging Technologies and Quality Assurance in Technical Education, 350–354.

Kataria, A., Puri, V., Pareek, P. K., & Rani, S. (2023, July). Human activity classification using G-XGB. In *2023 International Conference on Data Science and Network Security (ICDSNS)* (pp. 1–5). IEEE.

Kothandaraman, D., Manickam, M., Balasundaram, A., Pradeep, D., Arulmurugan, A., Sivaraman, A. K., & Balakrishna, R. (2022). Decentralized link failure prevention routing (DLFPR) algorithm for efficient internet of things. *Intelligent Automation and Soft Computing*, *34*(1), 655–666.

Kumar, P., Banerjee, K., Singhal, N., Kumar, A., Rani, S., Kumar, R., & Lavinia, C. A. (2022). Verifiable, secure mobile agent migration in healthcare systems using a polynomial-based threshold secret sharing scheme with a blowfish algorithm. *Sensors*, *22*(22), 8620.

Lee, D., & Lee, S. (2021). Digital twin for supply chain coordination in modular construction. *Applied Sciences*, *11*(13), 5909.

Liu, S., Bao, J., Lu, Y., Li, J., Lu, S., & Sun, X. (2021). Digital twin modeling method based on biomimicry for machining aerospace components. *Journal of Manufacturing Systems*, *58*, 180–195.

Liu, Y., Zhang, L., Yang, Y., Zhou, L., Ren, L., Wang, F., … Deen, M. (2019). A novel cloud-based framework for the elderly healthcare services using digital twin. *IEEE Access*, *7*, 49088–49101.

Nagaraj, A. (2021). *Introduction to sensors in iot and cloud computing applications*. UAE: Bentham Science Publishers.

Nagaraj, A. (2022). Adapting blockchain for energy constrained IoT in healthcare environment. In K. Kaushik, S. Tayal, S. Dahiya, & A. O. Salau (eds.), *Sustainable and Advanced Applications of Blockchain in Smart Computational Technologies* (p. 103). Boca Raton, Florida: CRC press.

Onwude, D. B., Shrivastava, C., Berry, T., Cronje, P., North, J., Kirsten, N., … Defraeye, T. (2022). Physics-driven digital twins to quantify the impact of pre- and postharvest variability on the end quality evolution of orange fruit. *Resources, Conservation and Recycling*, *186*, 106585.

Park, Y., Woo, J., & Choi, S. (2020). A cloud-based digital twin manufacturing system based on an interoperable data schema for smart manufacturing. *International Journal of Computer Integrated Manufacturing*, *33*(12), 1259–1276.

Rani, S., Arya, V., & Kataria, A. (2022). Dynamic pricing-based e-commerce model for the produce of organic farming in India: A research roadmap with main advertence to vegetables. In *Proceedings of Data Analytics and Management: ICDAM 2021, Volume 2* (pp. 327–336). Springer Singapore.

Rani, S., Kataria, A., & Chauhan, M. (2022). Cyber security techniques, architectures, and design. In *Holistic Approach to Quantum Cryptography in Cyber Security* (pp. 41–66). CRC Press.

Rani, S., Kataria, A., Kumar, S., & Tiwari, P. (2023). Federated learning for secure IoMT-applications in smart healthcare systems: A comprehensive review. *Knowledge-based systems*, 110658.

Ruohomäki, T., Airaksinen, E., Huuska, P., Kesäniemi, O., Martikka, M., & Suomisto, J. (2018). Smart city platform enabling digital twin. In *International Conference on Intelligent Systems (IS)* (pp. 155–161). Funchal, Portugal: IEEE.

Singh, I., Salaria, D., & Bhambri, P. (2010). Comparative analysis of JAVA and AspectJ on the basis of various metrics. In *International Conference on Advanced Computing and Communication Technologies (IEEE Sponsored)* (pp. 714–720).

Singh, M., Srivastava, R., Fuenmayor, E., Kuts, V., Qiao, Y., Murray, N., & Devine, D. (2022). Applications of digital twin across industries: A review. *Applied Sciences, 12*, 5727.

Tanwar, R., Chhabra, Y., Rattan, P., & Rani, S. (2022, September). Blockchain in IoT networks for precision agriculture. In *International Conference on Innovative Computing and Communications: Proceedings of ICICC 2022, Volume 2* (pp. 137–147). Singapore: Springer Nature Singapore.

Thapar, V., & Bhambri, P. (2009, May). Context free language induction by evolution of deterministic pushdown automata using genetic programming. Paper presented at the International Conference on Downtrend Challenges in IT, pp. 33.

Tao, F., & Zhang, M. (2017). Digital twin shop-floor: A new shop-floor paradigm towards smart manufacturing. *IEEE Access, 5*, 20418–20427.

Wang, L., Deng, T., Shen, Z. J., Hu, H., & Qi, Y. (2022). Digital twin-driven smart supply chain. *Frontiers of Engineering Management, 231*, 1–15.

Xu, L., He, W., & Li, S. (2014). Internet of things in industries: A survey. *IEEE Transactions on industrial informatics, 10*(4), 2233–2243. https://api.semanticscholar.org/CorpusID: 13900209

Zhang, C., Zhou, G., He, J., Li, Z., & Cheng, W. (2019). A data-and knowledge-driven framework for digital twin manufacturing cell. *11th CIRP Conference on Industrial Product-Service Systems.83*, pp. 345–350. Zhuhai and Hong Kong, China: Elsevier.

Zhang, J., Li, L., Lin, G., Fang, D., Tai, Y., & Huang, J. (2020). Cyber resilience in healthcare digital twin on lung cancer. *IEEE Access, 8*, 201900–201913.

Zhang, L., Chen, X., Zhou, W., Cheng, T., Chen, L., Guo, Z., … Lu, L. (2020). Digital twins for additive manufacturing: A state-of-the-art review. *Applied Sciences, 10*(23), 8350.

5 Digital Twin in Industry 4.0

Application Areas and Challenges

Sandhya Soman, Gnanasankaran Natarajan,
and Piyush Kumar Pareek

5.1 INTRODUCTION

Computers, the Internet and smartphones - the most significant technological inventions - have fast-tracked how the world and this generation operate. We are so used to things being "instant" that if one waits to understand the impact of a new product after launching or cannot observe the concurrent performance of a new asset, it can pose a significant competitive threat. Digital Twinning is one of the greatest technological innovations that has revolutionised the way industry works today (Hu et al., 2022). Twinning provisioned the creation of replicas and early capture of possible failures in the production process (Gupta, O., Rani, S., & Pant, D. C., 2011). To understand the profundity with which this technical innovation can impact the current tech world, we must explore its genesis journey through Industry 4.0 (Boggess, M., 2023). Through this chapter, we have put forward this genesis journey - how it all began, the state of the art today and the future opportunities and challenges it poses.

5.1.1 FROM "STEAM POWER" TO AN ERA OF "SMART DEVICES" - THE HISTORY OF INDUSTRY 4.0

*   **Industry 1.0**
    The production process has significantly changed since the First Industrial Revolution (IBM, 2023). With the surge in population, there was a need to increase the production of goods and commodities. This scaling up was impossible by using man and animal power. Hence, the power of water and steam was used in the late 18th century, and this led to an era where, in the history of humankind, artefacts were manufactured using machines and not by hand (Singh et al., 2021a).
*   **Industry 2.0**
    Slowly, with the evolution of the needs of humankind, it became evident that steam and water alone could not fulfil the needs; hence, other power

DOI: 10.1201/9781003395416-5

sources like oil, gas and electricity were used in production lines. This second revolution also clarified that some parts of the production line needed to be automated to facilitate mass production (Bose et al., 2021).

- **Industry 3.0**
  The advancements in telecommunication brought a dramatic change in the production processes (Kaur, D., Singh, B., & Rani, S., 2023). Telecommunications, coupled with the computation power, enabled the automation of processes, speeding up the production process. As the storage became cheaper, the data generated in each iteration could be stored for future processing, and this also proved helpful in mining for further information (Jabeen et al., 2021).

- **Industry 4.0**
  The next revolutionary stage, also quoted as the "Fourth Industrial Revolution" or "Industry 4.0," began with the emergence of smart devices. These devices generate considerable data and can process a significant load (Kothandaraman, D., Manickam, M., Balasundaram, A., Pradeep, D., Arulmurugan, A., Sivaraman, A. K., & Balakrishna, R., 2022).

The customer of today is a lot more informed about his requirements. They have particular choices, and the market is too competitive. Customisation of products is not a choice but rather a norm. Industry 4.0 aims to make the entire production process customer-centric so that it can meet the needs of the customer with efficiency (Singh et al., 2021b).

The data at different levels is gathered to make models to understand the trends and better predict/suggest ways of optimising the process and the involved sub-processes.

The fourth stage of revolution is still advancing, with changes in business needs, evolving customer mindsets, and inventions happening at the technological fronts (Figure 5.1).

5.1.2 THE TECHNOLOGIES STEERING INDUSTRY 4.0

The critical technology forces (Cearley et al., 2017; Grübel, J. et al., 2022) that are driving the Fourth Industrial Revolution can be listed as follows (Figure 5.2):

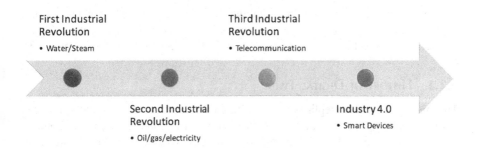

FIGURE 5.1 From the "steam" era to the "smart" era.

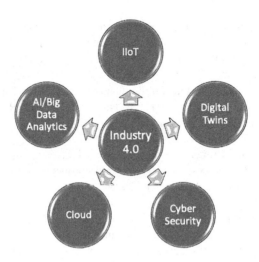

FIGURE 5.2 Technologies steering Industry 4.0.

- **AI/Big Data Analytics** plays a significant role in understanding the mammoth size of data generated, unveiling the trends hidden in the data, and using the same to make some strategic decisions.
- **Industrial IoT:** To optimise the processes used in Industrial IoT, the nuances of the process should be understood clearly. With the availability of advanced sensors, it is now possible to track the process progress and stages at a minuscule level and they can be used further for finetuning the process.
- **Digital Twins:** Reflecting the real world objects through models having virtual existence.
- **Cyber Security:** A secure process is "robust." In today's era, security is the most critical non-functional requirement, an unsaid prefix to all functional requirements.
- **Cloud:** With the advent of the cloud, space problems and process visibility issues have vanished. The data is now accessible to any remote corner of the world, and the inconsistency no longer bothers the organisation.

5.2 DIGITAL TWIN TECHNOLOGY

A twin is a replica of an object. A digital twin (DT) is a digital replica of a real-world entity. The entity may be an object, a process, or a service (Bhambri et al., 2022). Physical entities and twins are also used to replicate processes these days (Figure 5.3).

5.2.1 HISTORY OF DIGITAL TWIN

The history of digital replicas dates back to 1991 when D. Gelernter proposed "Mirror Worlds," which processed the information input and could generate software mimic model. In 2002, Michael Grieves worked with the Management of Product Lifecycle at the University of Michigan (Editor, 2021). He proposed a

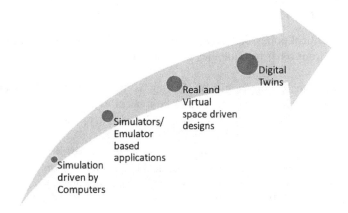

FIGURE 5.3   Journey of digital twin technology.

three-spaced model - an actual space, also known as the real space; the assumed space, also known as the virtual space; and a space whose primary purpose was to facilitate data flow between the former and latter spaces (Kumar, P., Banerjee, K., Singhal, N., Kumar, A., Rani, S., Kumar, R., & Lavinia, C. A., 2022). The new term "digital twins" was introduced by John Vickers of NASA in 2010. This concept has continued to grow, spread further, and found more applications in industries and different processes (Singh et al., 2021c).

Table 5.1 provides an overview of major events from 1960 till date in the journey of digital twin technology.

TABLE 5.1
History of Digital Twin

History of DTs	
Early 1960s–late 1980s	Pairing technique used by NASA in the Apollo 13 mission
	Computer simulators used in flight
	AutoCAD was introduced for creating 2D/3D models
1990–2000	AutoCAD improvised further, and its usage was spread to various engineering disciplines
2000–2010	The concept of Digital Twins introduced
2011–2017	NASA published papers in support of twinning
	GENIX - the digital twin framework by GE, gained popularity
	Digital Twin was listed as a major research trend
2018 onwards	Digital Twin is adopted by top companies to ally their manufacturing and industrial processes

5.2.2 How Do Digital Twins Differ from Other Technologies?

Some of the critical points that elaborate on how digital twins can be differentiated (IBM, 2023) from other technologies are listed in this section:

- The twin technology's ground footing is the connection between the physical component and its digital equivalent. The material component hosts sensors, which gather data that can be used to update the status of the twin (IBM, 2023).
- The physical component and the twin can be programmed again based on the analytics performed on the data collected from the sensors. This feature enables the enhancement of the entity's functionality and adds more value to the product (Bhambri, P., Aggarwal, M., Singh, H., Singh, A. P., & Rani, S., 2022).
- The diagnostic data available, also called "trace data," are enablers for quick comebacks of the components.

5.2.3 Features of Digital Twin

Since there is a lack of a unified definition of DT, these features have been derived from the common characteristics found in various purposes (Tao & Zhang, 2017) (Figure 5.4).

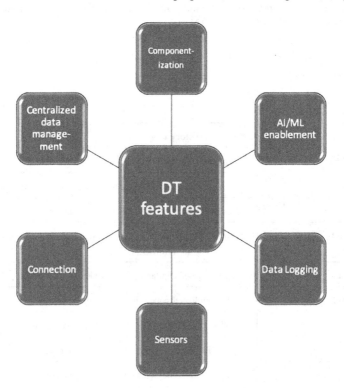

FIGURE 5.4 Features of digital twin.

1. Centralised management of the physical system's data enables efficient data transfer between the physical object and its DT.
2. Connection between the system and its DT facilitates real-time monitoring of the activities (Takyar, 2022).
3. Sensors capable of capturing real-time data to facilitate the creation of twins, which are as close in simulation as the actual object itself.
4. Provision to maintain data logs, which can be used to determine the source of problems/possible reasons for malfunctioning (Ritu & Bhambri, 2022).
5. Smart programming enables the usage of Artificial Intelligence (AI) and Machine Learning (ML) to facilitate intelligent analysis of collected data.
6. Componentisation is the ability to modularise the design. This will facilitate the localisation of errors and isolated handling of the errors (Sudevan, S., Barwani, B., Al Maani, E., Rani, S., & Sivaraman, A. K., 2021).

5.3 TYPES OF DIGITAL TWIN

The DT technology has been closely used for modelling a part of a system to an entire system. A close study of the existing classification reveals four major types of digital twins (Rani, S., Kataria, A., Kumar, S., & Tiwari, P., 2023).

5.3.1 COMPONENT TWIN

These are twins of a part of a system *or* product. They can be used to model parts critical for the product's performance or crucial while combining different parts (Rani, S., Mishra, A. K., Kataria, A., Mallik, S., & Qin, H., 2023). This type of twinning is beneficial when trying to understand the other features of a product's part, like its physical characteristics, thermal characteristics, electromagnetic effect, etc.

5.3.2 ASSET TWIN

They represent the entire system/product. An asset twin is generally a combination of several component twins. They aid in understanding the interaction between these components and how composition affects them as a single system.

5.3.3 SYSTEM TWINS

While asset twins only capture the components of a product, the system twins take it to the next higher level of integration. It captures the different products integrated and working together as a system. This is particularly beneficial in understanding the interaction between the product components and the data flow from one component to another and in understanding the integration issues.

5.3.4 PROCESS TWINS

They are used to capture the entire lifecycle of a product. To put it in simple terms, a process twin captures a set of systems working together as a single unit (Jabeen et al., 2021) (Figure 5.5).

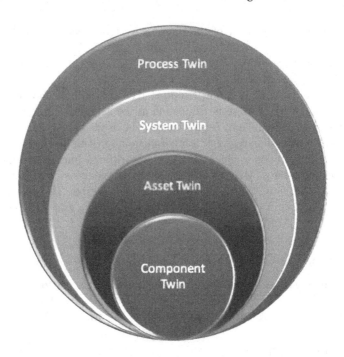

FIGURE 5.5 Types of digital twin.

5.4 TWINS VS SIMULATION

An important area that confuses most readers is whether there is any similarity between a digital twin and a simulation *or whether they* are synonyms (Rani, S., & Kaur, S., 2012). The best way to understand this is to focus on the fact that DT is a concept that has been materialised into a reality through various technologies like IoT, simulation in the 3D plane and AI/ML (Raghunathan, 2019). The following three points can help us understand the differences between the two:

- While simulation optimises a process offline, twins collect real-time information, enable changing parameters at run time, and see the cause-effect relationship of the change incorporated. The primary advantage of the DT in this scenario is that it can help save time and cost and can also help pinpoint the pain areas in a shorter time.
- Another perspective is that, through DT, we can understand what has been happening in a process and the current status. We can get a clear picture of the various components of the process interacting with each other and understand the areas of defect or improvement (Lucke et al., 2008). This is an advantage over having to go through lengthy reports. The information is available in an easy-to-use manner, is comprehendible, and does not require too much process and, hence, can be utilised more effectively for timely decision-making.

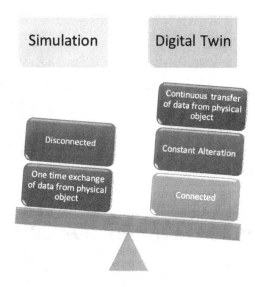

FIGURE 5.6 DT vs simulation.

- DT has been critical in understanding the behaviour of a process when two or more binding entities interact (X., 2022). It helps to unveil clashes occurring during the interaction of these processes/entities. The information gathered from simulations is passed on to DTs, which can use technologies like *data analytics* for performing predictive analysis to gain further insight into the process (Figure 5.6).

5.5 DIGITAL TWIN ARCHITECTURE

A typical twin system architecture can be visualised as a collection of three interacting integrands - the physical environment (Grübel, J. et al., 2022; Rana et al., 2021) or the hardware component (Da Silva Mendonca, R. et al., 2022), the virtual environment or the software component, the data/analytical environment, or the middleware component (Guo, J., 2021).

5.5.1 PHYSICAL ENVIRONMENT

The actual state of the physical environment is captured by the IoT sensors, which initiate the exchange of data between the physical and virtual environment. The hardware part contains all the devices required to facilitate data transfer and convert signals to machine-needed actions (Rani, S., Bhambri, P., & Gupta, O. P., 2022).

5.5.2 THE SOFTWARE ENVIRONMENT

The twin converts the data collected at various levels by different sensors into meaningful insights by applying other machine learning models. It also permits real-time visualisation of the current state of the physical process (Sumathi et al., 2021).

FIGURE 5.7   Architecture of DT.

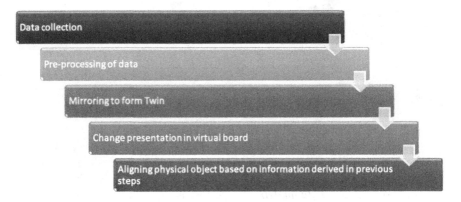

FIGURE 5.8   Steps of digital twin loop represented in a sequential manner.

5.5.3   MIDDLEWARE

The two worlds are connected through the **middleware**. It collects data from myriad sources and contains layers that further manipulate data, including finding patterns in the data, modelling it, and using it for strategic decision-making (Figure 5.7).

1. A digital twin has been portrayed as a loop interconnecting physical systems with their virtual realities. The loop intertwines the following operations, carried out iteratively (Wikipedia contributors, 2023) (Figure 5.8).

5.6   HOW DOES A DT WORK?

Several versions of the working of a DT can be found in the literature. This section explains a generic lifecycle applicable to DTs across application domains. A digital twin follows the lifecycle, encompassing the following stages.

- The first stage is the collection of data through sensors. This is used to understand the background of the process to be replicated.

- Once the data has been gathered, it is converted into a model that can virtually represent this physical object/process. The model must be able to capture the attributes and behaviour of the original object.
- The twin monitors the object in real time and continuously captures data to find the occurrence of any defect. This data analysis also reveals areas where the object stands weak, i.e., areas of improvement.
- The pain point that led to the creation of DT was the introduction of changes to the original object/process, and the ripple effect caused by these changes. DTs can be used to simulate these changes and further test the impact of these changes on the original object. This provides flexibility in introducing new changes and can also help identify any unintended adverse effects caused in the original system due to the introduction of a difference (Bakshi et al., 2021).
- The data collected so far can be used for process optimisation and increasing the performance and efficiency of the process/object. It also enables timely feedback to the stakeholders to make informed strategic decisions, saving time and cost-effectively (Figure 5.9).

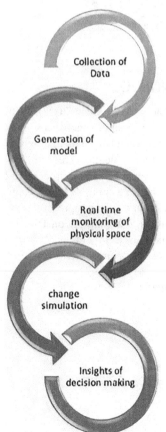

FIGURE 5.9   Functionality of a digital twin.

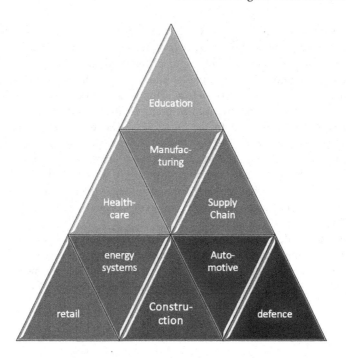

FIGURE 5.10   Use cases of digital twin technology.

5.7   USE CASES OF DIGITAL TWIN TECHNOLOGY

There are manifold applications of digital twin technology (Guo & Lv, 2022). With the advent of IoT, this technology has seen rapid adoption across industries. DTs have influenced almost all major sectors, from the manufacturing industry, where DTs have been used for production process optimisation, to health care, which is used for predicting patient's future health outcomes. DTs can be used to understand the utility trends of energy systems (Puri, V., Kataria, A., Solanki, V. K., & Rani, S., 2022, December). They have been beneficial in creating virtual representations of buildings and cities and used for smart management and planning of construction and cities (Pires et al., 2019). They have also been used in defence for the optimisation of the process of design and development of various defence systems (Kuzhaloli et al., 2020) (Figure 5.10).

In this section, we will focus on five primary domains, namely:

- manufacturing
- health care
- retail
- education

5.7.1   HEALTH CARE

The following points summarise some of the critical areas where Digital Twins have found applicability in health care (Bose et al., 2021):

FIGURE 5.11 Benefits of using DTs in health care.

- The structuring of the hospital layout can be optimised through DTs. They can be used to determine cost-effective ways of managing the various facilities and decide upon the most optimal usage pattern for critical resources.
- The twin of the human body can be used to see the effects of drugs and to conclude if it is safer to release the same to the larger public.
- It can be used effectively to educate students and trainees about medical concepts to students and trainees. They can experiment with the twin model to understand new medical techniques and procedures in a completely safe environment.
- At a higher level, DTs can be used to check the effect of different treatments on a patient and see their response level. This, in turn, can be utilised for creating optimised trials for the patients and can be beneficial in reducing the associated risks.
- One of the main advantages of having a twin is to facilitate constant monitoring of the real-world object/subject/process. This can be used to capture a patient's vitals and for rigorous tracking in patients requiring critical health care facilities (Arya, V., Rani, S., & Choudhary, N., 2022).
- It can also be used to understand the emotional quotient of the patient.
- The biomedical signals can also capture a patient's behavioural data and social determinants (Figure 5.11).

5.7.2 MANUFACTURING

The following points summarise some of the critical areas where Digital Twins have found applicability in manufacturing (Takyar, 2022):

- Manufacturing equipment is a capital expenditure for a Manufacturing Unit. Their health is critical for the seamless functioning of the entire production process. DTs can be used to track how each piece of equipment is performing and thus can be used to identify faults, if any, and reduce their unavailability due to malfunctioning or wear/tear of parts.
- Through constant monitoring of the process, the activities that do not add value, aka waste activities, can be identified and removed from the process for optimisation.

FIGURE 5.12 Benefits of using DTs in manufacturing.

- Digital twins can significantly reduce the need to create physical and virtual prototypes that resonate well with real-time changes.
- DTs are particularly helpful in predicting the demands and hence help optimise supply chain management.
- They can improve customer delight by reducing the wait time and enhancing the quality of the product (Figure 5.12).

5.7.3 RETAIL

The following points summarise some of the critical areas where Digital Twins have found applicability in manufacturing (Figure 5.13):

- The twins can be used to keep track of the store inventory and hence can facilitate the prediction of stock requirements and prevent under/over stocking.
- The second-to-second update of the store can be obtained, and hence, the store management process can be optimised, including the customer preference for product placement, the staff required, optimising the store structure, etc.
- DTs can help in understanding the needs and expectations of the customer.
- Here also, DT helps predict the demands and hence helps optimise the supply chain management.
- Real-time tracking enables retailers to identify any disruptions in the supply chain and can help them take timely action.

FIGURE 5.13 Benefits of using DTs in retail.

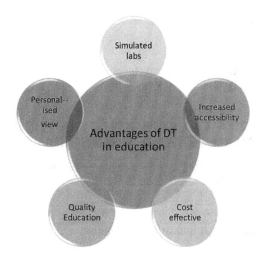

FIGURE 5.14 Benefits of using DTs in education.

- The twin resonates the health/condition of the actual physical equipment and hence can help to determine any wear/tear and thus can help reduce the non-availability of the resources.

5.7.4 EDUCATION

The following points summarise some of the critical areas where Digital Twins have found applicability in education (Figure 5.14):

- It provides a better experience to students as the twins act as virtual modes that can be used to understand the concepts better.
- They can experiment through the DTs and can create virtual projects.
- It expands the reach of education to specially abled children and even remote locations and enables students to collaborate and work on projects as a team.
- The teachers can get a personalised view of each student and use it to generate customised lesson plans for individual students.
- The twin can be used as a simulated lab setup and can be used to provide a safe learning experience for the students.

5.7.5 SUPPLY CHAIN

In the sector of the supply chain, digital twin can be used for the following (Kagermann et al., 2013):

- Identify roadblocks in the process
- Find the shortest path
- Determine bottlenecks in the path

- Make rapid fixes to the issues
- Test new courses/scenarios
- Assess the impact of changes
- Better collaboration between stakeholders
- Reduction in delays

5.8 CHALLENGES FACED BY DIGITAL TWIN TECHNOLOGY AND POSSIBLE MEASURES TO COUNTER THEM

The twin technology currently faces challenges in the following areas (Kritzinger et al., 2018; Lueth, 2021):

- The quality of data
- Possible integration with existing systems
- The privacy and security of data
- The handling of complexity
- The cost of implementation
- Establishment of regulatory norms

Table 5.2 lists these challenges in brief.

TABLE 5.2
Challenges Faced by DT Technology

Challenges Faced	
CH1: The quality of data	It refers to the data generated by the twin. The data must be integral and should not generate hallucinated versions of the physical world data. Also, the data must be updated in real-time to ensure that the information available is not obsolete and hence not fit for decision-making.
CH2: Possible integration with existing systems	The integration of DTs with the existing system is not a trivial process. If the integration is faulty, the replica cannot be created, which can consequently affect the usage of this DT technology.
CH3: The privacy and security of data	The twin technology is going to generate volumes of data. The management of this data requires special attention. Also, the privacy of the data should be maintained, and any security threats should be dealt with stringent measures.
CH4: The handling of complexity	The creation of twins requires specialised knowledge and resources. Acquiring such a skill set is a costly affair.
CH5: The cost of implementation	To date, due to technology and resource requirements, the cost of implementing a twin is a costly affair.
CH6: Establishment of regulatory norms	The ethical and privacy issues must be covered under the norms governing these twins' usage.

TABLE 5.3

Measures to Overcome the Challenges Faced by DT Technology

Overcoming Challenges	
CH1: The quality of data	• Use of high-quality sensors • The use of advanced data storage techniques ensures stored data privacy
CH2: Possible integration with existing systems	Creating open standards and APIs compliant with the existing system structure and functionality
CH3: The privacy and security of data	Usage of cryptosystems with robust algorithms for encryption
CH4: The handling of complexity	Creating a platform that hides the complexity and introduces user-friendly tools and APIs for interaction can ease the complexity
CH5: The cost of implementation	Opting for open-source technology and utilising the benefits of the cloud can significantly bring down the cost of implementation
CH6: Establishment of regulatory norms	The technical giants and industry groups must come together to create norms to govern the usage of digital twins and safeguard the privacy of the associated data

Having mentioned the challenges, let us now explore the possible measures that could be adopted to overcome these challenges. This is not an exhaustive list but a collection of plausible solutions (Singh et al., 2021c). The following Table 5.3 summarises the same:

5.9 IMPORTANCE OF DIGITAL TWIN IN IoT

We are moving towards an era more driven by data and technology than its predecessors. The most logical solution combines physical and virtual systems to generate optimised outputs. Digital twins can bring about a remarkable revolution in the IoT. Some of the vivid areas which will be benefitted can be listed below:

- The real-time monitoring of the state of the processes can be used to enhance the delight of customer experience.
- It can drastically reduce the need to create physical prototypes and, hence, can reduce the time for actual development. It can be a controlled playground for trying changes to the existing system and performing design changes.
- It can help determine activities that do not add value to the process lifecycle and eliminate or modify them.
- Through the constant monitoring mechanism of the twin, we can determine when the system would require maintenance.

FIGURE 5.15   Challenges in the widespread adoption of DT metaverse.

5.10   DIGITAL TWIN METAVERSE

By definition, a metaverse is an extension of the real world, accessible through the Internet, created to engage users and allow them to interact with each other. A "digital twin metaverse" creates a virtual world that constantly interacts with the real physical world. It is capable of interacting and manipulating the objects in the real world.

The DT metaverse is said to bring about a revolution in the field of IoT to optimise the design of products, prediction of outputs and creation of customer delight. The DT metaverse concept is still in its infancy. It's an up-and-coming concept that must overcome technical, ethical and regulatory hurdles (Figure 5.15).

The challenges can be listed below.

5.10.1   TECHNICAL CHALLENGES

- Generating accurate real-time simulations.
- Improvising the way humans interact with twins.
- Honouring the sensitivity and privacy of data.
- Merging these systems with already existing systems.
- Managing the time lag between event capture in the virtual and real world.

5.10.2   ETHICAL CHALLENGES

- Who will be responsible for these twins? The primary challenge is to define the level of autonomy for these DTs and determine the responsibility pyramid to ensure they are used in an ethically correct manner.
- Ensuring there is no interference with human interests and autonomy.
- DTs must not propagate existing bias but provide a true virtualisation of the physical world.

5.10.3 REGULATION-BASED CHALLENGES

- Protecting the intellectual property against any kind of malicious usage.
- Proper authorisation and authentication for collected data.
- Providing privacy and security to sensitive data and creating regulatory norms for data usage and other sensitive information.

Only if these issues are addressed and taken care of can the power of DT metaverse be truly unleashed and used for the benefit of the human race.

5.11 OPEN RESEARCH AREAS

Some of the areas in connection with the DT technology include:

- Using AI/ML and other intelligent algorithms to analyse the data generated by DT sensors.
- Improved algorithms for data cleansing.
- Portable system handling.
- Compatibility with existing technologies for seamless functioning.
- Devising algorithms for encrypting sensitive data during transmission.
- Ensuring that the twin functions well across platforms.
- Creating environment-friendly DTs.
- Bring the cost of the creation of DTs.
- Enhancing the privacy of associated data.
- Improve HCI to enhance the interaction of humans with DTs.
- Improving the accuracy of real-time data dissemination.

5.12 FUTURE OF DIGITAL TWIN

Digital twin technology is a rapidly evolving technology. The advancements in the twin technology go hand in hand with the advances in IoT, AI and ML. The twins are becoming increasingly sophisticated and accurate in capturing factual world information and have seen widespread adoption in many industries and domains. There is an expectation of multi-fold development in this field, which is expected to increase soon.

Some of the areas are listed below and have also been captured in Figure 5.16:

- Many businesses are likely to adapt DT shortly to streamline their production processes.
- With the improvement in simulation algorithms, real-time data collection and presentation accuracy will improve, making DT more accurate and reliable.
- Integration with technologies like AR and VR will make it more disruptive.
- It will bring down the downtime of the process components to a significant level.

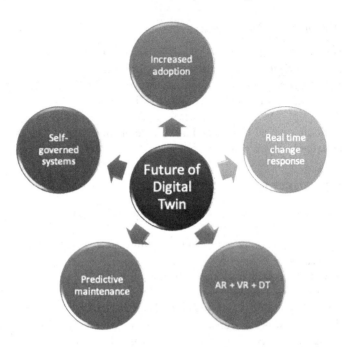

FIGURE 5.16 Future of digital twin.

- These systems are likely to be self-governed and autonomous in future, thereby aiding in developing independent processes.

5.13 CONCLUSION

Today's world has witnessed a significant revolution with the advent of twin technology. This book chapter throws light on the advancements that have taken place in the technological journey over the years, which have led to the beginning of Digital Twins. The different types of twins and their application areas have also been elaborated. Some primary application areas, such as education, supply chain management, health care and production, are already reaping the benefits of this technological revolution. The chapter also discusses the current research gaps in this area and the future of this rapidly evolving technology.

REFERENCES

Arya, V., Rani, S., & Choudhary, N. (2022). Enhanced bio-inspired trust and reputation model for wireless sensor networks. In *Proceedings of Second Doctoral Symposium on Computational Intelligence: DoSCI 2021* (pp. 569–579). Springer Singapore.

Bakshi, P., Bhambri, P., & Thapar, V. (2021). A review paper on wireless sensor network techniques in Internet of Things (IoT). *Wesleyan Journal of Research*, 14(7), 147–160.

Bhambri, P., Singh, M., Dhanoa, I. S., & Kumar, M. (2022). Deployment of ROBOT for HVAC duct and disaster management. *Oriental Journal of Computer Science and Technology*, 15, 1–8.

Bhambri, P., Aggarwal, M., Singh, H., Singh, A. P., & Rani, S. (2022). Uprising of EVs: Charging the future with demystified analytics and sustainable development. In *Decision Analytics for Sustainable Development in Smart Society 5.0: Issues, Challenges and Opportunities* (pp. 37–53). Singapore: Springer Nature Singapore.

Boggess, M. (2023, February 7). Industry 4.0 & the Future of Manufacturing. Hitachi Solutions. https://global.hitachi-solutions.com/blog/industry-4-0-technologies-outcomes-and-the-future-of-manufacturing/

Bose, M. M., Yadav, D., Bhambri, P., & Shankar, R. (2021). Electronic customer relationship management: Benefits and pre-implementation considerations. *Journal of Maharaja Sayajirao University of Baroda*, 55(01(VI)), 1343–1350. The Maharaja Sayajirao University of Baroda.

Cearley, D. W., Burke, B., Searle, S., & Walker, M. (2017). "Top 10 Strategic Technology Trends for 2018,". Gartner, Inc. I G00327329.

Da Silva Mendonca, R., De Oliveira Lins, S. R., Bessa, I., De Carvalho Ayres Júnior, F. A., De Medeiros, R. L. P., & De Lucena, V. F. (2022). Digital Twin applications: A survey of recent advances and challenges. *Processes*, 10(4), 744. 10.3390/pr10040744

Editor. (2021, September 16). Digital Twins: Components, Use Cases, and Implementation Tips. AltexSoft. https://www.altexsoft.com/blog/digital-twins/, last accessed on 2 Feb 2023.

Grübel, J., Thrash, T., Aguilar, L., Gath-Morad, M., Chatain, J., Sumner, R. W., Hölscher, C., & Schinazi, V. R. (2022). The Hitchhiker's guide to fused twins: A review of access to digital twins in situ in smart cities. *Remote Sensing*, 14(13), 3095. 10.3390/rs14133095

Guo, J. (2021). Digital twins are shaping future virtual worlds. *Service-Oriented Computing and Applications*, 15(2), 93–95.

Gupta, O., Rani, S., & Pant, D. C. (2011). Impact of parallel computing on bioinformatics algorithms. In *Proceedings 5th IEEE International Conference on Advanced Computing and Communication Technologies* (pp. 206–209).

Guo, J., & Lv, Z. (2022). Application of Digital Twins in multiple fields. *Multimedia Tools and Applications*, 81(19), 26941–26967. 10.1007/s11042-022-12536-5

Hu, W., Renke, L., & Cai, Y. (2022). Digital Twin and Industry 4.0 enablers in building and construction: A survey. *Buildings*, 12(11), 2004. 10.3390/buildings12112004

https://www.ibm.com/in-en/topics/industry-4-0, last accessed on 12 Jan 2023.

IBM. (2023). What is Industry 4.0, and how does it work? I IBM.

Jabeen, A., Pallathadka, H., Pallathadka, L. K., & Bhambri, P. (2021). E-CRM successful factors for business enterprises CASE STUDIES. *Journal of Maharaja Sayajirao University of Baroda*, 55(01(VI)), 1332–1342. The Maharaja Sayajirao University of Baroda.

Kagermann, H., Wahlster, W., & Helbig, J. (2013). Securing the future of German manufacturing industry: Recommendations for implementing the strategic initiative INDUSTRIE 4.0. *ACATECH, National Academy of Science and Engineering*.

Kaur, D., Singh, B., & Rani, S. (2023). Cyber security in the metaverse. In *Handbook of research on AI-based technologies and applications in the era of the metaverse* (pp. 418–435). IGI Global.

Kothandaraman, D., Manickam, M., Balasundaram, A., Pradeep, D., Arulmurugan, A., Sivaraman, A. K., & Balakrishna, R. (2022). Decentralized link failure prevention routing (DLFPR) algorithm for efficient internet of things. *Intelligent Automation and Soft Computing*, 34(1), 655–666.

Kumar, P., Banerjee, K., Singhal, N., Kumar, A., Rani, S., Kumar, R., & Lavinia, C. A. (2022). Verifiable, secure mobile agent migration in healthcare systems using a polynomial-based threshold secret sharing scheme with a blowfish algorithm. *Sensors*, 22(22), 8620.

Kritzinger, W. T., Karner, M., Traar, G., Henjes, J., & Sihn, W. (2018). Digital Twin in manufacturing: A categorical literature review and classification. *IFAC-PapersOnLine*, 51(11), 1016–1022. 10.1016/j.ifacol.2018.08.474

Kuzhaloli, S., Devaneyan, P., Sitaraman, N., Periyathanbi, P., Gurusamy, M., & Bhambri, P. (2020). IoT based Smart Kitchen Application for Gas Leakage Monitoring [Patent application number 202041049866A]. India.

Lucke, D., Constantinescu, C., & Westkämper, E. (2008). *Smart factory - A step towards the next generation of manufacturing.* Springer London EBooks, 115–118. 10.1007/978-1-84800-267-8_23

Lueth, K. L. (2021, June 1). How the world's 250 Digital Twins compare? Same, same but different. IoT Analytics. https://iot-analytics.com/how-the-worlds-250-digital-twins-compare/, last accessed on 1 Feb 2023.

Pires, F., Cachada, A., Barbosa, J., Moreira, A. C., & Leitão, P. (2019). Digital Twin in Industry 4.0: Technologies, applications and challenges. *International Conference on Industrial Informatics.* 10.1109/indin41052.2019.8972134

Puri, V., Kataria, A., Solanki, V. K., & Rani, S. (2022, December). AI-based botnet attack classification and detection in IoT devices. In *2022 IEEE International Conference on Machine Learning and Applied Network Technologies (ICMLANT)* (pp. 1–5). IEEE.

Raghunathan, V. (2019, May 13). Digital Twins vs Simulation: Three Key Differences. Entrepreneur. https://www.entrepreneur.com/en-au/technology/digital-twins-vs-simulation-three-key-differences/333645, last accessed on 1 Feb 2023.

Rana, R., Chhabra, Y., & Bhambri, P. (2021). Design and development of distributed clustering approach in wireless sensor network. *Webology*, 18(1), 696–712.

Rani, S., Bhambri, P., & Gupta, O. P. (2022). Green smart farming techniques and sustainable agriculture: Research roadmap towards organic farming for imperishable agricultural products. *Handbook of sustainable development through green engineering and technology*, 49–67.

Rani, S., & Kaur, S. (2012). Cluster analysis method for multiple sequence alignment. *International Journal of Computer Applications*, 43(14), 19–25.

Rani, S., Kataria, A., Kumar, S., & Tiwari, P. (2023). Federated learning for secure IoMT-applications in smart healthcare systems: A comprehensive review. *Knowledge-based systems*, 110658.

Ritu, & Bhambri, P. (2022). A CAD system for software effort estimation. Paper presented at the International Conference on Technological Advancements in Computational Sciences, 140–146. IEEE. DOI: 10.1109/ICTACS56270.2022.9988123.

Rani, S., Mishra, A. K., Kataria, A., Mallik, S., & Qin, H. (2023). Machine learning-based optimal crop selection system in smart agriculture. *Scientific Reports*, 13(1), 15997.

Singh, M., Fuenmayor, E., Hinchy, E. P., Qiao, Y., Murray, N., & Devine, D. M. (2021a). Digital Twin: Origin to future. *Applied System Innovation*, 4(2), 36. 10.3390/asi4020036

Singh, M., Bhambri, P., Lal, S., Singh, Y., Kaur, M., & Singh, J. (2021b). Design of the effective technique to improve memory and time constraints for sequence alignment. *International Journal of Applied Engineering Research (Netherlands)*, 6(02), 127–142. Roman Science Publications and Distributions.

Singh, Y. S., Lal, S., Bhambri, P., Kumar, A., & Dhanoa, I. S. (2021c). Advancements in social data security and encryption: A review. *Natural Volatiles & Essential Oils*, 8(4), 15353–15362. DergiPark.

Sumathi, N., Thirumagal, J., Jagannathan, S., Bhambri, P., & Ahamed, I. N. (2021). A comprehensive review on bionanotechnology for the 21st century. *Journal of the Maharaja Sayajirao University of Baroda*, 55(1), 114–131.

Sudevan, S., Barwani, B., Al Maani, E., Rani, S., & Sivaraman, A. K. (2021). Impact of blended learning during Covid-19 in Sultanate of Oman. *Annals of the Romanian Society for Cell Biology*, 23, 14978–14987.

Takyar, A. (2022, September 26). Digital Twin: A Complete Knowledge Guide. LeewayHertz - Software Development Company. https://www.leewayhertz.com/digital-twin/, last accessed on 31 Jan 2023.

Tao, F., & Zhang, R. (2017). Digital Twin shop-floor: A new shop-floor paradigm towards smart manufacturing. *IEEE Access*, 5, 20418–20427. 10.1109/access.2017.2756069

Wikipedia contributors. (2023, February 6). Digital twin. Wikipedia. https://en.wikipedia.org/wiki/Digital_twin

X. (2022, November 24). What is Industry 4.0, and what technologies are driving it? https://www.xmreality.com/blog/what-is-industry-4.0

6 Digital Twin

Enabling Technologies, Applications, and Challenges

Jaskiran Kaur, Pankaj Bhambri, and Sita Rani

6.1 INTRODUCTION

A digital twin is a cutting-edge technology that is gaining traction across many sectors because it improves the design, monitoring, and optimization of goods, processes, and systems. It is the digital analog of a physical system or process, which may be used to gain immediate information and do simulations (Jones, Snider, Nassehi, Yon, & Hicks, 2020; Tao, Xiao, Qi, Cheng, & Ji, 2022). The idea behind digital twins is to recreate a physical object in a digital form that is identical to it. This digital representation is updated frequently with facts from the real world to guarantee that it is an accurate portrayal of the physical equivalent. NASA made use of digital twins to model and monitor spacecraft in the early 2000s, which helped to popularize the idea. It has since grown throughout a variety of sectors, including industry, healthcare, transportation, and urban planning.

Physical assets and systems can have their lifespans and maintenance costs predicted with the help of digital twins (Tao, Zhang, Liu, & Nee, 2018). They help make the design and development processes more efficient, which in turn encourages new ideas and saves money. They help with decision making and risk assessment by modeling potential outcomes. In addition to their role as training tools and urban planning resources, digital twins also help to make cities smarter. They make individualized care planning and medication discovery possible in the medical field. By connecting the physical and digital worlds, digital twins boost efficiency, cost-effectiveness, and competitiveness across all sectors, all while enhancing decision-making, operational excellence, and the quality of the customer experience.

Digital twin uses a variety of technologies like sensors connected to the Internet of Things (IoT) (Rani, Kataria, Kumar, & Tiwari, 2023), cloud computing for storing and processing the collected data, 3D modeling and simulation for creating virtual representations, artificial intelligence (AI) for analyzing the collected data (Puri, Kataria, Solanki, & Rani, 2022), and augmented reality for visualizing and interacting with the virtual models.

DOI: 10.1201/9781003395416-6

The fundamental objectives of this chapter are:

- To present the basic framework and applications of digital twin.
- To emphasize the various technologies used to develop digital twin applications.
- To present the various challenges faced in deploying digital twin applications in various domains.

6.2 DIGITAL TWIN FRAMEWORK

The complexity and function of a system can greatly affect the nature of its digital twin. It's a fast-paced, rapidly developing industry where new tools and methods of integration are frequently developed. A digital twin usually consists of several significant components (shown in Figure 6.1) discussed below (Bhushan, Kumar, Kumar, Ravi, & Singh, 2022; Rani, Bhambri, & Chauhan, 2021):

- **Physical Object or System.** This is the physical object, structure, or system that the digital twin mimics in its digital form.
- **Sensors and Data Collection.** Sensors and other devices connected to the IoT are embedded within the physical object to monitor its environment in real time (Rani, Kataria, & Chauhan, 2022).
- **Data Communication.** Sensors collect information and send it to a centralized database, usually through wireless or wired networks, where it can be processed and analyzed (Rani, Pareek, Kaur, Chauhan, & Bhambri, 2023).
- **Data Processing and Analytics.** This layer is responsible for preparing the data for analysis and drawing conclusions. The information can be put through sophisticated analysis using machine learning (ML) and AI techniques.
- **Digital Representation.** A digital twin is a digital representation of a real-world object or system. It has rich information about geometry in three dimensions, physical characteristics, and sensor readings in real time. For convenience, this model might be stored in the cloud.

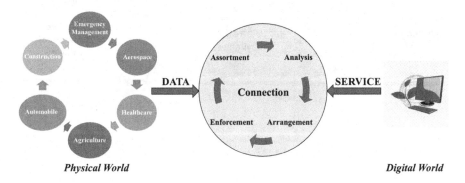

FIGURE 6.1   Digital twin framework.

- **Simulation and Modeling.** It is used to simulate the operation of a real-world system or component. These simulations are useful for performance forecasting, bug tracking, and scenario testing.
- **Visualization and Interaction.** Interfaces including visualizations, dashboards, and controls allow users to engage with the digital twin. The use of Augmented Reality and Virtual Reality (AR/VR) technology has the potential to improve the quality of user interactions.
- **Feedback Loop.** The digital twin can provide valuable insights and simulations that can guide real-world decision-making and operations. Modifications and enhancements can be made because of this feedback loop.
- **Security and Privacy.** As digital twins commonly deal with sensitive information, it is essential that they be protected by stringent security measures to preserve data integrity and guarantee privacy.
- **Communication and Integration.** In order to keep data and operations in sync, digital twins may need to exchange information with other systems like ERP or control systems.
- **Lifecycle Management.** Changes to the physical thing could cause the digital replica to change over time. The digital twin will always be up-to-date and reliable if proper version control and management procedures are in place.
- **Scalability and Redundancy.** For ever-increasing amounts of data, architectures should be built with redundancy in mind to keep things running smoothly and safely.

Prominent features of digital twin are depicted in Figure 6.2.

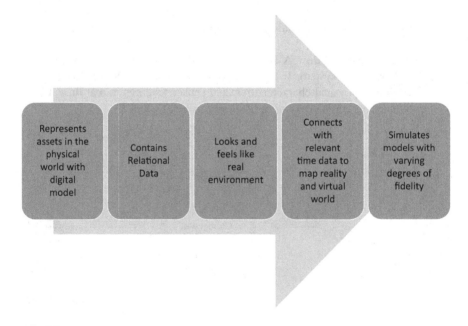

FIGURE 6.2 Digital twin - basic features.

6.3 LIFE CYCLE OF DIGITAL TWIN

There are many moving parts in the digital twin life cycle, from initial planning to implementation through maintenance. The ability to monitor, analyze, and optimize physical items, systems, or processes in real time is made possible by their digital twins. The various phases in the life cycle of a digital twin are briefed below (presented in Figure 6.3):

- **Conception and Planning.** Understanding the physical thing or system that will be digitally twinned is the first step in the digital twin's life cycle. At this point, the digital twin's goals, objectives, and expected outcomes are outlined, together with the particular data that will be collected and analyzed. Engineers, data scientists, and subject matter experts work together to create a detailed strategy.
- **Data Acquisition.** The creation of a reliable digital twin requires information from the physical object itself. To achieve this goal, sensors, cameras, IoT devices, and other data collectors must be deployed. For a digital twin to be effective, both the quality and amount of the data used are required (Hebbale et al., 2022).
- **Modeling and Simulation.** Once enough information has been gathered, it can be used to create a computer simulation of the real-world object or

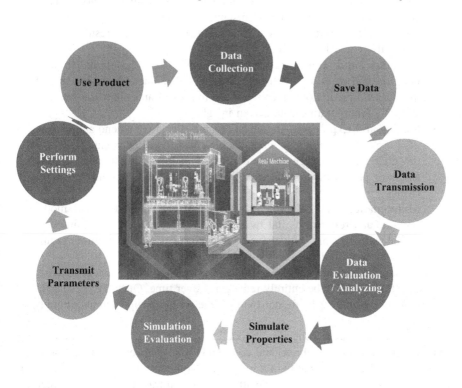

FIGURE 6.3 Digital twin life cycle.

system. A sophisticated simulation is generated by employing cutting-edge modeling strategies, be they 3D modeling, mathematical modeling, or ML methods. The digital twin relies on this idea as its foundation.

- **Integration and Connectivity.** Existing infrastructure and procedures must be adapted to work with the digital twin. Connectivity to other infrastructures is required, such as the IoT, control systems, and data storage solutions. For efficient control and data transfer, interoperability is essential.
- **Real-Time Monitoring.** Once the digital copy is in place, the real-world object may be tracked in near-real time. The current status of the physical system is reflected in the digital twin, which is constantly updated with data streams from sensors and devices. This information can be used for analysis and monitoring by engineers and operators.
- **Analysis and Predictive Maintenance.** Digital twins' ability to analyze data and predict behavior is one of their main advantages. Patterns, outliers, and potential problems can all be spotted using ML algorithms. Breakdowns can be avoided, and performance can be maximized, with the use of predictive maintenance procedures (Biradar, Nagaraj, Mohan, & Pareek, 2022).
- **Optimization and Control.** Decisions and the physical system's perform-ance are optimized based on the digital twin's insights. Algorithms for control can be used to make instantaneous changes to parameters or activate responses in response to incoming input. This step results in better productivity and lower costs.
- **Feedback and Iteration.** The effectiveness of the digital twin is monitored in real-time, with operator and stakeholder input used to hone the model's predictions. Decisions are improved and optimized continu-ously by incorporating data-driven insights.
- **Scaling and Expansion.** Organizations may decide to extend and increase their use of the digital twin when the benefits become apparent. To achieve this goal, it may be necessary to deploy additional digital twins for various assets or processes, thereby establishing a web of interconnected digital twins.
- **Maintenance and Lifecycle Management.** To keep data and models accurate and reliable, digital twins need regular upkeep. Maintaining the digital twin in sync with the evolving physical system requires regular updates, data validation, and software changes.
- **Decommissioning or Redesign.** The physical system may undergo radical transformations or be entirely redesigned over time. Once the new system is up and running, the digital twin can be retired or updated accordingly.

Conceptualization, data collection, modeling, integration, real-time monitoring, analysis, optimization, feedback, and continuing management are just a few of the phases that make up a digital twin's life cycle (Kothandaraman et al., 2022). From manufacturing and healthcare to smart cities and infrastructure management, it enables organizations to acquire insights, boost performance, and make decisions based on data. For this cutting-edge technology to deliver its full potential, efficient digital twin lifecycle management is essential.

6.4 DIGITAL TWIN APPLICATION DOMAINS

Digital twin technology has gained significant traction in various application domains, revolutionizing how industries operate, innovate, and optimize their processes.

- **Manufacturing and Industry 4.0.** For the purposes of process improvement, quality assurance, and preventative upkeep, digital twins have found widespread use in the manufacturing sector. They create a virtual version of the production line that can be monitored, simulated, and analyzed in real time. Improved productivity, less downtime, and quicker responses to interruptions are all made possible by this technology for manufacturing. Some of the digital twin application domains are shown in Figure 6.4.
- **Aerospace and Defence.** Digital twins are used in the aerospace and defence industry for a variety of purposes, including design, testing, and monitoring of very complex aircraft and military systems. They help engineers save money on development by simulating different situations, evaluating component performance, and checking for safety and reliability.

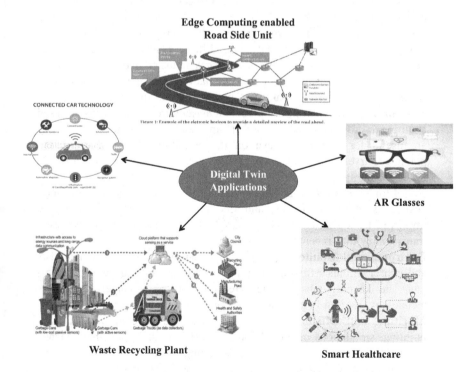

FIGURE 6.4 Digital twin application domains.

- **Healthcare and Medical Devices.** Patients' health conditions are modeled and tracked using digital twins, allowing for the development of individualized treatment plans. Virtual testing of medical devices allows for refinement of therapies, prostheses, and tools before they are really used on patients (Rani & Gupta, 2016).
- **Energy and Utilities.** Digital twins are used by the energy sector to improve electricity generation, delivery, and the use of renewable energy. Energy waste and environmental damage can be minimized with their assistance in grid management, failure prediction, and operational efficiency improvement.
- **Smart Cities and Infrastructure.** When it comes to planning and running a smart city, digital twins are indispensable. They are used by urban planners in the simulation of infrastructure like roads and water pipes. This technology facilitates operations in the areas of traffic control, energy efficiency, and emergency preparedness.
- **Automotive and Transportation.** Digital twins are employed in the automobile industry for purposes of design and testing, enhancing both safety and fuel efficiency. They also help with the research and development of autonomous vehicles by providing a platform for training AI algorithms and mimicking real-world scenarios.
- **Building and Construction.** Digital twins are utilized in construction to simulate building processes, predict project timelines, and optimize resource allocation. They help in detecting design flaws early, reducing construction costs, and improving the sustainability of structures.
- **Oil and Gas Exploration.** Offshore drilling platforms, pipelines, and refineries are modeled for the oil and gas industry using digital twins. These digital duplicates aid in risk evaluation, preventative maintenance scheduling, and decision making in potentially harmful settings.
- **Agriculture and Farming.** In precision agriculture, digital twins are used to improve crop management, soil quality, and resource allocation. They are useful for keeping an eye on the condition of crops, estimating potential harvests, and conserving both water and chemical inputs (Rani, Mishra, Kataria, Mallik, & Qin, 2023).
- **Retail and Supply Chain.** Digital twins help retailers test out new shop designs, study client habits, and fine-tune stock levels. Logistics are improved by digital twins in the supply chain because of the increased transparency into inventory and demand.
- **Environmental Monitoring.** Digital twins are used by environmentalists and conservationists for modeling ecosystems, monitoring wildlife habitats, and keeping tabs on the effects of climate change. Using this technology, we can better safeguard our planet.
- **Maritime and Offshore Industry.** Digital twins are utilized in shipbuilding, simulations of navigation, and offshore structural maintenance for maritime operations. They make shipping more secure, provide more efficient use of fuel, and lessen damage to the environment.

- **Entertainment and Gaming.** Digital twins are used in the media and entertainment industries to produce lifelike computer-generated worlds, characters, and simulations. As a result, media like video games, movies, and VR apps become more engrossing.

There is a wide variety of use cases for digital twins, each with its own set of problems and rewards. They are revolutionizing several sectors by creating a digital duplicate that can be tracked, simulated, analyzed, and optimized in real time. Because of the potential for digital twins to boost productivity and creativity in a wide range of industries, their use is anticipated to increase as technology develops further.

6.5 DIGITAL TWIN ENABLING TECHNOLOGIES

Many recent technological advancements have made it easier to create and maintain digital twins of real-world assets and systems. Among these are advanced analytics for simulation and modeling, ML for predictive capabilities, augmented reality for immersive visualization, and IoT sensors for data collecting. In addition, 5G connectivity guarantees instantaneous data transmission, while blockchain protects information authenticity. Broadly these technologies fall in the category of computational and communication technologies. Some of the prominent digital twin technologies are shown in Figure 6.5.

The ability to generate digital twins of physical assets or systems is a game-changer for businesses across a wide range of sectors thanks to the advent of digital twin technologies. These digital twins facilitate improved productivity, creativity, and choice-making through the provision of data, simulations, and real-time monitoring. Exploring the primary enabling technologies that allow for digital twins is crucial for comprehending their basis. By bridging the gap between the physical and digital worlds, these technologies allow sectors such as manufacturing, healthcare, and urban planning to optimize operations, improve decision-making, and spur innovation.

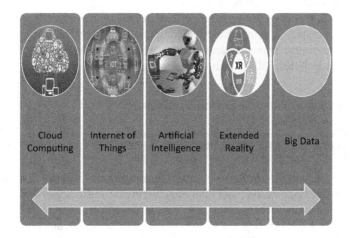

FIGURE 6.5 Digital twin enabling technologies.

6.5.1 DATA ACQUISITION AND SENSING TECHNOLOGIES

Real-world data from physical assets is essential to the development of digital twins. Several technological advancements are crucial to this procedure (Kumar et al., 2022):

- **IoT.** IoT devices with sensors and actuators play a crucial role in gathering information from a wide range of physical assets. These sensors can monitor and analyze a broad variety of parameters in real time, such as temperature, pressure, humidity, and more.
- **Remote Sensing.** Satellite imagery, drone photography, and LiDAR scanning are all ways that technology has improved our understanding of big landscapes. Create digital twins for use in agriculture, forestry, urban planning, and environmental monitoring with the help of these helpful tools.
- **Augmented Reality (AR) and Virtual Reality (VR).** Using augmented and virtual reality, digital twins can be more easily visualized and interacted with by their users. When used for design reviews, training, and maintenance operations, they provide an immersive environment that improves teamwork and decision-making.

6.5.2 DATA INTEGRATION AND MANAGEMENT TECHNOLOGIES

Organizations need efficient management and integration of data from various sources to construct accurate and comprehensive digital twins:

- **Data Lakes and Warehouses.** Data from multiple sources can be brought together by using these data storage options and then analyzed and modeled as needed. Commonly used tools for handling large datasets include Hadoop and Apache Spark.
- **Data Integration Platforms.** Data consistency, quality, and compatibility may be maintained across the business with the use of Extract, Transform, and Load (ETL) technologies.
- **Edge Computing.** By processing data in real time at the edge, where it was generated, solutions for edge computing can drastically cut down on response times. This is critical for uses where a lack of lag time is a must, such as in industrial automation and self-driving cars.

6.5.3 MODELING AND SIMULATION TECHNIQUES

The foundation of digital twin technology is precise modeling. Multiple methods are used to create reliable digital twin models, including:

- **Finite Element Analysis and Computational Fluid Dynamics.** Aerospace, automotive, and civil engineering all make heavy use of these modeling tools for structural analysis and fluid flow simulations.
- **ML and AI.** Predictive maintenance, anomaly detection, and optimization are all areas where ML and AI algorithms shine inside digital twins. They

can forecast the future based on past data and streamline the decision-making process with ease (Chethana, Pareek, de Albuquerque, Khanna, & Gupta, 2022; Pareek et al., 2022).

- **Physics-Based Models.** Physics-based models are crucial for understanding the behavior of systems governed by physical laws. These models are based on first principles, such as laws and equations; thus, they faithfully depict intricate systems like nuclear reactors and chemical reactions.

6.5.4 ANALYTICS AND DECISION SUPPORT

Massive volumes of data are produced by digital twins, which can be used to make educated decisions:

- **Predictive Analytics.** Organizations can foresee potential outcomes by using predictive models powered by ML. This helps with making forward-thinking choices and allocating resources (Chethana et al., 2022).
- **Prescriptive Analytics.** These models not only predict but also recommend the best course of action. They help people make educated decisions and fine-tune procedures to achieve peak efficiency.
- **Real-Time Monitoring.** Organizations can quickly react to outliers in behavior by constantly monitoring digital twin data. This is a must for keeping industrial systems running smoothly and efficiently (Shettar, Devangavi, & kumar Pareek, 2021).

6.5.5 VISUALIZATION AND USER INTERFACES

For digital twins to be useful, visualization must be done well.

- **3D Modeling and Rendering.** Intuitive visualization of physical assets and systems is made possible by 3D models. They provide a visual context for complex data, which aids in design, analysis, and training.
- **AR and VR.** By creating fully immersive experiences, AR and VR technologies provide real-time interaction between users and their digital doubles. In particular, these tools excel at training, maintenance, and reviewing designs.
- **Dashboards and Analytics Tools.** Stakeholders can quickly and easily access the crucial data and insights generated by digital twins through intuitive interfaces and dashboards. They make it easier for groups to work together and make sound decisions.

6.5.6 EMERGING TRENDS

Several currents are influencing the development of digital twin technology:

- **Digital Twin for Entire Cities.** Digital twins are being used by smart city programs to improve municipal planning, infrastructure management, and resident services. Both sustainability and quality of life can benefit from an all-encompassing strategy.

- **Quantum Computing.** The advent of quantum computing, which promises to exponentially increase computational capability, promises to revolutionize digital twins. This can drastically shorten the time it takes to run simulations, optimize models, and construct new ones.
- **Blockchain for Data Security.** Data security and trust are being investigated as potential benefits of blockchain technology inside digital twin ecosystems. Critical for secure applications, it guarantees data integrity, traceability, and access control.
- **Digital Twin in Healthcare.** Personalized medicine, medication discovery, and medical device development can all benefit from the use of digital twins for patients and organs in the healthcare industry. The potential for improved diagnosis and therapy is enhanced by this technology.

As a cutting-edge breakthrough, digital twin technology has the potential to revolutionize many different markets. Organizations that want to maximize the benefits of digital twins need to have a firm grasp of the underlying technologies that make them possible. New possibilities for optimization, efficiency, and competitiveness are emerging thanks to advances in areas ranging from data collecting and integration to cutting-edge modeling and analytics. Keeping abreast of new developments helps businesses adjust to the ever-changing, data-driven landscape.

6.6 MAJOR CHALLENGES IN THE DEPLOYMENT OF DIGITAL TWIN

While digital twins have the potential to greatly benefit businesses in terms of efficiency, cost savings, and decision making, there are a number of significant obstacles that must be overcome before any of those benefits can be realized as discussed below:

- **Data Integrity and Quality Assurance.** Integration of disparate data sources is a major hurdle for the widespread use of digital twins. To construct a faithful digital duplicate, digital twins make use of data collected in real time by sensors and IoT gadgets. The success of the digital twin depends on accurate, consistent data, which in turn requires strong data governance and quality assurance methods.
- **Scalability and Performance.** The widespread use of digital twins, however, may impose a burden on available computing power. It is crucial that the digital twin platform is able to process the massive amounts of data being produced without slowing down or crashing. This usually necessitates spending a lot of money on new facilities and machinery.
- **Security and Privacy.** The fact that digital twins store private data about real-world assets makes them tempting targets for hackers. To keep the digital twin and the physical system it represents safe, businesses must take strong precautions. The collection and processing of data from several

sources also raises privacy concerns and necessitates adherence to data protection standards.

- **Interoperability.** Within an organization, digital twins frequently require the use of additional systems, programs, and pieces of hardware. It can be difficult to ensure interoperability with preexisting IT ecosystems due to the potential usage of disparate technologies and standards, which can make integration more difficult.
- **Model Accuracy and Validation.** The success of the virtual system relies on a faithful representation of the real world. Continuous validation and refining of the digital twin is often necessary to ensure that its prediction capabilities are in line with the actual behavior of the system.
- **Cost of Return on Investment (RoI).** It might be pricey to create and maintain a digital twin. Data collecting, software creation, hardware infrastructure, and regular maintenance all have expenses that must be factored in by businesses. Proving a positive ROI is critical for digital twin projects to receive sustained funding and support.
- **Change Management and Organizational Culture.** Employees used to the status quo may push back against the introduction of digital twins into their workflows and operations. The successful deployment of digital twins requires effective change management methods and a culture that fosters digital transformation.
- **Regulatory Compliance.** Strict rules and regulations are imposed on industries like healthcare and aircraft. Deploying digital twins in these industries necessitates following difficult and time-consuming regulatory norms and procedures.
- **Data Ownership and Sharing.** Data ownership and the establishment of data sharing agreements can be difficult problems in collaborative organizations or supply chains. Data ownership, access rights, and obligations among stakeholders must be addressed within distinct governance and legal frameworks.
- **Ethical Considerations.** Concerns about data privacy, spying, and the loss of jobs to automation arise when digital twins are used. In order to preserve their credibility and moral standing, businesses must give serious thought to and solve these ethical issues.

6.7   FUTURE RESEARCH DIRECTIONS

It will be future research directions in digital twin deployment that will determine how this technology develops and how its current limits are overcome. Key issues that need attention are:

- **Advanced Analytics and AI Integration.** Integrating state-of-the-art AI and ML methods into digital twins will be investigated to improve their analytical capacities. Algorithms for proactive intelligence and maintenance of digital twins already exist, such as predictive maintenance, anomaly detection, and optimization.

- **Digital Twin Ecosystem.** To better reflect complex systems, researchers plan to investigate how to build ecosystems for digital twins that are both all-encompassing and interoperable.
- **Edge and Fog Computing.** Researching how edge and fog computing can be used in digital twin settings to improve real-time decision making by processing data closer to the source and lowering latency.
- **Quantum Computing.** Advances in modeling precision and performance are within reach as scientists investigate quantum computing's ability to solve complex simulations and optimizations in digital twin situations.
- **Human-Digital Twin Interaction.** It will be crucial to learn how people relate to and have faith in digital twins. In order to create more natural interactions, studies will look into user interfaces, AR, and VR software.
- **Energy Efficiency and Sustainability.** From smart cities to factories, researchers are focusing on the impact digital twins can have on reducing energy use and enhancing sustainability.
- **Blockchain and Data Security.** Looking into how blockchain technology can be used to create a more secure digital twin environment by keeping track of all modifications in a visible, unalterable ledger.
- **Ethical and Legal Considerations.** Research will center on establishing ethical norms and legal frameworks to govern the usage and privacy of digital twins in light of rising ethical concerns.
- **Muti-Domain Digital Twins.** Investigating the creation of digital twins to tackle intractable interdisciplinary problems. These twins would include cyber-physical systems, biological systems, and socio-technical systems.
- **Education and Workforce Development.** A trained workforce able to successfully manage and utilize digital twins is ensured by research into education, training, and skill development.

These lines of inquiry will help bring digital twins to full maturity and widespread use, opening the door for them to disrupt sectors, enhance decision-making, and fuel innovation in the years to come.

6.8 CONCLUSIONS

Digital twin is one of the most rapidly developing technologies across various sectors to improve design, optimize resources and processes, and develop efficient systems. It has revolutionized many application domains likewise smart cities, healthcare, defence, waste management, etc. However, the authors observed that the use of various enabling technologies causes many challenges in the deployment of various digital twin applications. The major challenges analyzed in this aspect are:

- Data integration and quality assurance
- Scalability
- Security of data and user's privacy

- Interoperability
- Deployment cost
- Regulatory compliance

These challenges lead to possible research directions for future work by engineers and scholars in the design and development of more efficient digital twin applications for various systems.

REFERENCES

Bhushan, S., Kumar, M., Kumar, P., Ravi, R. V., & Singh, A. K. (2022). *Holistic approach to quantum cryptography in cyber security*: CRC Press.

Biradar, V. G., Nagaraj, H., Mohan, S., & Pareek, P. K. (2022). Industrial fluids components health management using deep learning.

Chethana, C., Pareek, P. K., de Albuquerque, V. H. C., Khanna, A., & Gupta, D. (2022). *Deep learning technique based intrusion detection in cyber-security networks*. Paper presented at the 2022 IEEE 2nd Mysore Sub Section International Conference (MysuruCon).

Hebbale, S., Marndi, A., Kumar, B. M., Mohan, B., Achyutha, P., & Pareek, P. (2022). A survey on automated medical image classification using deep learning. *International Journal of Health Sciences*, 6(S1), 7850–7865.

Jones, D., Snider, C., Nassehi, A., Yon, J., & Hicks, B. (2020). Characterising the Digital Twin: A systematic literature review. *CIRP Journal of Manufacturing Science and Technology*, 29, 36–52.

Kothandaraman, D., Manickam, M., Balasundaram, A., Pradeep, D., Arulmurugan, A., Sivaraman, A. K., & Balakrishna, R. (2022). Decentralized link failure prevention routing (DLFPR) algorithm for efficient internet of things. *Intelligent Automation and Soft Computing*, 34(1), 655–666.

Kumar, P., Banerjee, K., Singhal, N., Kumar, A., Rani, S., Kumar, R., & Lavinia, C. A. (2022). Verifiable, secure mobile agent migration in healthcare systems using a polynomial-based threshold secret sharing scheme with a Blowfish algorithm. *Sensors*, 22(22), 8620.

Pareek, P. K., Surendhar S, P. A., Prasad, R., Ramkumar, G., Dixit, E., Subbiah, R., ... Jayadhas, S. A. (2022). Predicting the spread of vessels in initial stage cervical cancer through radiomics strategy based on deep learning approach. *Advances in Materials Science and Engineering*, 2022, 149–171.

Puri, V., Kataria, A., Solanki, V. K., & Rani, S. (2022). *AI-based botnet attack classification and detection in IoT devices*. Paper presented at the 2022 IEEE International Conference on Machine Learning and Applied Network Technologies (ICMLANT).

Rani, S., Bhambri, P., & Chauhan, M. (2021). *A machine learning model for kids' behavior analysis from facial emotions using principal component analysis*. Paper presented at the 2021 5th Asian Conference on Artificial Intelligence Technology (ACAIT).

Rani, S., & Gupta, O. (2016). Empirical analysis and performance evaluation of various GPU implementations of protein BLAST. *International Journal of Computer Applications*, 151(7), 22–27.

Rani, S., Kataria, A., & Chauhan, M. (2022). Cyber security techniques, architectures, and design. In *Holistic Approach to Quantum Cryptography in Cyber Security* (pp. 41–66): CRC Press.

Rani, S., Kataria, A., Kumar, S., & Tiwari, P. (2023). Federated learning for secure IoMT-applications in smart healthcare systems: A comprehensive review. *Knowledge-based systems*, 110658.

Rani, S., Mishra, A. K., Kataria, A., Mallik, S., & Qin, H. (2023). Machine learning-based optimal crop selection system in smart agriculture. *Scientific Reports, 13*(1), 15997.

Rani, S., Pareek, P. K., Kaur, J., Chauhan, M., & Bhambri, P. (2023). *Quantum machine learning in healthcare: Developments and challenges.* Paper presented at the 2023 IEEE International Conference on Integrated Circuits and Communication Systems (ICICACS).

Shettar, G. B., Devangavi, A. D., & kumar Pareek, P. (2021). *A Novel architecture for optimum association of cellular phone users to multi access edge computing (MAEC).* Paper presented at the 2021 IEEE Madras Section Conference (MASCON).

Tao, F., Xiao, B., Qi, Q., Cheng, J., & Ji, P. (2022). Digital twin modeling. *Journal of Manufacturing Systems, 64,* 372–389.

Tao, F., Zhang, H., Liu, A., & Nee, A. Y. (2018). Digital twin in industry: State-of-the-art. *IEEE Transactions on Industrial Informatics, 15*(4), 2405–2415.

7 Big Data Analytics with Digital Twin for Industrial Applications

Pankaj Bhambri, Sita Rani, Suresh Kumar, and Vijay Kumar Sinha

7.1 INTRODUCTION

"Big Data Analytics with Digital Twin for Industrial Applications" represents a cutting-edge exploration of how two transformative technologies, Big Data Analytics and Digital Twins, are reshaping the landscape of industrial operations. This book chapter offers a comprehensive overview of these concepts, shedding light on their individual significance and, most importantly, their synergistic potential when integrated (Kumar et al., 2022a, 2022b).

In the first section, the chapter lays the foundation by introducing the core components of Big Data Analytics, elucidating its pivotal role in processing and deriving actionable insights from the vast and complex data streams generated by industrial processes (Rani, S., Mishra, A. K., Kataria, A., Mallik, S., & Qin, H., 2023). Concurrently, it introduces Digital Twins as virtual replicas of physical assets and systems, underlining their role in revolutionizing real-time monitoring, optimization, and decision-making in various industrial sectors (Machała et al., 2022; Rani et al., 2023).

The heart of the chapter lies in its exploration of the seamless integration of Digital Twins with Big Data Analytics. It articulates how Digital Twins serve as data-rich virtual proxies for physical assets and systems, enabling the application of advanced analytics techniques to predict and optimize performance. Practical use cases across diverse industries - from predictive maintenance in manufacturing to supply chain management in logistics - are presented to illustrate the tangible benefits of this integrated approach (Rani et al. 2022a-c).

By offering both a theoretical framework and practical insights, "Big Data Analytics with Digital Twin for Industrial Applications" equips professionals, researchers, and industrial practitioners with the knowledge needed to harness the combined power of Big Data Analytics and Digital Twins (Kaur, D., Singh, B., & Rani, S., 2023). It not only addresses the transformative impact of this integration on operational efficiency but also delves into the challenges and considerations that must be navigated to implement these cutting-edge technologies effectively, ensuring

DOI: 10.1201/9781003395416-7

they remain at the forefront of the evolving industrial landscape (Kaur et al., 2006; Kamra & Bhambri, 2007; Jain & Bhambri, 2005; Habib & Chimsom, 2019).

7.1.1 OVERVIEW OF BIG DATA ANALYTICS

An overview of Big Data Analytics reveals it as a transformative field within data science, specializing in the handling, analysis, and interpretation of vast and complex datasets (Rani, S., Kataria, A., & Chauhan, M., 2022; Rani, S., Bhambri, P., & Gupta, O. P., 2022). At its core, Big Data Analytics is driven by the recognition that traditional data processing techniques and tools are often inadequate for dealing with the sheer volume, velocity, variety, and veracity of data generated in today's digital world (Gupta et al., 2007a-e; Goel & Gupta, 2020). It encompasses a wide array of techniques and technologies, including data mining, machine learning, statistical analysis, and data visualization, all aimed at uncovering valuable insights, patterns, and trends hidden within massive datasets.

Big Data Analytics finds applications across various domains, including business, healthcare, finance, and manufacturing, among others. In the business realm, it aids in understanding consumer behavior, optimizing marketing strategies, and improving operational efficiency. In healthcare, it enhances patient care by facilitating early disease detection and personalized treatment plans. Financial institutions employ it for fraud detection and risk assessment. In manufacturing, it plays a pivotal role in predictive maintenance, quality control, and supply chain optimization (Garg & Bhambri, 2011a, 2011b; Ghobakhloo, 2020). In essence, Big Data Analytics empowers organizations to make data-driven decisions, gain a competitive edge, and unlock previously untapped opportunities in an increasingly data-centric world.

7.1.2 INTRODUCTION TO DIGITAL TWINS

Digital Twins represent a groundbreaking concept at the intersection of the physical and digital worlds. Essentially, a Digital Twin is a virtual replica or digital counterpart of a physical object, system, or process. It goes beyond mere computer-aided design models by incorporating real-time data and information from sensors, IoT devices, and other sources to provide a dynamic, holistic view of the physical entity it mirrors. This means that Digital Twins continuously update themselves based on real-world changes, allowing for accurate simulations, monitoring, and analysis of their physical counterparts (Grewal & Bhambri, 2006; Rani et al., 2021; Rattan et al., 2005a, 2005b).

The applications of Digital Twins are vast and span across industries. In manufacturing, they are instrumental in optimizing production processes, predicting maintenance needs, and ensuring product quality. In healthcare, Digital Twins can simulate and analyze the behavior of organs, enabling personalized treatment plans. In urban planning, they help design smarter, more sustainable cities. Additionally, Digital Twins play a significant role in sectors such as aerospace, automotive, and energy, where they enhance product development, safety, and efficiency. The concept of Digital Twins is poised to revolutionize how we design, operate, and interact with the physical world, ushering in a new era of data-driven decision-making and innovation (Bhambri, 2010; Bhambri & Hans, 2010; Bhambri et al., 2010; Bhambri & Thapar, 2010; Bhambri & Hans, 2009; Dhanalakshmi et al., 2022).

7.1.3 SIGNIFICANCE OF INTEGRATION

The integration of Big Data Analytics with Digital Twins represents a significant leap forward in the realm of industrial applications and beyond. This integration offers a range of benefits and transformative potential that significantly impact various industries and sectors. Here are some key aspects of the significance of this integration (Chopra & Bhambri, 2011; Contreras et al., 2017; Bhambri et al., 2005a-c):

- Real-Time Monitoring and Predictive Insights: By combining Digital Twins, which provide real-time data on physical assets and processes, with Big Data Analytics, organizations can gain a deeper understanding of their operations. This allows for real-time monitoring of equipment and processes, enabling timely responses to anomalies and potential issues. Moreover, predictive analytics can be applied to anticipate maintenance needs and operational optimizations, reducing downtime and improving efficiency.
- Improved Decision-Making: The integration empowers decision-makers with data-driven insights. Managers and engineers can make informed choices based on a holistic view of their physical assets, as Digital Twins offer a virtual representation of the entire system. This leads to better resource allocation, more accurate planning, and the ability to respond swiftly to changing conditions or market demands (Gupta, O. P., 2017).
- Optimization of Processes: With Big Data Analytics, historical and real-time data from Digital Twins can be analyzed to identify patterns, inefficiencies, and opportunities for optimization. This can lead to streamlined processes, reduced waste, and improved overall performance. For instance, in manufacturing, it can result in better production yields and higher product quality (Arya, V., Rani, S., & Choudhary, N., 2022).
- Cost Reduction and Efficiency: The integration often leads to cost savings. Predictive maintenance, for example, can prevent unexpected equipment failures and reduce maintenance costs. Improved energy efficiency through data analysis can lead to reduced operational expenses. Overall, organizations can optimize their resource utilization and minimize operational inefficiencies.
- Enhanced Product Development: In product-centric industries, Digital Twins can be used to simulate product behavior and performance under various conditions. By integrating Big Data Analytics, organizations can gather valuable insights from product usage data in the field. This enables iterative product development, leading to better designed, more reliable products tailored to customer needs.

- Cross-Industry Applications: The integration is not limited to a single industry. It finds applications in manufacturing, healthcare, energy, transportation, and more. For instance, in healthcare, it can improve patient care by simulating and analyzing medical conditions, while in logistics, it can optimize supply chain operations.
- Sustainability: Organizations can leverage this integration to support sustainability initiatives. By optimizing processes, resource usage, and energy efficiency, they can reduce their environmental footprint. Sustainability is not only a corporate responsibility but also a market demand, and this integration helps meet those expectations.
- Competitive Advantage: Businesses that successfully integrate Big Data Analytics with Digital Twins can gain a competitive edge. They can respond more effectively to market changes, innovate faster, and deliver superior products or services, all of which are critical factors in today's fast-paced business environment.

The integration of Big Data Analytics with Digital Twins offers organizations a holistic, data-driven approach to understanding, monitoring, and optimizing their physical assets and processes. It is a significant enabler of efficiency, sustainability, and innovation across industries, providing a competitive advantage in an increasingly data-centric world.

7.2 DIGITAL TWINS IN INDUSTRIAL APPLICATIONS

Digital Twins in industrial applications represent a transformative approach where virtual replicas of physical assets, systems, or processes are employed to drive operational efficiency, innovation, and informed decision-making (Kataria, A., Puri, V., Pareek, P. K., & Rani, S., 2023, July). These digital counterparts, known as Digital Twins, capture real-time data and contextual information from sensors and IoT devices, enabling a comprehensive understanding of their physical counterparts. With applications spanning manufacturing, energy, healthcare, and beyond, Digital Twins empower industries to monitor, analyze, and optimize operations in real time, predict maintenance needs, enhance product development, and streamline processes. This technology-driven paradigm shift promises to revolutionize industrial sectors by offering unparalleled insights, cost savings, and competitive advantages, ultimately reshaping the way organizations interact with and leverage the physical world (Bhambri & Singh, 2005a, 2005b; Bhambri & Gupta, 2007; Bhambri et al., 2007a-c; Chen et al., 2017).

7.2.1 WHAT ARE DIGITAL TWINS?

Digital Twins are virtual replicas or digital counterparts of physical objects, systems, or processes. These digital representations are created by collecting real-time data and information from sensors, Internet of Things (IoT) devices, and other sources associated with their physical counterparts. Digital Twins are used in various domains, such as manufacturing, healthcare, urban planning, and more, to provide a dynamic and holistic view of physical assets. They continuously update themselves to reflect changes in the physical world, enabling real-time monitoring, analysis, and simulation. Digital Twins serve as invaluable tools for improving decision-making, optimizing operations, predicting maintenance needs, and enhancing innovation across industries, ultimately bridging the gap between the digital and physical realms (Bhambri et al., 2008a, 2008b; Cañas et al., 2021).

7.2.2 Types of Digital Twins

Digital Twins can take various forms and serve different purposes depending on the application and the complexity of the physical system they replicate. Here are the common types of Digital Twins (Singh & Bhambri, 2007; Yadav et al., 2022; Rani, S., Kataria, A., Kumar, S., & Tiwari, P., 2023):

- Component-level Digital Twins: These represent individual components or parts of a larger system, such as a single machine, sensor, or component. They focus on monitoring and optimizing the performance of specific elements within a system.
- System-level Digital Twins: System-level Digital Twins replicate entire systems or processes, encompassing multiple components and their interactions. These are used to gain insights into the overall behavior and efficiency of complex systems, like manufacturing production lines or energy grids.
- Product Digital Twins: Product Digital Twins are virtual replicas of physical products, such as cars, airplanes, or consumer electronics. They are used in product design, testing, and simulation to improve performance and reliability before physical production.
- Process Digital Twins: Process Digital Twins model and simulate specific processes or workflows within an organization. For example, they can be used to optimize supply chain logistics, healthcare procedures, or manufacturing workflows.
- Asset Digital Twins: Asset Digital Twins focus on individual assets, like buildings, bridges, or industrial equipment. They help monitor the condition, performance, and maintenance needs of these assets, ensuring their longevity and reliability.
- Human Digital Twins: These represent individuals in a virtual space, capturing data related to their health, behavior, and preferences. They find applications in healthcare for personalized medicine and wellness monitoring (Kaur, S., Kumar, R., Kaur, R., Singh, S., Rani, S., & Kaur, A., 2022).
- City Digital Twins: City Digital Twins create a digital representation of an entire city, including its infrastructure, transportation systems, and services. Urban planners use these to optimize city development and resource allocation (Sudevan, S., Barwani, B., Al Maani, E., Rani, S., & Sivaraman, A. K., 2021).
- Environmental Digital Twins: Environmental Digital Twins model natural ecosystems and environmental conditions. They are used to monitor and

predict environmental changes, such as weather patterns, pollution levels, or ecological shifts (Bhambri, P., Aggarwal, M., Singh, H., Singh, A. P., & Rani, S., 2022; Dhanalakshmi, R., Anand, J., Sivaraman, A. K., & Rani, S., 2022).

- Control Digital Twins: These are used to fine-tune and optimize control systems within industrial processes. They help ensure that systems operate efficiently and safely.
- Simulation Digital Twins: Simulation Digital Twins are focused on modeling and predicting how physical systems will behave under various conditions. They are used extensively in product design and testing to reduce costs and time-to-market (Rani, S., Bhambri, P., Kataria, A., & Khang, A., 2022).

These various types of Digital Twins cater to a wide range of industries and applications, providing tailored solutions to monitor, analyze, and optimize physical assets and processes in the digital realm.

7.2.3 CREATING DIGITAL TWINS

Creating Digital Twins involves a series of steps and technologies, depending on the complexity of the physical system you want to replicate (Rani 2021, October). Here's a simplified overview of how to create Digital Twins:

- Define the Objective: Clearly define the purpose and objectives of creating a Digital Twin. Determine what aspects of the physical system you want to replicate and what you aim to achieve with the Digital Twin (Tanwar, R., Chhabra, Y., Rattan, P., & Rani, S., 2022, September).
- Data Collection: Install sensors, IoT devices, and data collection points on the physical asset or system. These sensors should gather relevant data, including performance metrics, environmental conditions, and any other information necessary to replicate the physical system accurately.
- Data Integration: Aggregate and integrate data from various sources, ensuring compatibility and consistency. This often involves data preprocessing to clean, transform, and normalize the data.
- Data Storage and Management: Store the collected data in a secure and scalable database or data storage system. Ensure that the data is easily accessible for analysis and modeling.
- Digital Twin Model Development: Develop a mathematical or computational model that replicates the behavior of the physical system. This model should take into account the data collected, the physics governing the system, and any relevant algorithms or machine learning techniques (Rani, S., & Gupta, O. P., 2016; Gupta, O. P., & Rani, S., 2010).
- Real-Time Data Streaming: Establish real-time data streaming between the physical system and the Digital Twin model. This ensures that the Digital Twin remains up-to-date and accurately mirrors the physical system's behavior.

- Visualization and User Interface: Create a user-friendly interface to visualize the Digital Twin and its real-time data. Dashboards and visualization tools help users monitor and interact with the Digital Twin effectively.
- Simulation and Analysis: Use the Digital Twin to run simulations and analyze the behavior of the physical system under different conditions. This allows you to predict performance, identify potential issues, and optimize processes.
- Feedback Loop: Implement a feedback loop where insights and recommendations from the Digital Twin are used to make informed decisions and adjustments to the physical system. This closed-loop approach is crucial for continuous improvement.
- Security and Privacy: Ensure that the data collected, stored, and transmitted between the physical system and the Digital Twin is secure and compliant with relevant privacy regulations. Implement robust cybersecurity measures to protect the integrity of the Digital Twin.
- Scaling and Maintenance: As your Digital Twin evolves and new data becomes available, be prepared to scale the system accordingly. Regularly maintain and update the Digital Twin to reflect changes in the physical system and improve its accuracy and utility.
- Documentation and Training: Document the creation process, including data sources, algorithms, and modeling techniques used. Provide training to relevant stakeholders who will interact with or make decisions based on the Digital Twin.

Creating Digital Twins is a multidisciplinary endeavor that often requires collaboration between domain experts, data scientists, engineers, and IT professionals. The process should be driven by a clear understanding of the goals and potential benefits, as well as a commitment to ongoing improvement and adaptation as both the physical system and the Digital Twin evolve over time.

7.2.4 Data Sources for Digital Twins

Data sources for Digital Twins vary depending on the type of asset or system being replicated and the specific objectives of the Digital Twin. However, here are some common data sources that can provide valuable information for creating and maintaining Digital Twins:

- Sensors and IoT Devices: These are primary data sources for most Digital Twins. Sensors can monitor a wide range of parameters, including temperature, humidity, pressure, vibration, and more. IoT devices can provide data on the status and performance of equipment and assets.
- Machine and Equipment Data: Data generated by machines and equipment, such as production rates, energy consumption, error rates, and maintenance logs, can be crucial for manufacturing and industrial Digital Twins.

- Environmental Data: For assets exposed to environmental conditions, such as buildings or outdoor infrastructure, environmental sensors can provide data on weather conditions, air quality, and temperature.
- Location and Global Positioning System (GPS) Data: GPS data and geospatial information are important for assets that move or are geographically distributed. They can help track the location and movement of vehicles, ships, and other mobile assets.
- Process Control Systems: Data from process control systems and supervisory control and data acquisition systems can be used for process Digital Twins. These systems monitor and control industrial processes and provide data on variables like flow rates, pressures, and chemical concentrations.
- Cameras and Image Sensors: Visual data from cameras and image sensors can be used for object recognition, tracking, and monitoring. This is valuable in applications like surveillance, autonomous vehicles, and robotics.
- Health and Biometric Sensors: In healthcare and human-centric applications, data from health sensors (e.g., heart rate monitors, wearables) and biometric devices provide insights into an individual's health and behavior.
- Customer Data: In retail and customer-centric industries, customer data, such as purchase history, preferences, and feedback, can be used to create customer-centric Digital Twins for personalization and marketing.
- Energy and Utility Data: Energy consumption data, such as electricity, water, and gas usage, is important for monitoring and optimizing energy efficiency in buildings and industrial facilities.
- Supply Chain Data: For logistics and supply chain management, data on inventory levels, transportation routes, and delivery times can be integrated into Digital Twins to optimize supply chain operations.
- Maintenance and Repair Logs: Historical maintenance and repair logs provide insights into the performance and health of assets over time. This data is vital for predictive maintenance Digital Twins.
- Social Media and Online Data: In applications related to consumer sentiment analysis, social media data and online reviews can be used to gauge public opinion and sentiment regarding products or services.
- Simulated Data: In cases where real-time data is limited or unavailable, simulated data generated by models and simulations can be used to populate Digital Twins and test different scenarios.
- User Interaction Data: For Digital Twins with human-machine interaction, data on user interactions, preferences, and behavior can help refine and personalize the user experience.

These data sources collectively provide the input necessary to create and update Digital Twins, enabling them to accurately mirror the behavior and status of their physical counterparts. The choice of data sources depends on the specific use case and the information required for achieving the objectives of the Digital Twin.

7.3 BIG DATA ANALYTICS IN INDUSTRY

Big Data Analytics has emerged as a transformative force in various industries, revolutionizing the way organizations handle and derive value from vast and complex datasets. In the industrial sector, it plays a pivotal role in enhancing operational efficiency, reducing costs, and enabling data-driven decision-making. Industrial processes generate a wealth of data from sensors, machinery, and production lines, and Big Data Analytics processes this information to extract actionable insights (Bhambri et al., 2009; Bhambri & Singh, 2009; Bhambri & Thapar, 2009; Saucedo-Martínez et al., 2018). These insights enable predictive maintenance, where machinery issues are anticipated before they lead to costly breakdowns, optimizing production schedules and minimizing downtime (Thapar & Bhambri, 2009). Moreover, analytics tools help improve product quality by identifying patterns and anomalies, ensuring consistency and compliance with industry standards. From supply chain optimization to energy management, Big Data Analytics empowers industrial enterprises to achieve higher productivity and competitiveness.

Big Data Analytics supports product innovation and development by analyzing customer feedback and market trends (Singh, P., Gupta, O. P., & Saini, S., 2017). By collecting and analyzing data from various sources, including customer interactions, social media, and product usage, manufacturers gain a deeper understanding of consumer preferences, allowing them to design and deliver products tailored to market demands (Gupta, O. P., & Rani, S., 2013). Furthermore, it provides insights into cost optimization and resource allocation, enabling companies to streamline operations, reduce waste, and enhance sustainability (Abrol et al., 2005; Bai et al., 2020; Bhambri et al., 2011). In essence, Big Data Analytics has become a cornerstone of modern industrial strategies, fostering innovation, improving decision-making, and driving continuous improvement across the sector (Rani, S., Mishra, A. K., Kataria, A., Mallik, S., & Qin, H., 2023).

7.3.1 ROLE OF DATA IN INDUSTRIAL OPERATIONS

The role of data in industrial operations within the context of Big Data Analytics is paramount. Industrial processes generate an immense volume of data from various sources, including sensors, machines, supply chain activities, and quality control checks. This data holds a wealth of information that, when properly harnessed and analyzed, can lead to substantial improvements in efficiency, quality, and overall operational performance (Bathla et al., 2007a, 2007b; Kothandaraman et al., 2022).

First and foremost, data serves as the lifeblood of industrial operations by providing real-time insights into the status and health of machinery and processes. Sensors and monitoring devices continuously collect data on parameters like temperature, pressure, vibration, and product quality. Big Data Analytics processes this information to detect deviations from normal operating conditions, allowing for proactive maintenance. Predictive maintenance, driven by data analytics, helps organizations identify when equipment might fail and schedule maintenance activities precisely when needed, minimizing downtime and reducing operational costs.

Second, data plays a crucial role in supply chain management and optimization. Industrial operations often involve complex supply chains with numerous components and dependençies. Big Data Analytics enables the tracking and analysis of supply chain data, including inventory levels, transportation routes, and delivery times. By analyzing historical and real-time data, organizations can make more informed decisions about inventory management, logistics planning, and demand forecasting. This leads to smoother operations, reduced costs, and improved customer satisfaction through timely deliveries.

Last, data-driven decision-making is fundamental in ensuring product quality and process optimization. Manufacturers rely on data analytics to monitor production lines, detect defects or irregularities in real time, and make immediate adjustments to maintain quality standards. Historical data analysis helps identify the root causes of quality issues, enabling process improvements over time. In this way, data serves as a feedback loop for continuous improvement, driving higher product quality and operational excellence in industrial settings. Overall, data's role in industrial operations, facilitated by Big Data Analytics, is indispensable for efficiency, cost reduction, and quality assurance.

7.3.2 Data Preprocessing Techniques

Data preprocessing techniques are a crucial step in the Big Data Analytics process, especially in the context of industrial applications. These techniques are employed to clean, transform, and prepare raw data for analysis, ensuring that it is of high quality and suitable for extracting meaningful insights (Singh et al., 2010; Singh et al., 2006; Gupta & Bhambri, 2006). In the realm of industrial Big Data Analytics, several key data preprocessing techniques are commonly used:

- Data Cleaning: This involves identifying and handling missing data, duplicate records, and outliers. In industrial settings, missing sensor readings or erroneous data points can significantly affect analysis results. Data cleaning techniques include imputation (replacing missing values with estimated values), deduplication, and outlier detection.
- Data Integration: Industrial data often comes from multiple sources and formats, such as sensors, databases, and logs. Data integration techniques involve merging these heterogeneous data sources into a unified dataset for analysis. It ensures that data from various sensors and systems can be correlated and analyzed together (Rani, S., Arya, V., & Kataria, A., 2022).
- Data Transformation: Data transformation techniques are used to convert data into a suitable format for analysis. This may include scaling, normalization, or encoding categorical variables. In industrial applications, sensor data with different units or scales may need to be transformed to ensure compatibility (Gupta, O., Rani, S., & Pant, D. C., 2011).
- Feature Engineering: Feature engineering involves creating new variables (features) from existing data to enhance the performance of analytical models. For instance, engineers might derive features related to machinery

performance from raw sensor data, such as calculating average values or rolling averages over time.

- Time Series Analysis: In industrial settings, time series data is prevalent, where measurements are taken at regular intervals. Time series analysis techniques, such as smoothing, aggregation, and seasonality decomposition, help uncover patterns and trends in temporal data, facilitating predictive maintenance and process optimization.
- Dimensionality Reduction: In cases where data has a high dimensionality, dimensionality reduction techniques like Principal Component Analysis (PCA) or feature selection methods are used to reduce the number of variables without losing critical information. This can enhance the efficiency of analytics models and visualization.
- Data Sampling: When dealing with large volumes of data, data sampling techniques are applied to select a representative subset of the data for analysis. This reduces computational complexity while preserving the essential characteristics of the dataset.
- Data Imbalance Handling: In some industrial scenarios, data may be imbalanced, meaning that one class or outcome significantly outweighs the others. Techniques like oversampling, undersampling, or generating synthetic data are used to balance the dataset, ensuring that the analysis doesn't favor the majority class.
- Data Quality Validation: Validation techniques, such as data profiling and data quality rules, are applied to ensure that the data meets predefined quality criteria. This is particularly important in industries where data accuracy and reliability are critical, such as healthcare and manufacturing.

By applying these data preprocessing techniques, organizations can prepare their industrial data for meaningful analysis, leading to more accurate insights and informed decision-making in various domains, including predictive maintenance, quality control, and process optimization.

7.3.3 ADVANCED ANALYTICS METHODS

Advanced analytics methods represent a set of sophisticated techniques used in Big Data Analytics to extract deeper insights, make accurate predictions, and optimize industrial processes. These methods go beyond traditional descriptive analytics and basic statistical analysis, offering organizations in various industries the ability to leverage their data for more strategic decision-making (Bhambri & Singh, 2008a-c; Bhambri & Nischal, 2008a, 2008b; Rani, S., Bhambri, P., & Kataria, A., 2023). In the context of Big Data Analytics in industry, several advanced analytics methods are particularly relevant:

- Machine Learning: Machine learning algorithms play a central role in industrial Big Data Analytics. Supervised learning methods like regression and classification are used for predictive maintenance, quality control, and demand forecasting. Unsupervised learning techniques like clustering and dimensionality reduction help identify patterns and anomalies in data (Kataria, A., Agrawal, D., Rani, S., Karar, V., & Chauhan, M., 2022). Additionally, deep learning models, such as neural networks, are employed for complex tasks like image recognition and NLP.

- Time Series Analysis: Given the prevalence of time-stamped data in industrial settings, time series analysis methods are crucial. Techniques like ARIMA (AutoRegressive Integrated Moving Average), Exponential Smoothing, and LSTM (Long Short-Term Memory) networks are used for forecasting and anomaly detection in time series data, enabling predictive maintenance and efficient resource allocation (Bali, V., Bali, S., Gaur, D., Rani, S., & Kumar, R., 2023; Puri, V., Kataria, A., Solanki, V. K., & Rani, S., 2022, December).

- Optimization Algorithms: Optimization algorithms, such as linear programming, genetic algorithms, and simulated annealing, are applied to find the best solutions to complex industrial problems. These algorithms help optimize production schedules, supply chain logistics, and resource allocation, ultimately reducing costs and improving efficiency.

- Text Analytics and Natural Language Processing (NLP): In industries where textual data is abundant, such as customer feedback, maintenance logs, or quality reports, NLP techniques are employed to extract insights from unstructured text. Sentiment analysis, topic modeling, and named entity recognition help organizations understand customer sentiment, identify emerging issues, and improve communication.

- Spatial Analytics: Spatial analytics methods are used in industries like logistics and urban planning, where geographic data is critical. Geographic Information Systems and spatial analysis tools help organizations optimize routes, plan infrastructure, and assess the impact of location-based factors on operations.

- Prescriptive Analytics: This advanced analytics method goes beyond predicting outcomes and offers recommendations for optimal decision-making. Prescriptive analytics models, such as decision trees and optimization algorithms, provide actionable insights, guiding organizations on how to make the best choices in complex scenarios.

- Anomaly Detection: Anomaly detection methods, including statistical approaches and machine learning-based techniques, are employed to identify unusual patterns or outliers in data. Detecting anomalies in industrial processes is crucial for preventing equipment failures, ensuring safety, and maintaining product quality.

- Predictive Maintenance Models: Predictive maintenance models use historical and real-time data to predict when equipment or machinery is likely to fail. These models help organizations schedule maintenance activities proactively, minimizing downtime and reducing maintenance costs (Rani, S., & Kaur, S., 2012; Kaur, G., Kaur, R., & Rani, S., 2015).

- Simulation and Digital Twins: Simulation techniques, combined with Digital Twins, enable organizations to model and simulate various scenarios in a virtual environment. This allows for testing hypotheses, optimizing processes, and predicting outcomes before implementing changes in the physical world (Rani, S., & Gupta, O. P., 2017).

These advanced analytics methods empower industries to harness the full potential of their big data resources, driving innovation, cost savings, and competitive advantage. By leveraging these techniques, organizations can make data-driven decisions, optimize operations, and stay ahead in an increasingly data-centric industrial landscape.

7.3.4 PREDICTIVE MODELING

Predictive modeling is a core component of Big Data Analytics in the industrial sector, providing organizations with the ability to foresee future events and trends based on historical and real-time data. In the context of industry, predictive modeling is leveraged for a wide range of applications, with one of the most prominent being predictive maintenance. By analyzing large volumes of sensor data from machinery and equipment, organizations can build predictive models that identify patterns and anomalies, enabling them to anticipate when equipment is likely to fail (Bhambri & Singh, 2008a-c; Bhambri & Nischal, 2008a-b). This proactive approach to maintenance reduces unplanned downtime, lowers maintenance costs, and extends the lifespan of critical assets.

Additionally, predictive modeling plays a crucial role in optimizing production processes and quality control. Manufacturers can develop models that predict variations in product quality and process inefficiencies, allowing them to make real-time adjustments to production parameters. This leads to reduced waste, improved product consistency, and increased production efficiency. Furthermore, predictive modeling aids in demand forecasting and supply chain optimization, helping organizations optimize inventory levels, logistics planning, and distribution, ultimately improving overall operational efficiency and customer satisfaction. In summary, predictive modeling is a powerful tool within industrial Big Data Analytics, enabling organizations to make data-driven decisions that enhance operational efficiency, reduce costs, and maintain a competitive edge in the marketplace (Bilal, M., Kumari, B., & Rani, S., 2021, May; Rani, S., Pareek, P. K., Kaur, J., Chauhan, M., & Bhambri, P., 2023, February).

7.4 INTEGRATION OF DIGITAL TWINS AND BIG DATA ANALYTICS

The integration of Digital Twins and Big Data Analytics marks a groundbreaking synergy at the forefront of modern industrial and technological innovation. Digital Twins, as virtual replicas of physical assets or processes, offer a dynamic and real-time view of the physical world, while Big Data Analytics harnesses vast datasets to derive actionable insights. The convergence of these two transformative technologies holds immense promise across industries, enabling organizations to not only monitor and simulate the physical realm but also to analyze and optimize it in unprecedented ways. This integration empowers data-driven decision-making, predictive maintenance, process optimization, and the creation of more resilient and efficient systems, heralding a new era of operational excellence and competitiveness.

7.4.1 LEVERAGING DIGITAL TWINS FOR DATA ANALYTICS

Leveraging Digital Twins for data analytics represents a paradigm shift in how organizations harness the power of data to gain insights, make informed decisions, and optimize processes. Digital Twins, which are virtual replicas of physical assets, systems, or processes, offer a dynamic and data-rich environment for conducting advanced analytics. By integrating real-time data from sensors and IoT devices with these virtual counterparts, organizations can create an immersive and holistic representation of their physical entities. This synergy allows for continuous monitoring, predictive modeling, and data-driven simulations, enabling stakeholders to uncover hidden patterns, optimize performance, and enhance decision-making across a wide range of industries and applications. The convergence of Digital Twins and data analytics has the potential to drive innovation, efficiency, and competitiveness in an increasingly data-centric world.

7.4.2 REAL-TIME MONITORING AND CONTROL

In the integration of Digital Twins and Big Data Analytics, real-time monitoring and control represent a pivotal dimension that empowers organizations to continuously assess and manage the performance of physical assets and processes in a dynamic manner. Real-time monitoring involves the constant collection of data from sensors, IoT devices, and other sources embedded in the physical system, providing an up-to-the-minute view of its behavior. This influx of real-time data is then channeled into Big Data Analytics platforms, where advanced analytical techniques are applied to extract immediate insights (Singh et al., 2004; Singh et al., 2005a-f). Through this integration, organizations gain the ability to detect anomalies, deviations, or performance issues in real time, enabling swift decision-making and timely interventions to optimize operations, enhance productivity, and prevent potential breakdowns or disruptions.

7.4.3 OPTIMIZATION THROUGH DATA INSIGHTS

It represents a pivotal aspect of the integration between Digital Twins and Big Data Analytics, where data-driven strategies are employed to enhance the efficiency and effectiveness of industrial processes. This synergistic approach harnesses the capabilities of Digital Twins, which provide real-time virtual replicas of physical assets, and the analytical power of Big Data, enabling organizations to gain deeper insights into their operations. By analyzing vast volumes of data generated by these virtual counterparts, businesses can pinpoint areas for improvement, make informed decisions, and fine-tune processes in real time. This optimization not only streamlines production, reduces downtime, and enhances resource allocation but also ensures that industrial systems operate at their highest potential, thus driving competitiveness and innovation in the ever-evolving landscape of Industry 4.0.

7.4.4 Decision Support

Decision Support emerges as a critical facet that empowers organizations to make informed and timely choices based on the wealth of data and insights at their disposal. This synergy enables decision-makers to navigate complex industrial scenarios with unprecedented precision and confidence. By harnessing the real-time data from Digital Twins, coupled with the analytical prowess of Big Data Analytics, decision support mechanisms facilitate predictive maintenance, process optimization, and proactive resource allocation. This integrated approach ushers in a new era where decisions are driven not by intuition alone but by a comprehensive understanding of physical assets, processes, and the dynamic factors influencing them, leading to enhanced operational efficiency and competitive advantage.

7.5 USE CASES

A multitude of compelling use cases come to the forefront, demonstrating the transformative potential of integration with Big Data Analytics with Digital Twin for Industrial Applications. These use cases span various industries, from manufacturing to energy and logistics. For instance, in manufacturing, predictive maintenance Digital Twins enable organizations to preemptively identify machinery breakdowns and optimize maintenance schedules, reducing downtime and maintenance costs. In the energy sector, Digital Twins of power grids facilitate real-time monitoring and demand forecasting, enhancing grid reliability and energy distribution efficiency. Additionally, supply chain management benefits from Digital Twins by optimizing logistics and inventory management, ensuring timely deliveries and cost savings. These use cases underscore the versatility of Big Data Analytics and Digital Twins, reshaping how industries operate, innovate, and excel in an increasingly data-driven landscape.

7.5.1 Predictive Maintenance in Manufacturing

By integrating Digital Twins and Big Data Analytics, manufacturers can proactively monitor and predict the health of their machinery and equipment. Real-time data from sensors and IoT devices embedded in physical assets are fed into Digital Twins, allowing predictive models to anticipate maintenance needs and identify potential failures before they occur. This not only minimizes unplanned downtime but also optimizes maintenance schedules, reducing costs associated with unnecessary repairs. Predictive maintenance in manufacturing, enabled by the synergy of Digital Twins and Big Data Analytics, ensures that machines run at peak efficiency, production remains uninterrupted, and maintenance resources are allocated judiciously, ultimately enhancing productivity and competitiveness in the industrial sector.

7.5.2 Real-Time Process Optimization in Energy

By integrating Digital Twins with Big Data Analytics, energy companies gain the ability to monitor and fine-tune their energy generation and distribution systems in real time. For instance, in power generation, Digital Twins replicate the behavior of turbines, generators, and transmission lines, while Big Data Analytics processes continuous data streams from these assets. This synergy allows operators to detect anomalies, predict potential failures, and adjust operational parameters on the fly to optimize energy production and grid stability. Additionally, data analytics can uncover energy consumption patterns, enabling load balancing and demand response strategies, ultimately enhancing energy efficiency, reducing costs, and contributing to a more resilient and sustainable energy infrastructure.

7.5.3 Supply Chain Management in Logistics

Logistics companies can create Digital Twins of their entire supply chain, incorporating data from suppliers, warehouses, transportation, and delivery systems. Big Data Analytics then processes this information to predict demand fluctuations, optimize inventory levels, improve route planning, and enhance delivery schedules. By monitoring every link in the supply chain through Digital Twins and applying analytics, organizations can respond promptly to disruptions, reduce costs, minimize delays, and enhance customer service, ultimately achieving a streamlined and agile logistics operation. This use case exemplifies how the synergy of Digital Twins and Big Data Analytics is revolutionizing supply chain management, enabling companies to navigate the complexities of global logistics with unprecedented efficiency and resilience (Bhambri & Sharma, 2005).

7.6 CONCLUSION

The shared synergistic approach empowers organizations to harness the power of real-time data from Digital Twins, coupled with advanced analytics, to enhance decision-making, optimize processes, and predict and prevent issues. The use cases presented across various industrial sectors exemplify the tangible benefits, from predictive maintenance in manufacturing to supply chain optimization in logistics. While challenges such as data security and scalability exist, the chapter emphasizes that the rewards in terms of operational efficiency, cost savings, and innovation are well worth the investment. As we stand on the cusp of Industry 4.0 and beyond, the integration of Big Data Analytics with Digital Twins represents a pivotal step toward achieving smarter, more agile, and sustainable industrial ecosystems.

REFERENCES

Abrol, N., Shaifali, Rattan, M., & Bhambri, P. (2005). Implementation and performance evaluation of JPEG 2000 for medical images. In International Conference on Innovative Applications of Information Technology for Developing World.

Arya, V., Rani, S., & Choudhary, N. (2022). Enhanced bio-inspired trust and reputation model for wireless sensor networks. In Proceedings of Second Doctoral Symposium on Computational Intelligence: DoSCI 2021 (pp. 569–579). Springer Singapore.

Bai, C., Dallasega, P., Orzes, G., & Sarkis, J. (2020). Industry 4.0 technologies assessment: A sustainability perspective. *International Journal of Production Economics, 229,* 107776.

Bali, V., Bali, S., Gaur, D., Rani, S., & Kumar, R. (2023). Commercial-off-the shelf vendor selection: A multi-criteria decision-making approach using intuitionistic fuzzy sets and TOPSIS. *Operational research in engineering sciences: Theory and applications.*

Bathla, S., Bhambri, P., & Jindal, C. (2007a, May). Wearable computers: Smart era in computing. In Paper presented at the National Conference on Advances in Computer Technology and Applications.

Bathla, S., Jindal, C., & Bhambri, P. (2007b, March). Impact of technology on societal living. In International Conference on Convergence and Competition (pp. 14).

Bhambri, P. (2010). An adaptive and resource efficient hand off in recovery state in geographic adhoc networks. In International Conference on Engineering Innovations-A Fillip to Economic Development.

Bhambri, P., & Gupta, S. (2007, September). Interactive voice recognition system. In National Conference on Advancements in Modeling and Simulation (p. 107).

Bhambri, P., & Hans, S. (2009). Direct non iterative solution based neural network for image compression. *PIMT Journal of Research, 2*(2), 64–67.

Bhambri, P., & Hans, S. (2010). Evaluation of integrated development environments for embedded system design. *Apeejay Journal of Management and Technology, 5*(2), 138–146.

Bhambri, P., & Nischal, P. (2008a, September). Emerging trends of intersectoral growth of India with special reference to service sector. *PIMT Journal of Research, 1*(2), 10–18.

Bhambri, P., & Nischal, P. (2008b, May). Emerging new economy in telecommunication sector of india. In International Conference on Business Challenges & Strategies in Emerging Global Scenario (p. 26).

Bhambri, P., & Sharma, N. (2005, September). Priorities for sustainable civilization. Paper presented at the National Conference on Technical Education in Globalized Environment - Knowledge, Technology & The Teacher (pp. 108).

Bhambri, P., & Singh, I. (2005b, March). Electrical actuation systems. In Paper presented at the National Conference on Application of Mathematics in Engg. & Tech. (pp. 58–60).

Bhambri, P., & Singh, M. (2005a). Artificial intelligence. In Seminar on E-Governance - Pathway to Progress (pp. 14).

Bhambri, P., & Singh, M. (2008a). Direct non iterative solution based neural network for image compression. *PCTE Journal of Computer Sciences, 5*(2), 1–4.

Bhambri, P., & Singh, M. (2008b). Biometrics: Face recognition using eigen faces. *Apeejay Journal of Management and Technology, 3*(2), 160–164.

Bhambri, P., & Singh, M. (2008c). Image transport protocol for JPEG image over loss prone congested networks. *PIMT Journal of Research, 1*(1), 55–61.

Bhambri, P., & Singh, M. (2009). *Data mining model for protein sequence alignment.* Punjab Technical University, Jalandhar.

Bhambri, P., & Thapar, V. (2009, May). Power distribution challenges in VLSI: An introduction. In Paper presented at the International Conference on Downtrend Challenges in IT, pp. 63.

Bhambri, P., & Thapar, V. (2010). Iris biometric - A review. In Paper presented at the National Conference on Cellular and Molecular Medicine.

Bhambri, P., Singh, I., & Gupta, S. (2005a, March). Robotics systems. Paper presented at the National Conference on Emerging Computing Technologies (p. 27).

Bhambri, P., Sood, G., & Verma, A. (2005b). Robotics design: Major considerations. In National Conference on Emerging Computing Technologies (p. 100).

Bhambri, P., Singh, I., & Singh, J. (2005c). Role of programming and mathematics in the design of robotics. In National Conference on Application of Mathematics in Engg. & Tech. (p. 101).

Bhambri, P., Singh, H., & Gupta, S. (2007a, May). Generation of fuzzy rules and membership function from training examples. In Paper presented at the National Conference on Advances in Computer Technology and Applications.

Bhambri, P., Nischal, P., & Gupta, S. (2007b, April). Bioinformatics and computational biology. In National Conference on Some Aspects of Recent Trends in Engineering and Technology (p. 29).

Bhambri, P., Singh, R., & Singh, J. (2007c). Wireless security. In National Conference on Emerging Trends in Communication & IT (pp. 290).

Bhambri, P., Hans, S., & Singh, M. (2008a, November). Bioinformatics—Friendship between bits & genes. In International Conference on Advanced Computing & Communication Technologies (pp. 62–65).

Bhambri, P., Hans, S., & Singh, M. (2008b, November). Fractal image compression techniques: A fast fractal image compression method. In International Conference on Advanced Computing and Communication Technologies (pp. 6576–6660).

Bhambri, P., Hans, S., & Singh, M. (2009). Inharmonic signal synthesis & analysis. *Technia - International Journal of Computing Science and Communication Technologies*, *1*(2), 199–201.

Bhambri, P., Singh, M., Suresh, H., & Singh, I. (2010). Data mining model for protein sequence alignment. In Proceedings of the International Conference on Data Mining (pp. 612–617).

Bhambri, P., Gupta, O. P., Hans, S., & Singh, R. (2011). Conceptual translation as a part of gene expression. In International Conference on Advanced Computing and Communication Technologies (Sponsored by IEEE Delhi Section, IEEE Computer Society Chapter, Delhi Section and IETE Delhi Centre) (pp. 506–508).

Bhambri, P., Aggarwal, M., Singh, H., Singh, A. P., & Rani, S. (2022). Uprising of EVs: Charging the future with demystified analytics and sustainable development. In Decision Analytics for Sustainable Development in Smart Society 5.0: Issues, Challenges and Opportunities (pp. 37–53). Singapore: Springer Nature Singapore.

Bilal, M., Kumari, B., & Rani, S. (2021, May). An artificial intelligence supported E-commerce model to improve the export of Indian handloom and handicraft products in the world. In Proceedings of the International Conference on Innovative Computing & Communication (ICICC).

Cañas, H., Mula, J., Díaz-Madroñero, M., & Campuzano-Bolarín, F. (2021). Implementing Industry 4.0 principles. *Computers & Industrial Engineering*, *158*, 107379.

Chen, B., Wan, J., Shu, L., Li, P., Mukherjee, M., & Yin, B. (2017). Smart factory of industry 4.0: Key technologies, application case, and challenges. *IEEE Access*, *6*, 6505–6519.

Chopra, S. & Bhambri, P. (2011). *A new method of edge detection in mammographic images*. Punjab Technical University.

Contreras, J. D., Garcia, J. I., & Pastrana, J. D. (2017). Developing of Industry 4.0 applications. *International Journal of Online Engineering*, *13*(10).

Dhanalakshmi, R., Vijayaraghavan, N., Sivaraman, A. K., & Rani, S. (2022). Epidemic awareness spreading in smart cities using the artificial neural network. In *AI-centric smart city ecosystems* (pp. 187–207): CRC Press.

Dhanalakshmi, R., Anand, J., Sivaraman, A. K., & Rani, S. (2022). IoT-based water quality monitoring system using cloud for agriculture use. *Cloud and Fog Computing Platforms for Internet of Things*, *28*(3), 1–14.

Garg, D., & Bhambri, P. (2011a). A novel approach for fusion of multimodality medical images. *CiiT International Journal of Digital Image Processing, 3*(10), 576–580.

Garg, D., & Bhambri, P. (2011b). *A novel approach for fusion of multi-modality medical images.* Punjab Technical University, Jalandhar.

Ghobakhloo, M. (2020). Industry 4.0, digitization, and opportunities for sustainability. *Journal of Cleaner Production, 252,* 119869.

Goel, R., & Gupta, P. (2020). Robotics and industry 4.0. *A roadmap to Industry 4.0: Smart production, sharp business and sustainable development,* 157–169.

Grewal, H.K., & Bhambri, P. (2006). Globe-IT: Globalization of learning through open based education and information technology. In International Conference on Brand India: Issues, Challenges and Opportunities (p. 24).

Gupta, O., Rani, S., & Pant, D. C. (2011). Impact of parallel computing on bioinformatics algorithms. In Proceedings 5th IEEE International Conference on Advanced Computing and Communication Technologies (pp. 206–209).

Gupta, O. P. (2017). Study and analysis of various bioinformatics applications using protein BLAST: An overview. *Advances in Computational Sciences and Technology, 10*(8), 2587–2601.

Gupta, O. P., & Rani, S. (2010). Bioinformatics applications and tools: An overview. *CiiT-International Journal of Biometrics and Bioinformatics, 3*(3), 107–110.

Gupta, O. P., & Rani, S. (2013). Accelerating molecular sequence analysis using distributed computing environment. *International Journal of Scientific & Engineering Research–IJSER, 4*(10), 262–265.

Gupta, S., & Bhambri, P. (2006). A competitive market is pushing site search technology to new plateaus. In International Conference on Brand India: Issues, Challenges and Opportunities (p. 34).

Gupta, S., Nischal, P., & Bhambri, P. (2007a). Multimodal biometric: Enhancing security level of biometric system. In National Conference on Emerging Trends in Communication & IT (pp. 78–81).

Gupta, S., Nischal, P., & Bhambri, P. (2007b, March). Mathematical modeling of EMG (ELECTROMYOGRAM). In Paper presented at the International Conference on Global Trends in IT (p. 14).

Gupta, S., Nischal, P., & Bhambri, P. (2007c, February). DNA computing: An emerging trend. In Paper presented at the National Conference on Emerging Trends in Communication & IT (p. 267).

Gupta, S., Kaur, R., & Bhambri, P. (2007d). Common channel signaling system #7: A global standard for telecommunication. In National Conference on Emerging Trends in Communication & IT (pp. 130–134).

Gupta, S., Nischal, P., & Bhambri, P. (2007e). Data Encryption Standard (DES) Algorithm with Diffie-Hellman key exchange. In National Conference on Emerging Trends in Communication & IT (pp. 135–143).

Habib, M. K., & Chimsom, C. (2019). *Industry 4.0: Sustainability and design principles.* In Paper presented at the 2019 20th International Conference on Research and Education in Mechatronics (REM).

Jain, V. K., & Bhambri, P. (2005). Fundamentals of Information Technology & Computer Programming.

Kamra, A., & Bhambri, P. (2007). Computer peripherals & interfaces.

Kataria, A., Agrawal, D., Rani, S., Karar, V., & Chauhan, M. (2022). Prediction of blood screening parameters for preliminary analysis using neural networks. In *Predictive modeling in biomedical data mining and analysis* (pp. 157–169). Academic Press.

Kataria, A., Puri, V., Pareek, P. K., & Rani, S. (2023, July). Human activity classification using G-XGB. In 2023 International Conference on Data Science and Network Security (ICDSNS) (pp. 1–5). IEEE.

Kaur, D., Singh, B., & Rani, S. (2023). Cyber security in the metaverse. In *Handbook of research on AI-based technologies and applications in the era of the metaverse* (pp. 418–435). IGI Global.

Kaur, G., Bhambri, P., & Sohal, A. K. (2006, January). Review analysis of economic load dispatch. In National Conference on Future Trends in Information Technology.

Kaur, G., Kaur, R., & Rani, S. (2015). Cloud computing—a new trend in IT era. *International Journal of Scientific and Technology Management, 1*(3), 1–6.

Kaur, S., Kumar, R., Kaur, R., Singh, S., Rani, S., & Kaur, A. (2022). Piezoelectric materials in sensors: Bibliometric and visualization analysis. *Materials Today: Proceedings.*

Kothandaraman, D., Manickam, M., Balasundaram, A., Pradeep, D., Arulmurugan, A., Sivaraman, A. K., & Balakrishna, R. (2022). Decentralized link failure prevention routing (DLFPR) algorithm for efficient internet of things. *Intelligent Automation and Soft Computing, 34*(1), 655–666.

Kumar, P., Banerjee, K., Singhal, N., Kumar, A., Rani, S., Kumar, R., & Lavinia, C. A. (2022a). Verifiable, secure mobile agent migration in healthcare systems using a polynomial-based threshold secret sharing scheme with a Blowfish algorithm. *Sensors, 22*(22), 8620.

Kumar, R., Rani, S., & Awadh, M. A. (2022b). Exploring the application sphere of the internet of things in industry 4.0: A review, bibliometric and content analysis. *Sensors, 22*(11), 4276.

Machała, S., Chamier-Gliszczyński, N., & Królikowski, T. (2022). Application of AR/VR Technology in Industry 4.0. *Procedia Computer Science, 207,* 2990–2998.

Puri, V., Kataria, A., Solanki, V. K., & Rani, S. (2022, December). AI-based botnet attack classification and detection in IoT devices. In 2022 IEEE International Conference on Machine Learning and Applied Network Technologies (ICMLANT) (pp. 1–5). IEEE.

Rani, S., & Gupta, O. P. (2016). Empirical analysis and performance evaluation of various GPU implementations of protein BLAST. *International Journal of Computer Applications, 151*(7), 22–27.

Rani, S., & Gupta, O. P. (2017). CLUS_GPU-BLASTP: Accelerated protein sequence alignment using GPU-enabled cluster. *The Journal of Supercomputing, 73,* 4580–4595.

Rani, S., & Kaur, S. (2012). Cluster analysis method for multiple sequence alignment. *International Journal of Computer Applications, 43*(14), 19–25.

Rani, S., Bhambri, P., & Chauhan, M. (2021, October). A machine learning model for kids' behavior analysis from facial emotions using principal component analysis. In 2021 5th Asian Conference on Artificial Intelligence Technology (ACAIT) (pp. 522–525). IEEE.

Rani, S., Bhambri, P., & Gupta, O. P. (2022). Green smart farming techniques and sustainable agriculture: Research roadmap towards organic farming for imperishable agricultural products. *Handbook of sustainable development through green engineering and technology,* 49–67.

Rani, S., Arya, V., & Kataria, A. (2022). Dynamic pricing-based e-commerce model for the produce of organic farming in India: A research roadmap with main advertence to vegetables. In Proceedings of Data Analytics and Management: ICDAM 2021, *Volume 2* (pp. 327–336). Springer Singapore.

Rani, S., Kataria, A., & Chauhan, M. (2022). Cyber security techniques, architectures, and design. In *Holistic approach to quantum cryptography in cyber security* (pp. 41–66). CRC Press.

Rani, S., Bhambri, P., Kataria, A., & Khang, A. (2022). Smart City ecosystem: Concept, sustainability, design principles, and technologies. In *AI-centric smart city ecosystems* (pp. 1–20). CRC Press.

Rani, S., Kataria, A., & Chauhan, M. (2022a). Cyber security techniques, architectures, and design. In *Holistic approach to quantum cryptography in cyber security* (pp. 41–66): CRC Press.

Rani, S., Kataria, A., & Chauhan, M. (2022b). Fog computing in Industry 4.0: Applications and challenges—a research roadmap. *Energy conservation solutions for fog-edge computing paradigms*, 173–190.

Rani, S., Kataria, A., Chauhan, M., Rattan, P., Kumar, R., & Sivaraman, A. K. (2022c). Security and privacy challenges in the deployment of cyber-physical systems in smart city applications: State-of-art work. *Materials Today: Proceedings, 62*, 4671–4676.

Rani, S., Mishra, A. K., Kataria, A., Mallik, S., & Qin, H. (2023). Machine learning-based optimal crop selection system in smart agriculture. *Scientific Reports, 13*(1), 15997.

Rani, S., Pareek, P. K., Kaur, J., Chauhan, M., & Bhambri, P. (2023, February). Quantum machine learning in healthcare: Developments and challenges. In 2023 IEEE International Conference on Integrated Circuits and Communication Systems (ICICACS) (pp. 1–7). IEEE.

Rani, S., Bhambri, P., & Kataria, A. (2023). Integration of IoT, Big Data, and Cloud Computing technologies. *Big Data, Cloud Computing and IoT: Tools and applications.*

Rani, S., Kataria, A., Kumar, S., & Tiwari, P. (2023). Federated learning for secure IoMT-applications in smart healthcare systems: A comprehensive review. *Knowledge-based systems*, 110658.

Rani, S., Kataria, A., Kumar, S., & Tiwari, P. (2023). Federated learning for secure IoMT-applications in smart healthcare systems: A comprehensive review. *Knowledge-based systems*, 110658.

Rani, S., Mishra, A. K., Kataria, A., Mallik, S., & Qin, H. (2023). Machine learning-based optimal crop selection system in smart agriculture. *Scientific Reports, 13*(1), 15997.

Rattan, M., Bhambri, P., & Shaifali. (2005a, February). Information retrieval using soft computing techniques. In Paper presented at the National Conference on Bio-informatics Computing (p. 7).

Rattan, M., Bhambri, P., & Shaifali. (2005b, February). Institution for a sustainable civilization: Negotiating change in a technological culture. In Paper presented at the National Conference on Technical Education in Globalized Environment- Knowledge, Technology & The Teacher (p. 45).

Saucedo-Martínez, J. A., Pérez-Lara, M., Marmolejo-Saucedo, J. A., Salais-Fierro, T. E., & Vasant, P. (2018). Industry 4.0 framework for management and operations: A review. *Journal of Ambient Intelligence and Humanized Computing, 9*, 789–801.

Singh, I., Salaria, D., & Bhambri, P. (2010). Comparative analysis of JAVA and AspectJ on the basis of various metrics. In International Conference on Advanced Computing and Communication Technologies (IEEE Sponsored) (pp. 714–720).

Singh, M., Singh, P., Kaur, K., & Bhambri, P. (2005a, March). Database security. In Paper presented at the National Conference on Future Trends in Information Technology (pp. 57–62).

Singh, M., Bhambri, P., & Kaur, K. (2005b, March). Network security. In Paper presented at the National Conference on Future Trends in Information Technology (pp. 51–56).

Singh, M., Singh, P., Bhambri, P., & Sachdeva, R. (2005f). A Comparative study: Security algorithms. In *Seminar on Network Security and Its Implementations* (pp. 14).

Singh, P., & Bhambri, P. (2007). Alternate organizational models for ports. *Apeejay Journal of Management and Technology, 2*(2), 9–17.

Singh, P., Singh, M., & Bhambri, P. (2004, November). Interoperability: A problem of component reusability. In Paper presented at the International Conference on Emerging Technologies in IT Industry (p. 60).

Singh, P., Singh, M., & Bhambri, P. (2005c, March). Internet security. In Paper presented at the Seminar on Network Security and Its Implementations (p. 22).

Singh, P., Singh, M., & Bhambri, P. (2005d, March). Security in virtual private networks. In *Seminar on Network Security and Its Implementations* (pp. 11).

Singh, P., Singh, M., & Bhambri, P. (2005e, January). Embedded systems. In Paper presented at the Seminar on Embedded Systems (pp. 10–15).

Singh, P., Bhambri, P., & Sohal, A. K. (2006, January). Security in local networks. In Paper presented at the National Conference on Future Trends in Information Technology.

Singh, P., Gupta, O. P., & Saini, S. (2017). A brief research study of wireless sensor network. *Advances in Computational Sciences and Technology*, *10*(5), 733–739.

Sudevan, S., Barwani, B., Al Maani, E., Rani, S., & Sivaraman, A. K. (2021). Impact of blended learning during Covid-19 in Sultanate of Oman. *Annals of the Romanian Society for Cell Biology*, 14978–14987.

Tanwar, R., Chhabra, Y., Rattan, P., & Rani, S. (2022, September). Blockchain in IoT networks for precision agriculture. In International Conference on Innovative Computing and Communications: Proceedings of ICICC 2022, *Volume 2* (pp. 137–147). Singapore: Springer Nature Singapore.

Thapar, V., & Bhambri, P. (2009, May). Context free language induction by evolution of deterministic pushdown automata using genetic programming. In Paper presented at the International Conference on Downtrend Challenges in IT (p. 33).

Yadav, V. S., Singh, A., Raut, R. D., Mangla, S. K., Luthra, S., & Kumar, A. (2022). Exploring the application of Industry 4.0 technologies in the agricultural food supply chain: A systematic literature review. *Computers & Industrial Engineering*, *169*, 108304.

8 AI-Driven Digital Twin

Conceptual Framework and Applications

Maninder Pal Singh and Pankaj Bhambri

8.1 INTRODUCTION

Present-day technological advancements have transformed nearly every aspect of daily existence. It is significantly facilitating the development of improved facilities and enhancing the quality of life for users. Numerous spheres, including education, banking and finance, healthcare facilities, modern industry, and the agricultural sector, have benefited significantly from technological advancements. Artificial intelligence (AI), machine learning, deep learning, Internet of Things, Cloud Computing, Digital Twin, and the most recent connectivity services are the most prominent of the era's cutting-edge technologies that are assisting users intelligently and predicting their behavior, as well as providing the connectivity and convenience of data to satisfy the majority of their needs. The digital counterpart has the potential to be an indispensable concept for efficient intelligent construction. When AI and digital twins are combined, a new ray of hope emerges. A digital twin powered by AI is an electronic depiction of a tangible entity, system, or operation that integrates cutting-edge AI functionalities with real-time data in order to simulate, forecast, and optimize its operations and performance. Digital Twin is garnering the interest of both experts and intellectuals. In the present day, numerous tasks rely on technology to provide precise virtual representations of objects and models of surgical procedures (Mohsen, A., et al., 2023). A Gartner survey conducted in 2019 unveiled that digital twins were increasingly being adopted by enterprises. According to a forecast by Gartner (2019), 75% of Internet of Things (IoT) organizations are already utilizing Digital Twin technology or have intentions to do so by 2020. Additionally, by 2027, more than 40% of large companies globally will be utilizing Digital Twin in revenue-generating initiatives, according to Gartner (Groombridge, D., et al., 2021).

8.2 ARTIFICIAL INTELLIGENCE

AI is commonly understood as a field of knowledge that empowers technological systems to simulate a wide range of composite human abilities (Bhambri, 2016). However, that is insufficient to continue. Indeed, it merely serves to emphasize the

DOI: 10.1201/9781003395416-8

phrase 'artificial intelligence' in modified terminology. The precise nature of AI continues to be ambiguous in the absence of specification regarding these "combined human capabilities" (Rani, S., Kumar, S., Kataria, A., & Min, H., 2023). The aforementioned definition of AI remains unchanged: it refers to the execution of complex, multifarious tasks by computers in uncertain environments (Sheikh et al., 2023).

8.2.1 QUALITIES OF AN AI

*   **Ability of predicting and familiarizing -** AI implements algorithms that determine samples from enormous amounts of facts and figures.
*   **Makes decisions on its own -** AI is gifted to enhance human intelligence, provide insights and mend production.
*   **Uninterrupted learning -** AI practices algorithms to create analytical models. From those procedures, AI technology will discover how to achieve tasks through incalculable rounds of trial and error.
*   **AI is forward-looking -** AI is a tool that permits us to reassess how we examine data and incorporate information, and then customize these understandings to make good decisions (Ziyad, S., 2019).

It is reasonable that AI research continues to persist. The aforementioned sources propose natural language processing, science, planning, and education (Kaur et al., 2012; Rani, S., Bhambri, P., Kataria, A., Khang, A., & Sivaraman, A. K. (Eds.), 2023). Long-term collective objectives of common intelligence objects are the capacity to modify and alter objects and to think (Bansal et al., 2012). Statistical methods, intelligent computations, and mathematical exploration and optimization are employed to distinguish between traditional thematic AI coding and AI research. In addition to employing statistical methods and neural systems, our facility also encompasses mathematics, psychology, linguistics, philosophy, and numerous other disciplines (Chatterjee, R., 2020). Table 8.1 outlines the various classifications of AI.

8.2.2 FUTURE OF AI

The field of AI has had a transformative impact on society from its inception, as documented by Kaur and Bhambri (2015). The utilization of weak AI is predominantly controlled by individuals possessing extensive understanding of the field. This allows for the observation of AI's notable accomplishments as it diligently strives to enhance the quality of human lifestyles (Kataria, A., Puri, V., Pareek, P. K., & Rani, S., 2023, July). Researchers are currently collaborating with advanced AI systems that possess the capability to effectively address a variety of challenges across diverse contexts (Rani, Pareek, Kaur, Chauhan, & Bhambri, 2023, February). Researchers are persistently engaged in efforts to imbue machines with human-like behavior. However, the results obtained thus far have been varied. While the current state of the system has a certain degree of similarity to human behavior, it has not yet achieved perfect parity (Chauhan & Rani, 2021). According

TABLE 8.1
Types of AI (Ziyad, S., 2019)

Types of AI			
Reactive AI	**Limited Memory**	**Theory of Mind**	**Self-Aware**
1. Good for simple classification and pattern recognition task. 2. Great for scenarios where all parameters are known and can beat humans because it can make calculations much faster. 3. Incapable of dealing with scenarios including imperfect information and requires historical understanding.	1. Can handle a complex classification task. 2. Able to use historical data to make predictions. 3. Capable of complex tasks such as self-driving cars but still vulnerable to outliers or adversarial problems. 4. This is the current stage of AI and somehow we have to reach the mark.	1. Able to understand human motives and reasoning. Can deliver personal experience to everyone based on their motives and intent. 2. Consider the next milestone of AI's evolution.	1. Human-level intelligence that can bypass our intelligence too.

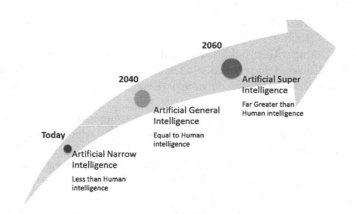

FIGURE 8.1   Future of AI (Ziyad, S., 2019).

to Ziyad (2019), the subsequent stage in AI development is the achievement of super AI, a concept that remains an aspiration for specialists in the field. Figure 8.1 illustrates the projected advancements in AI, showcasing the current accomplishments and the potential for achieving strong AI and Super AI in the future.

8.2.3 APPLICATION OF AI

AI has a wide range of applications across various industries and domains. Here are some key areas where AI is being applied (Kurfess et al., 2003)

- Healthcare: AI helps in Diagnosis and Treatment aspects. AI can assist in diagnosing diseases and recommending treatment plans. It also supports Drug Discovery; AI is used to accelerate drug discovery and development processes (Rani, S., Mishra, A. K., Kataria, A., Mallik, S., & Qin, H., 2023). It helps in plotting Medical Imaging, AI helps in interpreting medical images like X-rays, MRIs, and CT scans. AI is working well with Health Monitoring, AI-powered wearables and devices can monitor health conditions in real time (Rani, S., Bhambri, P., & Kataria, A., 2023).
- Finance: AI provides Algorithmic Trading; AI algorithms analyze financial data and execute trades autonomously (Singh et al., 2013). It helps in Fraud Detection, which means AI detects fraudulent transactions and activities. It helps in monitoring Credit Scores; AI assesses creditworthiness by analyzing credit data.
- Autonomous Vehicles: AI technologies like machine learning and computer vision enable self-driving cars and drones to work in very hard situations.
- Natural Language Processing (NLP): AI helps in enabling powerful chatbots for natural language, virtual assistants, and sentiment analysis (Paika & Bhambri, 2013). It helps in language translation, content generation, and text summarization (Dhanalakshmi, R., Vijayaraghavan, N., Sivaraman, A. K., & Rani, S., 2022).
- E-commerce: AI is used for recommendation systems to suggest products to users. It also provides Customer support chatbots by giving instant assistance (Kaur et al., 2014).
- Manufacturing: This field uses AI-driven robots and automation to enhance efficiency in production lines. It supports Predictive maintenance which reduces equipment downtime (Kaur, D., Singh, B., & Rani, S., 2023).
- Energy: AI helps in optimizing energy consumption in buildings and industries. It also provides predictive maintenance which reduces downtime in power plants.
- Education: AI assists in personalized learning by adapting educational content to individual students. It caters to grading system and assessment which can be automated using AI.
- Robotics: AI powers robots in various applications, from manufacturing to healthcare. By building Humanoid robots that can interact with humans in social contexts AI helps.
- Environmental Monitoring: AI processes data from satellites and sensors to monitor climate change, deforestation, and pollution (Bathla et al., 2007).
- Cybersecurity: AI detects and responds to cybersecurity threats in real time. It can analyze patterns to identify abnormal network behavior.
- Language Translation: AI-powered translation services bridge language barriers in communication.
- Government: AI aids in public policy analysis, fraud detection, and public service optimization (Garg & Bhambri, 2011).

The above applications of AI are continuing to expand into new areas as the technology evolves (Kurfess et al., 2003).

8.3 DIGITAL TWIN

The concept of a "digital twin" was first introduced in the context of creating a computer replica, or "twin," of Alan Alda's voice in the production titled "Alan Alda meets Alan Alda 2.0." According to Hodgins (1998), while a significant volume of literature has described the term, there seems to be little convention on the construction of a "digital twin." Referring to an object or creature as a "twin" implies an association with another entity; however, the extent of similarity might differ considerably, as observed in the cases of identical cities and humanoid twins (Boyes, H., et al., 2022). According to Kaur et al. (2022), DT is an innovative technology that has revolutionized the industry by replicating nearly all elements of a product, process, or service. According to Fu et al. (2022), there exists the potential to recreate all physical phenomena within the digital domain, enabling engineers to receive feedback from the virtual sphere. The scholar's suggested definition, as provided by Catapult (2021), is as follows: "A live digital connection between the current state of a physical asset or process and a virtual representation that produces a functional output." Based on our analysis, it may be inferred that this particular definition is the closest approximation to a universally accepted understanding. Digital twins are computer-generated copies of products, processes, or facilities that encompass the aforementioned capabilities (Schleich, B., et al., 2017). Grieves and Vickers (2017) provide a definition of the Digital Twin (DT) as a comprehensive representation of a physical synthetic product, encompassing both micro-atomic and macro-geometrical aspects (Tanwar, Chhabra, Rattan, & Rani, 2022, September). The Digital Twin has the potential to provide all relevant evidence that may be derived from the analysis of a physical manufactured product when it is in its ideal state. The application structure proposed by Zheng et al. (2019) consists of three distinct parts, including the physical space, information processing layer, and virtual space. It is demonstrated in Figure 8.2. This analysis offers a certain level of functional breakdown. However, it still falls short in terms of the necessary level of detail needed to effectively assess the composition and capabilities of digital twins (Bhambri, P., Rani, S., Gupta, G., & Khang, A. (Eds.), 2022).

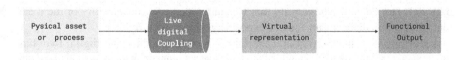

FIGURE 8.2   The application structure proposed by Zheng et al. (2019).

8.3.1 Approaches to Designing a Digital Twin

The current body of literature pertaining to digital twin design provides limited perspectives on the essential methodology required for their development. The focus is often placed on a very tiny physical entity, such as a production cell, rather than encompassing an entire plant or site. The study conducted by Jiang et al. (2021) examined the manifestation and implementation of the relationship between twins. Sharma and Bhambri (2013) advocated for the utilization of five fundamental components (namely, man, machine, material, technique, and environment) and two interconnections (production and logistics) to facilitate the process of analysis.

The approach employed in this study was based on the development of a hierarchical framework for representing distinct manufacturing processes through the utilization of finite state procedures (Kumar, R., Rani, S., & Khangura, S. S. (Eds.), 2023). Nevertheless, the authors assert that the adoption of this methodology presents difficulties in accurately delineating intricate systems. However, these are precisely the types of systems that could benefit from the implementation of a digital twin (Sudevan et al., 2021).

According to Ala-Laurinaho et al. (2020), it has been observed that there is a lack of standardized design for constructing digital twins. The diverse implementations of digital twins give rise to a complex challenge in achieving interoperability. The authors propose the utilization of a prefabricated methodology that operates with autonomous software units or systems, specifically well-structured modules. This technique facilitates adaptability in the creation and development of digital twins (Rani, S., Kataria, A., Kumar, S., & Tiwari, P., 2023). The implementation of this approach can enhance the process of substituting and combining specific functional elements to achieve scalability or enhance performance (Bilal, M., Kumari, B., & Rani, S., 2021, May).

A prevalent approach in software development for creating integrated designs involves the utilization of design outlines (Bali, V., Bali, S., Gaur, D., Rani, S., & Kumar, R., 2023). The scholarly discourse has examined the concept of designing digital twins through the utilization of a design outline catalogue, as discussed by Tekinerdogan and Verdouw (2020). However, Kumar et al. (2022) have identified two inconsistencies in their approach, despite the practical merits of employing design patterns. To begin with, it is important to note that the level of generalization in the given statement is quite high. The emphasis is mostly placed on the utilization of digital twins, rather than delving into the intricacies of their internal structure and organization. Additionally, the abstract paradigm of "control-based digital twins" proposes a direct integration of the digital twin with the actuators in the physical unit. The presence of a digital twin raises significant concerns regarding security and safety, as there is a possibility that it could supersede the authority of the local controller embedded within the corresponding physical entity.

According to Adamenko et al. (2020), it is recommended that a digital twin has adaptability, allowing it to be modified in order to accurately represent changes in the physical unit, as well as its surrounding environmental and functional conditions. The proposed approach is considered practicable because of the comparatively longer lifespan exhibited by cyber-physical structures in comparison to various IT systems. In order to facilitate the adaptability of digital twin systems, the implementation of a segmental architecture within the framework of system engineering drills is anticipated. This architectural approach enables the incorporation of gradual modifications, hence facilitating the verification and authentication of newly introduced or updated modules. The study conducted by Adamenko et al. (2020) does not discuss the concept of modularity. Instead, their focus is mostly on comparing the effectiveness of data-based strategies to system-based strategies.

According to Boschert and Rosen (2016), it is advisable for the framework to clearly establish its intended objectives and generate a collection of tasks, referred to as a method, that effectively accomplishes these objectives. By choosing this approach, the outline will prioritize the essential functioning mechanisms. The question of whether a digital twin is data-based or systems-based can be better understood by examining the fundamental activities involved, rather than relying solely on expert opinions.

8.3.2 How Is AI Driving Digital Twin?

In order to provide more clarification about the role of AI in the context of digital twins, it is important to underscore that a digital twin constitutes an integral element within a broader Digital Twin System (DTS) framework, as outlined by Emmert-Streib and Harja (2022) in Figure 8.3. In the depicted diagram, the concept of a virtual unit is employed as a parallel to a physical entity that is actualized by the utilization of a digital twin. Therefore, both virtual entities and digital twins are utilized interchangeably. The discussion of AI applications for a DTS is of utmost

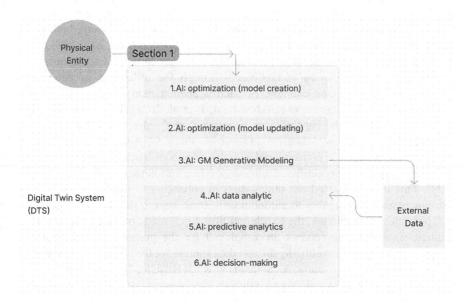

FIGURE 8.3 Digital twin system with an interface to a physical unit and peripheral data. (Emmert-Streib & Harja, 2022)

importance, as its structural design offers a direct platform for showcasing the various contributions that AI can give.

The operational architecture of the system enables the prioritization of different contributions that AI can provide in order to enhance the findings of a Digital Twin System. These contributions are emphasized from 1.AI to 6.AI.

The Digital Twin System encompasses a range of AI approaches, which can be categorized into six distinct components based on their fundamental architecture. The technique being referred to is commonly known as AI-DTS, which stands for Artificial Intelligence for Digital Twin Systems. 1. AI: Optimization via the construction of models. 2. AI: Optimization through the updating of models. 3. AI: Generative modeling. 4. AI: Data analytics. 5. AI: Predictive analytics. 6. AI: Decision making. In the subsequent section, a concise analysis is presented for each AI-DTS. The visualization depicted in Figure 8.3 illustrates that physical entities can be derived from a diverse range of applications, including but not limited to climate research, urban planning, engineering, manufacturing, health, and sustainability. According to Emmert-Streib (2023), a digital twin is created based on this process, wherein a dynamic model is constructed to accurately represent the key characteristics of the actual entity through computer simulation. Typically, this encompasses extraneous information from which the components of the digital twin are evaluated. The optimization method referred to as 1.AI: optimization (model development) is proposed in this study. In contrast to the initial approach, a distinct alternative optimization step incorporating AI is present. The second stage of optimization is validating the alignment between the digital twin and its physical counterparts throughout its operational cycle. The implementation of optimization techniques, specifically model updating, guarantees the enhancement of the informing apparatus of the DT referred to as 2.AI. In order to mitigate potential confusion between the processes of model design and model updating, braces are employed to offer additional information. This also highlights the issue elaborated upon thereafter, which is the lack of uniqueness among certain AI techniques.

The third AI association is facilitated through the utilization of generative modeling techniques. One example of such a phenomenon is the utilization of generative adversarial networks (GANs) (Gui, J. et al. 2021). In a comprehensive context, a GAN has the capability to generate factual information by extracting relevant features from large datasets. In some instances, a GAN can be employed to substitute or augment a conventional simulation model, such as those based on differential equations, agent-based models, or Boolean networks (Emmert-Streib, 2023). This implies that AI not only assists in enhancing a simulation model, but also possesses the capability to autonomously structure the simulation model.

Upon initial examination, the fourth and fifth applications of AI exhibit apparent similarities, as both approaches are employed for the purpose of data analysis. However, both parties are utilizing distinct data sources for the purpose of conducting their analysis (Puri, V., Kataria, A., Solanki, V. K., & Rani, S., 2022, December). The initial approach involves utilizing two distinct data sources, namely peripheral data and the digital twin. Consequently, it is possible to distinguish between two types of data exploration: data analytics and predictive analytics (referred to as 4. AI: data analytics and 5. AI: predictive analytics in Figure 8.3). The influence of data origin on the compilation of a research study is readily apparent (Emmert-Streib, 2023). The final AI application, referred to as 6.AI: decision making, serves the purpose of aggregating all individual outcomes achieved thus far and facilitating the process of decision-making. This phase encompasses the integration of all components, resulting in a comprehensive summary that may be observed as the ultimate result of a Digital Twin System, whether it is qualitative or quantitative in nature. Visual representations in the form of plots or charts are utilized to visually consolidate quantitative data. According to Emmert-Streib (2023), based on the presentation of these visual elements, it is possible for these facts to be interactive, enabling the investigation of outcomes. Considering the fact that the results of a DTS might have multiple dimensions, such an interactive examination holds significant value, especially for individuals who are not experts in AI, such as executives, clinicians, or supervisors (Kataria et al., 2022).

8.3.3 ADVANTAGES

AI-driven digital twins have a wide range of applications across various industries. These applications leverage the capabilities of AI, real-time data integration, simulation, and predictive analytics to enhance efficiency, improve decision-making, and optimize processes. Here are some notable applications of AI-driven digital twins:

- Manufacturing and Industry 4.0:
  - Production Optimization: Digital twins can simulate different production scenarios, helping optimize manufacturing processes, minimize downtime, and reduce waste.
  - Predictive Maintenance: AI-driven digital twins predict equipment failures, enabling proactive maintenance to avoid costly downtime.
  - Quality Control: Digital twins can analyze real-time data to detect defects and anomalies in manufacturing processes.
  - Supply Chain Optimization: Simulating supply chain operations helps in optimizing inventory management, logistics, and distribution.
- Smart Cities:
  - Urban Planning: Digital twins of cities help urban planners simulate the impact of infrastructure changes, traffic management, and zoning regulations.
  - Energy Management: Optimize energy consumption by simulating and predicting energy usage patterns in buildings, transportation systems, and utilities.
  - Environmental Monitoring: Digital twins monitor air quality, waste management, and other environmental factors for better sustainability planning.
- Healthcare:
  - Patient Care: Digital twins of patients can help personalize treatment plans based on real-time health data and predictive analytics.
  - Medical Training: Simulate medical procedures and scenarios for training healthcare professionals in a risk-free environment.

- Drug Development: Simulate the effects of drugs on virtual patient models to accelerate drug discovery and reduce development costs.
- Aerospace and Defense:
  - Design and Testing: Digital twins simulate aircraft performance, structural integrity, and operational scenarios for design and testing purposes.
  - Maintenance and Repair: Predictive maintenance in aviation improves aircraft reliability and minimizes unscheduled downtime.
  - Mission Planning: Military applications use digital twins to simulate and plan complex missions and operations.
- Energy and Utilities:
  - Power Plant Optimization: Simulate power plant operations to optimize efficiency, predict equipment failures, and manage energy distribution.
  - Renewable Energy Integration: Digital twins help manage and optimize the integration of renewable energy sources into the power grid.
  - Water Management: Simulate water distribution systems to optimize water usage, detect leaks, and improve infrastructure planning.
- Automotive Industry:
  - Vehicle Design: Digital twins simulate vehicle designs and performance characteristics, aiding in the development of safer and more efficient vehicles.
  - Autonomous Driving: Simulate and test autonomous vehicle behavior in various scenarios to ensure safety and reliability.
  - Manufacturing Optimization: Improve manufacturing processes and quality control in the automotive production line.
- Oil and Gas:
  - Asset Management: Digital twins of oil rigs and pipelines monitor equipment health and predict maintenance needs in remote locations.
  - Exploration and Drilling: Simulate subsurface conditions to optimize exploration and drilling processes.
  - Safety Training: Train personnel in hazardous environments by simulating emergency scenarios.
- Retail and Consumer Goods:
  - Inventory Management: Optimize inventory levels and supply chains by simulating demand patterns and trends.
  - Store Layout Optimization: Simulate store layouts to improve customer flow, product placement, and sales.

8.3.4 LIMITATIONS

While AI-driven digital twins offer numerous advantages, they also come with certain limitations and challenges that need to be considered:

- Data Dependency:
  - Quality and Accuracy: The accuracy and reliability of AI-driven digital twins heavily depend on the quality of the data they receive.

Inaccurate or incomplete data can lead to incorrect predictions and simulations.
- Data Volume: Handling and processing large volumes of real-time data can be challenging, requiring robust infrastructure and storage solutions.
- Complexity and Scalability:
  - Model Complexity: Creating a highly detailed digital twin model can be complex and resource-intensive, particularly for large and intricate physical systems.
  - Scalability: Scaling digital twin systems to represent entire cities or extensive industrial complexes can be technically challenging and expensive.
- Interoperability:
  - Integration with Legacy Systems: Integrating digital twins with existing legacy systems and infrastructure can be challenging, especially in industries with older technology stacks.
- Computational Resources:
  - High Computational Demands: Simulating complex systems in real time can require significant computational power, which may not always be readily available.
- Security and Privacy:
  - Data Security: Storing and transmitting sensitive data in a digital twin ecosystem can raise security concerns. Safeguarding against data breaches and cyberattacks is essential.
  - Privacy: Balancing the need for data collection with individuals' privacy rights can be a challenge, especially in smart city applications or healthcare.
- Cost:
  - Development and Maintenance Costs: Creating and maintaining a sophisticated AI-driven digital twin can be expensive, requiring investments in technology, personnel, and ongoing maintenance.
- Expertise Gap:
  - Skilled Workforce: Developing and managing AI-driven digital twins requires a skilled workforce with expertise in AI, data science, and domain-specific knowledge. Finding and retaining such talent can be challenging.
- Ethical Concerns:
  - Bias and Fairness: AI models used within digital twins can inherit biases from the data they are trained on, potentially leading to unfair or discriminatory outcomes.
  - Accountability: Determining responsibility and accountability in case of errors or adverse outcomes in AI-driven digital twin applications can be legally and ethically complex.
- Data Ownership:
  - Ownership and Access: Clarifying data ownership and access rights in multi-stakeholder environments can be a source of disputes.

- Limited Understanding of Complex Systems:
  - Behavioral Gaps: AI-driven digital twins may not fully capture the complexity and nuances of certain physical systems, leading to behavior gaps or unforeseen consequences.
- Maintenance and Updates:
  - Continuous Learning: Keeping the digital twin up-to-date with new data and knowledge requires ongoing maintenance efforts.
- Acceptance and Resistance:
  - Organizational Resistance: Some organizations or individuals may resist the adoption of AI-driven digital twins due to concerns about job displacement or distrust in AI.

8.4   RESEARCH DIRECTIONS

Some obstacles are encountered in the integration of various technologies, which may be subject to further investigation and support from scholars, engineers, and scientists in the future.

The expansion of Digital Twin is primarily driven by several causes, including the reduction in production time, cost, and product development time. Additionally, the visibility of operational processes facilitated by Digital Twin enhances transparency, while the centralization of data helps to mitigate redundancy in information systems. The integration of AI and DT facilitates the generation of predictive insights for Industry 4.0. More efficient AI algorithms have the capability to process large volumes of data in order to provide input to a DTS. AI plays a crucial role in the mapping of data collected from various devices by utilizing contemporary computing paradigms. This integration proves beneficial in achieving the intended outcomes for the Digital Twin system.

8.5   CONCLUSIONS

In contemporary society, a multitude of new technologies are playing a crucial role in various application fields that exhibit diversity. However, the optimal functionality of these technologies is achieved when they are properly mapped. The integration of technologies is facilitating the effective implementation of diverse applications. The focus of this study is on two primary technologies, namely AI and Digital Twin. The significant engagement in the integration of these technologies can be demonstrated by examining several domains of application. In addition to discussing the advantages, the author also emphasized the limitations and obstacles encountered in achieving precise and effective integration of the two components.

REFERENCES

Adamenko, D., Kunnen, S., Pluhnau, R., Loibl, A., & Nagarajah, A. (2020). Review and comparison of the methods of designing the digital twin. *Procedia CIRP*, 91, 27–32. 10.1016/j.procir.2020.02.146.

Ala-Laurinaho, R., Autiosalo, J., Nikander, A., Mattila, J., & Tammi, K. (2020). Data link for the creation of digital twins. *IEEE Access*, 8, 228675–228684.

Bansal, P., Bhambri, P., & Gupta, O. P. (2012). GOR method to predict protein secondary structure using different input formats. Paper presented at the International Conference on Advanced Computing and Communication Technologies (Sponsored by IEEE Computer Society Chapter, Delhi Section and IETE Delhi), 80–83.

Bilal, M., Kumari, B., & Rani, S. (2021, May). An artificial intelligence supported E-commerce model to improve the export of Indian handloom and handicraft products in the World. In Proceedings of the International Conference on Innovative Computing & Communication (ICICC).

Bathla, S., Jindal, C., & Bhambri, P. (2007, March). Impact of technology on societal living. In International Conference on Convergence and Competition (pp. 14).

Bali, V., Bali, S., Gaur, D., Rani, S., & Kumar, R. (2023). Commercial-off-the shelf vendor selection: A multi-criteria decision-making approach using intuitionistic fuzzy sets and TOPSIS. *Operational research in engineering sciences: Theory and applications*.

Bhambri, P. (2016). DNA to protein conversion. *PCTE Journal of Computer Sciences*, 14(2), 58–61.

Boschert, S., & Rosen, R. (2016). Digital Twin—the simulation aspect. In: Hehenberger, P., Bradley, D. (Eds.), *Mechatronic Futures*. Springer, Cham. 10.1007/ 978-3-319-32156-1_5.

Boyes, H., & Watson, T. (2022) Digital twins: An analysis framework and open issues. *Computers in Industry*, 143, 103763.

Bhambri, P., Rani, S., Gupta, G., & Khang, A. (Eds.). (2022). *Cloud and fog computing platforms for internet of things*. CRC Press.

Catapult, H. V. (2021). Untangling the requirements of a digital twin. *Univ. Sheff. Adv. Manuf. Res. Cent. (AMRC)*, 7.

Chatterjee, R. (2020). Fundamental concepts of artificial intelligence and its applications. *Journal of Mathematical Problems, Equations and Statistics*, 1(2), 13–24.

Chauhan, M., & Rani, S. (2021). Covid-19: A revolution in the field of education in India. *Learning how to learn using multimedia*, 23–42.

Dhanalakshmi, R., Vijayaraghavan, N., Sivaraman, A. K., & Rani, S. (2022). Epidemic awareness spreading in smart cities using the artificial neural network. In *AI-centric smart city ecosystems* (pp. 187–207). CRC Press.

Emmert-Streib, F. (2023). What is the role of AI for Digital Twins? *AI*, 4(3), 721–728.

Emmert-Streib, F., & Yli-Harja, O. (2022). What is a Digital Twin? Experimental design for a data-centric machine learning perspective in health. *International Journal of Molecular Sciences*, 23, 13149.

Fu, Y., Zhu, G., Zhu, M., & Xuan, F. (2022). Digital twin for integration of design-manufacturing-maintenance: An overview. *Chinese Journal of Mechanical Engineering*, 35(1), 80.

Garg, D., & Bhambri, P. (2011). A novel approach for fusion of multimodality medical images. *CiiT International Journal of Digital Image Processing*, 3(10), 576–580.

Gartner. (2019). *Gartner survey reveals digital twins are entering mainstream use*.

Grieves, M., & Vickers, J. (2017). Digital twin: Mitigating unpredictable, undesirable emergent behavior in complex systems. *Transdisciplinary perspectives on complex systems: New findings and approaches*, 85–113.

Groombridge, D., Karamouzis, F., & Chandrasekaran, A. (2021). Top strategic technology trends for 2022. Gartner Reprint, ID G00757234 Search in.

Gui, J., Sun, Z., Wen, Y., Tao, D., & Ye, J. (2021). A review on generative adversarial networks: Algorithms, theory, and applications. *IEEE Transactions on Knowledge and Data Engineering*, 35, 3313–3332.

Sheikh, H., Prins, C., & Schrijvers, E. (2023). Artificial intelligence: Definition and background, January 2023. DOI: 10.1007/978-3-031-21448-6_2 In Mission AI License CC BY 4.0.

Hodgins, J. K. (1998). Animating human motion. *Scientific American*, 278(3), 64–69.

Jiang, H., Qin, S., Fu, J., Zhang, J., & Ding, G. (2021). How to model and implement connections between physical and virtual models for digital twin application. *Journal of Manufacturing Systems*, 58, 36–51.

Kaur, A., Bhambri, P., & Gupta, O. P. (2012). A novel technique for robust image segmentation. *International Journal of Advanced Engineering Technology*, 3(4), 110–114.

Kaur, S., Kumar, R., Kaur, R., Singh, S., Rani, S., & Kaur, A. (2022). Piezoelectric materials in sensors: Bibliometric and visualization analysis. *Materials Today: Proceedings*.

Kataria, A., Puri, V., Pareek, P. K., & Rani, S. (2023, July). Human activity classification using G-XGB. In 2023 International Conference on Data Science and Network Security (ICDSNS) (pp. 1–5). IEEE.

Kaur, P. P., Singh, S., & Bhambri, P. (2014). A study on routing protocols behavior in MANETs. *International Journal of Research in Advent Technology*, 2(12), 26–31.

Kaur, R., & Bhambri, P. (2015). Information retrieval system for hospital management. *International Journal of Multidisciplinary Consortium*, 2(4), 16–21.

Kataria, A., Agrawal, D., Rani, S., Karar, V., & Chauhan, M. (2022). Prediction of blood screening parameters for preliminary analysis using neural networks. In *Predictive modeling in biomedical data mining and analysis* (pp. 157–169). Academic Press.

Kaur, D., Singh, B., & Rani, S. (2023). Cyber security in the metaverse. In *Handbook of Research on AI-Based Technologies and Applications in the Era of the Metaverse* (pp. 418–435). IGI Global.

Kurfess, Franz J. (2003). Encyclopedia of physical science and technology. *Artificial Intelligence*, 609–629. doi:10.1016/B0-12-227410-5/00027-2

Kumar, R., Rani, S., & Khangura, S. S. (Eds.). (2023). *Machine learning for sustainable manufacturing in Industry 4.0: Concept, concerns and applications*. CRC Press.

Kumar, P., Banerjee, K., Singhal, N., Kumar, A., Rani, S., Kumar, R., & Lavinia, C. A. (2022). Verifiable, Secure mobile agent migration in healthcare systems using a polynomial-based threshold secret sharing scheme with a Blowfish algorithm. *Sensors*, 22(22), 8620.

Mohsen, A., & Bilge, G. C. (2023). *Digital Twin: Benefits, use cases, challenges, and opportunities*, Decision Analytics Journal, Volume 6, 2023, 100165, ISSN 2772-6622.

Paika, V., & Bhambri, P. (2013). Fuzzy system based edge extraction techniques using device-dependent color spaces. *International Journal of Scientific & Engineering Research*, 4(8), 1467–1478.

Puri, V., Kataria, A., Solanki, V. K., & Rani, S. (2022, December). AI-based botnet attack classification and detection in IoT devices. In 2022 IEEE International Conference on Machine Learning and Applied Network Technologies (ICMLANT) (pp. 1–5). IEEE.

Rani, S., Bhambri, P., Kataria, A., Khang, A., & Sivaraman, A. K. (Eds.). (2023). Big data, cloud computing and IoT: Tools and applications. *Chapman and Hall/CRC*, 10(978100329833), 5.

Rani, S., Kataria, A., Kumar, S., & Tiwari, P. (2023). Federated learning for secure IoMT-applications in smart healthcare systems: A comprehensive review. *Knowledge-Based Systems*, 110658.

Rani, S., Mishra, A. K., Kataria, A., Mallik, S., & Qin, H. (2023). Machine learning-based optimal crop selection system in smart agriculture. *Scientific Reports*, 13(1), 15997.

Rani, S., Pareek, P. K., Kaur, J., Chauhan, M., & Bhambri, P. (2023, February). Quantum machine learning in healthcare: Developments and challenges. In 2023 IEEE International Conference on Integrated Circuits and Communication Systems (ICICACS) (pp. 1–7). IEEE.

Rani, S., Bhambri, P., & Kataria, A. (2023). Integration of IoT, Big Data, and Cloud Computing technologies. *Big Data, Cloud Computing and IoT: Tools and applications.*

Rani, S., Kumar, S., Kataria, A., & Min, H. (2023). SmartHealth: An intelligent framework to secure IoMT service applications using machine learning. *ICT Express*, 2(43), 342–367.

Schleich, B., Anwer, N., Mathieu, L., & Wartzack, S. (2017). Shaping the digital twin for design and production engineering. *CIRP Annals*, 66(1), 141–144.

Sharma, M., & Bhambri, P. (2013). A study of GENE prediction program of metagenomic data on various GENE prediction software. *International Journal of Advanced Research*, 1(7), 394–399.

Sudevan, S., Barwani, B., Al Maani, E., Rani, S., & Sivaraman, A. K. (2021). Impact of blended learning during Covid-19 in Sultanate of Oman. *Annals of the Romanian Society for Cell Biology*, 14978–14987.

Singh, S., Kakkar, P., & Bhambri, P. (2013). A study of the impact of random waypoint and vector mobility models on various routing protocols in MANET. *International Journal of Advances in Computing and Information Technology*, 2(3), 41–51.

Tanwar, R., Chhabra, Y., Rattan, P., & Rani, S. (2022, September). Blockchain in IoT networks for precision agriculture. In International Conference on Innovative Computing and Communications: Proceedings of ICICC 2022, Volume 2 (pp. 137–147). Singapore: Springer Nature Singapore.

Tekinerdogan, B., & Verdouw, C. (2020). Systems architecture design pattern catalog for developing digital twins. *Sensors*, 20(18), 5103. 10.3390/s20185103.

Zheng, Y., Yang, S., & Cheng, H. (2019). An application framework of digital twin and its case study. *Journal of Ambient Intelligence and Humanized Computing*, 10, 1141–1153.

Ziyad, S. (2019). Artificial Intelligence Definition, Ethics and Standards, April 2019.

9 AI-Driven Digital Twin for Healthcare Applications

K. Aditya Shastry and B. A. Manjunatha

9.1 INTRODUCTION

Artificial intelligence (AI) is a subfield of computer science that concentrates on the creation of scientific concepts, procedures, and programmes for mimicking, augmenting, and augmenting human cognitive skills. In 1950, Alan Turing devised the "Turing test" and defined AI as being both comparable to and more complicated than the human intellect (Liu et al., 2021).

AI is being used more and more these days, especially even though deep learning (DL) (a collection of training techniques that serve as the foundation of the latest generation of AI skills, with the capability to effectively learn from big-data analysis and then make choices based on that understanding) came out (Mintz et al., 2019). Many different neural networks are used in this type of AI. AI is being utilised in so many various ways and helping to make so many technological advances that a fresh concept has come up: AI plus. "AI plus" is the procedure of combining AI's technological advancements and successes with more traditional approaches to business to increase productivity, innovation, and growth (Kaul et al., 2020). AI researchers have discovered that the proportion of advantages to resources spent in the healthcare profession is greater compared to any other segment they have looked at to date. When AI is used in healthcare, it leads to big changes in the way healthcare is done now (Gomez et al., 2019, Jabeen et al., 2021). Healthcare uses of AI have also gotten a lot of attention due to their great potential (Patel et al., 2009).

People are wondering if AI technology could likely overtake doctors because of how quickly it is being used in the medical sector (Bakshi et al., 2021). Feasibly, AI systems may not be capable of substituting doctors; however, they may help doctors get better results and be more precise in the medical sector. Obtaining access to health records is a key part of the development of these AI medical apps (Manne et al., 2021). AI is not a standalone system, but a group of methods. Some of these methods are often used in healthcare, like "machine learning" (ML). ML is a process where methods are trained using information that already exists so that, based on what they've already learned, they can recognise the test input when given

 DOI: 10.1201/9781003395416-9

the information used for testing (Bose et al., 2021). ML is a type of AI that is used a lot (Lee et al., 2018).

AI software, which includes ML and the ability to learn on its own, opens up new possibilities for advancement in many disciplines, including financial services, pharmaceutics, business, trade, distribution channels, transportation, and energy (Esmaeilzadeh et al., 2020; Lopez et al., 2019). AI might be used in clinical information systems to help doctors make decisions about diagnosis and treatment and to perform predictive modelling on a population (Brufau et al., 2019). Several businesses have made the development of AI-based products a key part of their plans (Coombs et al., 2020). AI has made a lot of big changes, which has led to new research that looks at the effects of these technologies and AI (Babu et al., 2021). To reach this goal, though, you need to know a lot about the factors that affect how customers in different service and manufacturing industries will react to AI-based solutions. Studies from the past have shown how important AI is in healthcare, especially healthcare analytics (Khanna et al., 2013). AI can improve patient safety, diagnosis, and the way medical information is analysed (Dreyer et al., 2018). According to research (Houssami et al., 2017), using AI knowledge to diagnose "breast cancer" reduces the number of mistakes made by humans. However, several connected moral and social trust factors, as well as AI dependency, still need to be made (Bali, V., Bali, S., Gaur, D., Rani, S., & Kumar, R., 2023). AI-driven suggestions may be used differently in the medical field than in other industries because health information is sensitive, and customers are more likely to make mistakes with their medications.

Effective methods of AI in the medical field are discussed in this chapter. The rest of this section is scheduled to go as follows. The several AI methods used in healthcare are discussed in Section 2.

9.2 AI METHODS IN HEALTHCARE

There is a gradual shift toward applying the ubiquitous AI tools of business and routine activities to the medical industry. AI has the potential to assist medical practitioners in many different aspects of patient service and administration, allowing them to quickly adjust their procedures to new circumstances (Rani, S., Mishra, A. K., Kataria, A., Mallik, S., & Qin, H., 2023). Although the majority of AI and healthcare advances have far-reaching effects on the healthcare sector, the approaches they facilitate can vary greatly amongst hospitals and other medical institutions. Regardless of the fact that various research have demonstrated that AI might perform medical assignments comparable to or better than humans (Manne et al., 2021), it will be a long time before AI in healthcare is able to completely replace humans.

Figure 9.1 shows the commonly used AI methods in healthcare.

Prior to visiting a physician, a patient may interact with a machine as part of "normal" clinical practice in the coming years. With advancements in AI, it seems that the era of wrong diagnosis and addressing clinical manifestations as opposed to their underlying cause may soon be a thing of the past. Consider how

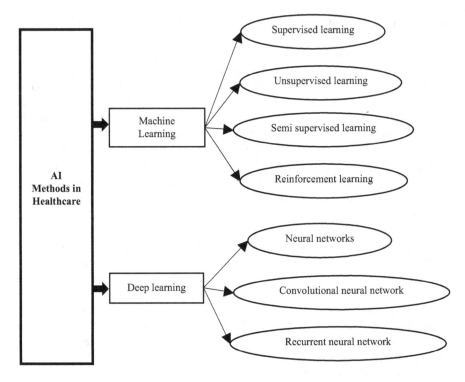

FIGURE 9.1 AI methods in healthcare.

several decades of "blood pressure" metrics you possess or how much storage you would need to erase in order to put a 3D representation of an organ on your laptop (Kaur, D., Singh, B., & Rani, S., 2023). The information recorded in hospitals and kept in electronic medical records via common tests and diagnostic imaging enables additional applications of AI and information-driven medicine with superior performance. These technologies have altered and will continue to alter physicians' and academics' therapeutic conflict resolving strategies (Basu et al., 2020).

Although certain techniques may perform as well as or better than doctors in a range of duties, they have not been completely incorporated into standard clinical practice (Kumar, P., Banerjee, K., Singhal, N., Kumar, A., Rani, S., Kumar, R., & Lavinia, C. A., 2022). Although these systems could greatly impact healthcare and improve the efficacy of surgical treatments, they face considerable initial legal challenges that must be overcome before they can be implemented. Similar to how doctors hone their skills over the course of years in medical school by taking classes, taking exams, practising on patients, and gaining feedback, AI systems need time to train and make mistakes before they can perform well (Puri, V., Kataria, A., Solanki, V. K., & Rani, S., 2022, December). Human intelligence is required for tasks like pattern and voice recognition, picture processing, and decision-making, but these may theoretically be completed by AI methods. For an algorithm to make use of a given

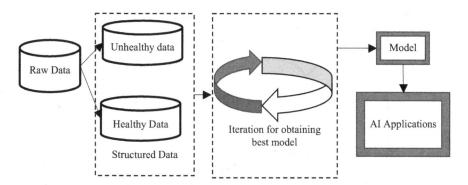

FIGURE 9.2   AI algorithms.

image, for instance, human beings must provide explicit instructions on what else to look for. In conclusion, AI algorithms are highly effective at carrying out repetitive tasks, often outperforming humans in the tasks for which they were designed (Amisha et al., 2019).

To construct an effective AI system, systems are frequently provided with content, indicating that each data item does have a tag or tag that the technique could identify (Figure 9.2). After the approach has been subjected to a necessary number of distinct data sets and related explanations, its behaviour is assessed to check its accuracy, just as students are given exams (Dhanalakshmi, R., Vijayaraghavan, N., Sivaraman, A. K., & Rani, S., 2022). These technique "tests" often involve the input of test dataset that the designers already possess the solutions, allowing researchers to assess the approaches' capacity to recognise the correct response (Tanwar, R., Chhabra, Y., Rattan, P., & Rani, S., 2022, September). In response to the results of evaluation, the methods may be changed, provided with more information, or built to aid the programmer in making decisions (Briganti et al., 2020).

Figure 9.2 is an illustration of a method that might comprehend the fundamental structure of a wrist and recreate the placement of a missing digit. The input is a set of palm X-rays, and the output is a map displaying the locations of missing hand components. The prototype in this instance is the arm shape, which can be applied to various pictures. This could assist clinicians in determining where to reconstruct or replace a leg (Gomez et al., 2019).

There are various data-driven learning strategies available. Most of the data input for AI-based medical applications is numeric (such as pulse rate or pressure) or graphical (like the MRI scans or Imaging of Tumour Clinical Specimens). Following learning from the data, the approaches enable determining if it is a likelihood or a categorisation. For instance, a useful outcome could be the likelihood of getting an arterial thrombus depending on pulse rate and hypertensive data, or the cancerous or benign categorisation of an image biopsy. In medical applications, the diagnostics performance of a technique is compared to that of a physician in order to determine the technique's capabilities and usefulness in healthcare (Secinaro et al., 2021).

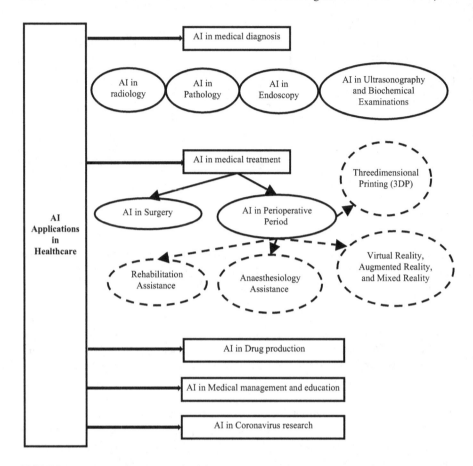

FIGURE 9.3   AI applications in healthcare.

Numerous medical challenges are ideally suited for AI applications as a result of developments in computing power and the huge amounts of data generated by healthcare facilities. Two contemporary uses of precise and medically beneficial procedures that facilitate identification mutually for patients and doctors are presented below.

Figure 9.3 shows the various applications of AI in healthcare.

9.3   AI IN MEDICAL TREATMENT

9.3.1   AI IN SURGERY

To date, the medical AI system has been the most clinically meaningful use of AI technology. Machines such as the PUMA-560, Probot, AESOP, Robodoc, and Acrobot (Jakopec et al., 2001; Cowley, 1992; Stefano, 2017) were utilised as helpful surgery adjuncts 20 years ago. Nevertheless, traditional treatment gadgets were limited in their effectiveness since they still needed personal supervision and interaction (Rani, S., Pareek, P. K., Kaur, J., Chauhan, M., & Bhambri, P., 2023, February).

The concept of an AI-based treatment model has evolved with the development of AI technology. The "Da Vinci surgical" AI system constitutes its most cutting-edge use of this principle in the current era. The debut of the "Da Vinci medical" machine as a remarkable, one-of-a-kind advancement in human history permits less intense medical assistance, with the advantages of improved sight, extra accurate and straightforward therapy, and some even remote control. Major surgical treatments can now be performed with surgical techniques that were formerly difficult to implement (Kataria, A., Agrawal, D., Rani, S., Karar, V., & Chauhan, M., 2022). The Da Vinci surgical AI system has three parts: the doctor connection, the robotic operating system, and the imaging system (Kataria, A., Puri, V., Pareek, P. K., & Rani, S., 2023, July). In 2000, the FDA of the United States approved the real use of Da Vinci surgical gear. The standard treatment model was altered by this AI system. With the execution of the Da Vinci surgical AI system, for example, the pituitary process was improved in terms of post-operative symptomatic treatment and verbal results (Zuo et al., 2017), mesiodistal operation was improved in regards to accuracy and security (Stefanelli et al., 2020), bowel, nephrotoxicity, and bulbourethral glands medical intervention was improved as demonstrated by an increased surgical intervention beneficial result, but a low attrition (Lenfant et al., 2020; Winder et al., 2020; Jones et al., 2020), and respiratory cancer surgery was beneficial for patients as a result of a lower attrition (Wang et al., 2020).

The primary distinguishing feature of AI surgical technologies, relative to conventional surgical processes, is "AI," which indicates that the surgery processes have evolved to an intelligent state. Assisted by AI techniques such as DL, histologic analysis in the course of surgery is now a reality, allowing for fast incisal edge pathologic investigation and genuine cell biopsies (Zuo et al., 2017). Utilising DL, the AI method could also self-deduce centred on the plentiful experimentations from diagnostic physicians and recreate clinical digitised data by posting the surgical programme to an AI surgical scheme to smartly aid the surgical procedure, such as minimally invasive resection scope composition, postoperative endocrine remnant quantity health coverage, and prognostication of lymphatic system with potentially positive metastatic disease (Navarrete et al., 2020).

9.3.2 AI IN DRUG PRODUCTION

Unfortunately, even after extensive research, exploratory medicines may well not operate as expected because of the extended and complicated time frame required for their production in the traditional system, which includes functional target studies, drug food product layout, performance monitoring, screening procedures, experimentation, and progress. However, advancements in AI have changed healthcare's organic medication firms and sped up the discovery and production of new medications (Bajorath et al., 2020) (Table 9.1).

TABLE 9.1

AI Applications and Techniques in Healthcare

AI Application	Reference	Task	AI Technique
Radiology	(Stefanelli et al., 2020; Heydon et al., 2021; Xie et al., 2020)	Early detection, prompt treatment, and classification of retinal disorders	Deep neural network
	(Gong et al., 2018a, 2018b)	Identify cancerous and harmless pulmonary nodules	AI-aided diagnostic (CADx)
	(Rodriguez et al., 2019; McKinney et al., 2020; Rodriguez et al., 2019)	Detection of Breast Cancer	CNN
	(Stoel et al., 2019)	Premature arthritis diagnosis	CNN
Ultrasonography and biochemical examinations	(Nguyen et al., 2019; Sun et al., 2020; Chen et al., 2020a, 2020b)	Categorisation of thyroid nodules	CNN, Resnet
	(Fujioka et al., 2019; Chen et al., 2019)	Pancreatic, ovarian, bronchial, pectoralis major tendon, and urinary interval cancers, various obstetrics and gynaecological abnormalities were detected with ultrasonography.	CNN ensemble
	(Abelson et al., 2018)	Surveillance and identification of chronic lymphocytic leukaemia	Deep neural network
	(Sun et al., 2018)	Anti-PD-1/PDL1 monoclonal antibodies: Estimation of the radiomic signal and diagnostic procedures	technique of elastic–net regularised analysis
	(Li et al., 2019)	Diagnosis of Noonan syndrome,	CNN
	(Tomita et al., 2019)	Prediction and diagnosis of asthma	DNN
Surgery	(Demircioglu, 2019; Cowley, 1992; Stefano, 2017)	Surgical systems	PUMA-560, Probot, AESOP, Robodoc, and Acrobo
	(Tae, 2020)	Thyroid surgery	Da Vinci surgical AI system
	(Lenfant et al., 2020; Winder et al., 2020; Jones et al., 2020)	Gastric, nephritic, and prostatic surgery	
	(Wang et al., 2020)	Lung cancer surgery	
	(Zuo, 2017)	Real-time tissue biopsy	
	(Navarrete et al., 2020)	Lymph node forecasting, organ leftover size assurance, and surgical resection area definition	Multi-support vector regression, SVM, CNN

Category	References	Description	AI methods
Virtual reality	(Nikoyan et al., 2020; Skelley et al., 2019; Yamaguchi, 2019)	Improvement in Anterior Lumbar Disk herniation Procedure Success Through the Use of Virtual Reality Technology.	ANN
Augmented reality	(Bangeas et al., 2019; Feng et al., 2018; Kashyap et al., 2018)	Recognition of the difficulty in navigating intricate vasculature throughout operation	Digital holographic imaging technology
Mixed reality	(Corona et al., 2018; Sun et al., 2020; Zhou et al., 2020; Park et al., 2021; Gomez et al., 2019; Salah et al., 2020; Alkhaibary et al., 2020; Vidal et al., 2020; Xing et al., 2020; Rey et al., 2020; Boso et al., 2020)	Perioperative guiding support for a variety of procedures including spinal, orthopaedic, hepatic, renal, and cranial operations; postoperative rehabilitation and routine training	The Hololens is Microsoft's newest portable MR gadget and technical creation
Anaesthesiology assistance	(Ettinger et al., 2020; Levin et al., 2020; Farmer et al., 2020)	Assessing anaesthetic level, controlling anaesthesia, predicting abnormalities, using ultrasonography to help with discomfort and suffering control, and managing the surgical site	ANN, Fuzzy logic, ML, computer vision
Rehabilitation assistance	(Edgar et al., 2020; Mirchi et al., 2020; Sadeghi et al., 2020; Fertleman et al., 2018; Creighton et al., 2020; Gibby et al., 2020; Hu et al., 2019)	To gather data, lessen the likelihood of false alarms, aid in patient rehabilitation, evaluate the patient's development, and ensure the patient's condition	SVM, ANN, principal component analysis
Drug production	(Goo et al., 2020; Salmas et al., 2020; Wu et al., 2018; Chytas et al., 2021; Zeiger et al., 2020; Yoshida et al., 2020; Rojas et al., 2020; Held et al., 2020; Chen et al., 2020a, 2020b)	New drug discovery and assembly, target proteins, making medications for cancer victims, small molecule drug therapy, decisions on the dosage, form, and composition of medications	"Deep neural nets (DNNs)," CNNs, and RNNs have been shown to outperform other popular methods such as Random Forest, Gradient Boosted Trees, and Gaussian Processes
Medical management and education	(Hashimoto et al., 2020; Seger et al., 2020; Kamdar et al., 2020; Poncette et al., 2020; Angehrn et al., 2020; Dai et al., 2020; Averta et al., 2020; Zhao et al., 2020; De et al., 2020; Ramezani et al., 2019; Bajorath et al., 2020)	In comparison to widely used techniques like Random Forest, Gradient Boosted Trees, and Gaussian Processes, "deep neural nets" (DNNs), CNNs, and RNNs were demonstrated to achieve superior results and individualised clinical care	Long-short-term memory (LSTM), ANN, RNN, explainable AI

9.4 CONCLUSION AND FUTURE SCOPE

Since AI software is a product of the contemporary era, its development tracks the progression of technological advancements. Both the locomotive revolutionary and the electrical invention profoundly impacted person's existence and pushed civilisation forward during humanity's history. Contemporary scientific and technological development has already proven an inexorable trend that has burst in appeal like a flame, and AI technology is a key part of this. Physician diagnosis using computed tomography, deleterious, laparotomy, ultrasonographic, and physical and chemical exams has been effectively supported with a higher level of accuracy and a reduced human work volume thanks to novel AI methods, which have also significantly altered the conventional healthcare setting in the medicine field. Although prior preparation, the surgical procedure itself, and the postpartum recovery period all contributed to amazing healthcare outcomes, the quality of the healthcare delivered during the perioperative period was significantly enhanced. Further, AI has played a critical role in transforming healthcare management, expert exams, and medication research. Various AI techniques and their practical implementations were discussed in this chapter. A new phase of AI has begun, and we expect it to bring about unprecedented transformations in healthcare delivery.

REFERENCES

Abelson, S., Collord, G., Ng, S., et al. (2018). Prediction of acute myeloid leukemia risk in healthy individuals. *Nature*, 559(7714), 400–404.

Alkhaibary, A., Alharbi, A., Alnefaie, N., et al. (2020). Cranioplasty: A comprehensive review of the history, materials, surgical aspects, and complications. *World Neurosurgery*, 139, 445–452.

Amisha, Malik, P., Pathania, M., & Rathaur, V. K. (2019). Overview of artificial intelligence in medicine. *Journal of Family Medicine and Primary Care*, 8(7), 2328–2331. 10.41 03/jfmpc.jfmpc_440_19

Angehrn, Z., Haldna, L., Zandvliet, A. S., et al. (2020). Artificial intelligence and machine learning applied at the point of care. *Frontiers in Pharmacology*, 11, 759.

Averta, G., Della, S. C., Valenza, G., et al. (2020). Exploiting upper-limb functional principal components for human-like motion generation of anthropomorphic robots. *Journal of Neuroengineering and Rehabilitation*, 17(1), 63.

Babu, G. C. N., Gupta, S., Bhambri, P., Leo, L. M., Rao, B. H., & Kumar, S. (2021). A semantic health observation system development based on the IoT sensors. *Turkish Journal of Physiotherapy and Rehabilitation*, 32(3), 1721–1729.

Bajorath, J., Kearnes, S., Walters, W. P., et al. (2020). Artificial intelligence in drug discovery: Into the great wide open. *Journal of Medicinal Chemistry*, 63(16), 8651–8652.

Bakshi, P., Bhambri, P., & Thapar, V. (2021). A review paper on wireless sensor network techniques in Internet of Things (IoT). *Wesleyan Journal of Research*, 14(7), 147–160.

Bali, V., Bali, S., Gaur, D., Rani, S., & Kumar, R. (2023). Commercial-off-the shelf vendor selection: A multi-criteria decision-making approach using intuitionistic fuzzy sets and TOPSIS. *Operational Research in engineering sciences: Theory and applications*.

Bangeas, P., Tsioukas, V., Papadopoulos, V. N., et al. (2019). Role of innovative 3D printing models in the management of hepatobiliary malignancies. *World Journal of Hepatology*, 11(7), 574–585.

Basu, K., Sinha, R., Ong, A., & Basu, T. (2020). Artificial Intelligence: How is it changing medical sciences and its future? *Indian Journal of Dermatology*, 65(5), 365–370. 10. 4103/ijd.IJD_421_20

Bose, M. M., Yadav, D., Bhambri, P., & Shankar, R. (2021). Electronic customer relationship management: Benefits and pre-implementation considerations. *Journal of Maharaja Sayajirao University of Baroda*, 55(01(VI)), 1343–1350. The Maharaja Sayajirao University of Baroda.

Boso, D., Maghin, E., Carraro, E., et al. (2020). Extracellular matrix-derived hydrogels as biomaterial for different skeletal muscle tissue replacements. *Materials (Basel)*, 13(11), 2483.

Briganti, G., & Le Moine, O. (2020). Artificial intelligence in medicine: Today and tomorrow. *Frontiers in Medicine*, 7, 27. 10.3389/fmed.2020.00027

Brufau, S. R., Wyatt, K. D., Boyum, P., Mickelson, M., Moore, M., & Cognetta-Rieke, C. (2019). A lesson in implementation: A pre-post study of providers' experience with artificial intelligence-based clinical decision support. *International Journal of Medical Informatics*, 137, 104072.

Chen, C. H., Lee, Y. W., Huang, Y. S., et al. (2019). Computer-aided diagnosis of endobronchial ultrasound images using convolutional neural network. *Computers in Biology and Medicine*, 177, 175–182.

Chen, J., You, H., & Li, K. (2020)a. A review of thyroid gland segmentation and thyroid nodule segmentation methods for medical ultrasound images. *Computers in Biology and Medicine*, 185, 105329.

Chen, P. J., Penn, I. W., Wei, S. H., et al. (2020)b. Augmented reality-assisted training with selected Tai-Chi movements improves balance control and increases lower limb muscle strength in older adults: A prospective randomized trial. *Journal of Exercise Science & Fitness*, 18(3), 142–147.

Chytas, D., Chronopoulos, E., Salmas, M., et al. (2021). Comment on: "Intraoperative 3D Hologram Support with Mixed Reality Techniques in Liver Surgery". *Annals of Surgery*, 274(6), e761–e762.

Coombs, C., Hislop, D., Taneva, S. K., & Barnard, S. (2020). The strategic impacts of Intelligent Automation for knowledge and service work: An interdisciplinary review. *The Journal of Strategic Information Systems*, 29(4), 101600. 10.1016/j.jsis.2020. 101600

Corona, P. S., Vicente, M., Tetsworth, K., et al. (2018). Preliminary results using patient-specific 3D printed models to improve preoperative planning for correction of post-traumatic tibial deformities with circular frames. *Injury*, 49(Suppl 2), S51–S59.

Cowley, G. (1992). Introducing "Robodoc". *Newsweek*, 120(21), 86.

Creighton, F. X., Unberath, M., Song, T., et al. (2020). Early Feasibility Studies of Augmented Reality Navigation for Lateral Skull Base Surgery. *Otol Neurotol*, 41(7), 883–888.

Dai, B., Yu, Y., Huang, L., et al. (2020). Application of neural network model in assisting device fitting for low vision patients. *Annals of Translational Medicine*, 8(11), 702.

De, C. H., Corradi, F., Smeets, C., et al. (2020). Wearable monitoring and interpretable machine learning can objectively track progression in patients during cardiac rehabilitation. *Sensors (Basel)*, 20(12), 3601.

Demircioglu, A. (2019). Radiomics-AI-based image analysis. *Pathologe*, 40(Suppl 3), 271–276.

Dhanalakshmi, R., Vijayaraghavan, N., Sivaraman, A. K., & Rani, S. (2022). Epidemic awareness spreading in smart cities using the artificial neural network. In *AI-centric smart city ecosystems* (pp. 187–207). CRC Press.

Dreyer, K., & Allen, B. (2018). Artificial intelligence in health care: Brave new world or golden opportunity? *Journal of the American College of Radiology*, 15(4), 655–657.

Edgar, L., Pu, T., Porter, B., et al. (2020). Regenerative medicine, organ bioengineering and transplantation. *British Journal of Surgery*, 107(7), 793–800.

Esmaeilzadeh, P. (2020). Use of AI-based tools for healthcare purposes: a survey study from consumers' perspectives. *BMC Medical Informatics and Decision Making*, 20(1), 170. 10.1186/s12911-020-01191-1

Ettinger, M., & Windhagen, H. (2020). Individual revision arthroplasty of the knee joint. *Orthopade*, 49(5), 396–402.

Farmer, Z. L., Dominguez, R. J., Mancinelli, C., et al. (2020). Urogynecological surgical mesh implants: New trends in materials, manufacturing and therapeutic approaches. *International Journal of Pharmaceutics*, 585, 119512.

Feng, Z. H., Li, X. B., Phan, K., et al. (2018). Design of a 3D navigation template to guide the screw trajectory in spine: A step-by-step approach using Mimics and 3-Matic software. *Journal of Spine Surgery*, 4(3), 645–653.

Fertleman, C., Aubugeau, W. P., Sher, C., et al. (2018). A Discussion of virtual reality as a new tool for training healthcare professionals. *Frontiers in Public Health*, 6, 44.

Fujioka, T., Mori, M., Kubota, K., & Others. (2019). Breast ultrasound image synthesis using deep convolutional generative adversarial networks. *Diagnostics (Basel)*, 9(4), 17643.

Gibby, J., Cvetko, S., Javan, R., et al. (2020). Use of augmented reality for image-guided spine procedures. *European Spine Journal*, 29(8), 1823–1832.

Gomez, J. M., Estades, F. J., Meschian, C. S., et al. (2019). Internal hemipelvectomy and reconstruction assisted by 3D printing technology using premade intraoperative cutting and placement guides in a patient with pelvic sarcoma: A case report. *JBJS Case Connect*, 9(4), e60.

Gong, J., Liu, J. Y., Jiang, Y. J., et al. (2018)a. Fusion of quantitative imaging features and serum biomarkers to improve performance of computer-aided diagnosis scheme for lung cancer: A preliminary study. *Medical Physics*, 45(12), 5472–5481.

Gong, J., Liu, J.Y., Sun, X.W., et al. (2018)b. Computer-aided diagnosis of lung cancer: the effect of training data sets on classification accuracy of lung nodules. *Physics in Medicine and Biology*, 63(3), 35036.

Goo, H. W., Park, S. J., & Yoo, S. J. (2020). Advanced medical use of three-dimensional imaging in congenital heart disease: Augmented reality, mixed reality, virtual reality, and three-dimensional printing. *Korean Journal of Radiology*, 21(2), 133–145.

Hashimoto, D. A., Witkowski, E., Gao, L., et al. (2020). Artificial intelligence in anesthesiology: Current techniques, clinical applications, and limitations. *Anesthesiology*, 132(2), 379–394.

Held, J., Yu, K., Pyles, C., et al. (2020). Augmented reality-based rehabilitation of gait impairments: Case report. *JMIR mHealth uHealth*, 8(5), e17804.

Heydon, P., Egan, C., Bolter, L., & et al. (2021). Prospective evaluation of an artificial intelligence-enabled algorithm for automated diabetic retinopathy screening of 30 000 patients. *British Journal of Ophthalmology*, 105(5), 723–728.

Houssami, N., Turner, R. M., & Morrow, M. (2017). Meta-analysis of pre-operative magnetic resonance imaging (MRI) and surgical treatment for breast cancer. *Breast Cancer Research and Treatment*, 165(2), 273–283.

Hu, H. Z., Feng, X. B., Shao, Z. W., et al. (2019). Application and prospect of mixed reality technology in medical field. *Current Medical Science*, 39(1), 1–6.

Jabeen, A., Pallathadka, H., Pallathadka, L. K., & Bhambri, P. (2021). E-CRM successful factors for business enterprises CASE STUDIES. *Journal of Maharaja Sayajirao University of Baroda*, 55(01(VI)), 1332–1342. The Maharaja Sayajirao University of Baroda.

Jakopec, M., Harris, S. J., Rodriguez, Y. B., et al. (2001). The first clinical application of a "hands-on" robotic knee surgery system. *Computer Aided Surgery*, 6(6), 329–339.

Jones, R., Dobbs, R. W., Halgrimson, W. R., et al. (2020). Single port robotic radical prostatectomy with the da Vinci SP platform: a step-by-step approach. *Canadian Journal of Urology*, 27(3), 10263–10269.

Kamdar, N., & Jalilian, L. (2020). Telemedicine: A digital interface for perioperative anesthetic care. *Anesthesia & Analgesia*, 130(2), 272–275.

Kashyap, A., Kadur, S., Mishra, A., et al. (2018). Cervical pedicle screw guiding jig, an innovative solution. *Journal of Clinical Orthopaedics and Trauma*, 9(3), 226–229.

Kataria, A., Agrawal, D., Rani, S., Karar, V., & Chauhan, M. (2022). Prediction of blood screening parameters for preliminary analysis using neural networks. In *Predictive modeling in biomedical data mining and analysis* (pp. 157–169). Academic Press.

Kataria, A., Puri, V., Pareek, P. K., & Rani, S. (2023, July). Human activity classification using G-XGB. In *2023 International Conference on Data Science and Network Security (ICDSNS)* (pp. 1–5). IEEE.

Kaul, V., Enslin, S., & Gross, S. A. (2020). The history of artificial intelligence in medicine. *Gastrointestinal Endoscopy*, 92(4), 807–812. 10.1016/j.gie.2020.06.040

Kaur, D., Singh, B., & Rani, S. (2023). Cyber security in the metaverse. In *Handbook of research on AI-based technologies and applications in the era of the metaverse* (pp. 418–435). IGI Global.

Khanna, S., Sattar, A., & Hansen, D. (2013). Artificial intelligence in health–the three big challenges. *Australasian Medical Journal*, 6(5), 315.

Kumar, P., Banerjee, K., Singhal, N., Kumar, A., Rani, S., Kumar, R., & Lavinia, C. A. (2022). Verifiable, secure mobile agent migration in healthcare systems using a polynomial-based threshold secret sharing scheme with a Blowfish algorithm. *Sensors*, 22(22), 8620.

Lee, S. I., Celik, S., Logsdon, B. A., Lundberg, S. M., Martins, T. J., Oehler, V. G., Estey, E. H., Miller, C. P., Chien, S., Dai, J., Saxena, A., Blau, C. A., & Becker, P. S. (2018). Machine learning approach to integrate big data for precision medicine in acute myeloid leukemia. *Nature Communications*, 9(1), 42. 10.1038/s41467-017-02691-x

Lenfant, L., Wilson, C. A., Sawczyn, G., et al. (2020). Single-port robot-assisted dismembered pyeloplasty with mini-pfannenstiel or peri-umbilical access: Initial experience in a single center. *Urology*, 143, 147–152.

Levin, D., Mackensen, G. B., Reisman, M., et al. (2020). 3D printing applications for transcatheter aortic valve replacement. *Current Cardiology Reports*, 22(4), 23.

Li, X., Yao, R., Tan, X., et al. (2019). Molecular and phenotypic spectrum of Noonan syndrome in Chinese patients. *Clinical Genetics*, 96(4), 290–299.

Liu, P. R., Lu, L., Zhang, J. Y., Huo, T. T., Liu, S. X., & Ye, Z. W. (2021). Application of artificial intelligence in medicine: An overview. *Current Medical Science*, 41(6), 1105–1115. 10.1007/s11596-021-2474-3

López-Robles, J. R., Otegi-Olaso, J. R., Gómez, I. P., & Cobo, M. J. (2019). 30 years of intelligence models in management and business: A bibliometric review. *International Journal of Information Management*, 48, 22–38. 10.1016/j.ijinfomgt.2018.11.004

Manne, R., & Kantheti, S. (2021). Application of artificial intelligence in healthcare: Chances and challenges. *Current Journal of Applied Science and Technology*, 40, 78–89. 10.9734/CJAST/2021/v40i631320

McKinney, S. M., Sieniek, M., Godbole, V., et al. (2020). International evaluation of an AI system for breast cancer screening. *Nature*, 577(7788), 89–94.

Mintz, Y., & Brodie, R. (2019). Introduction to artificial intelligence in medicine. *Minimally Invasive Therapy & Allied Technologies*, 28(2), 73–81. 10.1080/13645706.2019. 1575882

Mirchi, N., Bissonnette, V., Ledwos, N., et al. (2020). Artificial neural networks to assess virtual reality anterior cervical discectomy performance. *Operative Neurosurgery (Hagerstown)*, 19(1), 65–75.

Navarrete, A. J., & Hashimoto, D. A. (2020). Current applications of artificial intelligence for intraoperative decision support in surgery. *Frontiers in Medicine*, 14(4), 369–381.

Nguyen, D. T., Pham, T. D., Batchuluun, G., & Others. (2019). Artificial intelligence-based thyroid nodule classification using information from spatial and frequency domains. *Journal of Clinical Medicine*, 8(11), 1976.

Nikoyan, L., & Patel, R. (2020). Intraoral scanner, three-dimensional imaging, and three-dimensional printing in the dental office. *Dental Clinics of North America*, 64(2), 365–378.

Park, J. W., Kang, H. G., Kim, J. H., et al. (2021). The application of 3D-printing technology in pelvic bone tumor surgery. *Journal of Orthopaedic Science*, 26(2), 276–283.

Patel, V. L., Shortliffe, E. H., Stefanelli, M., et al. (2009). The coming of age of artificial intelligence in medicine. *Artificial Intelligence in Medicine*, 46(1), 5–17. 10.1016/j.artmed.2008.07.017

Poncette, A. S., Mosch, L., Spies, C., et al. (2020). Improvements in patient monitoring in the intensive care unit: Survey study. *Journal of Medical Internet Research*, 22(6), e19091.

Puri, V., Kataria, A., Solanki, V. K., & Rani, S. (2022, December). AI-based botnet attack classification and detection in IoT devices. In *2022 IEEE International Conference on Machine Learning and Applied Network Technologies (ICMLANT)* (pp. 1–5). IEEE.

Ramezani, R., Zhang, W., Xie, Z., et al. (2019). A combination of indoor localization and wearable sensor-based physical activity recognition to assess older patients undergoing subacute rehabilitation: Baseline study results. *JMIR mHealth and uHealth*, 7(7), e14090.

Rani, S., Mishra, A. K., Kataria, A., Mallik, S., & Qin, H. (2023). Machine learning-based optimal crop selection system in smart agriculture. *Scientific Reports*, 13(1), 15997.

Rani, S., Pareek, P. K., Kaur, J., Chauhan, M., & Bhambri, P. (2023, February). Quantum machine learning in healthcare: Developments and challenges. In *2023 IEEE International Conference on Integrated Circuits and Communication Systems (ICICACS)* (pp. 1–7). IEEE.

Rey, F., Barzaghini, B., Nardini, A., et al. (2020). Advances in tissue engineering and innovative fabrication techniques for 3-D-structures: Translational applications in neurodegenerative diseases. *Cells*, 9(7), 1636.

Rodriguez, R. A., Lang, K., Gubern, M. A., et al. (2019). Stand-alone artificial intelligence for breast cancer detection in mammography: Comparison with 101 radiologists. *Journal of the National Cancer Institute*, 111(9), 916–922.

Rojas, M. E., Cabrera, M. E., Lin, C., et al. (2020). The System for Telementoring with Augmented Reality (STAR): A head-mounted display to improve surgical coaching and confidence in remote areas. *Surgery*, 167(4), 724–731.

Sadeghi, A. H., Taverne, Y., Bogers, A., et al. (2020). Immersive virtual reality surgical planning of minimally invasive coronary artery bypass for Kawasaki disease. *European Heart Journal*, 41(34), 3279.

Salah, M., Tayebi, L., Moharamzadeh, K., et al. (2020). Three-dimensional bio-printing and bone tissue engineering: Technical innovations and potential applications in maxillofacial reconstructive surgery. *Maxillofacial Plastic and Reconstructive Surgery*, 42(1), 18.

Salmas, M., Chronopoulos, E., & Chytas, D. (2020). Comment on: "A Novel Evaluation Model for a Mixed-Reality Surgical Navigation System: Where Microsoft HoloLens Meets the Operating Room". *Surgical Innovation*, 27(4), 421–422.

Secinaro, S., Calandra, D., Secinaro, A., et al. (2021). The role of artificial intelligence in healthcare: A structured literature review. *BMC Medical Informatics and Decision Making*, 21, 125. 10.1186/s12911-021-01488-9

Seger, C., & Cannesson, M. (2020). Recent advances in the technology of anesthesia. *F1000Research*, 9, F1000 Faculty Review-375.

Skelley, N. W., Smith, M. J., Ma, R., et al. (2019). Three-dimensional printing technology in orthopedics. *Journal of the American Academy of Orthopaedic Surgeons*, 27(24), 918–925.

Stefanelli, L. V., Mandelaris, G. A., Franchina, A., et al. (2020). Accuracy evaluation of 14 maxillary full arch implant treatments performed with da Vinci bridge: A case series. *Materials*, 13(12), 2806.

Stefano, G. B. (2017). Robotic surgery: Fast forward to telemedicine. *Medical Science Monitor*, 23, 1856.

Stoel, B. C. (2019). Artificial intelligence in detecting early RA. *Seminars in Arthritis & Rheumatism*, 49(3S), S25–S28.

Sun, C., Zhang, Y., Chang, Q., & Others. (2020). Evaluation of a deep learning-based computer-aided diagnosis system for distinguishing benign from malignant thyroid nodules in ultrasound images. *Medical Physics*, 47(9), 3952–3960.

Sun, M. L., Zhang, Y., Peng, Y., et al. (2020). Accuracy of a novel 3D-printed patient-specific intramedullary guide to control femoral component rotation in total knee arthroplasty. *Orthopaedic Surgery*, 12(2), 429–441.

Sun, R., Limkin, E. J., Vakalopoulou, M., et al. (2018). A radiomics approach to assess tumor-infiltrating CD8 cells and response to anti-PD-1 or anti-PD-L1 immunotherapy: An imaging biomarker, retrospective multicohort study. *Lancet Oncology*, 19(9), 1180–1191.

Tae, K. (2020). Robotic thyroid surgery. *Auris, Nasus, Larynx*, 48(3), 331–338.

Tanwar, R., Chhabra, Y., Rattan, P., & Rani, S. (2022, September). Blockchain in IoT networks for precision agriculture. In *International Conference on Innovative Computing and Communications: Proceedings of ICICC 2022*, Volume 2 (pp. 137–147). Singapore: Springer Nature Singapore.

Tomita, K., Nagao, R., Touge, H., et al. (2019). Deep learning facilitates the diagnosis of adult asthma. *Allergology International*, 68(4), 456–461.

Vidal, L., Kampleitner, C., Brennan, M. A., et al. (2020). Reconstruction of large skeletal defects: Current clinical therapeutic strategies and future directions using 3D printing. *Frontiers in Bioengineering and Biotechnology*, 8, 61.

Wang, Y., Meng, D., Sun, X., et al. (2020). A prospective study of da Vinci surgical robotic system with chest wall external nursing interventions. *Chinese Journal of Lung Cancer*, 23(6), 487–491.

Winder, A., Strauss, D. C., Jones, R. L., et al. (2020). Robotic surgery for gastric gastrointestinal stromal tumors: A single center case series. *Journal of Surgical Oncology*, doi: 10.1002/jso.26053.

Wu, X., Liu, R., Yu, J., et al. (2018). Mixed reality technology launches in orthopedic surgery for comprehensive preoperative management of complicated cervical fractures. *Surgical Innovation*, 25(4), 421–422.

Xie, Q., Liu, Y., Huang, H., & et al. (2020). An innovative method for screening and evaluating the degree of diabetic retinopathy and drug treatment based on artificial intelligence algorithms. *Pharmacological Research*, 159, 104986.

Xing, F., Xiang, Z., Rommens, P. M., et al. (2020). 3D bioprinting for vascularized tissue-engineered bone fabrication. *Materials (Basel)*, 13(10), 2278.

Yamaguchi, J. T., & Hsu, W. K. (2019). Three-dimensional printing in minimally invasive spine surgery. *Current Reviews in Musculoskeletal Medicine*, 12(4), 425–435.

Yoshida, S., Sugimoto, M., Fukuda, S., et al. (2020). Mixed reality computed tomography-based surgical planning for partial nephrectomy using a head-mounted holographic computer. *International Journal of Urology*, 26(6), 681–682.

Zeiger, J., Costa, A., Bederson, J., et al. (2020). Use of mixed reality visualization in endoscopic endonasal skull base surgery. *Operative Neurosurgery (Hagerstown)*, 19(1), 43–52.

Zhao, Y., Liang, C., Gu, Z., et al. (2020). A new design scheme for intelligent upper limb rehabilitation training robot. *International Journal of Environmental Research and Public Health*, 17(8), 2948.

Zhou, F., Xue, F., & Zhang, S. (2020). The application of 3D printing patient specific instrumentation model in total knee arthroplasty. *Saudi Journal of Biological Sciences*, 27(5), 1217–1221.

Zuo, S., & Yang, G. Z. (2017). Endomicroscopy for computer and robot assisted intervention. *IEEE Reviews in Biomedical Engineering*, 10, 12–25.

10 Application of Artificial Intelligence in Resource-Poor Healthcare

P. Priyanga, N. C. Naveen, and K. R. Pradeep

10.1 INTRODUCTION

First formulated in 1956 by John McCarthy, Artificial Intelligence (AI) comprises machines that can accomplish tasks that are distinctive to the humanoid intelligence along with the capacity to acquire without being specially programmed. AI involves processing, recognizing, understanding, planning, problem-solving, and learning. Machine Learning (ML) techniques are in which machines can learn on their own. This can be achieved without being clearly automated. ML is a functionality of AI which delivers a structure to learn and progress the analysis from knowledge automatically. ML algorithms can be generated by assimilating the input and output of a code (Reese et al., 2017). The differences between AI-Expert Systems and ML-Machine Intelligence are as in Table 10.1.

10.1.1 Chapter Learning Objective

The Healthcare industry has been a bit slow to accept ML for several valid reasons, but in the near future, ML will transform healthcare. This is possible by systematically applying ML to leverage unstructured data that is available as blood tests, biopsy results, vital signs, medical histories, medicine histories, images, genomic profiles, epidemiological data, physician notes, and even medical research papers. AI, Cognitive Learning (CL), and Deep Learning (DL) are composed to restructure the world by developing tools that can use both structured and unstructured data to generate relationships, rules, and patterns. ML is already applied to telecommunication, retail, financial services, entertainment, and transportation businesses (Bhambri et al., 2020). Users can experience the application of ML daily in the form of targeted online advertisements, etc. ML can be applied in HcA to diagnose, predict outcomes, provide follow-up, tailor treatments, and can make healthcare more intelligent, efficient, safe, and cost-effective for all. The prospective application of AI and ML in the healthcare industry is significant and substantial with the data available. The main objective of this chapter is to identify the challenges to applying AI and ML techniques from developers and researchers to implement and provide technology

DOI: 10.1201/9781003395416-10

TABLE 10.1

Differences - AI and ML

SI. No	AI-Expert Systems	ML-Machine Intelligence
1	AI is well-defined as the capacity to gain and put on knowledge	ML is characterized as the pursuit of skill or knowledge
2	Increase the chances of success as compared to the accuracy	Increase of accuracy as compared to the success
3	A program that can do smart work	Takes the data and learns from it
4	Simulates natural intelligence that solves a complex problem	Learn from data on a specific task to achieve the attainment
5	Used for decision-making	Learn new things from data
6	Mimic humans that can respond and behave to circumstances	Create self-learning algorithms
7	Finds the optimal solution	Finds the solution and analyses, whether it is optimal or not
8	Passes on the intellect and wisdom	Passes on the knowledge

infrastructure, storage capacity and processing that will enable them to create ML solutions.

10.2 BACKGROUND AND SUMMARY

AI systems are being used in healthcare organizations and are quickly transforming both administrative and medical procedures (Omar Ali et al., 2023). This shift shows how crucial AI is to many procedures, especially those in medicine that deal with early detection and diagnosis. Previous research suggests that AI may improve the standard of care provided in the healthcare sector. AI-based technologies are said to enhance the quality of human existence by making it simpler, safer, and more productive (Rani, S., Pareek, P. K., Kaur, J., Chauhan, M., & Bhambri, P., 2023, February).

In order to make medical judgements, particularly in the management of health services, including predictive analysis for patient diagnosis and treatment, it is necessary to apply AI to the field of health services (Sri Sunarti et al., 2021). The difficulties include promoting early acceptance, long-term deployment in the healthcare system, disregard for the user's perspective, and inefficient use of technology despite the necessity for the adoption of AI in the public health sector. Safety, efficacy, privacy, information and consent, the freedom to choose, "the right to try," costs and access are some of the ethical issues that AI clinical applications face (Dhanoa and Bhambri, 2020).

In the field of computer science known as AI, robots are given the ability to be programmed to carry out intelligent tasks that are typically performed by humans (Tsang et al., 2020). Through delicately designed algorithms, computers and other machines use AI techniques to comprehend, analyze, and learn from data. For instance, using today's AI technology, cameras can recognize faces automatically, computers can translate between languages, it is simple to search for and identify things in e-commerce, computers can help doctors with decision-making, and so on (Sasubilli et al., 2020).

Big data encompasses tasks like acquiring information from enormous datasets and organizing, analyzing, and processing it in order to perform different operations on it. Although working with data remains a challenge, computing has gained value (Kataria, A., Agrawal, D., Rani, S., Karar, V., & Chauhan, M., 2022). The job of big data systems is to handle a lot of data. As a result, it has a variety of techniques that allow it to work with these variously structured and stored data. Big Data heterogeneity, timeliness, scale, privacy, and complexity issues impede all phases of ML's ability to extract value from data. The problems start initially from the data acquisition stage itself when from the large dataset, it is required to make decisions in an ad hoc manner. Understanding the data, maintaining, rejecting, or reliably saving the data, and producing appropriate metadata are the real research challenges with the data set. Another major challenge is that the data available on the Web will not be in a structured format. Examples include blogs and messages that are not adequately structured texts, while videos and images are maintained and structured for display and storage, but not for semantic content and search (Kumar, P., Banerjee, K., Singhal, N., Kumar, A., Rani, S., Kumar, R., & Lavinia, C. A., 2022). Changing this content to a properly structured format for future reference or research is a significantly challenging work. Data linking techniques are used to bring together data from different sources to create a new richer dataset that is helpful in improving the value (Bali, V., Bali, S., Gaur, D., Rani, S., & Kumar, R., 2023). Currently, on the Web, data is available in digital format, and facilitating and creating a link for the data have a lot of opportunities and equally is challenging work. Most linking techniques in healthcare can combine records from different records if they refer to the same entity. (An entity may be a patient, organization, geographic region, etc.) A few other real challenges are analyzing the data, retrieving, organizing and modeling that is due to the complexity of the data and lack of scalability of the algorithms that need to be analyzed.

Wei Fan and Albert Bifet have identified 3-V in Big Data Mining (Wei Fan et al., 2012):

1. Volume: Web has a larger amount of data than in the past, and the size of the data is rapidly growing, but the tools currently available can process a small amount of data available.
2. Variety: Various types of data are currently accessible in the form of text, video, audio, graph, GPS, sensor data, and many more with the advent of IoT.
3. Velocity: A large set of data is available in real-time as data streams, but current research is only interested in getting useful and selective data.

Nowadays, there are more Vs getting added, such as:

4. Variability: The user wants to use the data in various structures.
5. Value: It is possible to form decisions based on answering the questions which were not measured possible previously. This provides value to the business for an organization with compelling advantages.

The advancement in ML techniques can assist the Web Analytics (WA) in finding the exciting patterns, but the challenge is still open in the areas like:

1. Data from multiple sources: This requires understanding various datasets available on the Internet.
2. Data format: The data may come from different sources and hence in different formats and different languages.
3. Data preparation: The collected data must be prepared for analytics.
4. Data security: The collected and prepared data must be secured and must satisfy confidentiality, integrity, and availability.

There are several Big Data, Data Mining (DM), and Warehouse tools accessible in the market but these tools are not just right for tasks such as

1. Association: Finding relationships among different data.
2. Classification: Identifying and arranging data into a set of groups created on a few similar features of the data.
3. Clustering: Identifying and presenting visually, the facts which were unnoticed and not recognized before.
4. Forecasting: Finding data patterns that can provide sensible predictions.

The research challenge is to tackle these classical problems in WA and build a novel solution to find exciting patterns by harnessing the streams from the real-time Web (Kaur, D., Singh, B., & Rani, S., 2023).

10.3   CURRENT PERSPECTIVE

The Internet is majorly used, rapidly growing and is the largest data storage platform. The Internet became the main source of information because of its diversity and magnitude of data. As data format and web content are highly diverse, the accuracy of data is dependent on Web Mining (WM) algorithms. Current Internet usage is as follows: Google handles 1 billion queries in a day. Twitter gets 250 million messages in a day (Kataria, A., Puri, V., Pareek, P. K., & Rani, S., 2023, July). Facebook and YouTube get views of 800 million and 4 billion, respectively. More than 90% of web data has been created in the past couple of years, and every year data growth is estimated at 40%, and it is measured in zettabytes (Rani, S., Mishra, A. K., Kataria, A., Mallik, S., & Qin, H., 2023). The main reason behind this is that the Internet is readily available around the world, and every single person and company generates a lot of data every day (Dhanalakshmi, R., Vijayaraghavan, N., Sivaraman, A. K., & Rani, S., 2022). In a decade, the Internet has evolved and plays a major role in day-to-day activities like shopping, reading the newspaper, and seeking information and services provided by governments and enterprises. This has helped web marketing to grow rapidly in many developed countries and investment in web advertisements have grown big compared to television and newspaper. This growth is going to continue and is evident for the significance of the Internet (Sharma et al., 2020).

In 2005, 11.5 billion estimated pages were present on the Web; as of today, this is estimated at around 100 billion pages, and the growth rate is faster than Moore's law. The number of pages is doubling every eight months and, as a result generating a large quantity of data with rapidly developing value.

The current healthcare system is a highly interconnected network with various clinical and administrative healthcare professionals generating complex data from various systems and medical equipment. Further expansion of the Web helped to create a web-based Personal Health Record concept, and this gives lifelong health information accessible to people. Researchers and clinicians can access this health information using various tools to provide necessary vital aspects such as the patient's health condition, various test details of patients, human resources, medical unit coordination, etc. Currently, healthcare and the medical field are facing problems such as increasing medical expenses, aging factor, and the rise of chronic patients, hence requirements for providing excellent medical services are much needed. The aging population in many developed countries causes a shortage of medical resources and healthcare, leading to the difference between people's demand for healthcare and available medical resources. To address this demand a new medical service system needs to be created and information technologies started to play a major role in improving and creating a central service system. The healthcare community started to take the necessary steps to adopt and develop medical care using information technologies. National Health Information Infrastructure has introduced a blueprint to establish national healthcare infrastructure in three aspects: public health, personal health, and medical institution (Bilal, M., Kumari, B., & Rani, S., 2021, May; Tanwar, R., Chhabra, Y., Rattan, P., & Rani, S., 2022, September). To improve the healthcare system, a large amount of peer-patient information should be exchanged, and this process will help the patients and also provide medical knowledge for the moderators. The healthcare system is required to deliver quality, better access, and continuous care of patients with low investment and operation costs in infrastructures and technology.

In the past few years, there have been significant developments in how ML can be used in various industries and research. Many ML techniques have been applied in the field of healthcare, among which classification is the predominant one. In the realm of medicine, classification techniques are frequently used to analyze patient data and produce a predictive model or set of association rules. Researchers have utilized a hybrid intelligent system to introduce a unique form of classification of medical data based on the hybrid combinatorial structure of the Fuzzy max-min neural network, and the data classification is done using the Random forest. This methodology is put into effect on a variety of datasets together with Breast Cancer and primary immunodeficiency disorder (PIDD) that performed better compared to other existing methods.

1. A better diagnosis of diabetes was proposed by (Pradeep K R et al., 2016) predicting the blood glucose level. The proposed methodology demonstrates that the Support Vector Machine provides superior accuracy and illustrates that the performance and accuracy of the disease prediction are affected by the data set's pre-processing (Pradeep K R et al., 2013). Early

Diagnosis of diabetes disease with less cost is always preferable and showed that the J48 algorithm is noted for its accuracy.

2. Naïve Bayes weighted approach technique was used to advance a decision aid function for the heart disease prediction system proposed by (P. Priyanga et al., 2017). The adoption of this method will help doctors make better decisions and give quality views. These systems used a weighted approach technique to increase the accuracy of prediction.

3. ML techniques have been widely used in diverse areas such as education, pharmacy, manufacturing sectors, business, and engineering as described by (Zahra Beheshti et al., 2013). Currently, in the medical epidemic analysis field, ML can be used to select a proper architecture and learning algorithms that can provide better efficiency. ML is a convoluted task, but current, effective learning algorithms are available which can play a powerful role in enhancing accuracy and performance.

By applying AI and ML techniques, it is possible to bring high quality and efficiency improvements in delivering improved healthcare. Victoria Espinel, president, and CEO of BSA, says AI has the potential to enhance health outcomes by 30% to 40%, according to predictions by 2020. It was also mentioned that by giving healthcare professionals new insights into the vast amounts of available data, AI and ML will lead to better outcomes for their decision-making. "AI tools are powering machine-assisted diagnosis, and surgical applications are being used to improve treatment options and outcomes," testified Espinel. Pathologists are using image analysis algorithms to properly evaluate patient data and assist doctors in giving patients better care (Rana et al., 2020).

Research in the fields of biomedicine and epidemiology has advanced significantly as a result of the power of machine learning algorithms to handle enormous amounts of data and uncover intriguing patterns from many sources. AI and ML are significantly applied in the medical imaging field, and neuroradiologists are using these techniques to find genetic markers in MRI scans and predict brain tumors. Researchers from Stanford have developed algorithms that can diagnose 14 different types of medical conditions and can diagnose pneumonia from medical images. Memorial Sloan Kettering Cancer Center is working on images that can improve the diagnosis of prostate cancer. ML algorithms can help radiologists gain more information with efficiency to cope with rising patient healthcare requirements.

10.4 ADVANCES IN ML

An extensive set of ML algorithms are established towards framing the models and attain methods for analysis. Based on the learning method, these algorithms can be classified as:

10.4.1 INSTANCE-BASED ALGORITHMS (I-BA)

This is a decision type problem amongst the incidences of training data that are dynamic to the model. These types of approaches are regularly collected through training data and then evaluate test data and build a prediction model called as lazy learner. This prediction model basically accumulates the training data and delays till it caters with the test data (Kaur et al., 2020). So, an indolent learner accepts a compact period in training, and then additional time in forecasting. Stanford researchers have created popular I-bA algorithms capable of diagnosing 14 distinct medical diseases and identifying pneumonia from medical photos. Memorial Sloan Kettering Cancer Centre is developing imaging to enhance the detection of prostate cancer.

10.4.2 Clustering Algorithms

Clustering involves classification of data into similar groups, and every subset permits a frequently limited regular attribute, correlated to a limited specific distance matrix. General clustering techniques are Hierarchical Clustering, k-Means, Expectation-Maximization (EM) and k-Medians.

10.4.3 Regression Algorithms

These algorithms process by generating the association among variables which continually advances via error rate in predictions. The mission of predicting the value of a regularly fluctuating variable includes most popular algorithms such as Logistic Regression Multivariate Adaptive Regression Splines (MARS), Locally Estimated Scatterplot Smoothing (LOESS) and Stepwise Ordinary Least Squares Regression (OLSR).

10.4.4 Decision Tree Algorithms

These algorithms convey classification techniques and regression techniques by effectively partitioning the dataset. Here the unconditional target values reinforced by the decision trees are fast and accurate with a widespread choice associated to ML. The popular decision tree algorithms are Decision Stump and Conditional Decision Trees, Chi-squared Automatic Interaction Detection (CHAID), ID3 along with C4.5 and C5.0 algorithm, Classification and Regression Tree (CART) algorithm.

10.4.5 Artificial Neural Network Algorithms (ANN)

The ANN model utilizes supervised learning techniques, created based on the structure of Genetic Neural Networks (GNN) having a weighted interrelationship in the intermediate units. This is also known as parallel distributed processing networks that include algorithms such as Hopfield Network, Radial Basis Function Network (RBFN) and Back-Propagation.

10.4.6 Deep Learning Algorithms

DL methods are a new improvement towards ANN that takes the lead of gainful design and develops complex neural networks. DL algorithms include Deep Belief

Network (DBN), Stacked Auto encoders, Convolutional Neural Network (CNN), and Restricted Boltzmann Machine (RBM).

10.4.7 ENSEMBLE ALGORITHMS

Ensemble algorithms are dependent upon unsupervised learning that splits the training data into subsets of the data base on which self-governing learning models are created. The popular ensemble algorithms are AdaBoost, Random Forest, Gradient Boosting Machines (GBM), Bootstrapped Aggregation, Stacked Generalization (blending), Bagging, Boosting, and Gradient Boosted Regression Trees (GBRT).

10.5 FUTURE TRENDS

Data analysis is an actual challenge in application as well as presenting the results by domain experts who do not have technical knowledge. These challenges require advanced research in Big Data that gives a good overview with a future forecast, especially in the field of healthcare. Other substantial work in Big Data instituted in many of the conferences or journals specified to "DM and KDD" or "ML" show that the following research is still required.

1. Scalable BD Structure: Twitter data experienced (Jimmy Lin et al., 2012) gives clear facts about infrastructures of Big Data that provide the experience of analyzing the Twitter data. The author indicates that this is not straightforward, and it is difficult to perform analytics due to the lack of DM tools available currently. It is also indicated that preparing the application of DM methods and changing pilot models into efficient results consumes most of the time.
2. Mining Heterogeneous Information Networks (MHIN): An Organizational Analysis Method (Yizhou Sun et al., 2010), shows promising new research for Big Data is mining HIN. The work considers structured, unstructured, and semi-structured HIN. These semi-structured HIN models influence the ironic interpretation of captured links and nodes in a grid in revealing exciting information (Puri, V., Kataria, A., Solanki, V. K., & Rani, S., 2022, December).
3. Big Graph Mining (BGM): Procedures and findings (U Kang et al., 2012), present mining big graphs, usage of the Pegasus tool, and the work shows approximately interesting results in Twitter and Web Graph. This research work gives research directions for future work in big graph mining.

10.6 USE CASES CHALLENGES RELATING TO ML IN HEALTHCARE

The challenges of ML in the field of healthcare comprises

1. Designing an extensive and receptive computational architecture for ML appropriate for healthcare.

2. Ability to determine, build, and distinguish the exclusiveness of data in advance of administering ML algorithms and tools.
3. It requires the ability to simplify the data and to learn several levels with the combination of learning.
4. Scope to attain numerical base development with Structured Prediction through obstinate implication.

Substantial ML techniques such as association rule learning, ensemble learning, large-scale recommender systems, and Natural Language Processing (NLP) are still undergoing scalability complications. The serious problems raised to enable ML systems that are unsuitable for determining the Big Data classification are

1. Training on a specified dataset based on ML methods, are not suitable for alternate dataset, here, classification efficacy may not be more useful over dissimilar types of datasets.
2. With the existing Big Data having numerous learning tasks followed ML techniques is not suitable.
3. Training on a certain number of class types is generally followed by ML techniques.

Conventional algorithms in ML typically don't scale to BD. The key intricacy deceits with memory limitations. Despite the fact that the algorithms normally assume that training data trials survive only within primary memory where BD doesn't succeed into it. The normal approach of getting knowledge on a vast dataset is done by data distribution. Here by varying the batch size on the exclusive training dataset is done through separate calculations proceeding to the discrete subgroups. Based on this, training the different prediction models surrenders the precision. The other approach is done over online learning, where memory usage doesn't count on dataset size. Correspondingly, distributed learning and online learning are no more adequate for learning BD division due to resulting challenges as stated below:

1. More important uncertainty relates to data size, which is adaptable to online or dispersed learning. Sequential online learning on BD requires a significant amount of training time on a specific system. Contrarily, distributed learning for the large quantity of machines, limits down the accomplished efficiency for each machine and modifies the complete performance.
2. Linking instantaneous training and prediction has no more been considered for the BD. Where BD operated once is being kept in the distributed storage, as an outcome of it, the learning process approves of the attempt provided in the batch technique.

The future challenge for researchers is to develop medical imaging ML algorithms that can create a technology infrastructure that can support intensive unstructured data that is currently available. The major problem in these algorithms needs a considerable amount of computing power and storage performance. Applications using machine learning (ML) must prevent "GPU starvation," which happens when a processor malfunctions because it cannot access the necessary data. Currently, the amount of computing power required by ML algorithms is increasing rapidly, and the computing power delivered by GPUs has increased by a factor of 10. The main challenge for an organization is to develop ML applications that can have a significant impact on efficiency and quality in healthcare.

To summarize the following are some of the scope, services and benefits for healthcare if ML is applied

1. Internet in clinics will have positive support to patients and can also be used for better communications
2. Doctors at urban referral hospitals can respond quickly to consultation requests from the remote health workers
3. Doctors can plan and diagnose the same way as a remote healthcare worker
4. Doctors from the same or different country need not physically visit the remote locations but can help healthcare workers efficiently
5. Primary care and specialists can use live interactive video for better treatment
6. Use of store and forward communication of diagnostic pictures, very important signs, and video clips in conjunction with patient information can be done efficiently
7. Remote patient monitoring as well as consumer health &medical information
8. The Internet and wireless devices are used by patients to access specialized health information and engage in online team discussions to provide peer-to-peer assistance.

10.7 CONCLUSION

Current healthcare research agonizes from decreasing achievement rates, and hence Big Data and ML with useful analytics could be a key element and are being accepted across the industries as well as pharmaceuticals. It is projected that handling Big Data strategies leads to good decision-making where it could generate up to $100 billion in the healthcare structure, and ML is playing an integral role in the field of medical diagnostics. The trials are to enhance the innovation, improve the efficiency of clinical trials and research, and build novel tools for physicians, consumers, etc.

In the healthcare industry, data growths are generated from several sources, and effectively using this data will help organizations to identify better and develop a predictive model of being successful that is safe and effective. Many ML diagnostic applications fall under Chatbots that use AI with speech recognition ability that can identify patterns in patient symptoms for better diagnosis and provide appropriate treatment. The challenge to organizations is to create value-based healthcare that can optimize clinical, financial, and technical operations since patient's data include structured data, unstructured data, high-definition 3D medical images, and videos. Organizations should secure patient data which is generated by including biometric readings, safety medical devices, or wearable activity trackers. They also need to simplify storage architecture that is flexible enough to manage Big Data with proper backup performance. Researchers are using DL algorithms to recognize and develop models that are comparable to physicians. Machine vision and other ML technologies can enhance clinicians to diagnose rare diseases. Organizations have to create a better infrastructure that is flexible and supports performance, advanced data analytics, use of private, hybrid, or public clouds, and changing clinical workflows.

REFERENCES

Bhambri, P., Sinha, V.K., & Dhanoa, I.S. (2020). Diabetes prediction with WEKA Tool. Journal of Critical Reviews, 7(9), 2366–2371.

Bilal, M., Kumari, B., & Rani, S. (2021, May). An artificial intelligence supported E-commerce model to improve the export of Indian handloom and handicraft products in the World. In *Proceedings of the International Conference on Innovative Computing & Communication (ICICC)*.

Bali, V., Bali, S., Gaur, D., Rani, S., & Kumar, R. (2023). Commercial-off-the shelf vendor selection: A multi-criteria decision-making approach using intuitionistic fuzzy sets and TOPSIS. Operational research in engineering sciences: Theory and applications.

Dhanalakshmi, R., Vijayaraghavan, N., Sivaraman, A. K., & Rani, S. (2022). Epidemic awareness spreading in smart cities using the artificial neural network. In AI-centric smart city ecosystems (pp. 187–207). CRC Press.

Dhanoa, I.S., & Bhambri, P. (2020). Traffic-aware energy efficient VM migrations. Journal of Critical Reviews, 7(19), 177–183.

Jimmy Lin, & Dmitriy, Ryaboy (2012). Scaling big data mining infrastructure: The Twitter experience. ACM SIGKDD ExplorationsNew York, USA, 14(2), 6–19.

Kataria, A., Agrawal, D., Rani, S., Karar, V., & Chauhan, M. (2022). Prediction of blood screening parameters for preliminary analysis using neural networks. In Predictive modeling in biomedical data mining and analysis (pp. 157–169). Academic Press.

K R Pradeep & Dr. Naveen N C (2016). Predictive analysis of diabetes using J48 algorithm of classification techniques. In *2nd International Conference on Contemporary Computing and Informatics (IC3I), Noida, India*.

K R Pradeep, & Dr. Naveen N C (2013). A collective study of Machine Learning (ML) algorithms with Big Data Analytics (BDA) for Healthcare Analytics (HcA). International Journal of Computer Trends and Technology (IJCTT), 47(3), 149–155.

Kaur, K., Dhanoa, I.S., Bhambri, P., & Singh, G. (2020). Energy saving VM migration techniques. Journal of Critical Reviews, 7(9), 2359–2365.

Kataria, A., Puri, V., Pareek, P. K., & Rani, S. (2023, July). Human activity classification using G-XGB. In *2023 International Conference on Data Science and Network Security (ICDSNS)* (pp. 1–5). IEEE.

Kaur, D., Singh, B., & Rani, S. (2023). Cyber security in the metaverse. In Handbook of research on ai-based technologies and applications in the era of the metaverse (pp. 418–435). IGI Global.

Kumar, P., Banerjee, K., Singhal, N., Kumar, A., Rani, S., Kumar, R., & Lavinia, C. A. (2022). Verifiable, secure mobile agent migration in healthcare systems using a polynomial-based threshold secret sharing scheme with a Blowfish algorithm. Sensors, 22(22), 8620.

Omar Ali, Wiem Abdelbaki, Anup Shrestha, Ersin Elbasi, Mohammad Abdallah Ali Alryalat, Yogesh K Dwivedi (2023). A systematic literature review of artificial Intelligence in the healthcare sector: Benefits, challenges, methodologies, and functionalities. Journal of Innovation & Knowledge, 8(2023), 100333, *Published by Elsevier Espana*, 10.1016/ j.jik.2023.100333, pp. 1–19.

Priyanga, P. & Naveen, N. C. (2017). Web analytics support system for prediction of heart disease using Naïve Bayes weighted approach (NBwa), Paper presented *IEEE - Eleventh Asia International Conference on Mathematical Modelling and Computer Simulation, AMS2017, Malaysia.*

Puri, V., Kataria, A., Solanki, V. K., & Rani, S. (2022, December). AI-based botnet attack classification and detection in IoT devices. In *2022 IEEE International Conference on Machine Learning and Applied Network Technologies (ICMLANT)* (pp. 1–5). IEEE.

Rana, R., Chhabra, Y., & Bhambri, P. (2020). Comparison of clustering approaches for enhancing sustainability performance in WSNs: A study. In *Proceedings of the International Congress on Sustainable Development through Engineering Innovations* (pp. 62–71). ISBN 978-93-89947-14-4.

Rani, S., Mishra, A. K., Kataria, A., Mallik, S., & Qin, H. (2023). Machine learning-based optimal crop selection system in smart agriculture. Scientific Reports, 13(1), 15997.

Rani, S., Pareek, P. K., Kaur, J., Chauhan, M., & Bhambri, P. (2023, February). Quantum machine learning in healthcare: Developments and challenges. In *2023 IEEE International Conference on Integrated Circuits and Communication Systems (ICICACS)* (pp. 1–7). IEEE.

Reese, H (2017). Understanding the differences between AI, machine learning, and deep learning, from https://www.techrepublic.com/article/understanding-the-differences-Between-ai-machine-learning-and-deep-learning.

Sasubilli et al. (2020). Machine learning implementation on medical domain to identify disease insights using TMS. In *The International Conference on Advances in Computing and communication Engineering* (pp. 1–4).

Sharma, R., Bhambri, P., & Sohal, A.K. (2020). Mobile adhoc networks. Journal of Composition Theory, 13(2), 982–985.

Sri Sunarti, Ferry Fadzlul Rahman, Muhammad Naufal, Muhammad Risky, KresnaFebriyanto, RusniMasnina (2021). Artificial intelligence in healthcare: Opportunities and risk for future. *Published by Elsevier Espana*, 10.1016/j.gaceta.2020.12.019 *Gaceta Sanitaria, Volume 35, Supplement 1, 2021*, Pages S67-S70.

Tsang et al. (2020). Application of machine learning to support self-management of asthma with mHealth. In *The 42nd Annual International Conference of the IEEE Engineering in Medicine & Biology Society* (pp. 5673–5677).

Tanwar, R., Chhabra, Y., Rattan, P., & Rani, S. (2022, September). Blockchain in IoT networks for precision agriculture. In *International Conference on Innovative Computing and Communications: Proceedings of ICICC 2022, Volume 2* (pp. 137–147). Singapore: Springer Nature Singapore.

U Kang, & Christos, Faloutsos (2012). Big graph mining: Algorithms and discoveries. ACM SIGKDD Explorations, New York, USA, 14(2), 29–36.

Wei Fan, & Albert Bifet (2012). Mining Big Data: Current status, and forecast to the future. ACM SIGKDD Explorations, New York, USA, 14(2), 1–5.

Yizhou Sun, Xifeng Yan & Philip, S. Yu (2010). Mining knowledge from databases: An information network analysis approach. In *ACM SIGMOD International Conference on Management of data. Indiana, USA.*

Zahra Beheshti, SitiMariyamH, Shamsuddin, EbrahimBeheshti, & Siti Sophiayati Yuhaniz (2013). Enhancement of artificial neural network learning using centripetal accelerated particle swarm optimization for medical diseases diagnosis. Soft Computing Berlin, Germany, 18(11),2253–2270.

11 Artificial Intelligence and Internet of Things (IoT) Facilitated Digital Twin for Industry 4.0 Application Domains

Rachna Rana and Pankaj Bhambri

11.1 INTRODUCTION

11.1.1 DIGITAL TWIN

Digital Twin (DT) expertise is the procedure of building a numerical copy of a corporal object (e.g., car, building, city). The digital double simulates the processes that a physical object goes through and predicts how it will perform in different environments. A Digital Twin algorithm uses real data and leading-edge knowledge such as an Artificial Intelligence (AI) and Internet of Things (IoT), and information analytics to analyze a product or process's performance and make more precise predictions.

A Digital Twin typically includes additional information (hardware firmware type, hardware conformation, correction, setpoint evidence, etc.). With enough information, a DT can suggest customized keys based on each user's unique history and statistics. Physical assets are linked to sensors that collect information about operating conditions and real-time status or location in order to create a DT. The sensor data is analyzed along with industrial and contextual information. DT expertise requires a strong digital philosophy.

By gradually implementing the technology and testing, companies can assist engineers and analysts in adopting this new approach. The DT is constantly restructured with the most conversant data, and can be modified as required. Industry 4.0 is a game-changer that promises to revolutionize the manufacturing industry through the use of leading-edge technologies. Nevertheless, there are several challenges that must be overcome so as to successfully apply Industry 4.0.

One of the main constraints is the large investment needed in leading-edge base imitation and technologies. For smaller businesses or those with limited budgets, this can be a challenge. Industry 4.0 also necessitates a high-skilled workforce with

DOI: 10.1201/9781003395416-11

digital expertise. This means that employees need to be trained or new employees need to be hired to fill these roles.

Another restriction is the rising danger of imitation-attacks on online data brought on by the expansion of Internet-connected products and systems. Therefore, putting Industry 4.0 into practice calls for robust well-being measures to safeguard private information and property rights. Industry 4.0 also depends on dependable and quick communication networks, but not all businesses have admittance to the mandatory base, which might make implementation tough (Kaur, D., Singh, B., & Rani, S., 2023).

Businesses may think about integrating Industry 4.0 into the sub-production process to get around these constraints. This strategy starts with small-scale deployments to gather knowledge and experience before extending to bigger businesses. Investments in training and retraining programs for the workforce can also aid in the development of the abilities and proficiency essential to help and affirm Industry 4.0 expertise. Finally, organizations may lessen the dangers involved in data collecting and analysis by putting robust data protection and data well-being processes in place.

IoT expertise is used in intelligent workshops to link diverse equipment, gadgets, and sensors to a main network. This minimizes downtime and improves the production process. An Industry 4.0 description of the production procedure that is more effective, flexible, and acceptable is known as an intelligent factory. Companies may sustain their competitiveness under challenging market conditions in this way. With the help of interconnected equipment, systems, and devices, manufacturing procedures are automated, adaptable, and more efficient in an intelligent factory (Rani, S., Pareek, P. K., Kaur, J., Chauhan, M., & Bhambri, P., 2023, February).

This makes it possible for smart workshops to scrutinize and manage numerous parts of the production process using IoT devices. For instance, networked devices may supply real-time data on their location and routines, while sensors can creatively scrutinize temperature, humidity, and pressure. AI and appliance acquiring procedures can be utilized to examine the resultant data in order to find trends and improve production procedures (Evangeline & Anandhakumar, 2020, p. 49).

11.1.2 AI AND IoT

Smart workshops use IoT devices to advance developments, moderate slowdown, and protect currency in the downriver progression. IoT gadgets can perceive fluctuations in progressions and attentive labour to possible security menaces, counteracting misfortunes and damages. This can be predominantly convenient in engineering productions that comprise dangerous constituents or thick mechanisms. Conversely, handling and integrating a large number of IoT campaigns can be stimulating. It wants dedicated proficiency and substantial possessions to confirm that the campaigns are correctly organized and sustained. Furthermore, IoT devices are vulnerable to imitation-attacks, which can conciliation the truthfulness of the engineering procedure and subtle information. This is especially concerning given that hackers may target IoT devices as an entry point to access a larger network (Dhanalakshmi, R., Anand, J., Sivaraman, A. K., & Rani, S., 2022).

Additionally, unlike IoT, campaigns use different message resolutions, making it hard to add them into a sole classification. To address this, manufacturers need to use specialized software and hardware to ensure that the devices can communicate effectively with each other. This can be a significant investment, but the benefits of a fully integrated IoT system can be substantial. Finally, IoT strategies create an immense amount of information, which can be irresistible to accomplish and analyze. Manufacturers need to use advanced analytics tools and techniques to gain insights from this data and make informed decisions. This can include using appliance acquiring methods to identify patterns and trends in the data, which can help constructors enhance procedures, diminish charges, and improve creation quality (Fuller et al., 2020, p. 91).

Intelligent workshops have revolutionized the manufacturing industry by incorporating Industry 4.0 sensor expertise to measure various production process conditions and parameters. These sensors are capable of detecting factors such as hotness, clamminess, heaviness, and other neighbouring situations to ensure optimal efficiency and productivity. By gathering and analyzing data in actual period, intelligent workshops can speedily recognize and criticize any issues that may arise, leading to reduced downtime and increased output. Overall, the integration of these advanced technologies has enabled workshops to operate with greater precision and accuracy, ultimately resulting in a more streamlined and efficient production process (Rachna et al., 2020).

IoT sensors have become an integral part of smart workshops. These beams can be used to scrutinize the entire production process, including the handling of natural resources, construction stages, and the final product. By collecting real-time data, manufacturers can get a detailed insight into their production efficiency and product quality. This information enables them to identify areas that require improvements and optimize their processes accordingly. Moreover, it provides manufacturers with the ability to predict and prevent potential malfunctions, thereby reducing downtime and maintenance costs. Overall, IoT sensors have revolutionized the manufacturing industry by providing a comprehensive and detailed view of the production process. (Rachna et al., 2021).

IoT sensors play a crucial role in predictive maintenance by detecting and analyzing data from machines to predict when maintenance will be necessary. By utilizing IoT beams, productions can avoid unexpected machine failures, which can lead to costly downtime. Additionally, IoT beams can be used to scrutinize the engineering climate and identify probable well-being threats or data well-being breaches. This information can be used to identify areas that need enhancement and to take upbeat measures to prevent well-being breaches (Rana, 2018; Rana et al., 2019). The integration of a network of connected sensors and machines has revolutionized the way industries operate. One of the key benefits of this technological advancement is the enhanced safety it provides for workers, equipment, and assets (Kaur, G., Kaur, R., & Rani, S., 2015).

By leveraging a network of interconnected sensors and machines, companies can scrutinize and analyze information in actual time period, allowing them to identify potential safety hazards and take necessary precautions to prevent accidents. For instance, if a machine is operating outside of its normal parameters, the network can automatically shut down the machine or trigger an alert to notify a technician to take immediate action (Rani, S., & Gupta, O. P., 2017).

Moreover, this expertise also provides greater protection for equipment and assets. The network can scrutinize the condition of equipment and assets in real time, allowing companies to proactively identify issues before they become major problems that could lead to costly repairs or replacements. In summary, the integration of a network of connected sensors and machines has transformed the way industries operate by providing enhanced safety measures and increased protection for valuable equipment and assets (Fuller et al., 2020, p. 13-43).

As the engineering productions evolves, it is becoming increasingly decisive for businesses to optimize their production processes to remain competitive. One key way to do this is through enhanced connectivity and coordination, which can lead to greater efficiency and productivity while minimizing waste and downtime. By leveraging the power of the IoT, manufacturers can track inventory, manage supply chains, and make informed decisions regarding production and distribution (Rachna et al., 2022). This can result in reduced downtime, lower costs, and improved productivity. Industry 4.0 has brought about a new era of manufacturing, where expertise plays a critical role in driving efficiency and quality control (Singh, P., Gupta, O. P., & Saini, S., 2017). By implementing power-protecting modes, beams, and software program, constructers can harness the power of connected devices to strengthen effectiveness, growth throughput, and boost superiority method. With the wealth of information gathered through intelligent and machine learning analysis, plant managers can optimize production processes, minimize downtime, and ensure quality control. In summary, the integration of IoT expertise and Industry 4.0 principles can help manufacturers achieve greater efficiency, productivity, and quality control while reducing costs and minimizing downtime (Ghosh et al., 2019, p. 133).

Predictive maintenance is a proactive maintenance strategy that utilizes IoT expertise to scrutinize equipment performance and detect potential faults and failures. In smart workshops, this approach is used to minimize unintentional interruption by recognizing and addressing issues before they lead to equipment breakdowns. By collecting and analyzing information from measuring device connected on apparatus and production equipment, predictive maintenance systems can find configurations and movements that show probable questions, such as uncharacteristic sensations or warmth revolutions (Gupta, O. P., & Rani, S., 2013).

This enables maintenance teams to take corrective action before failures occur, reducing the risk of costly downtime and improving overall equipment effectiveness (Rana et al., 2021a; Rana et al., 2021b). Incorporating IoT-enabled sensors into manufacturing equipment enables factory managers to predict and prevent equipment failures, thus facilitating the development of effective maintenance schedules (Rani, S., Arya, V., & Kataria, A., 2022). This advanced expertise allows for the avoidance of downtime, ultimately enhancing the efficiency and productivity of the manufacturing process (Guo et al., 2020, p. 156-163).

The IoT has proven to be versatile and useful in various fields, including inventory management, energy management, and asset tracking. In smart workshops, IoT devices allow for a connected and computerized location that licences actual period scrutinizing, scrutiny, and resistor of construction progress (Gupta, O. P., & Rani, S., 2010). By combining blockchain expertise with imitation well-being industries, we can improve blockchain applications in intelligent engineering, contributing to the development of Industry 4.0. Sustainable smart manufacturing also looks into exploring IoT and arterial intelligence to create imitation-physical manufacturing networks (Ivanov & Dolgui, 2020, p. 65).

Research is exploring the use of smart manufacturing technologies to enhance the production process for advanced parts in IoT manufacturing (Rani, S., & Gupta, O. P., 2016). Resolution maintenance procedures for smart workshops using the IoT are being developed through big data analysis in green manufacturing (Kataria, A., Puri, V., Pareek, P. K., & Rani, S., 2023, July). The study of intelligent workshops in the Industry 4.0 era aims to improve the throughput of fragment construction. The Industry 4.0 intelligent production system is being examined to deliver presentations to the IoT in forward-thinking engineering and to enhance the proficiency of part production (Javaid et al., 2023, p. 89).

This study aims to create an imitation well-being system that is reliable and efficient for scrutinizing information visualization and automated guided vehicle (AGV) status. It uses an IoT architecture based on deep neural networks. The study also explores the potential of using IoT and deep learning technologies to detect and repair faults in short-circuit motors. Additionally, the study investigates the use of IoT platforms and neural network deep learning algorithms to prevent computer numerical control (CNC) mechanical imitation-attacks through online scrutinizing systems (Rani, S., & Kaur, S., 2012). Lastly, the study explores how convolutional neural networks can be used for disease detection and classification, to increase the productivity of tomato cultivation (Gupta, O., Rani, S., & Pant, D. C., 2011). The language used in the study is kept simple and familiar, with an emphasis on clear communication (Karadeniz et al., 2019, p. 66–77).

We are currently investigating the use of Bash Bunny as a means of filtering military and police units without the need for privilege escalation (Kothandaraman, D., Manickam, M., Balasundaram, A., Pradeep, D., Arulmurugan, A., Sivaraman, A. K., & Balakrishna, R., 2022). This is to improve network well-being against imitation-attacks. Additionally, we are exploring the use of a robust Kalman strainer to improve the well-being of positioning automated vehicles against various imitation-attacks (Kenett& Bortman, 2021, p. 45–65).

11.2 CHALLENGES OF AI AND IoT FACILITATED DT FOR INDUSTRY 4.0

The application of the DT is widespread, including in the automobile, alternative solutions, and power generating industries. It has provided solutions for issues including improving racing performance and emissions testing. In order to enhance staffing and processes, it is also utilized in hospital modelling (Knapp et al., 2017). The DT is a potent tool that lets users build a digital clone of a real system or product. The design, performance information, and maintenance history of the original device are all included in this duplicate. Users can investigate a variety of options to enhance product processes, increase a product's lifespan, develop new goods, and test prototypes by utilizing this DT.

The ability to design and test programs programmatically is one of the main benefits of utilizing a DT. Due to the lack of reliance on actual implementation, users are able to test various solutions and simulate various scenarios. This can help identify possible problems early on and save time and resources.

DTs can be utilized for performance improvement and predictive maintenance in addition to enhancing product development and testing. Users may enhance performance based on real-time information by keeping an eye on the DT and seeing possible problems before they become serious. A valuable tool for enhancing product development, testing, and maintenance, DTs are being used more often across a wide range of businesses (Kochhar, 2023, p. 74).

Companies have a serious difficulty when it comes to the safety and correct training of new personnel. Although safety and skill-related content is covered in class, it might not be contextually relevant enough for new hires to completely understand their new workplace. In addition, busy activities and noise in a plant or factory might restrict onsite training by making it difficult to visit particular areas or ask questions (Rani, S., Bhambri, P., & Chauhan, M., 2021, October).

DTs, however, provide a novel approach to this problem. DTs allow new hires to get acclimated to their new workplace without putting themselves in danger or having their job interrupted. The actual setting in which they will be using their abilities can be better understood by new employees by traversing the DT and completing pertinent training material. This gives them the assurance and under-standing of their surroundings they need to begin their new career (Li et al., 2022, p.67).

Space planning may be a difficult and complicated procedure in the manufac-turing sector. The way in which space is used can be greatly affected by changes, such as the addition of new machinery or adjustments to workflow. Traditional planning techniques, including simple floor plans, diagrams, and images, do not always give the degree of precision needed for the best planning, which might result in mistakes or errors.

Expertise developments have made it feasible to circumvent these difficulties, nevertheless. You may now attain dimensional precision and a photorealistic perspective of your production plant with the aid of DTs. You can map asset layouts, construction projects, and compliance with important Occupational Safety and Health Administration (OSHA) rules like smoke alarms, fire extinguishers, and automated external defibrillator (AED) thanks to this expertise. This guarantees that your facility is secure and complies with all applicable laws.

Through connections and tags, DTs also facilitate collaborations by enabling other users to study and record the information required to make crucial choices (Rani, S., Kumar, S., Kataria, A., & Min, H., 2023). With the use of this expertise, you can see your facilities in a more precise and thorough manner, which may assist you in seeing future problems and making wise decisions. Utilizing DTs will help you design your space more effectively and make sure that your manufacturing facility is secure, effective, and legal (Liu et al., 2022, p. 67).

- **Maintenance and repair challenge:** Unforeseen breakdowns of machinery can cause process delays and loss of revenue. Locating and scheduling repairs, however, may be made easier by directly integrating asset repair information, manuals, and other paperwork into each DT. By integrating DTs with IoT-connected devices, predictive maintenance information can be obtained outside of the physical context, enabling you to plan and schedule repairs proactively (Lünnemann et al., 2023, p. 78).
- **Remote site visits challenge:** Effective communication and conversant information transfer are crucial in the global footprint of many organizations. However, this can be challenging to achieve between different locations. Sending a DT of the manufacturing floor to important stakeholders would promote alignment throughout your firm, which would solve this challenge. As a result, there is no longer a need for costly travel or bringing documents or pictures. Decision-makers may easily view virtual models of the manufacturing line and fully comprehend the area around it using their mobile devices (Rani et al. 2023).
- **Tours and guests challenge:** It's always great to welcome guests who are enthusiastic and invested in what you do. However, it's crucial to maintain a balance between allowing visitors to explore your space and minimizing potential distractions, disruptions, and risks. To address this concern, an immersive 3D digital replica of your space can be created, enabling guests and caterers to experience it on any device, including virtual reality (VR), without actually having to be there. This provides a genuine experience for your guests without having to schedule visits to the production area (Ritu et al. 2023, February 17).

11.3 BENEFITS OF AI AND IoT FACILITATED DT FOR INDUSTRY 4.0

- **Real-time remote scrutinizing:** Real-time comprehension of a complicated physical system might be difficult to ascertain in its entirety. The idea of "DTs" is helpful in this situation. A DT, which offers real-time information and analytics, is essentially a virtual version of a physical system. With DTs, users may access and track the operation of the physical system from a distance, learning about its behaviour, forecasting its future performance, and seeing possible faults before they turn into major concerns. Large and sophisticated systems need continual scrutinizing and maintenance in fields like aerospace, manufacturing, and healthcare; hence, this expertise is very helpful in such fields (Malini et al., 2023, p. 89).
- **Assess risk and accelerate production time:** DTs are virtual representations of actual systems, procedures, or goods. Before a product or process is created or put into use, engineers and designers may detect and evaluate any possible problems or flaws in it using real-time information and simulations. Engineers may optimize designs, save on expenses and time spent developing a product or process, and raise the calibre of the finished

item or process by constructing a precise digital model of it and simulating its behaviour. In sectors where safety and dependability are crucial, including aerospace, automotive, and healthcare, this expertise is being employed more and more (Mandolla et al., 2019, p. 67). Engineers can tamper with the system to test the system's response, create contingencies, and determine conforming justification policies. It enhances threat calculation, speeds up the improvement of new products and improves production line reliability.

- **Better team collaboration:** In today's fast-paced world, technicians need to focus on both collaboration and efficiency to stay ahead of the competition. By having 24/7 access to system information and automating processes, technicians can streamline their work and devote more time to team collaboration. This allows them to share ideas, identify and solve problems more efficiently, and ultimately improve overall operational effectiveness. With the help of advanced expertise, technicians can achieve optimal results and drive success for their organizations.
- **Predictive maintenance:** DT systems utilize IoT sensors that generate vast amounts of real-time information. Companies can analyze this information to proactively identify system issues, enabling them to plan more accurately for predictive maintenance. This enhances production line efficiency and reduces maintenance costs.

11.4 APPLICATION DOMAINS OF AI AND IoT FACILITATED DT FOR INDUSTRY 4.0

A simulated mock-up of a warehouse, facility, equipment, invention, or organization is referred to as a product digital duplicate. When operators can see the essential integrated system information coupled with the actual physical space occupied, it helps them make decisions and improves operations. This is made possible by DT expertise, which offers real-time views of production facilities. A 3D digital double offers an immersive digital depiction of real space, from machinery to the factory floor layout, for the industrial sector. DTs for productions enable access to locations for planning, tours, and training without posing any well-being or disruption concerns or necessitating any trip (Mohammadi & Taylor, 2021, p. 202-210).

The first engineering rebellion was glimmered by strengthening supremacy and methodisation at the beginning of the 19th century. Twenty years later, we are in the midst of Industry 4.0, a digital revolution that blends digital dual modelling, augmented reality, the IoT, and appliance acquiring to boost industrial output and automate a number of crucial procedures. Approximately 69% of respondents in the industrial industry said they have smart expertise efforts, according to a 2022 poll by the expertise consultancy firm ISG (Rani, S., Kataria, A., Kumar, S., & Tiwari, P., 2023). In addition, over two-thirds of respondents said businesses are employing smart manufacturing to cut expenses. Teams may access a visual DT that models one physical place at a time using Matterport. Your DTs can advance by offering real-time information and significant insights into your industrial operations when coupled with

IoT sensors. Together, these cutting-edge technologies assist businesses in auto-mating manufacturing procedures and optimizing safety (Moiceanu & Paraschiv, 2022, p. 132).

11.4.1 USE CASES OF DT IN PRODUCTION

DT helps increase productivity and efficiency. DT can also reduce downtime, streamline onsite production processes, and help you gain better visibility into the physical assets you are responsible for. Five applications of DT in manufacturing are listed below (Murata et al., 2022, p. 43):

- Training without hazardous risks
- Field inspection quality
- Easy access to monitor and organize field information
- Inspection and international tour.
- Virtual tours and reception waiting for guests

11.4.2 APPLICATIONS

DT expertise is used in fabricating and it can be functional to multi-fold disparate diligence. Below are some of the DT applications that have set new standards in various industries (Murata et al., 2022, p. 341-360). These are the following applications:

Manufacturing: DTs can simulate the entire production process in detail. It can help optimize internal processes such as manufacturing and product design when applied to production. A DT allows a troupe to precisely augur the coming address of an affair or process. This way, the manufacturer can identify flaws in the design before production begins, which can save them a lot of money (Su et al., 2022, p. 38).

Energy: Since DT uses real information to run simulations, it is easier to optimize energy production and consumption. The expertise uses real-world information to identify growing energy needs and identify machines that may be consuming too much energy. This, of course, leads to optimization of energy requirements and reduced operating costs (Su et al., 2022, p. 73).

Automotive: Traditionally, the automotive industry is heavily involved in product development and testing. We all have problems when automakers have to pull millions of vehicles off the market because of a single design flaw, costing them billions of dollars. DT expertise can help prevent damage before production starts, effectively reducing production costs. In addition, it can help identify bottlenecks in operations and reduce development time (Sit & Lee, 2023, p. 141).

- **Logistics Supply chain management:** This can also be a real nightmare, especially if the company employs thousands of people in different workshops. Even for the best manager, making sure the flow of materials and people is always in optimal condition is an impossible task. DT expertise can help by administering miniatures in disparate scripts. He can spot problems throughout the entire supply chain and suggest solutions to increase efficiency and improve overall decision-making.

- **Smart Cities:** The use of DTs can aid in making cities more sustainable by guiding planning decisions and providing solutions to common urban challenges.
- **Healthcare:** DTs have proven to be invaluable in the field of medical services. They have shown exceptional benefits in zones such as surgical exercise, voice input, and peril minimization during surgeries. In addition, the system is capable of modelling the movement of people throughout the hospital and identifying potential infection hotspots, thus enabling healthcare professionals to take necessary actions to prevent the spread of infections.
- **Production:** DT is being used in various industries like construction and retail to improve efficiency and consumer proficiency.
- **Catastrophe Supervision:** Universal temperature modification variation has exaggerated the sphere in modern years. Consequently, DTs can help resolve this problem by generating smarter base, temperature variation scrutinizing and danger answer devices.

DTs are computer programs that collect information from the real world to build models that can forecast how well a process or product will function. To increase efficiency, these systems can combine software analytics, AI, and IoT. These virtual models are now a crucial component of the newest technologies to spur innovation and boost performance thanks to developments in appliance acquiring and big information. Essentially, developing one makes it possible to advance key technological trends, eliminates expensive failures of physical items, and makes use of extrapolative abilities, amenities, high-level analytics, challenging practises, and scrutinizing (Thapliyal, 2022, p. 199-233).

An IoT device's working dynamics and physical components can be virtually represented by the DT. It's more than just a strategy. It is not only a picture. It goes beyond "virtual reality" goggles. It is a cybernetic depiction of the dynamics and elements that affect how an IoT scheme answers through its lifespan. There are a lot of things, including buildings, industry operations, jet engines, etc. Digital replicas are simply computer programs that take information from the actual world to build simulations that forecast how a process or product will behave. To increase performance, these programs can combine software analytics, AI, and IoT (Trauer et al., 2021, p. 196).

These virtual models are now an essential component of the newest technologies to promote innovation and boost performance thanks to developments in machine learning and big information. To put it simply, it develops a tool that enhances strategic technological trends, prevents expensive physical item failures, and makes use of cutting-edge predictive, service, analytics, process inspection, and supervision (Wang et al., 2021, p. 51).

11.5 CONCLUSION

DTexpertise involves a complicated process of collecting, analyzing and simulating information. Sensors and other devices can be used by manufacturers to gather real-time information about the status of a process or a product. The information is then processed and analyzed using IoT sensors to generate a virtual representation. DTs can be used to create cybernetic imitations of any equipment, tool, product, process or anything else that a manufacturer would like to improve at the factory. Machine learning algorithms can analyze the information generated by these DTs to gain insight into the behaviour of the assets in the real world and make decisions that improve the company's performance. To sum up, DTs are an essential part of Industry 4.0. They allow manufacturers to build virtual replicas of their assets, optimize processes and make real-time decisions based on information. As DTs continue to develop, they will likely continue to play an increasingly significant role in manufacturing and beyond.

Geopolitical tensions, technical advancements, shifts in international markets, and the effects of temperature variations are just a few of the problems that the industrial world is facing today. To solve these issues, digitization and automation are paradigm-shifting technologies. The large quantity of information created by the Industrial IoT must be gathered, understood, and used. This is precisely what digital commerce accomplishes by merging the physical and digital worlds. Through the use of DTs, the corporeal machineries and operational dynamics of an IoT device may be represented virtually. It is more than just a map or a strategy. Not just a picture, however. More than "virtual reality" goggles are involved. The components and dynamics of how an IoT device behaves throughout its life cycle are virtually represented. There are several items, including manufacturing floor operations, buildings, and jet engines.

Businesses may add value, develop new income sources, and answer important strategic questions by working with digital twins. Organizations are starting a path to develop DTs with less effort and time than ever before due to new technological features, adaptability, capabilities, cost reduction, and flexibility. As more and more cognitive capacity is utilized, the potential for digital twins is virtually limitless. As a consequence, the digital twin is always acquiring new knowledge and skills, allowing one to continue to provide the data necessary to improve procedures, develop fresh ideas, and produce better goods in the future.

REFERENCES

Ammar, M., Haleem, A., Javaid, M., Walia, R., & Bahl, S. (2021). Improving material quality management and manufacturing organizations systems through industry 4.0 technologies. *Materials Today: Proceedings*, *45*, 5089–5096. 10.1016/j.matpr.2021.01.585

Bilberg, A., & Malik, A. A. (2019). Digital twin-driven human–robot collaborative assembly. *CIRP Annals*, *68*(1), 499–502. 10.1016/j.cirp.2019.04.011

Developing marketing strategies for cone ice cream: A case study of brand X ice cream Indonesia. (2022). *Asian Journal of Entrepreneurship*. 10.55057/aje.2022.3.3.3

Digital twin-driven smart human-machine collaboration: Theory, enabling technologies and applications. (2022). *Journal of Mechanical Engineering*, *58*(18), 279. 10.3901/jme. 2022.18.279

Dhanalakshmi, R., Anand, J., Sivaraman, A. K., & Rani, S. (2022). IoT-based water quality monitoring system using cloud for agriculture use. *Cloud and Fog Computing Platforms for Internet of Things*, *28*(3), 1–14.

Evangeline, P., & Anandhakumar. (2020). Digital twin expertise for "smart manufacturing". *Advances in Computers*, 35–49. 10.1016/bs.adcom.2019.10.009

Fuller, A., Fan, Z., Day, C., & Barlow, C. (2020). Digital twin: Enabling technologies, challenges and open research. *IEEE Access*, 8, 108952–108971. 10.1109/access.2020. 2998358

Ghosh, A. K., Ullah, A. S., & Kubo, A. (2019). Hidden Markov model-based digital twin construction for futuristic manufacturing systems. *Artificial Intelligence for Engineering Design, Analysis and Manufacturing*, 33(03), 317–331. 10.1017/s089006041900012x

Guo, D., Ling, S., Li, H., Ao, D., Zhang, T., Rong, Y., & Huang, G. Q. (2020). A framework for personalized production based on digital twin, blockchain and additive manufacturing in the context of Industry 4.0. In *2020 IEEE 16th International Conference on Automation Science and Engineering (CASE)*. 10.1109/case48305.2020.9216732

Gupta, O., Rani, S., & Pant, D. C. (2011). Impact of parallel computing on bioinformatics algorithms. In *Proceedings 5th IEEE International Conference on Advanced Computing and Communication Technologies* (pp. 206–209).

Gupta, O. P., & Rani, S. (2010). Bioinformatics applications and tools: An overview. *CiiT-International Journal of Biometrics and Bioinformatics*, 3(3), 107–110.

Gupta, O. P., & Rani, S. (2013). Accelerating molecular sequence analysis using distributed computing environment. *International Journal of Scientific & Engineering Research–IJSER*, 4(10), 262–265.

Ivanov, D., & Dolgui, A. (2020). A digital supply chain twin for managing the disruption risks and resilience in the era of Industry 4.0. *Production Planning & Control*, 32(9), 775–788. 10.1080/09537287.2020.1768450

Javaid, M., Haleem, A., & Suman, R. (2023). Digital twin applications toward industry 4.0: A review. *Cognitive Robotics*, 3, 71–92. 10.1016/j.cogr.2023.04.003

Karadeniz, A. M., Arif, I., Kanak, A., & Ergun, S. (2019). A digital twin of gastronomic things: A case study for ice cream machines. In *2019 IEEE International Symposium on Circuits and Systems (ISCAS)*. 10.1109/iscas.2019.8702679

Kataria, A., Puri, V., Pareek, P. K., & Rani, S. (2023, July). Human Activity Classification using G-XGB. In *2023 International Conference on Data Science and Network Security (ICDSNS)* (pp. 1–5). IEEE.

Kaur, D., Singh, B., & Rani, S. (2023). Cyber security in the metaverse. In *Handbook of Research on AI-Based Technologies and Applications in the Era of the Metaverse* (pp. 418–435). IGI Global.

Kaur, G., Kaur, R., & Rani, S. (2015). Cloud computing – a new trend in IT era. *International Journal of Scientific and Technology Management*, 1(3), 1–6.

Kenett, R. S., & Bortman, J. (2021). The digital twin in industry 4.0: A wide-angle perspective. *Quality and Reliability Engineering International*, 38(3), 1357–1366. 10. 1002/qre.2948

Knapp, G., Mukherjee, T., Zuback, J., Wei, H., Palmer, T., De, A., & DebRoy, T. (2017). Building blocks for a digital twin of additive manufacturing. *Acta Materialia*, 135, 390–399. 10.1016/j.actamat.2017.06.039

Kochhar, N. (2023). Leading the transformation in the automotive industry through the digital twin. *The Digital Twin*, 773–797. 10.1007/978-3-031-21343-4_27

Kothandaraman, D., Manickam, M., Balasundaram, A., Pradeep, D., Arulmurugan, A., Sivaraman, A. K., & Balakrishna, R. (2022). Decentralized link failure prevention routing (DLFPR) algorithm for efficient internet of things. *Intelligent Automation and Soft Computing*, 34(1), 655–666.

Li, J., Zheng, H., & Bao, J. (2022). Development of digital twin-based WEEE recycling workshop: Initial approaches and future challenges. In *2022 6th International Conference on Robotics and Automation Sciences (ICRAS)*. 10.1109/icras55217. 2022.9842043

Liu, S., Wang, X. V., & Wang, L. (2022). Digital twin-enabled advanced execution for human-robot collaborative assembly. *CIRP Annals, 71*(1), 25–28. 10.1016/j.cirp.2022. 03.024

Lünnemann, P., Fresemann, C., & Richter, F. (2023). The digital twin for operations, maintenance, repair and overhaul. *The Digital Twin,* 661–675. 10.1007/978-3-031-21343-4_23

Malini, A., Rajasekaran, U., Sriram, G., & Ramyavarshini, P. (2023). Industry 4.0: Survey of digital twin in smart manufacturing and smart cities. *Digital Twin for Smart Manufacturing,* 89–110. 10.1016/b978-0-323-99205-3.00013-4

Mandolla, C., Petruzzelli, A. M., Percoco, G., & Urbinati, A. (2019). Building a digital twin for additive manufacturing through the exploitation of blockchain: A case analysis of the aircraft industry. *Computers in Industry, 109,* 134–152. 10.1016/j.compind. 2019.04.011

Mohammadi, N., & Taylor, J. E. (2021). Thinking fast and slow in disaster decision-making with smart city digital twins. *Nature Computational Science, 1*(12), 771–773. 10.1038/s43588-021-00174-0

Moiceanu, G., & Paraschiv, G. (2022). Digital twin and smart manufacturing in industries: A bibliometric analysis focusing on industry 4.0. *Sensors, 22*(4), 1388. 10.3390/s22 041388

Murata, A., Doi, T., & Karwowski, W. (2022). Sensitivity of PERCLOS70 to drowsiness level: Effectiveness of PERCLOS70 to prevent crashes caused by drowsiness. *IEEE Access, 10,* 70806–70814. 10.1109/access.2022.3187995

Murata, A., Doi, T., & Karwowski, W. (2022). Effectiveness of tactile warning and voice command for enhancing the safety of drivers. *IEEE Access, 10,* 93854–93866. 10. 1109/access.2022.3204045

Rachna, C. Y., & Bhambri, P. (2020). Comparison of clustering approaches for enhancing sustainability performance in WSNSL a study. In *TEQIP-III sponsored International Conference on Sustainable Development Through Engineering Innovations* (pp. 62–71), ISBN: 978-93-89947-14-4.

Rachna, Bhambri, P., & Chhabra, Y. (2022). Deployment of distributed clustering approach in WSNs and IoTs. *Cloud and Fog Computing Platforms for Internet of Things,* 85–98. 10.1201/9781003213888-7

Rachna, Chhabra, Y., & Bhambri, P. (2021). Various approaches and algorithms for scrutiniseing the energy efficiency of wireless sensor networks. *Lecture Notes in Civil Engineering,* 761–770. 10.1007/978-981-15-9554-7_68

Rana, R. (2018, March). A Review of the evolution of Wireless sensor networks. *International Journal of Advanced Research Trends in Engineering and Technology (IJARTET), 5,* Special issue, March 2018, ISSN2394-3777 (Print), ISSN2394-3785 (Online), Available online at www.ijartet.com

Rana, R., Chhabra, Y., & Bhambri, P. (2019). A review on development and challenges in Wireless Sensor Networks. In *International Multidisciplinary Academic Research Conference (IMARC, 2019),* (pp. 184–188), ISBN: 978-81-942282-0-2.

Rana, R., Chhabra, Y., & Bhambri, P. (2021a). Comparison and evaluation of various QoS parameters in WSNs with the implementation of enhanced low energy adaptive efficient distributed clustering approach, Webology (ISSN: 1735-188X) Volume 18, Number 1, 2021.

Rana, R., Chhabra, Y., & Bhambri, P. (2021b). Design and development of distributed clustering approach in a wireless sensor network. Webology (ISSN: 1735-188X) Volume 18, Number 1, 2021.

Rani, S., & Gupta, O. P. (2016). Empirical analysis and performance evaluation of various GPU implementations of protein BLAST. *International Journal of Computer Applications, 151*(7), 22–27.

Rani, S., & Gupta, O. P. (2017). CLUS_GPU-BLASTP: Accelerated protein sequence alignment using GPU-enabled cluster. *The Journal of Supercomputing*, *73*, 4580–4595.

Rani, S., & Kaur, S. (2012). Cluster analysis method for multiple sequence alignment. *International Journal of Computer Applications*, *43*(14), 19–25.

Rani, S., Bhambri, P., & Chauhan, M. (2021, October). A machine learning model for kids' behavior analysis from facial emotions using principal component analysis. In *2021 5th Asian Conference on Artificial Intelligence Technology (ACAIT)* (pp. 522–525). IEEE.

Rani, S., Arya, V., & Kataria, A. (2022). Dynamic pricing-based e-commerce model for the produce of organic farming in India: A research roadmap with main advertence to vegetables. In *Proceedings of Data Analytics and Management: ICDAM 2021, Volume 2* (pp. 327–336). Springer Singapore.

Rani, S., Mishra, A. K., Kataria, A., Mallik, S., & Qin, H. (2023). Machine learning-based optimal crop selection system in smart agriculture. *Scientific Reports*, *13*(1), 15997.

Rani, S., Bhambri, P., & Kataria, A. (2023). Integration of IoT, big data, and cloud computing technologies. *Big Data, Cloud Computing, and IoT: Tools and Applications*.

Rani, S., Bhambri, P., Kataria, A., & Khang, A. (2023). Smart city ecosystem: Concept, sustainability, design principles, and technologies. In *AI-Centric Smart City Ecosystems* (pp. 1–20). CRC Press.

Rani, S., Pareek, P. K., Kaur, J., Chauhan, M., & Bhambri, P. (2023, February). Quantum machine learning in healthcare: Developments and challenges. In *2023 IEEE International Conference on Integrated Circuits and Communication Systems (ICICACS)* (pp. 1–7). IEEE.

Rani, S., Kumar, S., Kataria, A., & Min, H. (2023). SmartHealth: An intelligent framework to secure IoMT service applications using machine learning. *ICT Express*.

Rani, S., Pareek, P. K., Kaur, J., Chauhan, M., & Bhambri, P. (2023). Quantum Machine Learning in Healthcare: Developments and Challenges. In *Paper presented at the International Conference on Integrated Circuits and Communication Systems*, 1–7.

Rani, S., Kataria, A., Kumar, S., & Tiwari, P. (2023). Federated learning for secure IoMT-applications in smart healthcare systems: A comprehensive review. *Knowledge-Based Systems*, 110658.

Ritu, P., & Bhambri, P. (2023, February 17). Software Effort Estimation with Machine Learning – A Systematic Literature Review. In Editor(s) (Ed.), *Agile Software Development: Trends, Challenges and Applications* (pp. 291–308). John Wiley & Sons, Inc.

Singh, P., Gupta, O. P., & Saini, S. (2017). A brief research study of wireless sensor network. *Advances in Computational Sciences and Technology*, *10*(5), 733–739.

Sit, S. K., & Lee, C. K. (2023). Design of a digital twin in low-volume, high-mix job allocation and scheduling for achieving mass personalisation. *Systems*, *11*(9), 454. 10.3390/systems11090454

Su, S., Zhong, R. Y., & Jiang, Y. (2022). Digital twin and its applications in the construction industry: A state-of-art systematic review. *Digital Twin*, *2*, 15. 10.12688/digitaltwin. 17664.1

Thapliyal, K. (2022). Digital twin in healthcare present and future scope. *Digital Twins and Healthcare*, 69–87. 10.4018/978-1-6684-5925-6.ch005

Trauer, J., Pfingstl, S., Finsterer, M., & Zimmermann, M. (2021). Improving production efficiency with a digital twin based on anomaly detection. *Sustainability*, *13*(18), 10155. 10.3390/su131810155

Wang, Y., Cao, Y., & Wang, F. (2021). Anomaly detection in digital twin model. In *2021 IEEE 1st International Conference on Digital Twins and Parallel Intelligence (DTPI)*. 10.1109/dtpi52967.2021.9540116

12 AI-Driven Digital Twin and Resource Optimization in Industry 4.0 Ecosystem

Pankaj Bhambri, Sita Rani, Alex Khang, and Rashmi Soni

12.1 INTRODUCTION

It represents a cutting-edge exploration into the transformative convergence of artificial intelligence (AI), Digital Twins, and the Industry 4.0 revolution. At its core, this concept revolves around the idea that digital representations of physical assets, known as Digital Twins, enhanced and empowered by AI technologies, can usher in a new era of industrial excellence (Abrol et al., 2005; Bai et al., 2020; Bhambri et al., 2011). These Digital Twins, often virtual replicas of real-world objects or systems, harness AI's capabilities to simulate, monitor, and optimize their physical counterparts in real time (Bathla et al., 2007a, 2007b, Kothandaraman et al., 2022). Within the context of Industry 4.0, characterized by the pervasive digitization of industrial processes and the Internet of Things (IoT), this conceptual framework offers a structured approach to maximize the potential of AI-driven Digital Twins (Kumar et al., 2022a, 2022b). It spans diverse domains, from manufacturing to infrastructure management, predictive maintenance, and resource optimization, fundamentally changing how industries operate, innovate, and thrive in an increasingly digital and interconnected world. This concept reflects the transformative power of AI and Digital Twins as catalysts for the evolution of modern industry, pushing the boundaries of efficiency, sustainability, and competitiveness (Machała et al., 2022; Rani et al., 2023).

12.1.1 AI in Industry 4.0

AI is well used in Industry 4.0 and thus helpful for the AI-driven Digital Twin applications and resource optimization in the Industry 4.0 Ecosystem (Rani et al., 2022a-c). The closely associated relation between these terms is as elaborated below:

- Context of Industry 4.0: "AI in Industry 4.0" refers to the integration and utilization of AI technologies within the framework of Industry 4.0

 DOI: 10.1201/9781003395416-12

(Rani, S., Kataria, A., Kumar, S., & Tiwari, P., 2023). Industry 4.0 is characterized by the digitization and automation of industrial processes, emphasizing the use of advanced technologies for enhanced productivity, efficiency, and competitiveness (Kaur et al., 2006; Kamra & Bhambri, 2007; Jain & Bhambri, 2005; Habib & Chimsom, 2019).

- AI-Driven Digital Twins: "AI-driven Digital Twin and Resource Optimization in the Industry 4.0 Ecosystem" zooms in on a specific application of AI within the broader context of Industry 4.0. In this context, AI is applied to Digital Twins, which are virtual representations of physical assets or systems (Puri, V., Kataria, A., Solanki, V. K., & Rani, S., 2022, December; Bali, V., Bali, S., Gaur, D., Rani, S., & Kumar, R., 2023). These Digital Twins are enhanced by AI capabilities, allowing them to simulate, monitor, and optimize real-world assets in real time. This application is a key component of how AI contributes to Industry 4.0 (Gupta et al., 2007a–e; Goel & Gupta, 2020; Tanwar, R., Chhabra, Y., Rattan, P., & Rani, S., 2022, September).
- Resource Optimization: The chapter also highlights resource optimization, another critical aspect of Industry 4.0. By leveraging AI-driven Digital Twins, organizations can optimize the allocation of resources such as manpower, materials, energy, and equipment. This optimization is essential for achieving the efficiency and sustainability goals of Industry 4.0 (Garg & Bhambri, 2011a, 2011b; Ghobakhloo, 2020).
- Efficiency and Innovation: Both concepts share the common goal of enhancing efficiency, reducing costs, and fostering innovation within industrial processes. AI in Industry 4.0 and AI-driven Digital Twins contribute to achieving these objectives by enabling data-driven decision-making, predictive maintenance, and intelligent resource allocation (Grewal & Bhambri, 2006; Rani et al., 2021; Rattan et al., 2005a, 2005b).

In essence, "AI in Industry 4.0" provides the overarching context and framework for the application of AI-driven Digital Twins and resource optimization within the Industry 4.0 ecosystem. It underscores the transformative role of AI in reshaping industrial practices and driving advancements in the digital age.

12.1.2 DIGITAL TWIN TECHNOLOGY

Digital Twin Technology is very much effective for Resource Optimization in the Industry 4.0 Ecosystem. The closely associated relation is elaborated below:

- Foundation of Digital Twin Technology: Digital Twin Technology forms the basis for the concept of AI-driven Digital Twin. Digital Twin Technology involves creating virtual replicas or digital representations of physical assets, processes, or systems. These digital twins are updated in real time, reflecting the current state and behavior of their physical counterparts (Bhambri, 2010; Bhambri & Hans, 2010; Bhambri et al., 2010; Bhambri & Thapar, 2010; Bhambri and Hans, 2009; Dhanalakshmi et al., 2022).

- Enhanced by AI: In "AI-driven Digital Twin and Resource Optimization in the Industry 4.0 Ecosystem," Digital Twin Technology is taken a step further by incorporating AI. AI-driven Digital Twins are virtual representations enriched with AI capabilities. These AI-driven Digital Twins can analyze data, make predictions, and optimize operations in ways that traditional Digital Twins cannot (Chopra & Bhambri, 2011; Contreras et al., 2017; Bhambri et al., 2005a-c).
- Resource Optimization: AI-driven Digital Twins are central to the optimization of resources in the Industry 4.0 ecosystem. They can simulate and predict the performance of physical assets and processes, enabling organizations to allocate resources more efficiently. For example, AI-driven Digital Twins can optimize the allocation of manufacturing equipment or energy consumption based on real-time data and predictive analytics (Bhambri & Singh, 2005a-b; Bhambri & Gupta, 2007; Bhambri et al., 2007a-c; Chen et al., 2017).
- Real-Time Data Integration: Both Digital Twin Technology and AI-driven Digital Twins rely on real-time data integration. Digital Twin Technology captures and updates data from physical assets in real time to maintain an accurate representation. AI-driven Digital Twins take this a step further by using AI algorithms to analyze and interpret the data, providing actionable insights for resource optimization (Bhambri et al., 2008a-b; Cañas et al., 2021).
- Industry 4.0 Context: Both concepts are integral to the Industry 4.0 paradigm, which emphasizes the digitization and connectivity of industrial processes (Bilal, M., Kumari, B., & Rani, S., 2021, May). Digital Twin Technology and AI-driven Digital Twins contribute to achieving the goals of Industry 4.0 by enabling data-driven decision-making, predictive maintenance, and efficient resource allocation (Singh & Bhambri, 2007; Yadav et al., 2022).

Digital Twin Technology represents the initial step in creating digital representations of physical assets, and AI-driven Digital Twins enhance these representations with advanced AI capabilities for the optimization of resources and processes in Industry 4.0.

12.2 PREDICTIVE MAINTENANCE

Predictive Maintenance revolves around the proactive and data-driven approach to maintaining industrial machinery and equipment. In this framework, Predictive Maintenance utilizes AI-driven Digital Twins to continuously collect and analyze real-time data from sensors and IoT devices embedded within the machinery (Rani, S., Mishra, R. K., Usman, M., Kataria, A., Kumar, P., Bhambri, P., & Mishra, A. K., 2021). By harnessing the power of AI and advanced analytics, Predictive Maintenance models can predict when equipment is likely to fail or require maintenance well in advance of an actual breakdown. This enables organizations to schedule maintenance activities during planned downtime, reducing costly unscheduled downtime and preventing unexpected failures. Additionally, Predictive Maintenance optimizes resource allocation by ensuring that maintenance personnel, spare parts, and tools are available precisely when needed. Predictive Maintenance, as implemented within the framework of AI-driven Digital Twins and Industry 4.0, represents a paradigm shift in industrial maintenance practices. It harnesses the power of real-time data, AI, and predictive analytics to optimize maintenance activities, enhance asset reliability, reduce costs, and promote sustainability - a transformational approach that is at the forefront of modern industrial practices (Thapar & Bhambri, 2009).

In the broader context of Industry 4.0, Predictive Maintenance is a crucial component as it enhances operational efficiency, extends the lifespan of equipment, reduces maintenance costs, and contributes to overall competitiveness and sustainability. By proactively addressing maintenance needs using AI-driven Digital Twins, organizations can transform their maintenance practices from a reactive model to a proactive and data-driven one, reaping significant benefits in terms of reliability and cost savings (Bhambri & Gupta, 2005; Bhambri & Bhandari, 2005; Bhambri & Mangat, 2005; Chauhan & Rani, 2021).

12.2.1 DATA-DRIVEN MONITORING

Predictive Maintenance starts with the continuous and real-time monitoring of industrial equipment and assets. This monitoring is facilitated by a network of sensors and IoT devices that are embedded within machinery and connected to AI-driven Digital Twins. These sensors collect a wealth of data on various parameters, including temperature, pressure, vibration, and performance metrics.

12.2.2 AI AND MACHINE LEARNING

The collected data is then processed and analyzed using advanced AI and machine learning algorithms. AI-driven Digital Twins play a crucial role in this stage. These virtual replicas of physical assets incorporate AI models that can identify patterns, anomalies, and trends in the data. They learn from historical data and use this knowledge to make predictions about future equipment behavior.

12.2.3 CONDITION MONITORING

Predictive Maintenance continuously assesses the condition of machinery and assets in real time. By comparing current data with historical benchmarks and established thresholds, the AI-driven system can detect early signs of wear, degradation, or impending failure. For example, it can identify irregular vibrations in a motor that may indicate impending bearing failure.

12.2.4 PREDICTIVE ANALYTICS

The AI-driven system generates predictive insights based on the condition monitoring data. It can predict when a specific component or piece of equipment is likely to fail or require maintenance. These predictions are not calendar-based but are instead tailored to the actual condition and performance of the asset (Banerjee, K., Bali, V., Nawaz, N., Bali, S., Mathur, S., Mishra, R. K., & Rani, S., 2022).

12.2.5 PROACTIVE PLANNING

Armed with predictive insights, organizations can proactively plan maintenance activities. This involves scheduling maintenance during planned downtime periods when it is most cost-effective and least disruptive to operations. It also ensures that maintenance personnel have the necessary tools and spare parts ready.

12.2.6 COST REDUCTION AND EFFICIENCY

Predictive Maintenance offers significant cost savings by reducing unplanned downtime, preventing catastrophic failures, and optimizing resource allocation. It extends the lifespan of equipment, reduces maintenance costs, and enhances operational efficiency.

12.2.7 ASSET AVAILABILITY AND RELIABILITY

By predicting and preventing failures, Predictive Maintenance enhances the reliability and availability of critical assets. This is especially vital in industries like manufacturing and energy, where downtime can result in significant financial losses.

12.2.8 SUSTAINABILITY

Predictive Maintenance aligns with sustainability goals by reducing the consumption of resources associated with unscheduled repairs and replacements. It also minimizes waste and contributes to environmental responsibility.

12.3 REAL-TIME DATA ANALYTICS

Real-time data analytics is a critical component of the modern data-driven landscape, allowing organizations to process and derive insights from data as it is generated, enabling rapid decision-making and responsiveness. In real-time data analytics, data is collected, processed, and analyzed without delay, often within milliseconds or seconds of its generation. This capability is particularly valuable in industries such as finance, healthcare, manufacturing, and IoT, where timely insights can have a substantial impact. Real-time data analytics systems typically employ technologies like stream processing and complex event processing to handle high volumes of data swiftly. These systems can detect patterns, anomalies, and trends in real time, enabling organizations to respond to changing conditions, optimize operations, enhance customer experiences, and even prevent issues before they escalate. The importance of real-time data analytics continues to grow in the era of Industry 4.0 and digital transformation, where the speed and accuracy of decision-making are critical for success. Real-time data analytics can be used in AI-driven digital twin and Industry 4.0 in the following ways (Bhambri et al., 2009; Bhambri & Singh, 2009; Bhambri & Thapar, 2009; Saucedo-Martínez et al., 2018):

12.3.1 DATA COLLECTION AND INTEGRATION

In the context of Industry 4.0, numerous sensors and IoT devices continuously generate vast amounts of data from industrial equipment and processes. "Real-time Data Analytics" is essential for collecting, processing, and integrating this data into a usable format. This data forms the foundation for AI-driven Digital Twins, which rely on up-to-the-minute information about the physical assets they represent.

12.3.2 IMMEDIATE INSIGHTS

Real-time data analytics enables the rapid analysis of incoming data streams. AI-driven Digital Twins leverage this capability by processing the data in real time. As data is collected and integrated, AI algorithms within Digital Twins can immediately derive insights, detect anomalies, and identify patterns. These insights can then be used to make real-time decisions and optimizations.

12.3.3 PREDICTIVE AND PRESCRIPTIVE ANALYTICS

Beyond descriptive analytics, real-time data analytics in AI-driven Digital Twins extends to predictive and prescriptive analytics. Machine learning algorithms can predict future equipment behavior, identify potential maintenance needs, and prescribe actions to optimize resource allocation. For example, if a machine shows signs of impending failure, the system can proactively schedule maintenance to prevent downtime.

12.3.4 OPTIMIZING RESOURCE ALLOCATION

Resource optimization, a core theme in both concepts, is greatly empowered by real-time data analytics. AI-driven Digital Twins use real-time data to make informed decisions about resource allocation. This includes allocating labor, materials, energy, and machinery to maximize efficiency while minimizing costs and waste (Kataria, A., Puri, V., Pareek, P. K., & Rani, S., 2023, July).

12.3.5 ADAPTIVE AND RESPONSIVE OPERATIONS

In Industry 4.0, operations need to be adaptive and responsive to changing conditions. Real-time data analytics in AI-driven Digital Twins enables systems to adapt and make decisions on the fly. For instance, in manufacturing, production schedules can be adjusted in real time based on fluctuations in demand or unexpected equipment behavior.

12.3.6 Enhanced Efficiency and Competitiveness

The combination of real-time data analytics and AI-driven Digital Twins enhances efficiency, reduces operational costs, and fosters competitiveness. By making data-driven decisions in real time, organizations can optimize their processes and stay agile in a rapidly evolving industrial landscape.

Real-time Data Analytics provides the live data feed and analytical capabilities necessary for AI-driven Digital Twins to simulate, monitor, and optimize physical assets and processes in real time. These technologies together empower organizations to harness data for greater efficiency, sustainability, and competitiveness in the Industry 4.0 ecosystem.

12.4 SMART MANUFACTURING

Smart manufacturing is very effective for utilization with AI-Driven Digital Twin and Industry 4.0. These terms are intricately intertwined, representing a paradigm shift in industrial practices. Smart manufacturing, driven by the principles of Industry 4.0, leverages technologies like the IoT, real-time data analytics, and automation to create highly efficient and agile production systems. AI-driven Digital Twins play a pivotal role in this landscape by providing a virtual replica of physical assets and processes, enriched with AI capabilities. This dynamic duo enhances productivity and quality through real-time monitoring, predictive maintenance, and resource optimization. Smart manufacturing relies on AI-driven Digital Twins for their ability to simulate, predict, and optimize production operations in ways that were previously unimaginable. Together, they empower organizations to achieve unprecedented levels of efficiency, responsiveness, and competitiveness, reshaping the future of manufacturing in the digital age (Singh et al., 2010; Singh et al., 2006; Gupta & Bhambri, 2006).

12.4.1 Manufacturing Optimization

Manufacturing optimization is a critical facet of smart manufacturing, a transformative approach that leverages advanced technologies to enhance the efficiency, quality, and agility of industrial production processes (Rani, S., Kataria, A., Sharma, V., Ghosh, S., Karar, V., Lee, K., & Choi, C., 2021). Within the context of smart manufacturing, manufacturing optimization involves the systematic improvement of various aspects of the manufacturing process to achieve the best possible outcomes. Here are key aspects of manufacturing optimization within smart manufacturing:

- Data-Driven Decision-Making: Smart manufacturing relies heavily on real-time data acquisition and analysis. Sensors and IoT devices collect data from machinery and processes, and this data is used to make informed decisions. Manufacturing optimization leverages this data to identify areas where improvements can be made, such as reducing defects, minimizing downtime, or optimizing resource utilization.

- Predictive Maintenance: Predictive maintenance is a core component of manufacturing optimization. By using AI-driven analytics and models, smart manufacturing systems can predict when equipment is likely to fail or require maintenance. This allows organizations to schedule maintenance activities proactively, reducing unplanned downtime and minimizing disruptions to production.
- Resource Allocation: Efficient resource allocation is crucial for manufacturing optimization. Smart manufacturing systems can allocate resources such as labor, materials, and energy in real time based on current conditions and production demands. This ensures that resources are used optimally, reducing waste and maximizing productivity (Rani, S., Pareek, P. K., Kaur, J., Chauhan, M., & Bhambri, P., 2023, February).
- Quality Control: Quality control is a key focus of manufacturing optimization. Smart manufacturing systems can monitor product quality in real time, identifying defects or deviations from quality standards. This enables immediate adjustments to be made to production processes to maintain consistent product quality.
- Process Optimization: Manufacturing optimization involves continuous process improvement. Smart manufacturing systems analyze data to identify bottlenecks, inefficiencies, or areas where processes can be streamlined. This leads to more efficient production workflows and reduced lead times.
- Customization and Flexibility: Smart manufacturing allows for greater customization and flexibility in production. Manufacturing processes can be adapted quickly to produce different products or accommodate changing customer demands. This flexibility enhances responsiveness and competitiveness.
- Energy Efficiency: Resource optimization within smart manufacturing extends to energy usage. Systems can monitor and control energy consumption in real time, adjusting operations to minimize energy waste and reduce environmental impact.
- Cost Reduction: Ultimately, manufacturing optimization leads to cost reduction. By improving efficiency, reducing waste, and minimizing downtime, organizations can lower production costs and improve their bottom line.

Manufacturing optimization is at the core of smart manufacturing, driven by real-time data analytics, predictive maintenance, resource allocation, and process improvement. It empowers organizations to produce higher quality products more efficiently, respond quickly to changing market demands, and remain competitive in a rapidly evolving industrial landscape.

12.4.2 SUPPLY CHAIN MANAGEMENT

Supply chain management (SCM) is a critical component of smart manufacturing, playing a pivotal role in ensuring the efficient flow of materials, information, and products throughout the production process (Rani, S., Kataria, A., & Chauhan, M., 2022). Within the context of smart manufacturing, SCM is enhanced and transformed by advanced technologies, data-driven insights, and real-time coordination. Here are key aspects of SCM within smart manufacturing:

- Real-time Visibility: Smart manufacturing leverages IoT sensors and real-time data analytics to provide unprecedented visibility into the supply chain. This visibility allows organizations to track the location and status of raw materials, components, and finished products at every stage of production and distribution.
- Predictive Demand Planning: Data analytics and machine learning are used to predict demand patterns more accurately. This enables organizations to optimize inventory levels, reduce overstocking or under-stocking, and respond swiftly to changes in customer demand.
- Supplier Collaboration: Smart manufacturing fosters closer collaboration with suppliers. Through real-time data sharing and analytics, organizations can work closely with suppliers to ensure the timely delivery of materials and components, optimize pricing and quality, and reduce lead times (Rani, S., Kataria, A., Chauhan, M., Rattan, P., Kumar, R., & Sivaraman, A. K., 2022).
- Inventory Optimization: Real-time data analytics are used to optimize inventory levels. This includes identifying slow-moving or obsolete inventory and dynamically adjusting inventory levels to meet production demands while minimizing carrying costs.
- Transportation Management: Smart manufacturing extends real-time visibility to transportation and logistics. It allows organizations to track the movement of products, monitor transportation conditions (e.g., temperature for perishables), and optimize transportation routes for efficiency and cost savings.
- Quality Assurance: Smart manufacturing systems can monitor product quality in real time. This includes tracking quality metrics throughout the supply chain, identifying defects or deviations, and taking corrective actions swiftly to maintain quality standards.
- Traceability and Compliance: Traceability is enhanced through blockchain and other technologies, ensuring that the origin and journey of products can be tracked transparently. Compliance with regulatory requirements is also simplified and automated.
- Risk Management: Advanced analytics and AI-driven models help identify and mitigate supply chain risks. This includes assessing the impact of disruptions, such as natural disasters or geopolitical events, and developing contingency plans (Kumar, R., Rani, S., & Awadh, M. A., 2022).
- Sustainability: Smart manufacturing considers sustainability factors in supply chain decisions. This includes reducing waste, minimizing energy consumption in transportation, and selecting suppliers with eco-friendly practices.
- Agility and Responsiveness: Smart manufacturing enables a more agile and responsive supply chain. Organizations can adjust production schedules and sourcing decisions in real time to respond to unexpected events or changing market conditions.

SCM in smart manufacturing is about leveraging data, analytics, and technology to create a more transparent, efficient, and responsive supply chain. It enables organizations to optimize inventory, improve quality, reduce costs, and enhance their overall competitiveness in a rapidly evolving global marketplace (Rani, S., Mishra, A. K., Kataria, A., Mallik, S., & Qin, H., 2023).

12.5 SUSTAINABILITY IN INDUSTRY 4.0

Sustainability in Industry 4.0 is a compelling and essential concept that addresses the intersection of advanced technologies like AI-driven digital twins with the principles of environmental, economic, and social sustainability. Industry 4.0, characterized by the fusion of digital technologies with physical systems, has revolutionized manufacturing and industrial processes. AI-driven digital twins, in particular, play a pivotal role in this paradigm shift (Kataria, A., Agrawal, D., Rani, S., Karar, V., & Chauhan, M., 2022).

Digital twins are virtual replicas of physical assets or systems, utilizing real-time data from sensors and IoT devices to monitor, simulate, and optimize their real-world counterparts. When powered by AI, these digital twins become incredibly sophisticated, capable of predictive analytics, adaptive decision-making, and continuous improvement. This AI-driven approach in Industry 4.0 contributes significantly to sustainability in several ways (Kaur, D., Singh, B., & Rani, S., 2023).

Firstly, it enhances resource efficiency by optimizing operations, reducing waste, and minimizing energy consumption. AI-driven digital twins can predict equipment failures before they happen, allowing for preventive maintenance, which not only reduces downtime but also conserves resources. Additionally, they optimize production processes by fine-tuning parameters and managing supply chains, thereby reducing energy and material usage.

Secondly, sustainability is improved through better product design and lifecycle management. AI-driven digital twins enable companies to design products with environmental impact in mind from the start, facilitating eco-friendly materials selection and efficient manufacturing processes. Moreover, they provide insights into the entire product lifecycle, enabling companies to extend product life, recycle components, and reduce waste generation (Rani, S., Bhambri, P., & Kataria, A., 2023).

Furthermore, these advanced digital twins support sustainability by enhancing safety in the workplace. They can simulate potentially hazardous situations, allowing for risk assessment and the development of safety protocols, ultimately reducing accidents and their associated environmental and human costs. Sustainability in Industry 4.0, with the integration of AI-driven digital twins, is a multifaceted approach. It optimizes resource usage, promotes eco-friendly product design, extends product lifecycles, and enhances workplace safety. As businesses increasingly adopt these technologies, they not only improve their bottom line but also contribute to a more sustainable and environmentally responsible industrial landscape. It demonstrates the powerful synergy between technology and sustainability, reinforcing the idea that the future of industry must be both smart and green. Sustainability in Industry 4.0, particularly in the context of AI-driven digital twins and Industry 4.0, can be classified into several key categories (Bhambri & Singh, 2008a-c; Bhambri & Nischal, 2008a-b).

12.5.1 Resource Efficiency

AI-driven digital twins help optimize resource utilization by continuously monitoring and adjusting manufacturing processes. This leads to reduced waste, minimized energy consumption, and improved overall resource efficiency. By using data analytics and predictive maintenance, resources can be allocated more judiciously, reducing the environmental impact of industrial operations.

12.5.2 Eco-friendly Product Design

Sustainability in Industry 4.0 involves the development of environmentally friendly products. Digital twins enable companies to simulate and test product designs in a virtual environment, facilitating the selection of eco-friendly materials and the creation of products with a reduced environmental footprint. This category emphasizes the importance of sustainable product development and innovation.

12.5.3 Extended Product Lifecycle

AI-driven digital twins support the entire lifecycle of products. They can monitor products in real time, predict maintenance needs, and facilitate repair and refurbishment, thus extending the life of products. This approach promotes the concept of a circular economy, where products are reused, recycled, or remanufactured, reducing the volume of waste generated.

12.5.4 Supply Chain Optimization

Sustainability in Industry 4.0 encompasses SCM. Digital twins can optimize supply chains by predicting demand, managing inventory efficiently, and minimizing transportation-related emissions. This not only reduces operational costs but also lowers the environmental impact associated with logistics and transportation.

12.5.5 Safety and Environmental Risk Mitigation

AI-driven digital twins can simulate and assess potential safety hazards and environmental risks in industrial processes. By identifying and mitigating these risks proactively, companies can prevent accidents, minimize environmental damage, and protect the well-being of workers and the surrounding community.

12.5.6 Regulatory Compliance

Ensuring compliance with environmental and sustainability regulations is a crucial aspect of sustainability in Industry 4.0. Digital twins can assist in tracking and documenting compliance data, making it easier for companies to adhere to increasingly stringent environmental regulations and report their sustainability efforts transparently (Rani, S., Kumar, S., Kataria, A., & Min, H., 2023).

12.5.7 DATA-DRIVEN DECISION-MAKING

Industry 4.0 relies on data-driven decision-making, and sustainability efforts are no exception. AI-driven digital twins provide valuable insights and predictive analytics that guide sustainability initiatives. This category underscores the importance of leveraging data to make informed choices that align with sustainable practices.

12.5.8 EMPLOYEE AND COMMUNITY WELL-BEING

Sustainability extends beyond environmental concerns to encompass social and community aspects. Industry 4.0 technologies, including digital twins, can enhance workplace safety and job satisfaction for employees. Additionally, sustainable practices can benefit local communities by reducing pollution and resource depletion.

Sustainability in the context of AI-driven digital twins and Industry 4.0 can be categorized into resource efficiency, eco-friendly product design, extended product lifecycle, supply chain optimization, risk mitigation, regulatory compliance, data-driven decision-making, and considerations for employee and community well-being. These categories collectively illustrate the multidimensional approach necessary for achieving sustainability in the modern industrial landscape (Bhambri and Sharma, 2005).

12.6 INTEROPERABILITY IN INDUSTRY 4.0

Interoperability in Industry 4.0, is a fundamental concept that addresses the seamless integration and communication of various technologies and systems within a manufacturing or industrial environment. Industry 4.0 is characterized by the convergence of digital technologies, such as IoT sensors, AI, and automation, to create smart and interconnected systems. AI-driven digital twins play a pivotal role in this ecosystem, serving as virtual replicas of physical assets and systems. Interoperability ensures that these digital twins can effectively communicate and exchange data with other components of the Industry 4.0 infrastructure (Singh et al., 2004; Singh et al., 2005a-f). This capability is essential for several reasons:

12.6.1 DATA INTEGRATION

Digital twins rely on real-time data from sensors, machines, and other sources to simulate and monitor physical assets. Interoperability allows for the seamless integration of this data, ensuring that all relevant information is accessible within the digital twin environment. This comprehensive data integration enhances the accuracy and effectiveness of decision-making processes.

12.6.2 SYSTEM COORDINATION

In a manufacturing setting, multiple systems and devices need to work in coordination. Interoperability enables digital twins to communicate with automation systems, robotics, and other machinery, ensuring that processes are synchronized for optimal efficiency and productivity. This coordination reduces bottlenecks and minimizes downtime.

12.6.3 PREDICTIVE ANALYTICS

AI-driven digital twins excel at predictive analytics, identifying potential issues and recommending proactive actions. Interoperability allows digital twins to share these insights with maintenance systems, enabling predictive maintenance and reducing the risk of equipment failures and costly disruptions.

12.6.4 SUPPLY CHAIN INTEGRATION

Within the broader Industry 4.0 framework, interoperability extends to SCM. Digital twins can exchange data with suppliers, logistics providers, and distributors, allowing for real-time tracking of inventory, demand forecasting, and efficient order fulfillment. This integration optimizes the supply chain, reduces lead times, and minimizes excess inventory.

12.6.5 CROSS-PLATFORM COMPATIBILITY

Interoperability ensures that digital twins can operate across different platforms and software environments. This flexibility is essential for scalability and adaptability as companies expand their Industry 4.0 capabilities. It enables the integration of new technologies and systems seamlessly.

12.6.6 SECURITY AND DATA PRIVACY

Interoperability also encompasses security considerations. Ensuring secure data exchange between digital twins and other systems is crucial to protect sensitive information and maintain data privacy. Robust security measures are essential to prevent cyber threats and data breaches.

Interoperability in Industry 4.0, particularly within the context of AI-driven digital twins, is the linchpin that enables the full potential of this technological revolution. It fosters efficient data exchange, system coordination, predictive analytics, supply chain optimization, cross-platform compatibility, and security. Ultimately, interoperability facilitates a cohesive and responsive industrial eco-system, where digital twins serve as the central intelligence that connects and optimizes all components of the modern manufacturing and industrial landscape.

12.7 CASE STUDIES

While AI-driven digital twins and Industry 4.0 are relatively new concepts in India, there are emerging examples of their application in various sectors. Here are two case studies showcasing how these technologies are being used for resource optimization in the Indian context:

12.7.1 CASE STUDY 1: TATA STEEL'S SMART MANUFACTURING

Tata Steel, one of India's leading steel manufacturers, embarked on a journey to enhance resource optimization and sustainability in their steel production processes. Tata Steel adopted AI-driven digital twins within their steel manufacturing plants, creating virtual replicas of critical equipment and production lines. These digital twins were equipped with AI algorithms that collected and analyzed real-time data from sensors, cameras, and historical production records.

- Resource Optimization
  - Energy Efficiency: The digital twins continuously monitored energy consumption patterns and recommended adjustments. They optimized the operation of blast furnaces and rolling mills based on demand, resulting in significant energy savings.
  - Maintenance Predictions: By analyzing data from equipment sensors, digital twins predicted maintenance needs, allowing Tata Steel to schedule repairs during planned downtime. This approach reduced unplanned shutdowns and optimized resource allocation.
  - Quality Control: The digital twins monitored product quality throughout the production process. In case of deviations from quality standards, adjustments were made automatically to prevent the production of defective steel, reducing material waste.
- Results: Tata Steel reported substantial improvements in their resource optimization efforts:
  - Energy consumption decreased by 12%.
  - Maintenance costs reduced by 15%.
  - Productivity increased by 8% due to reduced downtime.
  - A 10% reduction in raw material consumption, contributing to cost savings and sustainability.

12.7.2 CASE STUDY 2: PRECISION AGRICULTURE WITH MAHINDRA AGRIBUSINESS

Mahindra Agribusiness, a division of the Mahindra Group, implemented AI-driven digital twins in their agricultural operations to optimize resource usage in farming. Mahindra Agribusiness introduced digital twins into their tractors and farming equipment, allowing farmers to create digital representations of their fields. These digital twins were connected to IoT devices, weather stations, and soil sensors, providing real-time data.

- Resource Optimization:
  - Precision Farming: Farmers used digital twins to make data-driven decisions on irrigation, fertilization, and pest control. The digital twins helped optimize resource usage by providing insights into when and where these interventions were needed, reducing water and chemical usage.
  - Crop Monitoring: AI-driven digital twins monitored crop health using remote sensing and satellite imagery. They identified areas with stress or disease, enabling targeted interventions and minimizing crop loss.
  - Data-Driven Crop Planning: Farmers used historical data and predictive analytics from digital twins to plan their crop cycles. This resulted in improved yields and reduced resource wastage.
- Results: Mahindra Agribusiness witnessed several positive outcomes from their adoption of AI-driven digital twins:
  - A 25% reduction in water usage through optimized irrigation.
  - A 20% decrease in chemical usage, benefiting both the environment and farmers' profitability.
  - A 12% increase in overall crop yield due to precise resource management and data-driven decision-making.

These case studies from India demonstrate that AI-driven digital twins and Industry 4.0 technologies are making strides in optimizing resource utilization across diverse industries. As India continues to embrace these innovations, they have the potential to significantly enhance sustainability, efficiency, and competitiveness in the country's industrial ecosystem.

12.8 CONCLUSION

Here, we shared a comprehensive and illuminating exploration of the transformative synergy between AI-driven digital twins and the Industry 4.0 paradigm. It elucidates the pivotal role these technologies play in reshaping the industrial landscape, emphasizing their capacity to optimize resources, enhance sustainability, and foster operational efficiency. Through real-world case studies and thoughtful analysis, the chapter effectively underscores how these innovations are not merely theoretical concepts but practical solutions with tangible benefits across industries. Moreover, it accentuates the necessity of addressing issues like interoperability, data security, and ethical considerations as we journey deeper into the Industry 4.0 era. As we conclude, the chapter inspires a vision of a future where AI-driven digital twins are integral to intelligent, data-driven decision-making, and where industries harness their potential to create a more sustainable, efficient, and resilient industrial ecosystem. It serves as a valuable reference for both scholars and practitioners seeking to navigate and capitalize on the transformative forces of Industry 4.0 in the modern world.

REFERENCES

Abrol, N., Shaifali, Rattan, M., & Bhambri, P. (2005). Implementation and performance evaluation of JPEG 2000 for medical images. In International Conference on Innovative Applications of Information Technology for Developing World.

Bai, C., Dallasega, P., Orzes, G., & Sarkis, J. (2020). Industry 4.0 technologies assessment: A sustainability perspective. *International Journal of Production Economics*, 229, 107776.

Bathla, S., Bhambri, P., & Jindal, C. (2007a, May). Wearable computers: Smart era in computing. Paper presented at the National Conference on Advances in Computer Technology and Applications.

Bathla, S., Jindal, C., & Bhambri, P. (2007b, March). Impact of technology on societal living. In International Conference on Convergence and Competition (pp. 14).

Bali, V., Bali, S., Gaur, D., Rani, S., & Kumar, R. (2023). Commercial-off-the shelf vendor selection: A multi-criteria decision-making approach using intuitionistic fuzzy sets and TOPSIS. *Operational Research in Engineering Sciences: Theory and Applications*.

Bhambri, P., Gupta, O. P., Hans, S., & Singh, R. (2011). Conceptual Translation as a part of gene expression. In International Conference on Advanced Computing and Communication Technologies (Sponsored by IEEE Delhi Section, IEEE Computer Society Chapter, Delhi Section and IETE Delhi Centre) (pp. 506–508).

Bhambri, P. (2010). An Adaptive and resource efficient hand off in recovery state in geographic adhoc networks. In International Conference on Engineering Innovations-A Fillip to Economic Development.

Bhambri, P., & Hans, S. (2010). Evaluation of integrated development environments for embedded system design. *Apeejay Journal of Management and Technology*, 5(2), 138–146.

Bhambri, P., Singh, M., Suresh, H., & Singh, I. (2010). Data mining model for protein sequence alignment. In Proceedings of the International Conference on Data Mining (pp. 612–617).

Bhambri, P., & Thapar, V. (2010). Iris biometric - A review. Paper presented at the National Conference on Cellular and Molecular Medicine.

Bhambri, P., & Hans, S. (2009). Direct non iterative solution based neural network for image compression. *PIMT Journal of Research*, 2(2), 64–67.

Bhambri, P., Hans, S., & Singh, M. (2009). Inharmonic signal synthesis & analysis. *Technia - International Journal of Computing Science and Communication Technologies*, 1(2), 199–201.

Bhambri, P., & Singh, M. (2009). *Data mining model for protein sequence alignment*. Punjab Technical University, Jalandhar.

Bhambri, P., & Thapar, V. (2009, May). Power distribution challenges in VLSI: An introduction. Paper presented at the International Conference on Downtrend Challenges in IT, pp. 63.

Bhambri, P., Hans, S., & Singh, M. (2008a, November). Bioinformatics - Friendship between bits & genes. In International Conference on Advanced Computing & Communication Technologies (pp. 62–65).

Bhambri, P., Hans, S., & Singh, M. (2008b, November). Fractal image compression techniques: A fast fractal image compression method. In International Conference on Advanced Computing and Communication Technologies (pp. 6576–6660).

Bhambri, P., & Singh, M. (2008a). Direct non iterative solution based neural network for image compression. *PCTE Journal of Computer Sciences*, 5(2), 1–4.

Bhambri, P., & Singh, M. (2008b). Biometrics: Face recognition using eigen faces. *Apeejay Journal of Management and Technology*, 3(2), 160–164.

Bhambri, P., & Singh, M. (2008c). Image transport protocol for JPEG image over loss prone congested networks. *PIMT Journal of Research*, 1(1), 55–61.

Bhambri, P., & Nischal, P. (2008a, September). Emerging trends of intersectoral growth of India with special reference to service sector. *PIMT Journal of Research*, 1(2), 10–18.

Bhambri, P., & Nischal, P. (2008b, May). Emerging new economy in telecommunication sector of india. In International Conference on Business Challenges & Strategies in Emerging Global Scenario (p. 26).

Bhambri, P., Singh, H., & Gupta, S. (2007a, May). Generation of fuzzy rules and membership function from training examples. Paper presented at the National Conference on Advances in Computer Technology and Applications.

Bhambri, P., Nischal, P., & Gupta, S. (2007b, April). Bioinformatics and computational biology. In National Conference on Some Aspects of Recent Trends in Engineering and Technology (p. 29).

Banerjee, K., Bali, V., Nawaz, N., Bali, S., Mathur, S., Mishra, R. K., & Rani, S. (2022). A machine-learning approach for prediction of water contamination using latitude, longitude, and elevation. *Water*, 14(5), 728.

Bhambri, P., Singh, R., & Singh, J. (2007c). Wireless security. In National Conference on Emerging Trends in Communication & IT (pp. 290).

Bhambri, P., & Gupta, S. (2007, September). Interactive voice recognition system. In National Conference on Advancements in Modeling and simulation (p. 107).

Bhambri, P., & Singh, M. (2005a). Artificial intelligence. In *Seminar on E-Governance—Pathway to Progress* (pp. 14).

Bhambri, P., & Sharma, N. (2005, September). Priorities for sustainable civilization. Paper presented at the National Conference on Technical Education in Globalized Environment - Knowledge, Technology & The Teacher, pp. 108.

Bhambri, P., & Gupta, S. (2005, March). A survey & comparison of permutation possibility of fault tolerant multistage interconnection networks. Paper presented at the National Conference on Application of Mathematics in Engg. & Tech., 13.

Bhambri, P., & Bhandari, A. (2005, March). Different protocols for wireless security. Paper presented at the National Conference on Advancements in Modeling and Simulation, 8.

Bhambri, P., Singh, I., & Gupta, S. (2005a, March). Robotics systems. Paper presented at the National Conference on Emerging Computing Technologies, 27.

Bhambri, P., & Singh, I. (2005b, March). Electrical actuation systems. Paper presented at the National Conference on Application of Mathematics in Engg. & Tech., 58–60.

Bhambri, P., & Mangat, A. S. (2005, March). Wireless security. Paper presented at the National Conference on Emerging Computing Technologies, 155–161.

Bhambri, P., Sood, G., & Verma, A. (2005b). Robotics design: Major considerations. In National Conference on Emerging Computing Technologies (pp. 100).

Bhambri, P., Singh, I., & Singh, J. (2005c). Role of programming and mathematics in the design of robotics. In National Conference on Application of Mathematics in Engg. & Tech. (pp. 101).

Bilal, M., Kumari, B., & Rani, S. (2021, May). An artificial intelligence supported E-commerce model to improve the export of Indian handloom and handicraft products in the World. In *Proceedings of the International Conference on Innovative Computing & Communication (ICICC)*.

Cañas, H., Mula, J., Díaz-Madroñero, M., & Campuzano-Bolarín, F. (2021). Implementing industry 4.0 principles. *Computers & Industrial Engineering*, 158, 107379.

Chauhan, M., & Rani, S. (2021). Covid-19: A revolution in the field of education in India. *Learning how to learn using multimedia*, 23–42.

Chen, B., Wan, J., Shu, L., Li, P., Mukherjee, M., & Yin, B. (2017). Smart factory of industry 4.0: Key technologies, application case, and challenges. *IEEE Access*, 6, 6505–6519.

Contreras, J. D., Garcia, J. I., & Pastrana, J. D. (2017). Developing of Industry 4.0 Applications. *International Journal of Online Engineering*, 13(10), 546–559.

Chopra, S. & Bhambri, P. (2011). *A new method of edge detection in mammographic images.* Punjab Technical University.

Dhanalakshmi, R., Vijayaraghavan, N., Sivaraman, A. K., & Rani, S. (2022). Epidemic awareness spreading in smart cities using the artificial neural network. In *AI-Centric Smart City Ecosystems* (pp. 187–207): CRC Press.

Garg, D., & Bhambri, P. (2011a). A novel approach for fusion of multimodality medical images. *CiiT International Journal of Digital Image Processing*, 3(10), 576–580.

Garg, D., & Bhambri, P. (2011b). *A Novel Approach for Fusion of Multi-Modality Medical Images.* Punjab Technical University, Jalandhar.

Ghobakhloo, M. (2020). Industry 4.0, digitization, and opportunities for sustainability. *Journal of Cleaner Production*, 252, 119869.

Goel, R., & Gupta, P. (2020). Robotics and industry 4.0. *A roadmap to Industry 4.0: Smart production, sharp business and sustainable development*, 157–169.

Grewal, H.K., & Bhambri, P. (2006). Globe-IT: Globalization of learning through open based education and information technology. In *International Conference on Brand India: Issues, Challenges and Opportunities* (pp. 24).

Gupta, S., Nischal, P., & Bhambri, P. (2007a). Multimodal biometric: Enhancing security level of biometric system. In National Conference on Emerging Trends in Communication & IT (pp. 78–81).

Gupta, S., Nischal, P., & Bhambri, P. (2007b, March). Mathematical modeling of EMG (ELECTROMYOGRAM). Paper presented at the International Conference on Global Trends in IT, pp. 14.

Gupta, S., Nischal, P., & Bhambri, P. (2007c, February). DNA computing: An emerging trend. Paper presented at the National Conference on Emerging Trends in Communication & IT, pp. 267.

Gupta, S., Kaur, R., & Bhambri, P. (2007d). Common channel signaling system #7: A global standard for telecommunication. In National Conference on Emerging Trends in Communication & IT (pp. 130–134).

Gupta, S., Nischal, P., & Bhambri, P. (2007e). Data Encryption Standard (DES) algorithm with Diffie-Hellman key exchange. In National Conference on Emerging Trends in Communication & IT (pp. 135–143).

Gupta, S., & Bhambri, P. (2006). A competitive market is pushing site search technology to new plateaus. In *International Conference on Brand India: Issues, Challenges and Opportunities* (pp. 34).

Habib, M. K., & Chimsom, C. (2019). Industry 4.0: Sustainability and design principles. Paper presented at the 2019 20th International Conference on Research and Education in Mechatronics (REM).

Jain, V. K., & Bhambri, P. (2005). Fundamentals of Information Technology & Computer Programming.

Kataria, A., Agrawal, D., Rani, S., Karar, V., & Chauhan, M. (2022). Prediction of blood screening parameters for preliminary analysis using neural networks. In *Predictive Modeling in Biomedical Data Mining and Analysis* (pp. 157–169). Academic Press.

Kamra, A., & Bhambri, P. (2007). Computer peripherals & interfaces.

Kaur, G., Bhambri, P., & Sohal, A. K. (2006, January). Review analysis of economic load dispatch. In National Conference on Future Trends in Information Technology.

Kothandaraman, D., Manickam, M., Balasundaram, A., Pradeep, D., Arulmurugan, A., Sivaraman, A. K., & Balakrishna, R. (2022). Decentralized link failure prevention routing (DLFPR) algorithm for efficient internet of things. *Intelligent Automation and Soft Computing*, 34(1), 655–666.

Kumar, P., Banerjee, K., Singhal, N., Kumar, A., Rani, S., Kumar, R., & Lavinia, C. A. (2022a). Verifiable, secure mobile agent migration in healthcare systems using a polynomial-based threshold secret sharing scheme with a Blowfish algorithm. *Sensors*, 22(22), 8620.

Kumar, R., Rani, S., & Awadh, M. A. (2022). Exploring the application sphere of the internet of things in industry 4.0: A review, bibliometric and content analysis. *Sensors*, 22(11), 4276.

Kataria, A., Puri, V., Pareek, P. K., & Rani, S. (2023, July). Human activity classification using G-XGB. In *2023 International Conference on Data Science and Network Security (ICDSNS)* (pp. 1–5). IEEE.

Kaur, D., Singh, B., & Rani, S. (2023). Cyber security in the metaverse. In *Handbook of Research on AI-Based Technologies and Applications in the Era of the Metaverse* (pp. 418–435). IGI Global.

Kumar, R., Rani, S., & Awadh, M. A. (2022b). Exploring the application sphere of the internet of things in industry 4.0: A review, bibliometric and content analysis. *Sensors*, 22(11), 4276.

Machała, S., Chamier-Gliszczyński, N., & Królikowski, T. (2022). Application of AR/VR technology in Industry 4.0. *Procedia Computer Science*, 207, 2990–2998.

Puri, V., Kataria, A., Solanki, V. K., & Rani, S. (2022, December). AI-based botnet attack classification and detection in IoT devices. In *2022 IEEE International Conference on Machine Learning and Applied Network Technologies (ICMLANT)* (pp. 1–5). IEEE.

Rani, S., Kataria, A., Kumar, S., & Tiwari, P. (2023). Federated learning for secure IoMT-applications in smart healthcare systems: A comprehensive review. *Knowledge-based systems*, 110658.

Rani, S., Kataria, A., & Chauhan, M. (2022). Fog computing in industry 4.0: Applications and challenges—A research roadmap. *Energy conservation solutions for fog-edge computing paradigms*, 173–190.

Rani, S., Kataria, A., & Chauhan, M. (2022a). Cyber security techniques, architectures, and design. In *Holistic approach to quantum cryptography in cyber security* (pp. 41–66): CRC Press.

Rani, S., Kataria, A., & Chauhan, M. (2022b). Fog computing in industry 4.0: Applications and challenges—A research roadmap. *Energy conservation solutions for fog-edge computing paradigms*, 173–190.

Rani, S., Pareek, P. K., Kaur, J., Chauhan, M., & Bhambri, P. (2023, February). Quantum machine learning in healthcare: Developments and challenges. In *2023 IEEE International Conference on Integrated Circuits and Communication Systems (ICICACS)* (pp. 1–7). IEEE.

Rani, S., Kataria, A., Chauhan, M., Rattan, P., Kumar, R., & Sivaraman, A. K. (2022c). Security and privacy challenges in the deployment of cyber-physical systems in smart city applications: State-of-art work. *Materials Today: Proceedings*, 62, 4671–4676.

Rani, S., Kataria, A., Sharma, V., Ghosh, S., Karar, V., Lee, K., & Choi, C. (2021). Threats and corrective measures for IoT security with observance of cybercrime: A survey. *Wireless Communications and Mobile Computing*, 2021, 1–30.

Rani, S., Kumar, S., Kataria, A., & Min, H. (2023). SmartHealth: An intelligent framework to secure IoMT service applications using machine learning. *ICT Express*.

Rani, S., Kataria, A., Chauhan, M., Rattan, P., Kumar, R., & Sivaraman, A. K. (2022). Security and privacy challenges in the deployment of cyber-physical systems in smart city applications: State-of-art work. *Materials Today: Proceedings*, 62, 4671–4676.

Rani, S., Mishra, R. K., Usman, M., Kataria, A., Kumar, P., Bhambri, P., & Mishra, A. K. (2021). Amalgamation of advanced technologies for sustainable development of smart city environment: A review. *IEEE Access*, 9, 150060–150087.

Rani, S., Mishra, A. K., Kataria, A., Mallik, S., & Qin, H. (2023). Machine learning-based optimal crop selection system in smart agriculture. *Scientific Reports*, 13(1), 15997.

Rani, S., Bhambri, P., & Kataria, A. (2023). Integration of IoT, Big Data, and Cloud Computing Technologies. *Big Data, Cloud Computing and IoT: Tools and applications.*

Rattan, M., Bhambri, P., & Shaifali. (2005a, February). Information retrieval using soft computing techniques. Paper presented at the National Conference on Bio-informatics Computing, 7.

Rattan, M., Bhambri, P., & Shaifali. (2005b, February). Institution for a sustainable civilization: Negotiating change in a technological culture. Paper presented at the National Conference on Technical Education in Globalized Environment - Knowledge, Technology & The Teacher, 45.

Salkin, C., Oner, M., Ustundag, A., & Cevikcan, E. (2018). A conceptual framework for Industry 4.0. *Industry 4.0: Managing the digital transformation,* 3–23.

Saucedo-Martínez, J. A., Pérez-Lara, M., Marmolejo-Saucedo, J. A., Salais-Fierro, T. E., & Vasant, P. (2018). Industry 4.0 framework for management and operations: A review. *Journal of Ambient Intelligence and Humanized Computing,* 9, 789–801.

Singh, I., Salaria, D., & Bhambri, P. (2010). Comparative analysis of JAVA and AspectJ on the basis of various metrics. In *International Conference on Advanced Computing and Communication Technologies (IEEE Sponsored)* (pp. 714–720).

Singh, P., & Bhambri, P. (2007). Alternate organizational models for ports. *Apeejay Journal of Management and Technology,* 2(2), 9–17.

Singh, P., Bhambri, P., & Sohal, A. K. (2006, January). Security in local networks. Paper presented at the National Conference on Future Trends in Information Technology.

Singh, M., Singh, P., Kaur, K., & Bhambri, P. (2005a, March). Database security. Paper presented at the National Conference on Future Trends in Information Technology, 57–62.

Singh, M., Bhambri, P., & Kaur, K. (2005b, March). Network security. Paper presented at the National Conference on Future Trends in Information Technology, 51–56.

Singh, P., Singh, M., & Bhambri, P. (2005c, March). Internet security. Paper presented at the Seminar on Network Security and Its Implementations, 22.

Singh, P., Singh, M., & Bhambri, P. (2005d, March). Security in virtual private networks. In *Seminar on Network Security and Its Implementations* (pp. 11).

Singh, P., Singh, M., & Bhambri, P. (2005e, January). Embedded systems. Paper presented at the Seminar on Embedded Systems, 10–15.

Singh, M., Singh, P., Bhambri, P., & Sachdeva, R. (2005f). A comparative study: Security algorithms. In *Seminar on Network Security and Its Implementations* (pp. 14).

Singh, P., Singh, M., & Bhambri, P. (2004, November). Interoperability: A problem of component reusability. Paper presented at the International Conference on Emerging Technologies in IT Industry, 60.

Tanwar, R., Chhabra, Y., Rattan, P., & Rani, S. (2022, September). Blockchain in IoT Networks for Precision Agriculture. In *International Conference on Innovative Computing and Communications: Proceedings of ICICC 2022, Volume 2* (pp. 137–147). Singapore: Springer Nature Singapore.

Thapar, V., & Bhambri, P. (2009, May). Context free language induction by evolution of deterministic pushdown automata using genetic programming. Paper presented at the International Conference on Downtrend Challenges in IT, pp. 33.

Yadav, V. S., Singh, A., Raut, R. D., Mangla, S. K., Luthra, S., & Kumar, A. (2022). Exploring the application of Industry 4.0 technologies in the agricultural food supply chain: A systematic literature review. *Computers & industrial engineering,* 169, 108304.

13 Digital Twin for Sustainable Industrial Development

Pawan Whig, Nikhitha Yathiraju,
Venugopal Reddy Modhugu, and
Ashima Bhatnagar Bhatia

13.1 INTRODUCTION

In recent years, the global push for sustainability has become an urgent imperative, driven by concerns over climate change, resource depletion, and environmental degradation. The industrial sector, being a significant contributor to greenhouse gas emissions and resource consumption, plays a pivotal role in the pursuit of sustainable development. To address these challenges and create a more eco-friendly and resource-efficient industrial landscape, innovative technologies are required. One such promising technology is the Digital Twin. The concept of the Digital Twin traces its origins to the early 2000s, primarily emerging from the aerospace and manufacturing industries. A Digital Twin is a virtual representation or simulation of a physical asset, process, or system that mirrors its real-world counterpart in real time. It relies on a network of sensors, Internet of Things (IoT) devices, and advanced analytics to continuously collect data from the physical entity. This data is then used to create a digital model, enabling real-time monitoring, analysis, and prediction of the asset's behavior and performance. The integration of Digital Twins into industrial processes opens up new horizons for sustainable development. By creating a digital replica of assets, companies can optimize their operations, enhance resource efficiency, and reduce their environmental footprint. As industries continue to explore the potential of Digital Twins, the drive toward sustainability is poised to gain significant momentum. In this book chapter, we delve into the transformative potential of Digital Twins in fostering sustainable industrial development. We aim to provide a comprehensive overview of the benefits, challenges, and innovations surrounding this technology. The term "Digital Twin" was first coined in 2002 by Dr. Michael Grieves of the University of Michigan, and it refers to a digital replica of a physical object or system that can be used for simulation, analysis, and control. In recent years, digital twins have gained significant attention in the industrial sector, as they offer a powerful tool for optimizing processes, improving efficiency, and reducing costs (Whig, Velu, & Naddikatu, 2022; Botín-Sanabria et al., 2022). A digital twin is a virtual

 DOI: 10.1201/9781003395416-13

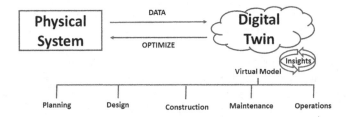

FIGURE 13.1   Introduction to digital twin.

representation of a physical object or system that is used to simulate, monitor, and analyze its real-world behavior. The concept of digital twin has been gaining popularity in recent years and has been applied across various industries including manufacturing, healthcare, and smart cities. In the literature, a digital twin is often defined as a dynamic digital replica of a physical object or system that is updated in real time using data from sensors and other sources. It is used to analyze the physical object's behavior and improve decision-making by providing a virtual environment for testing and experimentation (Alkali et al., 2022a).

Studies have shown that the implementation of digital twins can lead to improved efficiency and cost savings in various industries. In manufacturing, digital twins can be used to optimize production processes, reduce downtime, and improve product quality. In healthcare, they can be used to monitor patient health and improve treatment outcomes (Whig, Velu, & Sharma, 2022; He, & Bai, 2021). However, there are also challenges associated with the implementation of digital twins, including the need for large amounts of data, the complexity of integrating different systems, and the need for privacy and security measures. Overall, the use of digital twins is a rapidly evolving field and there is a growing body of literature exploring its applications, benefits, and challenges. As technology continues to advance, it is likely that the use of digital twins will become increasingly widespread and lead to further innovations in various industries (Whig, Kouser, Velu, et al., 2022; Bauer, Stevens, & Hazeleger, 2021). The concept of digital twins is closely related to the field of IoT, as it relies on the ability to collect and analyze data from various sensors and devices. This data is then used to create a digital replica of the physical system, which can be used for simulation, analysis, and control as shown in Figure 13.1.

Digital twins have a wide range of applications in the industrial sector, including manufacturing, energy, and transportation. In this chapter, we will explore the use of digital twins in industrial processes and discuss the benefits they offer.

13.2   IMPORTANCE OF DIGITAL TWINS FOR SUSTAINABLE INDUSTRIAL DEVELOPMENT

The importance of Digital Twins for sustainable industrial development cannot be overstated (Tanwar, R., Chhabra, Y., Rattan, P., & Rani, S., 2022, September). As industries grapple with the urgent need to reduce their environmental impact and transition toward more sustainable practices, Digital Twins offer a multitude of benefits that can revolutionize the industrial landscape. Below are some key reasons why Digital Twins are crucial for driving sustainability in the industrial sector:

1. Real-time Monitoring and Predictive Maintenance: Digital Twins enable continuous real-time monitoring of industrial assets, processes, and systems. By analyzing data from sensors and IoT devices, companies can detect anomalies and potential issues before they escalate into costly breakdowns (Bhambri, 2021). This proactive approach to maintenance minimizes downtime, reduces the need for resource-intensive emergency repairs, and extends the lifespan of assets - all of which contribute to improved sustainability and reduced environmental impact.

2. Resource Optimization: Digital Twins provide insights into the performance of industrial processes, allowing for data-driven decision-making to optimize resource utilization. By identifying inefficiencies and areas of improvement, industries can reduce waste, minimize energy and water consumption, and make more sustainable use of raw materials. This resource optimization not only lowers operational costs but also supports the transition toward circular economy principles.

3. Process Enhancement and Simulation: Digital Twins enable companies to simulate different scenarios and configurations, facilitating process optimization. By experimenting in the virtual environment, industries can identify the most energy-efficient and eco-friendly processes before implementing them in the physical world. This capability significantly contributes to reducing the environmental footprint of industrial operations (Singh et al., 2021).

4. Emission Reduction and Environmental Compliance: Industrial activities are a significant source of greenhouse gas emissions and pollution. Digital Twins help industries track and analyze emissions data, allowing them to set emission reduction targets and develop strategies to achieve them. Moreover, Digital Twins aid in ensuring compliance with environmental regulations, leading to more responsible and sustainable practices.

5. Supply Chain Management: Digital Twins can extend beyond individual industrial entities and be utilized across the entire supply chain. By monitoring and optimizing the movement of raw materials, components, and finished products, industries can reduce transportation-related emissions and enhance overall supply chain efficiency, contributing to a more sustainable industrial ecosystem.

6. Design and Construction: Digital Twins are valuable during the design and construction phases of industrial assets. By creating virtual models, engineers can optimize building designs for energy efficiency, incorporate sustainable materials, and simulate the environmental impact of construction projects. This early integration of sustainability principles leads to greener, more environmentally responsible infrastructure.

7. Training and Safety: Digital Twins can be employed for training purposes, allowing operators and employees to familiarize themselves with industrial processes in a safe and controlled environment. Well-trained staff are less

likely to cause accidents or environmental mishaps, contributing to improved safety and sustainability (Rani, S., Mishra, A. K., Kataria, A., Mallik, S., & Qin, H., 2023).

8. Continuous Improvement and Innovation: Digital Twins facilitate data-driven continuous improvement and innovation. By constantly analyzing performance data and learning from virtual simulations, industries can iteratively enhance their operations, adopt new sustainable practices, and stay at the forefront of sustainable industrial development.

In conclusion, Digital Twins are a transformative technology that holds immense promise for driving sustainable industrial development (Rani, S., Kumar, S., Kataria, A., & Min, H., 2023). By offering real-time monitoring, predictive maintenance, resource optimization, process simulation, and emission reduction capabilities, Digital Twins empower industries to transition toward more eco-friendly and resource-efficient practices. As the world faces pressing environmental challenges, the adoption of Digital Twins can play a pivotal role in achieving the delicate balance between industrial growth and environmental preservation (Bhambri et al., 2020). Embracing Digital Twins as a core component of sustainable development is not just a strategic choice for industries; it is a collective responsibility toward creating a more sustainable and resilient future for generations to come (Bakshi et al., 2021).

A digital twin is a digital representation of a physical asset, such as a machine or building, that can be used for simulation and analysis (Rana et al., 2021). In industry, digital twins can be used to improve the performance and efficiency of physical assets, as well as reduce downtime and maintenance costs as shown in Figure 13.2. For example, a digital twin of a machine can be used to simulate its operation and predict when maintenance will be needed, allowing for proactive

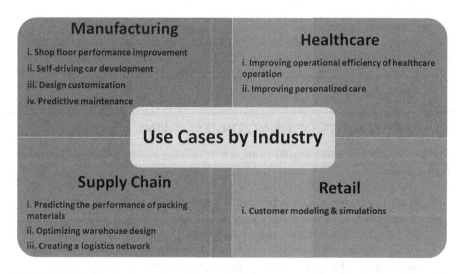

FIGURE 13.2 Importance of digital twins in industry.

maintenance to be scheduled. Additionally, digital twins can be used to optimize the performance of a system by simulating different scenarios and identifying the best course of action. They can also be used to train operators and engineers, and to improve the design of new products and systems. Overall, digital twins can provide a powerful tool for improving the performance and efficiency of industrial processes (Whig, Velu, & Nadikattu, 2022).

A digital twin is a virtual representation of a physical asset or system, such as a machine, building, or process. It can be used to simulate and analyze the performance of the physical asset, allowing industries to optimize its performance, predict and prevent failures, and improve decision-making (Whig, Velu, & Ready, 2022; Lo, C. K., 2021). The process of using a digital twin typically involves the following steps:

1. **Data collection**: Collect data from the physical asset or system, such as sensor readings, performance metrics, and maintenance records.
2. **Modeling**: Use the collected data to create a digital twin model of the physical asset or system. This model can include information about the asset's geometry, materials, and behavior.
3. **Simulation**: Use the digital twin model to simulate the behavior of the physical asset or system under different conditions and scenarios. This can be used to predict performance, identify potential issues, and evaluate potential changes.
4. **Analysis**: Analyze the simulation results to gain insights into the performance of the physical asset or system. This can include identifying potential issues, optimizing performance, and making decisions about maintenance, repairs, or upgrades.
5. **Feedback**: Feed the insights and learnings from the analysis back into the physical asset or system to improve its performance and prevent issues.
6. **Continual monitoring**: Continuously monitor the physical asset or system, and update the digital twin model as necessary to reflect the current state of the physical asset; this helps to identify any issues early on and take necessary action (Whig, Velu, & Bhatia, 2022; Shahat, Hyun, & Yeom, 2021).

13.3 KEY BENEFITS OF USING DIGITAL TWINS

The key benefits of using digital twins are as follows and some are also listed in Figure 13.3.

- Predictive maintenance: Digital twins can be used to simulate the operation of a physical asset and predict when maintenance will be needed, allowing for proactive maintenance to be scheduled.
- Optimization: Digital twins can be used to simulate different scenarios and identify the best course of action to optimize the performance of a system.

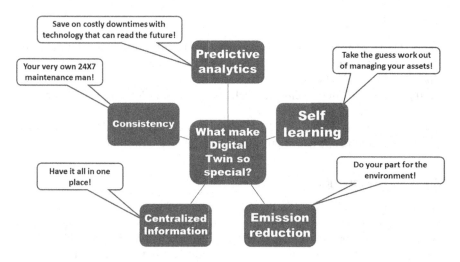

FIGURE 13.3 Benefits of using digital twins.

- Training and simulation: Digital twins can be used to train operators and engineers, and to improve the design of new products and systems.
- Remote monitoring and control: Digital twins can be used to remotely monitor and control physical assets, which can be especially useful for assets that are located in remote or dangerous locations (Kaur, D., Singh, B., & Rani, S., 2023).
- Increased efficiency: Digital twins can help increase the efficiency of industrial processes by identifying bottlenecks and inefficiencies, and by providing real-time data on the performance of physical assets.
- Cost savings: By reducing downtime and maintenance costs, digital twins can lead to significant cost savings for industrial organizations.
- Improved decision-making: Digital twins provide data-driven insights that can help organizations make better decisions.
- Increased safety: By identifying potential hazards and providing real-time data on the performance of physical assets, digital twins can help to improve safety in industrial environments.

13.4 DIGITAL TWIN APPLICATIONS IN INDUSTRY

Digital twin technology is rapidly gaining popularity in the industrial sector, as it provides a powerful tool for improving the performance and efficiency of industrial processes. By creating a digital replica of a physical asset, such as a machine or building, digital twins enable organizations to simulate, analyze and optimize the performance of these assets. This technology is being applied in a wide range of industries, including manufacturing, transportation, energy, healthcare and construction (Jupalle et al., 2022). In this section, we will look at some of the key applications of digital twin technology in industry and the benefits it can provide (Rani, S., Pareek, P. K., Kaur, J., Chauhan, M., & Bhambri, P., 2023, February).

13.4.1 MANUFACTURING

Digital twin technology is being used in manufacturing to optimize the performance of equipment and production lines. By creating a digital replica of a machine or production line, manufacturers can simulate its operation and identify areas for improvement, such as reducing downtime or increasing efficiency (Tomar et al., 2021).

Digital twins can also be used for predictive maintenance, allowing manufacturers to schedule maintenance proactively and reduce downtime.

13.4.2 CONSTRUCTION

Digital twins are being used in the construction industry to improve the design, planning, and construction of buildings and infrastructure. By creating a digital replica of a building or infrastructure, architects, engineers, and construction teams can simulate and analyze different design options, identify potential issues, and optimize the construction process. Digital twins can also be used for remote monitoring and management of buildings and infrastructure, allowing teams to identify and address issues in real time (Whig, Nadikattu, & Velu, 2022).

Energy and utilities: Digital twin technology is being used in the energy and utilities sector to optimize the performance of power plants, transmission and distribution networks, and renewable energy systems. By creating a digital replica of a power plant or transmission network, energy companies can simulate and analyze different scenarios, optimize the performance of the system, and reduce downtime (Anand et al., 2022). Digital twins can also be used for predictive maintenance, allowing energy companies to schedule maintenance proactively and reduce downtime. Some digital twin applications in industry are shown in Figure 13.4.

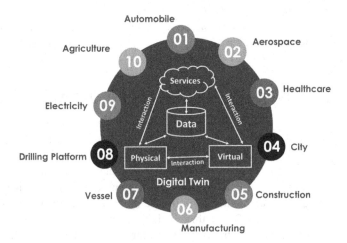

FIGURE 13.4 Digital twin applications in industry.

13.4.3 SUPPLY CHAIN AND LOGISTICS

Digital twin technology is being used in the supply chain and logistics industry to optimize the performance of logistics networks, transportation systems, and warehouses. By creating a digital replica of a logistics network or transportation system, supply chain managers can simulate and analyze different scenarios, optimize the performance of the system, and reduce downtime. Digital twins can also be used for predictive maintenance, allowing supply chain managers to schedule maintenance proactively and reduce downtime (Alkali et al., 2022b).

13.4.4 MAINTENANCE AND ASSET MANAGEMENT

Digital twin technology is being used in maintenance and asset management to improve the performance and efficiency of industrial assets (Kataria, A., Agrawal, D., Rani, S., Karar, V., & Chauhan, M., 2022). By creating a digital replica of an asset, such as a machine or building, maintenance teams can simulate and analyze its operation, identify areas for improvement, and optimize the performance of the asset. Digital twins can also be used for predictive maintenance, allowing maintenance teams to schedule maintenance proactively and reduce downtime.

13.5 CREATING AND MANAGING DIGITAL TWINS

A Digital Twin is a digital replica of a physical object or system that can be used for simulation, analysis, and monitoring. Creating a Digital Twin involves capturing and digitizing data from the physical object or system, and then using this data to create a virtual model. Managing a Digital Twin involves updating and maintaining the virtual model to ensure it remains accurate and relevant. Digital Twins can be used in a variety of industries, such as manufacturing, construction, and healthcare, to improve efficiency, reduce costs, and enhance decision-making (Chopra & WHIG, 2022).

Creating and managing a digital twin for an airplane would involve several steps, including data collection, modeling, simulation, analysis, and feedback. For example, let's say an airline wants to create a digital twin of one of their airplanes as shown in Figure 13.5.

The process would involve the following steps:

- Data collection: The airline would install sensors on the airplane to collect data on its performance, such as flight data, engine performance, and maintenance records. They would also gather information about the airplane's design and specifications (Kataria, A., Puri, V., Pareek, P. K., & Rani, S., 2023, July).
- Modeling: Using the collected data, the airline would create a digital twin model of the airplane. This model would include information about the airplane's geometry, materials, and behavior. The model would also take into account the different systems such as flight control, navigation, and power systems.

DIGITAL TWIN – AN EXAMPLE

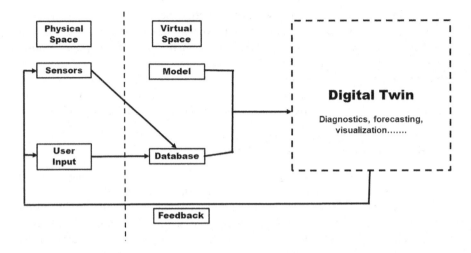

FIGURE 13.5   Creating and managing a digital twin for an airplane.

- Simulation: Using the digital twin model, the airline would simulate the airplane's performance under different conditions, such as different flight paths, weather conditions, and maintenance scenarios. This would allow them to predict how the airplane would behave in the real world and identify potential issues before they occur.
- Analysis: The airline would analyze the simulation results to gain insights into the airplane's performance. This could include identifying potential issues, optimizing performance, and making decisions about maintenance, repairs, or upgrades.
- Feedback: The airline would feed the insights and learnings from the analysis back into the real airplane to improve its performance and prevent issues. For example, if the simulation identified a potential problem with a certain component, the airline would schedule maintenance or replacement to address it.
- Continual monitoring: The airline would continuously monitor the airplane, and update the digital twin model as necessary to reflect the current state of the real airplane. This would help the airline to identify any issues early on and take necessary action.

13.6   DATA COLLECTION AND INTEGRATION

Data collection and integration is a critical step in creating and managing a Digital Twin. This involves capturing data from various sources, such as sensors, cameras, and other IoT devices, and integrating it into a single, unified model (Kataria, Ghosh & Karar, 2020). The data collected can include information on the physical characteristics of the object or system, such as dimensions, materials, and performance data. Additionally, data on the environment in which the object or system operates, such as temperature, humidity, and vibration, can also be collected. The data collected must be accurate, consistent, and up-to-date in order for the Digital Twin to be an accurate representation of the physical object or system. This step also involves using data analytics tools to extract insights from the collected data and feed it back to the digital twin model (Kataria & Puri, 2022).

13.6.1 MODELING AND SIMULATION

Modeling and simulation is the process of creating a virtual representation of a physical object or system using the data collected and integrated in the previous step. This involves using computer-aided design software and other tools to create a detailed and accurate digital replica of the object or system (Mamza, 2021). This replica can then be used to simulate different scenarios and test various designs and configurations. The goal of modeling and simulation is to improve the performance and reliability of the physical object or system and reduce the need for physical testing and prototyping as shown in Figure 13.6.

There are several steps involved in the modeling and simulation of a Digital Twin:

- Defining the scope of the project: This involves identifying the objectives of the simulation and the specific aspects of the physical object or system that need to be modeled.
- Collecting and integrating data: This involves capturing data from various sources, such as sensors, cameras, and other IoT devices, and integrating it into a single, unified model. This step also involves using data analytics tools to extract insights from the collected data and feed it back to the digital twin model.
- Creating the virtual model: This involves using computer-aided design software and other tools to create a detailed and accurate digital replica of the object or system. The model should be based on the data collected and integrated in the previous step.

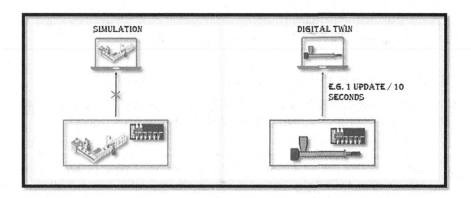

FIGURE 13.6 Physical testing and prototyping.

- Running simulations: This involves using the virtual model to simulate different scenarios and test various designs and configurations. The simulations should be based on the specific objectives defined in the first step.
- Analyzing the results: This involves reviewing the results of the simulations and extracting insights from the data. The insights gained can be used to improve the performance and efficiency of the physical object or system, and to make more informed decisions.
- Communicating and Collaborating: This step involves sharing the model and data with other stakeholders, such as engineers, managers, and decision-makers, allowing different teams and individuals to collaborate and communicate on the same model, and to access and contribute to the same data.
- Iteration: This step involves repeating the above steps as necessary to improve the accuracy and relevance of the Digital twin model.

13.6.2 ANALYTICS AND VISUALIZATION

Analytics and visualization is the process of extracting insights from the data collected and integrated in the previous step. This involves using data analytics tools and techniques to identify patterns, trends, and anomalies in the data (Kataria et al., 2020). The insights gained can be used to improve the performance and efficiency of the physical object or system, and to make more informed decisions. Visualization techniques, such as 3D modeling and interactive dashboards, can be used to present the data and insights in a user-friendly and easy-to-understand format (Khera et al., 2021).

13.6.3 COLLABORATION AND COMMUNICATION

Collaboration and communication is the process of sharing the Digital Twin model and data with other stakeholders, such as engineers, managers, and decision-makers. This allows different teams and individuals to collaborate and communicate on the same model, and to access and contribute to the same data. Collaboration tools, such as cloud-based platforms and virtual reality, can be used to enable remote collaboration and communication. This allows for faster and more efficient decision-making, as well as better communication between different teams and departments.

13.6.4 CHALLENGES AND CONSIDERATIONS IN DIGITAL TWIN

Creating and managing a Digital Twin can present a number of challenges and considerations. Some of the most significant challenges include:

1. Data collection and integration: Capturing and integrating data from various sources can be a complex and time-consuming process. Ensuring that the data collected is accurate, consistent, and up-to-date is critical for the Digital Twin to be an accurate representation of the physical object or system.

**Person expanding activities from
the Real World to Cyberspace**

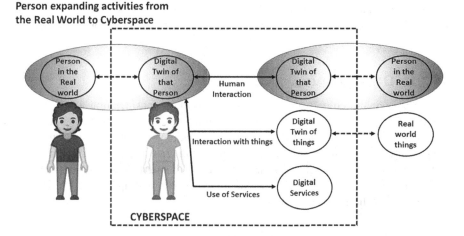

FIGURE 13.7   Collaboration and communication in digital twin.

2. Modeling and simulation: Creating a detailed and accurate virtual model of a physical object or system can be challenging, especially for complex systems with many interacting components.
3. Analytics and visualization: Extracting insights from the data collected and integrated can be a complex process, and requires specialized tools and techniques.
4. Collaboration and communication: Sharing the Digital Twin model and data with other stakeholders can be challenging, especially when working with remote teams or in highly regulated industries as shown in Figure 13.7.
5. Data Security and privacy: The Digital twin model will include sensitive information and data, so it is important to consider the security and privacy of the data.
6. Cost and scalability: Creating and maintaining a Digital twin model can be costly, especially for large or complex systems. It is important to consider the scalability and long-term costs of the project (Velu & Whig, 2021).
7. Integration with existing systems: Integrating the Digital twin model with existing systems and infrastructure can be challenging, and may require significant changes to existing processes and systems.
8. Maintenance and updates: Keeping the Digital twin model up-to-date and relevant requires ongoing maintenance and updates, which can be time-consuming and resource-intensive.

13.7   DATA PRIVACY AND SECURITY

Data privacy and security are important considerations when creating and managing a Digital Twin, as the model will include sensitive information and data. This includes personal data, as well as confidential business information. Ensuring the security and privacy of the data is critical to protect the interests of the organization and its stakeholders. This can involve implementing measures such as encryption, firewalls, and access controls to protect the data from unauthorized access or breaches.

13.7.1 Data Accuracy and Completeness

Data accuracy and completeness is another important consideration when creating and managing a Digital Twin. The model should be based on accurate and complete data in order to be an accurate representation of the physical object or system (Arun Velu, 2021). This can involve using sensors, cameras, and other IoT devices to capture data, as well as using data analytics tools to extract insights from the data. Ensuring that the data collected is accurate, consistent, and up-to-date is critical to the success of the Digital Twin project.

13.7.2 Technical and Organizational Integration

Technical and organizational integration is a consideration when creating and managing a Digital Twin, as the model may need to be integrated with existing systems and infrastructure. This can involve making changes to existing processes and systems to ensure that the Digital Twin model is integrated with the organization's existing IT infrastructure. It also requires coordination with different teams and departments to ensure that the Digital Twin model is aligned with the organization's overall strategy and goals (Kumar et al., 2022).

13.7.3 Cost and Return on Investment (ROI)

Cost and return on investment (ROI) analysis is a consideration when creating and managing a Digital Twin, as the project can be costly, especially for large or complex systems. It is important to consider the long-term costs of the project, as well as the potential benefits, such as improved performance and efficiency, in order to determine the overall ROI. This can involve using tools such as cost-benefit analysis and discounted cash flow to evaluate the costs and benefits of the project (Bhatia & Bhatia, 2013).

13.7.4 Future of Digital Twins

The future of Digital Twins is promising, as the technology continues to evolve and new applications are being discovered. In the coming years, we can expect to see Digital Twins being used in a wide range of industries, including manufacturing, healthcare, construction, and transportation. The future of digital twin can be understood by levels shown in Figure 13.8.

Some of the key trends and developments that are likely to shape the future of Digital Twins include:

1. Advancements in AI and machine learning, which will enable Digital Twins to become more intelligent and autonomous.

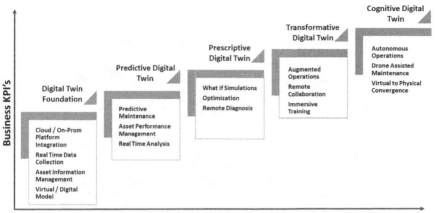

FIGURE 13.8   Levels of digital twin.

2. Increased use of IoT devices and sensors, which will enable Digital Twins to capture more data and provide more accurate and detailed insights.
3. Greater use of AR and VR technologies, which will enable Digital Twins to be used for training, simulation, and collaboration.
4. More widespread adoption of Digital Twins by organizations of all sizes and across all industries, as the benefits of the technology become more widely understood and accepted.
5. An increased emphasis on data privacy and security, as Digital Twins will involve the collection and processing of large amounts of personal and sensitive data.
6. The use of digital twin to improve the performance and efficiency of systems, such as in the case of smart cities, and improve the sustainability and overall livability of our cities.
7. Advancements in data visualization tools, which will enable users to better understand the data and insights generated by Digital Twins.
8. The use of digital twin in the field of autonomous systems, such as self-driving cars, drones, and robots, to improve their performance and safety.

Azure Digital Twins is a platform provided by Microsoft that allows organizations to create and manage digital twins of their physical assets and environments as shown in Figure 13.9. It uses IoT data and machine learning to create a virtual representation of the real world, and provides a variety of tools for modeling, simulation, and analysis.

For example, let's say a company wants to use Azure Digital Twins to create a digital twin of a building. The process would involve the following steps:

1. Data collection: The company would install IoT sensors in the building to collect data on temperature, humidity, lighting, and occupancy. They would also gather information about the building's design and layout.

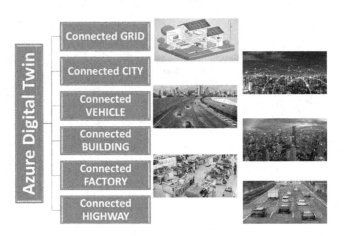

FIGURE 13.9   Azure digital twins: a case study.

2. Modeling: Using the collected data, the company would create a digital twin of the building using Azure Digital Twins. This model would include information about the building's layout, materials, and behavior.
3. Simulation: Using the digital twin, the company would simulate the building's performance under different scenarios, such as different occupancy levels, weather conditions, and energy usage. This would allow them to predict how the building would behave in the real world and identify potential issues before they occur.
4. Analysis: The company would analyze the simulation results to gain insights into the building's performance. This could include identifying potential issues, optimizing energy usage, and making decisions about maintenance, repairs, or upgrades.
5. Feedback: The company would feed the insights and learnings from the analysis back into the real building to improve its performance and prevent issues. For example, if the simulation identified a potential problem with a certain component, the company would schedule maintenance or replacement to address it.
6. Continual monitoring: The company would continuously monitor the building, and update the digital twin as necessary to reflect the current state of the real building. This would help the company to identify any issues early on and take necessary action.

Azure Digital Twins provide many features such as spatial intelligence, event-driven architecture, and integration with other Azure services like Azure IoT, Azure Event Grid, and Azure Time Series Insights that helps in building and managing digital twin.

13.7.5   ADVANCEMENTS IN TECHNOLOGY

Advancements in technology are likely to play a significant role in shaping the future of Digital Twins. As technology continues to evolve, Digital Twins will become more sophisticated and capable of handling larger and more complex data sets. Advancements in AI, machine learning, and IoT will enable Digital Twins to become more intelligent and autonomous, allowing for more accurate predictions and real-time adjustments. Furthermore, the use of augmented realty (AR) and virtual reality (VR) technologies will enable Digital Twins to be used for training, simulation, and collaboration, making it easier for teams to work together and make better decisions.

13.7.6 INDUSTRY ADOPTION AND CASE STUDIES

Industry adoption and case studies will help to demonstrate the value of Digital Twins and encourage more organizations to adopt the technology. As more companies start to use Digital Twins, we can expect to see a growing number of case studies and success stories that demonstrate the benefits of the technology. These case studies will provide valuable insights into how Digital Twins can be used to improve performance, reduce costs, and gain a competitive edge.

13.7.7 POTENTIAL IMPACT ON INDUSTRY AND SOCIETY

The potential impact of Digital Twins on industry and society is significant. The technology has the potential to revolutionize the way we work and live, by making systems more efficient and sustainable. In industry, Digital Twins can be used to improve the performance and efficiency of manufacturing, construction, and transportation systems. In healthcare, Digital Twins can be used to improve patient outcomes and reduce costs. In the field of smart cities, digital twins can be used to improve the performance and efficiency of city systems and infrastructure, as well as improve the overall livability of our cities. In the field of autonomous systems, digital twin can be used to improve their performance and safety. Overall, the potential impact of Digital Twins on industry and society is far-reaching and has the potential to bring about significant improvements in many areas of our lives.

13.8 CONCLUSION AND FUTURE SCOPE

In conclusion, the book chapter "Digital Twin for Sustainable Industrial Development" underscores the profound impact of Digital Twins in revolutionizing the industrial sector toward sustainability. By creating virtual replicas of physical assets and processes, Digital Twins empower industries to optimize resource utilization, predict and prevent downtime, and streamline operations, all while reducing their environmental impact. The integration of real-time data and advanced analytics provides decision-makers with valuable insights to drive eco-friendly practices, compliance with environmental regulations, and emission reduction strategies. However, it is essential to acknowledge the challenges surrounding the implementation of Digital Twins, including data security and compatibility with existing systems. Overcoming these hurdles through collaborative efforts and technological advancements will be crucial to fully harness the potential of Digital Twins and pave the way for a more sustainable, efficient, and responsible industrial future. As industries continue to adopt and innovate with Digital Twins, this chapter aims to inspire and guide stakeholders toward embracing this transformative technology to achieve a harmonious balance between economic growth and environmental preservation.

REFERENCES

Alkali, Y., Routray, I., & Whig, P. (2022a). Strategy for reliable, efficient and secure IoT using artificial intelligence. *IUP Journal of Computer Sciences*, 16(2), 543–556.

Alkali, Y., Routray, I., & Whig, P. (2022b). Study of various methods for reliable, efficient and Secured IoT using Artificial Intelligence. Available at SSRN 4020364.

Anand, M., Velu, A., & Whig, P. (2022). Prediction of loan behaviour with machine learning models for secure banking. *Journal of Computer Science and Engineering (JCSE)*, 3(1), 1–13.

Arun Velu, P. W. (2021). Impact of Covid vaccination on the globe using data analytics. *International Journal of Sustainable Development in Computing Science*, 3(2), 87–99.

Bakshi, P., Bhambri, P., & Thapar, V. (2021). A review paper on wireless sensor network techniques in internet of things (IoT). In *Proceedings of the International Conference on Contemporary Issues in Engineering & Technology*.

Bauer, P., Stevens, B., & Hazeleger, W. (2021). A digital twin of Earth for the green transition. *Nature Climate Change*, 11(2), 80–83.

Bhambri, P. (2021). Electronic evidence. In *Textbook of Cyber Heal* (pp. 86–120). AGAR Saliha Publication, Tamil Nadu. ISBN: 978-81-948141-7-7.

Bhambri, P., Kaur, H., Gupta, A., & Singh, J. (2020). Human activity recognition system. *Oriental Journal of Computer Science and Technology*, 13(2-3), 91–96.

Bhatia, V., & Bhatia, G. (2013). Room temperature based fan speed control system using pulse width modulation technique. *International Journal of Computer Applications*, 81(5), 34–45.

Botín-Sanabria, D. M., Mihaita, A. S., Peimbert-García, R. E., Ramírez-Moreno, M. A., Ramírez-Mendoza, R. A., & Lozoya-Santos, J. D. J. (2022). Digital twin technology challenges and applications: A comprehensive review. *Remote Sensing*, 13(6), 1335.

Chopra, G., & WHIG, P. (2022). A clustering approach based on support vectors. *International Journal of Machine Learning for Sustainable Development*, 4(1), 21–30.

He, B., & Bai, K. J. (2021). Digital twin-based sustainable intelligent manufacturing: A review. *Advances in Manufacturing*, 9, 1–21.

Jimenez, J. I., Jahankhani, H., & Kendzierskyj, S. (2020). Health care in the cyberspace: Medical cyber-physical system and digital twin challenges.

Jupalle, H., Kouser, S., Bhatia, A. B., Alam, N., Nadikattu, R. R., & Whig, P. (2022). Automation of human behaviors and its prediction using machine learning. *Microsystem Technologies*, 45, 1–9.

Kataria, A., & Puri, V. (2022). AI-and IoT-based hybrid model for air quality prediction in a smart city with network assistance. *IET Networks*, 11(6), 221–233.

Kataria, A., Ghosh, S., & Karar, V. (2020). Data prediction of electromagnetic head tracking using self healing neural model for head-mounted display. *Science and Technology*, 23(4), 354–367.

Kataria, A., Ghosh, S., Karar, V., Gupta, T., Srinivasan, K., & Hu, Y. C. (2020). Improved diver communication system by combining optical and electromagnetic trackers. *Sensors*, 20(18), 5084.

Kataria, A., Agrawal, D., Rani, S., Karar, V., & Chauhan, M. (2022). Prediction of blood screening parameters for preliminary analysis using neural networks. In *Predictive modeling in biomedical data mining and analysis* (pp. 157–169). Academic Press.

Kataria, A., Puri, V., Pareek, P. K., & Rani, S. (2023, July). Human activity classification using G-XGB. In *2023 International Conference on Data Science and Network Security (ICDSNS)* (pp. 1–5). IEEE.

Kaur, D., Singh, B., & Rani, S. (2023). Cyber security in the metaverse. In *Handbook of research on AI-based technologies and applications in the era of the metaverse* (pp. 418–435). IGI Global.

Kharchenko, V., Illiashenko, O., Morozova, O., et al. (2020). Combination of digital twin and artificial intelligence in manufacturing using industrial IoT. In 2020

Khera, Y., Whig, P., & Velu, A. (2021). efficient effective and secured electronic billing system using AI. *Vivekananda Journal of Research*, 10, 53–60.

Kumar, J., Saini, S. S., Agrawal, D., Kataria, A., & Karar, V. (2022, December). Effect of complexity and frequency of projected symbology of head-up display while flying in low visibility. In *2022 IEEE International Conference on Machine Learning and Applied Network Technologies (ICMLANT)* (pp. 1–4). IEEE.

Lo, C. K., Chen, C. H., & Zhong, R. Y. (2021). A review of digital twin in product design and development. *Advanced Engineering Informatics*, 48, 101297.

Mamza, E. S. (2021). Use of AIOT in health system. *International Journal of Sustainable Development in Computing Science*, 3(4), 21–30.

Rana, R., Chhabra, Y., & Bhambri, P. (2021). Comparison and evaluation of various QoS parameters in WSNs with the implementation of enhanced low energy adaptive efficient distributed clustering approach. *Webology*, 18(1), 677–695.

Rani, S., Kumar, S., Kataria, A., & Min, H. (2023). SmartHealth: An intelligent framework to secure IoMT service applications using machine learning. *ICT Express*.

Rani, S., Mishra, A. K., Kataria, A., Mallik, S., & Qin, H. (2023). Machine learning-based optimal crop selection system in smart agriculture. *Scientific Reports*, 13(1), 15997.

Rani, S., Pareek, P. K., Kaur, J., Chauhan, M., & Bhambri, P. (2023, February). Quantum machine learning in healthcare: Developments and challenges. In *2023 IEEE International Conference on Integrated Circuits and Communication Systems (ICICACS)* (pp. 1–7). IEEE.

Shahat, E., Hyun, C. T., & Yeom, C. (2021). City digital twin potentials: A review and research agenda. *Sustainability*, 13(6), 3386.

Singh, Y. S., Lal, S., Bhambri, P., Kumar, A., & Dhanoa, I. S. (2021). Advancements in social data security and encryption: A review. *Natural Volatiles & Essential Oils*, 8(4), 15353–15362. DergiPark.

Tanwar, R., Chhabra, Y., Rattan, P., & Rani, S. (2022, September). Blockchain in IoT networks for precision agriculture. In *International Conference on Innovative Computing and Communications: Proceedings of ICICC 2022, Volume 2* (pp. 137–147). Singapore: Springer Nature Singapore.

Tomar, U., Chakroborty, N., Sharma, H., & Whig, P. (2021). AI based smart agricuture system. *Transactions on Latest Trends in Artificial Intelligence*, 2(2), 23–32.

Velu, A., & Whig, P. (2021). Protect personal privacy and wasting time using Nlp: A comparative approach using AI. *Vivekananda Journal of Research*, 10, 42–52.

Whig, P., Kouser, S., Velu, A., & Nadikattu, R. R. (2022). Fog-IoT-assisted-based smart agriculture application. In *Demystifying federated learning for blockchain and industrial internet of things* (pp. 74–93). IGI Global.

Whig, P., Velu, A., & Sharma, P. (2022). Demystifying federated learning for blockchain: A case study. In *Demystifying federated learning for blockchain and industrial internet of things* (pp. 133–165). IGI Global.

Whig, P., Nadikattu, R. R., & Velu, A. (2022). COVID-19 pandemic analysis using application of AI. *Healthcare Monitoring and Data Analysis Using IoT: Technologies and Applications*, 1, 44–55.

Whig, P., Velu, A., & Naddikatu, R. R. (2022). The economic impact of AI-enabled blockchain in 6G-based industry. In *AI and blockchain technology in 6G wireless network* (pp. 205–224). Springer, Singapore.

Whig, P., Velu, A., & Nadikattu, R. R. (2022). Blockchain platform to resolve security issues in IoT and smart networks. In *AI-enabled agile internet of things for sustainable FinTech ecosystems* (pp. 46–65). IGI Global.

Whig, P., Velu, A., & Ready, R. (2022). Demystifying federated learning in artificial intelligence with human-computer interaction. In *Demystifying federated learning for blockchain and industrial internet of things* (pp. 94–122). IGI Global.

Whig, P., Velu, A., & Bhatia, A. B. (2022). Protect nature and reduce the carbon footprint with an application of blockchain for IIoT. In *Demystifying federated learning for blockchain and industrial internet of things* (pp. 123–132). IGI Global.

14 Environmental Impacts of Industrial Processes in Industry 4.0 Ecosystem
Artificial Intelligence Approach

Pankaj Bhambri, Sita Rani, Inderjit Singh Dhanoa, and Tien Anh Tran

14.1 INTRODUCTION

The environmental impacts of industrial processes in the Industry 4.0 ecosystem represent a pressing and multifaceted challenge in today's rapidly evolving industrial landscape. As Industry 4.0, characterized by the integration of digital technologies, automation, and the Internet of Things (IoT), continues to redefine manufacturing and production, there is a growing need to assess and address the consequences of these advancements on the environment (Kumar et al., 2022a, 2022b). This chapter explores the intricate relationship between Industry 4.0 and environmental sustainability, with a specific focus on the innovative application of artificial intelligence (AI) as a strategic approach (Machała et al., 2022; Rani et al., 2023; Rani, S., Chauhan, M., Kataria, A., & Khang, A., 2021). It delves into how AI-driven solutions can be employed to monitor, analyze, and mitigate the environmental footprints of industrial operations. From optimizing resource consumption to reducing emissions and minimizing waste generation, this chapter scrutinizes the potential of AI to not only enhance the efficiency and productivity of industrial processes but also align them with eco-conscious practices (Bathla et al., 2007a, 2007b, Kothandaraman et al., 2022). By providing insights, methodologies, and case studies, this chapter serves as a valuable resource for researchers, practitioners, and policymakers seeking to strike a balance between the advantages of Industry 4.0 and the imperative of environmental sustainability in the modern industrial ecosystem (Kumar, P., Banerjee, K., Singhal, N., Kumar, A., Rani, S., Kumar, R., & Lavinia, C. A., 2022).

14.1.1 ENVIRONMENTAL IMPACTS

Industry 4.0 represents a paradigm shift in manufacturing and industrial operations, marked by the integration of digital technologies, automation, AI, and the IoT.

DOI: 10.1201/9781003395416-14

While these advancements bring about numerous benefits, such as increased productivity, efficiency, and innovation, they also have significant environmental implications (Rani et al., 2022a-c):

- Energy Consumption: Industry 4.0 often involves the use of sophisticated machinery and data centers, which can consume substantial amounts of energy. Without proper management and energy-efficient technologies, this increased energy consumption can contribute to a larger carbon footprint.
- Resource Utilization: The optimization of production processes in Industry 4.0 may lead to increased resource utilization, including raw materials and water. Without sustainable practices, this can deplete finite resources and harm ecosystems.
- Emissions: Automation and robotics may lead to higher emissions if not managed effectively. For instance, increased transportation of goods through automated logistics systems can lead to more vehicle emissions, offsetting other energy-saving benefits.
- E-Waste: The rapid evolution of technology in Industry 4.0 can result in a higher rate of electronic waste (e-waste) when outdated equipment is discarded. This can pose significant environmental challenges if not properly recycled or disposed of.

However, it's essential to note that Industry 4.0 also offers potential solutions to these environmental challenges (Kaur et al., 2006; Kamra & Bhambri, 2007; Jain & Bhambri, 2005; Habib & Chimsom, 2019):

- Predictive Maintenance: AI-driven digital twins and predictive maintenance techniques can reduce energy waste by preventing unplanned downtime and optimizing machine operations (Dhanalakshmi, R., Anand, J., Sivaraman, A. K., & Rani, S., 2022).
- Resource Efficiency: IoT sensors and data analytics can help industries monitor and optimize resource consumption, leading to reduced waste and energy efficiency (Chauhan, M., & Rani, S., 2021).
- Sustainable Practices: Industry 4.0 can be leveraged to implement sustainable manufacturing practices, such as circular economy principles, which emphasize recycling and reusing materials (Khang, A., Bhambri, P., Rani, S., & Kataria, A., 2022).
- Eco-Friendly Product Design: Digital twins can assist in designing products with reduced environmental impact by simulating their lifecycle and identifying areas for improvement.

While Industry 4.0 has the potential to exacerbate environmental impacts, it also provides tools and strategies for mitigating them. The key lies in adopting a proactive approach, leveraging technologies like AI, IoT, and digital twins to monitor and optimize industrial processes with sustainability in mind (Gupta et al., 2007a-e; Goel & Gupta, 2020). This requires collaboration between industries, policymakers, and environmental experts to ensure that the benefits of Industry 4.0 can be harnessed while minimizing its negative effects on the environment (Garg & Bhambri, 2011a, 2011b; Ghobakhloo, 2020).

14.1.2 AI Approaches

AI approaches leverage AI technologies to monitor, analyze, and mitigate the environmental footprint of modern manufacturing and production operations (Gupta, O. P., 2017). Here are several ways in which AI is applied to address environmental concerns in Industry 4.0:

- Predictive Analytics: AI-driven predictive analytics is a powerful tool to anticipate and prevent environmental issues. By analyzing vast datasets from IoT sensors and other sources, AI algorithms can predict equipment failures, emissions spikes, or resource shortages (Gupta, O., Rani, S., & Pant, D. C., 2011). This allows for proactive interventions, reducing the risk of environmental incidents (Rani, S., & Gupta, O. P., 2017).
- Resource Optimization: AI is instrumental in optimizing resource utilization. Machine learning algorithms can analyze data related to energy consumption, water usage, and raw material inputs (Grewal & Bhambri, 2006; Rani et al., 2021; Rattan et al., 2005a, 2005b). By identifying inefficiencies and recommending adjustments, AI helps industries reduce waste and minimize their environmental impact.
- Energy Efficiency: AI-driven systems can continuously monitor energy consumption patterns within a manufacturing facility. Through real-time data analysis, these systems can suggest adjustments to machinery operations, lighting, and heating/cooling systems, optimizing energy efficiency and reducing carbon emissions.
- Emissions Reduction: AI can be used to monitor and control emissions from industrial processes. By integrating AI with environmental monitoring systems, industries can ensure compliance with emissions standards and implement strategies to minimize harmful pollutant releases (Rani, S., Bhambri, P., & Gupta, O. P., 2022).
- Waste Reduction: AI-driven digital twins can simulate production processes to identify opportunities for waste reduction and recycling (Gupta, O. P., & Rani, S., 2010; Sudevan, S., Barwani, B., Al Maani, E., Rani, S., & Sivaraman, A. K., 2021). By modeling and analyzing different production scenarios, AI can help industries minimize waste generation and adopt circular economy principles (Kaur, G., Kaur, R., & Rani, S., 2015).
- Supply Chain Sustainability: AI can be employed to optimize supply chains for sustainability. Machine learning algorithms can analyze transportation routes, inventory levels, and demand forecasts to reduce transportation-related emissions and minimize excess inventory (Kothandaraman, D., Manickam, M., Balasundaram, A., Pradeep, D., Arulmurugan, A., Sivaraman, A. K., & Balakrishna, R., 2022).

- Environmental Risk Assessment: AI can assess environmental risks associated with industrial processes (Kaur, S., Kumar, R., Kaur, R., Singh, S., Rani, S., & Kaur, A., 2022). By simulating potential hazards and their impacts, AI systems assist in the development of preventive measures and emergency response plans, ensuring the safety of both the environment and surrounding communities (Tanwar, R., Chhabra, Y., Rattan, P., & Rani, S., 2022, September; Rani, S., Arya, V., & Kataria, A., 2022).
- Real-time Monitoring: IoT sensors, when coupled with AI, provide real-time environmental monitoring. This enables industries to respond quickly to deviations from environmental standards and take corrective actions, preventing long-term environmental damage.
- Compliance and Reporting: AI can streamline environmental compliance by automating data collection, analysis, and reporting. This not only ensures adherence to regulations but also enhances transparency and accountability (Rani, S., & Kumar, R., 2022).

AI approaches in the context of Industry 4.0 are instrumental in mitigating the environmental impacts of industrial processes. They enable proactive and data-driven decision-making, optimize resource usage, reduce emissions, and promote sustainable practices (Bhambri, 2010; Bhambri & Hans, 2010; Bhambri et al., 2010; Bhambri & Thapar, 2010; Bhambri & Hans, 2009; Dhanalakshmi et al., 2022). As industries increasingly adopt AI technologies, they have the potential to not only enhance operational efficiency but also contribute to a more environmentally responsible and sustainable industrial ecosystem (Rani, S., Kataria, A., & Chauhan, M., 2022).

14.2 INDUSTRIAL PROCESSES

AI approaches leverage AI technologies to monitor, analyze, and mitigate the environmental footprint of modern manufacturing and production operations (Chopra & Bhambri, 2011; Contreras et al., 2017; Bhambri et al., 2005a-c). Here are several ways in which AI is applied to address environmental concerns in Industry 4.0:

- Predictive Analytics: AI-driven predictive analytics is a powerful tool to anticipate and prevent environmental issues. By analyzing vast datasets from IoT sensors and other sources, AI algorithms can predict equipment failures, emissions spikes, or resource shortages. This allows for proactive interventions, reducing the risk of environmental incidents.
- Resource Optimization: AI is instrumental in optimizing resource utilization. Machine learning algorithms can analyze data related to energy consumption, water usage, and raw material inputs. By identifying inefficiencies and recommending adjustments, AI helps industries reduce waste and minimize their environmental impact (Puri, V., Kataria, A., Solanki, V. K., & Rani, S., 2022, December).

- Energy Efficiency: AI-driven systems can continuously monitor energy consumption patterns within a manufacturing facility. Through real-time data analysis, these systems can suggest adjustments to machinery operations, lighting, and heating/cooling systems, optimizing energy efficiency and reducing carbon emissions (Bhambri, P., Rani, S., Gupta, G., & Khang, A. (Eds.), 2022).
- Emissions Reduction: AI can be used to monitor and control emissions from industrial processes. By integrating AI with environmental monitoring systems, industries can ensure compliance with emissions standards and implement strategies to minimize harmful pollutant releases.
- Waste Reduction: AI-driven digital twins can simulate production processes to identify opportunities for waste reduction and recycling. By modeling and analyzing different production scenarios, AI can help industries minimize waste generation and adopt circular economy principles.
- Supply Chain Sustainability: AI can be employed to optimize supply chains for sustainability. Machine learning algorithms can analyze transportation routes, inventory levels, and demand forecasts to reduce transportation-related emissions and minimize excess inventory (Puri, V., Kataria, A., Solanki, V. K., & Rani, S., 2022, December).
- Environmental Risk Assessment: AI can assess environmental risks associated with industrial processes. By simulating potential hazards and their impacts, AI systems assist in the development of preventive measures and emergency response plans, ensuring the safety of both the environment and surrounding communities (Rani, S., Bhambri, P., Kataria, A., Khang, A., & Sivaraman, A. K. (Eds.), 2023).
- Real-time Monitoring: IoT sensors, when coupled with AI, provide real-time environmental monitoring. This enables industries to respond quickly to deviations from environmental standards and take corrective actions, preventing long-term environmental damage.
- Compliance and Reporting: AI can streamline environmental compliance by automating data collection, analysis, and reporting. This not only ensures adherence to regulations but also enhances transparency and accountability.

AI approaches enable proactive and data-driven decision-making, optimize resource usage, reduce emissions, and promote sustainable practices (Bhambri & Singh, 2005a-b; Bhambri & Gupta, 2007; Bhambri et al., 2007a-c; Chen et al., 2017). As industries increasingly adopt AI technologies, they have the potential to not only enhance operational efficiency but also contribute to a more environmentally responsible and sustainable industrial ecosystem.

14.3   ECO-CONSCIOUS MANUFACTURING

It is an approach that emphasizes environmentally responsible practices and sustainability within the industrial context. It aligns with the broader goal of minimizing the environmental impacts of industrial processes in the Industry 4.0

ecosystem. Here's a discussion of eco-conscious manufacturing with reference to the environmental impacts of industrial processes in Industry 4.0 (Bhambri et al., 2008a-b; Cañas et al., 2021):

- Resource Efficiency: Eco-conscious manufacturing seeks to optimize resource usage, including raw materials, energy, and water. In the Industry 4.0 ecosystem, AI-driven digital twins and IoT sensors play a crucial role in monitoring resource consumption in real time (Arya, V., Rani, S., & Choudhary, N., 2022). This data is then used to identify opportunities for efficiency improvements, leading to reduced waste and lower resource intensity in production processes (Bhambri, P., Aggarwal, M., Singh, H., Singh, A. P., & Rani, S., 2022).
- Waste Reduction: Eco-conscious manufacturing prioritizes waste reduction and waste-to-value approaches. AI and data analytics can help identify sources of waste within industrial processes and suggest strategies to minimize it. Additionally, digital twins enable simulations and experiments to find innovative ways to reduce waste generation.
- Energy Efficiency: One of the central tenets of eco-conscious manufacturing is improving energy efficiency. Industry 4.0 technologies, such as AI-driven optimization algorithms, can fine-tune machine operations and processes to minimize energy consumption. This not only reduces environmental impacts but also lowers operational costs (Rani, S., Kataria, A., Kumar, S., & Tiwari, P., 2023).
- Circular Economy: Eco-conscious manufacturing promotes the principles of the circular economy, which involves designing products and processes with a focus on reuse, remanufacturing, and recycling (Rani, S., & Gupta, O. P., 2016). Digital twins can simulate the entire lifecycle of a product, helping manufacturers design products that are easier to disassemble and recycle.
- Emission Reduction: Minimizing emissions is a key aspect of eco-conscious manufacturing. AI can monitor emissions in real time, and digital twins can simulate the impact of different production scenarios on emissions levels (Rani, S., Bhambri, P., & Kataria, A., 2023). This information can guide decisions to reduce emissions and comply with environmental regulations (Rani, S., Kataria, A., Sharma, V., Ghosh, S., Karar, V., Lee, K., & Choi, C., 2021).
- Supply Chain Sustainability: Eco-conscious manufacturing extends beyond the factory floor to encompass the entire supply chain (Rani, S., Mishra, A. K., Kataria, A., Mallik, S., & Qin, H., 2023). Industry 4.0 technologies facilitate supply chain transparency and traceability, enabling companies to make sustainable sourcing decisions and reduce the environmental footprint of transportation and logistics (Banerjee, K., Bali, V., Nawaz, N., Bali, S., Mathur, S., Mishra, R. K., & Rani, S., 2022).
- Product Lifecycle Assessment: Understanding the environmental impact of products throughout their lifecycle is crucial. Digital twins can model a product's environmental footprint, from raw material extraction to end-of-life

disposal. This information informs decisions about product design, materials selection, and end-of-life strategies.

- Regulatory Compliance: Staying compliant with environmental regulations is a key component of eco-conscious manufacturing. AI can assist in tracking and managing compliance data, ensuring that industrial processes meet legal requirements related to environmental impact.

In the Industry 4.0 ecosystem, eco-conscious manufacturing leverages the power of data, connectivity, and AI-driven insights to reduce the environmental footprint of industrial processes (Singh and Bhambri, 2007; Yadav et al., 2022). By embracing sustainable practices and optimizing resource utilization, companies can not only mitigate their environmental impacts but also enhance their competitiveness, reputation, and resilience in an increasingly environmentally conscious world (Gupta, O. P., & Rani, S., 2013).

14.4 SUSTAINABLE PRODUCTION

It represents a strategic approach aimed at minimizing the adverse environmental effects associated with industrial operations while fostering long-term economic viability (Thapar & Bhambri, 2009). Industry 4.0 technologies, including AI, the IoT, and digital twins, are instrumental in achieving sustainable production goals (Bhambri & Gupta, 2005; Bhambri & Bhandari, 2005; Bhambri & Mangat, 2005; Chauhan & Rani, 2021). Here's an exploration of how sustainable production practices are integrated into Industry 4.0 and their implications for mitigating environmental impacts:

- Resource Efficiency: Sustainable production under Industry 4.0 focuses on optimizing resource utilization (Rani, S., Kumar, S., Kataria, A., & Min, H., 2023). AI-driven systems, combined with IoT sensors, continuously monitor resource consumption, such as energy, water, and raw materials, in real time. This data is then analyzed to identify inefficiencies and areas for improvement, ultimately reducing waste and conserving resources.
- Circular Economy: Industry 4.0 encourages the adoption of circular economy principles, wherein products and materials are designed, produced, and managed to maximize their utility and minimize waste. Digital twins simulate product lifecycles, enabling manufacturers to plan for product reuse, recycling, or remanufacturing. This minimizes the environmental impact of product disposal and contributes to a more sustainable production ecosystem.
- Emissions Reduction: Sustainable production places a strong emphasis on reducing emissions and pollutant releases. AI-driven systems can optimize manufacturing processes to minimize energy consumption and emissions. Predictive maintenance ensures that equipment operates at peak efficiency, reducing emissions associated with malfunctioning machinery (Rani, S., & Kaur, S., 2012).

- Real-Time Environmental Monitoring: The integration of IoT sensors and digital twins provides real-time environmental monitoring capabilities. Industries can continuously assess factors like air quality, water usage, and emissions, enabling immediate responses to deviations from environmental standards and facilitating regulatory compliance (Kataria, A., Agrawal, D., Rani, S., Karar, V., & Chauhan, M., 2022).
- Data-Driven Decision-Making: Sustainable production leverages AI to make data-driven decisions that align with environmental objectives (Rani, S., Pareek, P. K., Kaur, J., Chauhan, M., & Bhambri, P., 2023, February). AI algorithms analyze complex datasets to provide actionable insights, allowing industries to implement strategies that reduce environmental impacts, such as adjusting production schedules or optimizing transportation routes (Dhanalakshmi, R., Vijayaraghavan, N., Sivaraman, A. K., & Rani, S., 2022).
- Supply Chain Sustainability: Sustainability in Industry 4.0 extends beyond individual production facilities to encompass the entire supply chain. AI-driven supply chain optimization helps minimize transportation-related emissions, reduces excess inventory, and ensures that suppliers adhere to eco-friendly practices.
- Renewable Energy Integration: Sustainable production often involves the integration of renewable energy sources, such as solar and wind power, into manufacturing processes. AI can forecast energy generation patterns and optimize energy usage based on the availability of renewable energy, further reducing the carbon footprint of production.
- Environmental Compliance: Sustainable production practices prioritize adherence to environmental regulations and standards. AI-driven systems facilitate compliance by automating data collection and reporting, reducing the risk of non-compliance penalties and improving transparency (Kaur, D., Singh, B., & Rani, S., 2023).

Sustainable production in the Industry 4.0 ecosystem represents a holistic approach to mitigating the environmental impacts of industrial processes. It leverages digital technologies, particularly AI, to enhance resource efficiency, reduce emissions, and promote responsible resource management (Bhambri et al., 2009; Bhambri & Singh, 2009; Bhambri & Thapar, 2009; Saucedo-Martínez et al., 2018). By adopting sustainable production practices, industries can not only contribute to environmental preservation but also achieve long-term economic sustainability and competitiveness in a global market increasingly focused on eco-consciousness.

14.5 GREEN TECHNOLOGY

"Green technology," often referred to as "clean technology" or "sustainable technology," represents a critical aspect of addressing the environmental impacts of industrial processes within the Industry 4.0 ecosystem (Rani, S., Kataria, A., & Chauhan, M., 2022). Green technology encompasses innovative solutions, strategies, and practices aimed at reducing the environmental footprint of industrial activities and promoting sustainability (Singh et al., 2010; Singh et al., 2006; Gupta & Bhambri, 2006). In the context of "Environmental impacts of Industrial Processes in Industry 4.0 Ecosystem," here's how green technology plays a pivotal role:

- Renewable Energy Sources: One of the fundamental elements of green technology is the adoption of renewable energy sources such as solar, wind, hydroelectric, and geothermal power. In Industry 4.0, integrating renewable energy into manufacturing processes and operations helps reduce greenhouse gas emissions, energy costs, and reliance on fossil fuels (Kumar, R., Rani, S., & Khangura, S. S. (Eds.), 2023). AI-driven predictive analytics can optimize the use of renewable energy sources based on weather conditions and energy demand.
- Energy Efficiency: Green technology focuses on improving energy efficiency across industrial processes. This includes using advanced sensors, automation, and AI to monitor and control energy consumption in real time. Smart grids and energy management systems can balance energy supply and demand efficiently, reducing wastage and environmental impacts.
- Sustainable Materials: Green technology encourages the use of sustainable and eco-friendly materials in manufacturing. Industries are adopting recycled and biodegradable materials, as well as conducting life-cycle assessments to minimize the environmental impact of their products. AI can assist in material selection and supply chain optimization to reduce the carbon footprint of raw materials (Rani, S., Mishra, R. K., Usman, M., Kataria, A., Kumar, P., Bhambri, P., & Mishra, A. K., 2021).
- Waste Reduction and Recycling: Green technology emphasizes waste reduction and recycling. AI-driven robotic systems are employed in recycling facilities to sort and process recyclables more efficiently. Digital twins and IoT devices can monitor waste generation in real time, enabling better waste management practices and minimizing land filling.
- Cleaner Production Processes: Industry 4.0 enables the optimization of production processes for reduced environmental impact. AI-driven digital twins simulate manufacturing processes, allowing industries to identify inefficiencies and design more eco-friendly production methods. These results in lower emissions, reduced resource consumption, and minimized environmental pollution.
- Smart Agriculture: In agriculture, green technology involves precision farming techniques that use IoT sensors, drones, and AI to optimize crop cultivation. These technologies enable precise application of fertilizers, pesticides, and water, reducing chemical usage and minimizing runoff pollution.
- Circular Economy: Green technology promotes the concept of a circular economy, where products and materials are designed for reuse, remanufacturing, or recycling. Digital twins and AI can support this approach by optimizing product design for easy disassembly and recycling.

- Water Conservation: Sustainable water management is a key aspect of green technology. AI-driven systems can monitor water usage in industrial processes and agriculture, identify leaks, and optimize irrigation practices to reduce water wastage (Bilal, M., Kumari, B., & Rani, S., 2021, May).
- Environmental Monitoring: Green technology relies on advanced environmental monitoring tools, including sensors, satellites, and AI-driven analytics, to track air and water quality, biodiversity, and ecosystem health. This information is crucial for informed decision-making and early detection of environmental issues.

Green technology leverages digital technologies and sustainable practices to enhance energy efficiency, reduce emissions, minimize waste, and promote environmentally responsible industrial operations. As industries embrace green technology within the context of Industry 4.0, they contribute to a more sustainable and eco-conscious future while remaining competitive and innovative in the global market (Bhambri, P., Rani, S., Gupta, G., & Khang, A. (Eds.), 2022).

14.6 DATA-DRIVEN DECISIONS

Data-driven decisions are the cornerstone of addressing environmental impacts within the Industry 4.0 ecosystem. In this context, data serves as a powerful tool to monitor, analyze, and mitigate the environmental consequences of industrial processes. The integration of IoT sensors and digital technologies allows for real-time data collection on energy consumption, emissions, resource utilization, and production efficiency (Bhambri & Singh, 2008a-c; Bhambri & Nischal, 2008a-b). AI-driven analytics and predictive modeling harness this data to enable proactive interventions, reducing the risk of environmental incidents. Decision-makers can optimize resource allocation, track emissions in real time, and fine-tune production processes to minimize waste and energy consumption (Bhambri & Sharma, 2005). Furthermore, data-driven insights extend to supply chain optimization and environmental reporting, fostering a culture of continuous improvement and alignment with sustainability objectives (Singh et al., 2004; Singh et al., 2005a-f). Ultimately, data-driven decisions empower industries to harmonize their operations with environmental sustainability goals in the modern industrial landscape.

14.7 AI-DRIVEN SOLUTIONS

AI-driven solutions leverage AI technologies to collect, analyze, and interpret data, enabling industries to make informed decisions and optimize their operations for sustainability. Here are some details and examples of AI-driven solutions in this context:

- Predictive Maintenance: Predictive maintenance uses AI and machine learning algorithms to analyze sensor data from industrial equipment. By monitoring factors like temperature, vibration, and performance metrics in real time, AI can predict when equipment is likely to fail.

- Example: In a manufacturing plant, AI-driven predictive maintenance systems continuously analyze data from production machinery. When anomalies or patterns indicative of potential breakdowns are detected, the system alerts maintenance teams to perform proactive repairs, reducing downtime and preventing environmental impacts associated with sudden equipment failures.
- Energy Management: AI-based energy management systems optimize energy consumption by monitoring equipment and facility performance. They identify inefficiencies and recommend adjustments to reduce energy waste.
  - Example: An AI-driven energy management system in a factory analyzes historical energy usage, production schedules, and weather data. It then adjusts lighting, heating, ventilation, and air conditioning (HVAC), and machinery operation in real time to minimize energy consumption while maintaining comfort and productivity.
- Waste Reduction: AI-driven digital twins of production processes simulate various scenarios to identify opportunities for waste reduction and process optimization. By modeling and analyzing the entire production lifecycle, AI can pinpoint areas where resource efficiency can be improved.
  - Example: In an automotive manufacturing plant, a digital twin powered by AI analyzes production processes and identifies that certain steps in the painting process are resulting in excessive paint waste. Recommendations are made to adjust the process, reducing both paint consumption and hazardous waste generation.
- Emission Control: AI is used to monitor emissions in real time and make instant adjustments to reduce pollutant releases. This can involve adjusting combustion parameters in industrial boilers, optimizing fuel consumption, or controlling exhaust gas treatment systems.
  - Example: In a power plant, AI algorithms continuously monitor the combustion process. When emissions exceed permitted levels, the AI system adjusts the combustion parameters to optimize combustion efficiency and reduce emissions, ensuring compliance with environmental regulations (Rani, S., Bhambri, P., & Chauhan, M., 2021, October).
- Supply Chain Optimization: AI-driven supply chain optimization considers factors like transportation routes, inventory levels, and demand forecasts to minimize the environmental impact of logistics operations.
  - Example: An AI-based supply chain management system optimizes the routes for delivery trucks in a logistics company. By considering factors like traffic conditions, fuel efficiency, and load capacity, the system minimizes fuel consumption and emissions, reducing the environmental footprint of transportation.
- Environmental Risk Assessment: AI models can simulate environmental risks associated with industrial processes, such as chemical spills or air quality degradation. By modeling potential hazards and their impacts, industries can develop preventive measures and emergency response plans.

- Example: In a chemical plant, AI-driven simulations predict the potential consequences of a chemical spill. The model suggests safety measures and evacuation plans, ensuring that environmental risks are minimized in the event of an accident.

These examples demonstrate how AI-driven solutions are instrumental in addressing environmental impacts in Industry 4.0. By leveraging AI's capabilities for data analysis, prediction, and automation, industries can enhance sustainability, reduce resource consumption, and minimize negative environmental effects across a wide range of industrial processes.

14.8   ENVIRONMENTAL SUSTAINABILITY

Environmental sustainability refers to the practice of conducting industrial activities in a manner that minimizes harm to the environment, conserves resources, reduces waste, and mitigates greenhouse gas emissions. It involves adopting strategies and technologies that ensure the long-term well-being of the planet while maintaining economic viability. Here are some details and examples of environmental sustainability in this context:

- Resource Efficiency: Industrial processes in the Industry 4.0 ecosystem are optimized to use resources efficiently. For example, AI-driven systems monitor and control energy consumption, ensuring that machines and equipment operate at their most energy-efficient levels. This reduces resource waste and lowers operational costs.
- Waste Reduction: Sustainability efforts focus on minimizing waste generation and promoting recycling and reuse. In smart manufacturing environments, digital twins and IoT sensors help identify opportunities to reduce waste by adjusting production processes and material usage. For instance, excess material in 3D printing can be minimized, and defective parts can be caught early in the production process.
- Emissions Reduction: Environmental sustainability in Industry 4.0 involves actively reducing greenhouse gas emissions. AI algorithms analyze emissions data in real time, and decisions are made to optimize combustion processes, reduce energy consumption, or even switch to cleaner energy sources. For example, an AI-driven system might adjust the combustion parameters of a furnace to lower CO_2 emissions while maintaining production efficiency (Arunachalam, P., Janakiraman, N., Sivaraman, A. K., Balasundaram, A., Vincent, R., Rani, S., ... & Rajesh, M., 2022).
- Predictive Maintenance: Sustainability is also enhanced through predictive maintenance, which prevents unexpected equipment failures and costly downtime. AI-driven predictive models use historical data and sensor information to anticipate when machines need maintenance. This reduces the need for frequent, energy-intensive repairs or replacements and extends the life of equipment.

- Circular Economy: Industry 4.0 promotes circular economy principles by designing products with recyclability and reusability in mind. For instance, products can be designed to be easily disassembled and their components reused or recycled at the end of their life cycle. This minimizes the environmental impact of product disposal (Kataria, A., Puri, V., Pareek, P. K., & Rani, S., 2023, July).
- Smart Agriculture: In agriculture, environmental sustainability involves optimizing resource use and minimizing environmental impacts. IoT sensors monitor soil moisture, weather conditions, and crop health. AI-driven decision support systems recommend precise irrigation and fertilization, reducing water and chemical usage while maximizing crop yields.
- Renewable Energy Integration: Industry 4.0 encourages the integration of renewable energy sources like solar and wind into industrial operations. Smart grids and AI-based energy management systems enable industries to generate clean energy on-site and sell excess energy back to the grid (Rani, S., Bhambri, P., Kataria, A., & Khang, A., 2022).
- Environmental Reporting: Sustainability efforts include transparent reporting of environmental performance (Singh, P., Gupta, O. P., & Saini, S., 2017). Industries in the Industry 4.0 ecosystem use data-driven reporting systems to track and document their environmental achievements, ensuring compliance with regulations and providing stakeholders with clear insights into their sustainability efforts (Abrol et al., 2005; Bai et al., 2020; Bhambri et al., 2011).

Overall, environmental sustainability in the Industry 4.0 ecosystem is about leveraging digital technologies and data-driven decision-making to optimize industrial processes for minimal environmental impact. It requires a holistic approach that considers resource efficiency, waste reduction, emissions control, and a commitment to responsible environmental practices.

14.9 CONCLUSION

In conclusion, the exploration of the environmental impacts of industrial processes within the Industry 4.0 ecosystem, guided by an AI approach, reveals a promising trajectory towards sustainable industrialization. Industry 4.0's integration of digital technologies, IoT, and AI-driven systems empowers industries to monitor, analyze, and mitigate environmental footprints with unprecedented precision. Through real-time data collection, predictive analytics, and data-driven decision-making, businesses can optimize resource usage, reduce emissions, and minimize waste generation, all while enhancing production efficiency. As this chapter underscores, the intersection of Industry 4.0 and environmental sustainability is not merely a theoretical concept but a practical imperative, vital for fostering a future where industrial progress harmonizes with ecological responsibility. It emphasizes that the Fourth Industrial Revolution has the potential to reshape industrial practices, ushering in an era where economic growth goes hand in hand with environmental stewardship, ultimately ensuring a more sustainable and resilient industrial ecosystem.

REFERENCES

Abrol, N., Shaifali, Rattan, M., & Bhambri, P. (2005). Implementation and performance evaluation of JPEG 2000 for medical images. In International Conference on Innovative Applications of Information Technology for Developing World.

Arunachalam, P., Janakiraman, N., Sivaraman, A. K., Balasundaram, A., Vincent, R., Rani, S., ... & Rajesh, M. (2022). Synovial sarcoma classification technique using support vector machine and structure features. *Intelligent Automation & Soft Computing, 32*(2).

Arya, V., Rani, S., & Choudhary, N. (2022). Enhanced bio-inspired trust and reputation model for wireless sensor networks. In *Proceedings of Second Doctoral Symposium on Computational Intelligence: DoSCI 2021* (pp. 569–579). Springer Singapore.

Bai, C., Dallasega, P., Orzes, G., & Sarkis, J. (2020). Industry 4.0 technologies assessment: A sustainability perspective. *International Journal of Production Economics, 229*, 107776.

Banerjee, K., Bali, V., Nawaz, N., Bali, S., Mathur, S., Mishra, R. K., & Rani, S. (2022). A machine-learning approach for prediction of water contamination using latitude, longitude, and elevation. *Water, 14*(5), 728.

Bathla, S., Bhambri, P., & Jindal, C. (2007a, May). Wearable computers: Smart era in computing. Paper presented at the National Conference on Advances in Computer Technology and Applications.

Bathla, S., Jindal, C., & Bhambri, P. (2007b, March). Impact of technology on societal living. In International Conference on Convergence and Competition (pp. 14).

Bhambri, P. (2010). An adaptive and resource efficient hand off in recovery state in geographic adhoc networks. International Conference on Engineering Innovations - A Fillip to Economic Development.

Bhambri, P., & Bhandari, A. (2005, March). Different protocols for wireless security. Paper presented at the National Conference on Advancements in Modeling and Simulation, 8.

Bhambri, P., & Gupta, S. (2005, March). A Survey & Comparison of permutation possibility of fault tolerant multistage interconnection networks. Paper presented at the National Conference on Application of Mathematics in Engg. & Tech., 13.

Bhambri, P., & Gupta, S. (2007, September). Interactive voice recognition system. In National Conference on Advancements in Modeling and simulation (p. 107).

Bhambri, P., & Hans, S. (2009). Direct non iterative solution based neural network for image compression. *PIMT Journal of Research, 2*(2), 64–67.

Bhambri, P., & Hans, S. (2010). Evaluation of Integrated development environments for embedded system design. *Apeejay Journal of Management and Technology, 5*(2), 138–146.

Bhambri, P., & Mangat, A. S. (2005, March). Wireless security. Paper presented at the National Conference on Emerging Computing Technologies, 155–161.

Bhambri, P., & Nischal, P. (2008a, September). Emerging trends of intersectoral growth of India with special reference to service sector. *PIMT Journal of Research, 1*(2), 10–18.

Bhambri, P., & Nischal, P. (2008b, May). Emerging New Economy in Telecommunication Sector of India. In International Conference on Business Challenges & Strategies in Emerging Global Scenario (p. 26).

Bhambri, P., & Sharma, N. (2005, September). Priorities for sustainable civilization. Paper presented at the National Conference on Technical Education in Globalized Environment- Knowledge, Technology & The Teacher, pp. 108.

Bhambri, P., & Singh, I. (2005b, March). Electrical actuation systems. Paper presented at the National Conference on Application of Mathematics in Engg. & Tech., 58–60.

Bhambri, P., & Singh, M. (2005a). Artificial intelligence. In *Seminar on E-Governance— pathway to progress* (pp. 14).

Bhambri, P., & Singh, M. (2008a). Direct non iterative solution based neural network for image compression. *PCTE Journal of Computer Sciences, 5*(2), 1–4.

Bhambri, P., & Singh, M. (2008b). Biometrics: Face recognition using eigen faces. *Apeejay Journal of Management and Technology, 3*(2), 160–164.

Bhambri, P., & Singh, M. (2008c). Image transport protocol for JPEG image over loss prone congested networks. *PIMT Journal of Research, 1*(1), 55–61.

Bhambri, P., & Singh, M. (2009). *Data mining model for protein sequence alignment.* Punjab Technical University, Jalandhar.

Bhambri, P., & Thapar, V. (2009, May). Power distribution challenges in VLSI: An introduction. Paper presented at the International Conference on Downtrend Challenges in IT, pp. 63.

Bhambri, P., & Thapar, V. (2010). Iris biometric - A review. Paper presented at the National Conference on Cellular and Molecular Medicine.

Bhambri, P., Singh, I., & Gupta, S. (2005a, March). Robotics systems. Paper presented at the National Conference on Emerging Computing Technologies, 27.

Bhambri, P., Sood, G., & Verma, A. (2005b). Robotics design: Major considerations. In National Conference on Emerging Computing Technologies (pp. 100).

Bhambri, P., Singh, I., & Singh, J. (2005c). Role of programming and mathematics in the design of robotics. In National Conference on Application of Mathematics in Engg. & Tech. (pp. 101).

Bhambri, P., Singh, H., & Gupta, S. (2007a, May). Generation of fuzzy rules and membership function from training examples. Paper presented at the National Conference on Advances in Computer Technology and Applications.

Bhambri, P., Nischal, P., & Gupta, S. (2007b, April). Bioinformatics and computational Biology. In National Conference on Some Aspects of Recent Trends in Engineering and Technology (p. 29).

Bhambri, P., Singh, R., & Singh, J. (2007c). Wireless security. In National Conference on Emerging Trends in Communication & IT (pp. 290).

Bhambri, P., Hans, S., & Singh, M. (2008a, November). Bioinformatics - Friendship between bits & genes. In International Conference on Advanced Computing & Communication Technologies (pp. 62–65).

Bhambri, P., Hans, S., & Singh, M. (2008b, November). Fractal image compression techniques: A fast fractal image compression method. In International Conference on Advanced Computing and Communication Technologies (pp. 6576–6660).

Bhambri, P., Hans, S., & Singh, M. (2009). Inharmonic signal synthesis & analysis. *Technia - International Journal of Computing Science and Communication Technologies, 1*(2), 199–201.

Bhambri, P., Singh, M., Suresh, H., & Singh, I. (2010). Data mining model for protein sequence alignment. In Proceedings of the International Conference on Data Mining (pp. 612–617).

Bhambri, P., Gupta, O. P., Hans, S., & Singh, R. (2011). Conceptual translation as a part of gene expression. In International Conference on Advanced Computing and Communication Technologies (Sponsored by IEEE Delhi Section, IEEE Computer Society Chapter, Delhi Section and IETE Delhi Centre) (pp. 506–508).

Bhambri, P., Rani, S., Gupta, G., & Khang, A. (Eds.). (2022). *Cloud and fog computing platforms for internet of things.* CRC Press.

Bhambri, P., Aggarwal, M., Singh, H., Singh, A. P., & Rani, S. (2022). Uprising of EVs: Charging the future with demystified analytics and sustainable development. In *Decision Analytics for Sustainable Development in Smart Society 5.0: Issues, Challenges and Opportunities* (pp. 37–53). Singapore: Springer Nature Singapore.

Bilal, M., Kumari, B., & Rani, S. (2021, May). An artificial intelligence supported E-commerce model to improve the export of Indian handloom and handicraft products in the World. In *Proceedings of the International Conference on Innovative Computing & Communication (ICICC).*

Cañas, H., Mula, J., Díaz-Madroñero, M., & Campuzano-Bolarín, F. (2021). Implementing industry 4.0 principles. *Computers & Industrial Engineering, 158*, 107379.

Chauhan, M., & Rani, S. (2021). Covid-19: A revolution in the field of education in India. *Learning How to Learn Using Multimedia*, 23–42.

Chen, B., Wan, J., Shu, L., Li, P., Mukherjee, M., & Yin, B. (2017). Smart factory of industry 4.0: Key technologies, application case, and challenges. *IEEE Access, 6*, 6505–6519.

Chopra, S., & Bhambri, P. (2011). *A new method of edge detection in mammographic images*. Punjab Technical University.

Contreras, J. D., Garcia, J. I., & Pastrana, J. D. (2017). Developing of Industry 4.0 applications. *International Journal of Online Engineering, 13*(10).

Dhanalakshmi, R., Vijayaraghavan, N., Sivaraman, A. K., & Rani, S. (2022). Epidemic awareness spreading in smart cities using the artificial neural network. In *AI-centric smart city ecosystems* (pp. 187–207): CRC Press.

Dhanalakshmi, R., Anand, J., Sivaraman, A. K., & Rani, S. (2022). IoT-based water quality monitoring system using cloud for agriculture use. *Cloud and Fog Computing Platforms for Internet of Things, 28*(3), 1–14.

Garg, D., & Bhambri, P. (2011a). A novel approach for fusion of multimodality medical images. *CiiT International Journal of Digital Image Processing, 3*(10), 576–580.

Garg, D., & Bhambri, P. (2011b). *A novel approach for fusion of multi-modality medical images*. Punjab Technical University, Jalandhar.

Ghobakhloo, M. (2020). Industry 4.0, digitization, and opportunities for sustainability. *Journal of Cleaner Production, 252*, 119869.

Goel, R., & Gupta, P. (2020). Robotics and Industry 4.0. *A Roadmap to Industry 4.0: Smart production, sharp business and sustainable development*, 157–169.

Grewal, H.K., & Bhambri, P. (2006). Globe-IT: Globalization of learning through open based education and information technology. In International Conference on Brand India: Issues, Challenges and Opportunities (pp. 24).

Gupta, O., Rani, S., & Pant, D. C. (2011). Impact of parallel computing on bioinformatics algorithms. In *Proceedings 5th IEEE International Conference on Advanced Computing and Communication Technologies* (pp. 206–209).

Gupta, O. P. (2017). Study and analysis of various bioinformatics applications using protein BLAST: An overview. *Advances in Computational Sciences and Technology, 10*(8), 2587–2601.

Gupta, O. P., & Rani, S. (2010). Bioinformatics applications and tools: An overview. *CiiT-International Journal of Biometrics and Bioinformatics, 3*(3), 107–110.

Gupta, O. P., & Rani, S. (2013). Accelerating molecular sequence analysis using distributed computing environment. *International Journal of Scientific & Engineering Research–IJSER, 4*(10), 262–265.

Gupta, S., & Bhambri, P. (2006). A competitive market is pushing site search technology to new plateaus. In International Conference on Brand India: Issues, Challenges and Opportunities (pp. 34).

Gupta, S., Nischal, P., & Bhambri, P. (2007a). Multimodal biometric: Enhancing security level of biometric system. In National Conference on Emerging Trends in Communication & IT (pp. 78–81).

Gupta, S., Nischal, P., & Bhambri, P. (2007b, March). Mathematical modeling of EMG (ELECTROMYOGRAM). Paper presented at the International Conference on Global Trends in IT, pp. 14.

Gupta, S., Nischal, P., & Bhambri, P. (2007c, February). DNA computing: An emerging trend. Paper presented at the National Conference on Emerging Trends in Communication & IT, pp. 267.

Gupta, S., Kaur, R., & Bhambri, P. (2007d). Common channel signaling system #7: A global standard for telecommunication. In National Conference on Emerging Trends in Communication & IT (pp. 130–134).

Gupta, S., Nischal, P., & Bhambri, P. (2007e). Data encryption standard (DES) algorithm with Diffie-Hellman key exchange. In National Conference on Emerging Trends in Communication & IT (pp. 135–143).

Habib, M. K., & Chimsom, C. (2019). Industry 4.0: Sustainability and design principles. Paper presented at the 2019 20th International Conference on Research and Education in Mechatronics (REM).

Jain, V. K., & Bhambri, P. (2005). Fundamentals of information technology & computer programming.

Kamra, A., & Bhambri, P. (2007). Computer peripherals & interfaces.

Kataria, A., Agrawal, D., Rani, S., Karar, V., & Chauhan, M. (2022). Prediction of blood screening parameters for preliminary analysis using neural networks. In *Predictive modeling in biomedical data mining and analysis* (pp. 157–169). Academic Press.

Kataria, A., Puri, V., Pareek, P. K., & Rani, S. (2023, July). human activity classification using G-XGB. In *2023 International Conference on Data Science and Network Security (ICDSNS)* (pp. 1–5). IEEE.

Kaur, D., Singh, B., & Rani, S. (2023). Cyber security in the metaverse. In *Handbook of research on AI-based technologies and applications in the era of the metaverse* (pp. 418–435). IGI Global.

Kaur, G., Bhambri, P., & Sohal, A. K. (2006, January). Review analysis of economic load dispatch. In *National Conference on Future Trends in Information Technology*.

Kaur, G., Kaur, R., & Rani, S. (2015). Cloud computing - a new trend in IT era. *International Journal of Scientific and Technology Management, 1*(3), 1–6.

Kaur, S., Kumar, R., Kaur, R., Singh, S., Rani, S., & Kaur, A. (2022). Piezoelectric materials in sensors: Bibliometric and visualization analysis. *Materials Today: Proceedings*.

Khang, A., Bhambri, P., Rani, S., & Kataria, A. (2022). Big data, cloud computing and internet of things.

Kothandaraman, D., Manickam, M., Balasundaram, A., Pradeep, D., Arulmurugan, A., Sivaraman, A. K., & Balakrishna, R. (2022). Decentralized link failure prevention routing (DLFPR) algorithm for efficient internet of things. *Intelligent Automation and Soft Computing, 34*(1), 655–666.

Kumar, P., Banerjee, K., Singhal, N., Kumar, A., Rani, S., Kumar, R., & Lavinia, C. A. (2022). Verifiable, secure mobile agent migration in healthcare systems using a polynomial-based threshold secret sharing scheme with a Blowfish algorithm. *Sensors, 22*(22), 8620.

Kumar, P., Banerjee, K., Singhal, N., Kumar, A., Rani, S., Kumar, R., & Lavinia, C. A. (2022a). Verifiable, secure mobile agent migration in healthcare systems using a polynomial-based threshold secret sharing scheme with a Blowfish algorithm. *Sensors, 22*(22), 8620.

Kumar, R., Rani, S., & Awadh, M. A. (2022b). Exploring the application sphere of the internet of things in industry 4.0: A review, bibliometric and content analysis. *Sensors, 22*(11), 4276.

Kumar, R., Rani, S., & Khangura, S. S. (Eds.). (2023). *Machine learning for sustainable manufacturing in Industry 4.0: Concept, concerns and applications.* CRC Press.

Machała, S., Chamier-Gliszczyński, N., & Królikowski, T. (2022). Application of AR/VR technology in Industry 4.0. *Procedia Computer Science, 207*, 2990–2998.

Puri, V., Kataria, A., Solanki, V. K., & Rani, S. (2022, December). AI-based botnet attack classification and detection in IoT devices. In *2022 IEEE International Conference on Machine Learning and Applied Network Technologies (ICMLANT)* (pp. 1–5). IEEE.

Rani, S., & Gupta, O. P. (2016). Empirical analysis and performance evaluation of various GPU implementations of protein BLAST. *International Journal of Computer Applications, 151*(7), 22–27.

Rani, S., & Gupta, O. P. (2017). CLUS_GPU-BLASTP: Accelerated protein sequence alignment using GPU-enabled cluster. *The Journal of Supercomputing, 73,* 4580–4595.

Rani, S., & Kaur, S. (2012). Cluster analysis method for multiple sequence alignment. *International Journal of Computer Applications, 43*(14), 19–25.

Rani, S., & Kumar, R. (2022). Bibliometric review of actuators: Key automation technology in a smart city framework. *Materials Today: Proceedings, 60,* 1800–1807.

Rani, S., Bhambri, P., & Chauhan, M. (2021, October). A machine learning model for kids' behavior analysis from facial emotions using principal component analysis. In *2021 5th Asian Conference on Artificial Intelligence Technology (ACAIT)* (pp. 522–525). IEEE.

Rani, S., Chauhan, M., Kataria, A., & Khang, A. (2021). IoT equipped intelligent distributed framework for smart healthcare systems. *arXiv preprint arXiv:2110.04997.*

Rani, S., Kataria, A., Sharma, V., Ghosh, S., Karar, V., Lee, K., & Choi, C. (2021). Threats and corrective measures for IoT security with observance of cybercrime: A survey. *Wireless Communications and Mobile Computing, 2021,* 1–30.

Rani, S., Mishra, R. K., Usman, M., Kataria, A., Kumar, P., Bhambri, P., & Mishra, A. K. (2021). Amalgamation of advanced technologies for sustainable development of smart city environment: A review. *IEEE Access, 9,* 150060–150087.

Rani, S., Bhambri, P., & Gupta, O. P. (2022). Green smart farming techniques and sustainable agriculture: Research roadmap towards organic farming for imperishable agricultural products. *Handbook of sustainable development through green engineering and technology,* 49–67.

Rani, S., Bhambri, P., Kataria, A., & Khang, A. (2022). Smart city ecosystem: Concept, sustainability, design principles, and technologies. In *AI-centric smart city ecosystems* (pp. 1–20). CRC Press.

Rani, S., Arya, V., & Kataria, A. (2022). Dynamic pricing-based e-commerce model for the produce of organic farming in India: A research roadmap with main advertence to vegetables. In *Proceedings of Data Analytics and Management: ICDAM 2021, Volume 2* (pp. 327–336). Springer Singapore.

Rani, S., Kataria, A., & Chauhan, M. (2022). Fog computing in industry 4.0: Applications and challenges—A research roadmap. *Energy conservation solutions for fog-edge computing paradigms,* 173–190.

Rani, S., Kataria, A., & Chauhan, M. (2022). Cyber security techniques, architectures, and design. In *Holistic approach to quantum cryptography in cyber security* (pp. 41–66). CRC Press.

Rani, S., Kataria, A., & Chauhan, M. (2022a). Cyber security techniques, architectures, and design. In *Holistic approach to quantum cryptography in cyber security* (pp. 41–66): CRC Press.

Rani, S., Kataria, A., & Chauhan, M. (2022b). Fog computing in industry 4.0: Applications and challenges—A research roadmap. *Energy conservation solutions for fog-edge computing paradigms,* 173–190.

Rani, S., Kataria, A., Chauhan, M., Rattan, P., Kumar, R., & Sivaraman, A. K. (2022c). Security and privacy challenges in the deployment of cyber-physical systems in smart city applications: State-of-art work. *Materials Today: Proceedings, 62,* 4671–4676.

Rani, S., Bhambri, P., & Kataria, A. (2023). Integration of IoT, Big Data, and Cloud Computing technologies. *Big Data, Cloud Computing and IoT: Tools and applications.*

Rani, S., Mishra, A. K., Kataria, A., Mallik, S., & Qin, H. (2023). Machine learning-based optimal crop selection system in smart agriculture. *Scientific Reports, 13*(1), 15997.

Rani, S., Bhambri, P., Kataria, A., Khang, A., & Sivaraman, A. K. (Eds.). (2023). Big Data, Cloud Computing and IoT: Tools and applications. *Chapman and Hall/CRC, 10*(978100329833), 5.

Rani, S., Kataria, A., Kumar, S., & Tiwari, P. (2023). Federated learning for secure IoMT-applications in smart healthcare systems: A comprehensive review. *Knowledge-based systems*, 110658.

Rani, S., Kumar, S., Kataria, A., & Min, H. (2023). SmartHealth: An intelligent framework to secure IoMT service applications using machine learning. *ICT Express*.

Rani, S., Pareek, P. K., Kaur, J., Chauhan, M., & Bhambri, P. (2023, February). Quantum Machine Learning in Healthcare: Developments and Challenges. In *2023 IEEE International Conference on Integrated Circuits and Communication Systems (ICICACS)* (pp. 1–7). IEEE.

Rattan, M., Bhambri, P., & Shaifali. (2005a, February). Information Retrieval Using Soft Computing Techniques. Paper presented at the National Conference on Bio-informatics Computing, 7.

Rattan, M., Bhambri, P., & Shaifali. (2005b, February). Institution for a Sustainable Civilization: Negotiating Change in a Technological Culture. Paper presented at the National Conference on Technical Education in Globalized Environment - Knowledge, Technology & The Teacher, 45.

Saucedo-Martínez, J. A., Pérez-Lara, M., Marmolejo-Saucedo, J. A., Salais-Fierro, T. E., & Vasant, P. (2018). Industry 4.0 framework for management and operations: A review. *Journal of Ambient Intelligence and Humanized Computing, 9*, 789–801.

Singh, I., Salaria, D., & Bhambri, P. (2010). Comparative Analysis of JAVA and AspectJ on the basis of Various Metrics. In International Conference on Advanced Computing and Communication Technologies (IEEE Sponsored) (pp. 714–720).

Singh, M., Singh, P., Kaur, K., & Bhambri, P. (2005a, March). Database Security. Paper presented at the National Conference on Future Trends in Information Technology, 57–62.

Singh, M., Bhambri, P., & Kaur, K. (2005b, March). Network Security. Paper presented at the National Conference on Future Trends in Information Technology, 51–56.

Singh, M., Singh, P., Bhambri, P., & Sachdeva, R. (2005f). A comparative study: Security algorithms. In *Seminar on Network Security and Its Implementations* (pp. 14).

Singh, P., & Bhambri, P. (2007). Alternate organizational models for ports. *Apeejay Journal of Management and Technology, 2*(2), 9–17.

Singh, P., Singh, M., & Bhambri, P. (2004, November). Interoperability: A problem of component reusability. Paper presented at the International Conference on Emerging Technologies in IT Industry, 60.

Singh, P., Singh, M., & Bhambri, P. (2005c, March). Internet security. Paper presented at the Seminar on Network Security and Its Implementations, 22.

Singh, P., Singh, M., & Bhambri, P. (2005d, March). Security in virtual private networks. In *Seminar on network security and its implementations* (pp. 11).

Singh, P., Singh, M., & Bhambri, P. (2005e, January). Embedded Systems. Paper presented at the Seminar on Embedded Systems, 10–15.

Singh, P., Bhambri, P., & Sohal, A. K. (2006, January). Security in local networks. Paper presented at the National Conference on Future Trends in Information Technology.

Singh, P., Gupta, O. P., & Saini, S. (2017). A brief research study of wireless sensor network. *Advances in Computational Sciences and Technology, 10*(5), 733–739.

Sudevan, S., Barwani, B., Al Maani, E., Rani, S., & Sivaraman, A. K. (2021). Impact of blended learning during Covid-19 in Sultanate of Oman. *Annals of the Romanian Society for Cell Biology, 33*, 14978–14987.

Tanwar, R., Chhabra, Y., Rattan, P., & Rani, S. (2022, September). Blockchain in IoT networks for precision agriculture. In *International Conference on Innovative Computing and Communications: Proceedings of ICICC 2022, Volume 2* (pp. 137–147). Singapore: Springer Nature Singapore.

Thapar, V., & Bhambri, P. (2009, May). Context free language induction by evolution of deterministic pushdown automata using genetic programming. Paper presented at the International Conference on Downtrend Challenges in IT, pp. 33.

Yadav, V. S., Singh, A., Raut, R. D., Mangla, S. K., Luthra, S., & Kumar, A. (2022). Exploring the application of Industry 4.0 technologies in the agricultural food supply chain: A systematic literature review. *Computers & Industrial Engineering, 169,* 108304.

15 Digital Twin for Sustainable Industrial Development

Rachna Rana and Pankaj Bhambri

15.1 INTRODUCTION OF SUSTAINABILITY OF DIGITAL TWIN

As the industry progresses, the advent of Information and Communication Technologies (ICT) provides a plethora of opportunities for sustainable development of all the tools available to support production and maintenance processes. Digital Twin (DT) knowledge has long been recognized as a key enabler of sustainability objectives. In this study, we review the existing literature on DT and explore how DT can be leveraged to support sustainable engineering conservation practices and operations. The outputs display that there is an emphasis on the economic aspects of sustainability, while environmental and social considerations are secondary. We also note the increasing attention in this extent of investigation. DT has been leveraged in many engineering applications to investigate different conservation and production events. In addition, we look at how much sustainability issues are addressed in the existing literature, including a detailed list of criteria, and how often they are addressed.

In conclusion, DT technology can lead to sustainable industrial practices. Sustainability refers to the three sides of financial, ecological and social development, which must be achieved at the same time (Franciosi, 2020). New pieces of knowledge such as Internet of Things (IoT), large information analysis, AI, and cloud computing have digitized many industries (Qi, 2021). DTs are the result of these developments. However, there are many descriptions of DT in the information. DT refers to the expansion of a self-motivated figure image of a connected mechanical object (social scheme, device, machine, or production process) (Omrany et al., 2023, p. 65) (Figure 15.1).

DT has many advantages for improving industrial performance: it can be used for simulation, verification, monitoring, optimization, diagnosis and prediction, and decision support (Qi et al., 2018). Therefore, DT is particularly effective in achieving sustainable production and maintenance (Rani, S., Bhambri, P., & Kataria, A., 2023). In the context of digitalization, interdisciplinary collaboration between production planning and maintenance is a priority area for improving system performance (Franciosi et al., 2021). Consequently, it is worthwhile to explore the use of DT in maintenance and production activities to improve the sustainability performance of

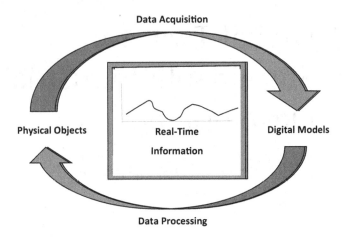

FIGURE 15.1 An architecture of digital twin technology.

industrial companies. This study conducts a systematic literature review to explore the state of research at the intersection of DT and sustainability applied to industrial maintenance and production (Kataria, A., Puri, V., Pareek, P. K., & Rani, S., 2023, July). The main contribution of this chapter is to present a comprehensive analysis of studies in the literature that use DT to improve sustainability (Ritu et al., 2023, February 17).

The maintenance and production activities covered in these documents were identified and the sustainability aspects considered in these studies were also explored (Rani et al., 2023; Bali, V., Bali, S., Gaur, D., Rani, S., & Kumar, R., 2023). For this reason, a list of economic, environmental, and social criteria, including sustainability indicators, with their respective frequency of use, was created. Indeed, recent literature reviews have focused on the use of DT in industrial sectors, but without explicitly considering the relationships with the various sustainability aspects (Puri, V., Kataria, A., Solanki, V. K., & Rani, S., 2022, December). Examples include reviews on the applications of DT for maintenance (Errandonea et al., 2020) and DT in industrial operations (Melesse et al., 2021). Other studies that consider sustainability address emerging technologies and do not provide details on the potential of DT, for example, describe recent trends in maintenance in the context of digitization and sustainability, and addresses the sustainability functions of Industry 4.0 (Rani, S., Mishra, A. K., Kataria, A., Mallik, S., & Qin, H., 2023).

In today's global competitive environment, manufacturing companies are facing the challenge of moving from mass-produced products to mass customization (Dhanalakshmi, R., Vijayaraghavan, N., Sivaraman, A. K., & Rani, S., 2022). Meeting individual client prospects and achieving the loftiest position of client satisfaction requires one to fleetly establish business relations (Rana, 2018; Rana et al., 2019). This presents companies with a series of business challenges, similar to manufacturing a high variety of high-quality, high-performance (Glatt et al., 2021, p. 165), low-cost, smart, largely tailored personalized products (Rani, S.,

Kumar, S., Kataria, A., & Min, H., 2023). Being part of a mass customization request implies giving the client the occurrence to be part of the value creation process through the design and description of their own individual products and/or services (Rana et al., 2021a; Rana et al., 2021b) by combining functions and factorsand producing them in small lot sizes, immaculately, a batch size of one, with quick delivery conditions, and without paying a high price for decoration, that is, maintaining the profitable conditions of mass production (Kaur, D., Singh, B., & Rani, S., 2023; Kataria, A., Agrawal, D., Rani, S., Karar, V., & Chauhan, M., 2022).

Industry 4.0 combines technologies similar to the IoT, Big Data, cyber-physical systems (CPS), DT, etc., to integrate the artificial value creation process chains via the real-time vacuity/sharing of applicable information between humans and machines (Rachna et al., 2022), a commodity that has big counter accusations for sustainability. More specifically, the main tasks of these Industry 4.0 core technologies are the digitization of data, analysis, and knowledge birth, which can be used to apply robotization inflexibility (Rachna et al., 2020); to increase the position of manufacturing effectiveness, inflexibility, and competitiveness/productivity; and to integrate all the value-adding chains (Rachna et al., 2021).

A large number of studies now support the notion that the 4.0 concept has the potential to meet affordable/profitable mass customization requirements, as there is a need for reconfigurable, adaptive, smart-manufacturing, evolving-manufacturing, etc. The 4.0 concept is seen as a response to the challenges of mass customization, since it necessitates the use of innovation-driven technological product approaches (Bilal, M., Kumari, B., & Rani, S., 2021, May).

According to Rani et al., 2023, one of the prerequisites of 4.0 when enforced to meet the challenges of the mass customization request, is to achieve a high status of sustainability (see Xie et al. 2021, p. 43). According to Vignesh and Arunachalam (2021), the idea of 4.0 must take mass customization requirements into account. In order to achieve this, the value creation chain must be optimized through fully automated, digitized processes. Sustainable competitiveness must also be considered from a social and environmental perspective. In the era of Industry 4.0, this means having a real-time information flow model that can quickly identify customer needs and simplify the customization process, as described by Kaewunruen et al. (2021). A digital network of production processes and resources is needed for systematic data storage and processing to support a transparent and responsive support system, as noted by Kaewunruen and Lian (2019). The product environment should be scalable without additional costs. This scalability refers to the reconfiguration of the construction scheme, which can be achieved through the mixing of a fully automated, digitalized, extremely cost-effective and intelligent new production unit, as explained by Jasiulewicz-Kaczmarek et al. (2023) and Glatt et al. (2021). To increase customer satisfaction, businesses must use new efficient reconfigurable production methods, such as CPS, with real-time production coordination capabilities, as stated by Jain and Narayanan (2023). This requires efficient processing of large amounts of data, which are then transformed into optimized decisions, as noted by Gupta and Basu (2019).

15.2 VARIETIES OF DTS

15.2.1 Twins or Fraternal Twins

There are dissimilar levels of DTs. The first and most fundamental level is the twin model of a single component, such as a device or part of a larger system (Kumar, P., Banerjee, K., Singhal, N., Kumar, A., Rani, S., Kumar, R., & Lavinia, C. A., 2022). Engineers use DT models to understand the characteristics of the component and to test its durability, stability, and performance. They may perform stress tests and perform other tasks that simulate real-world conditions and ensure the part is working correctly. For example, at a product factory, a pair of components can be used by engineers to monitor a product's performance, track its degradation, and bringout root source investigation in the event of failure or product quality decrease. This approach enhances the performance and life of the component and provides more precise predictions of when it might need to be repaired or replaced (Rani, S., Pareek, P. K., Kaur, J., Chauhan, M., & Bhambri, P., 2023, February).

15.2.2 Asset or Product Twins

Asset (or product) twins are the next level after component (or part) twins. An asset can be composed of more than one partial twin, or it can be composed of information from component (or component) twins. By aggregating components into a bigger asset/product, asset twins enable you to monitor and analyze the whole asset. They allow users to better understand how individual components interact with one another and the environment, as well as how they work together. Asset Twins help you optimize your manufacturing processes and increase efficiency by optimizing each individual part. Engineers commonly use asset twins to reduce MTBF (mean time to failure) and MTTR (mean time to repair), reduce water or power consumption and improve overall performance. An example of an asset twin would be an early part of a raw materials heating process, or a group of component parts of a conveyor belt, furnace, valve, temperature sensor, etc. System (or unit) twins are groups of asset (or component parts of a system. System twins reveal how assets interact with one another. System twins are used by plant managers to optimize asset-to-asset collaboration to enhance performance and minimize wear and tear. Pairing devices enable users to evaluate systems to find efficiencies and insights into new business opportunities to optimize all associated processes. For instance, a chemical plant's dual system can contain all resources and processes associated with the production of a particular basic product which is the first stage in the production of specific chemicals. By utilizing system twins, you gain insight into how assets operate together and how to optimize their performance (Bhambri, P., Rani, S., Gupta, G., & Khang, A. (Eds.)., 2022).

15.2.3 Process Twins

Process twins are the most advanced of the DTs. They link system twins to bigger and more intricate workflows, often across the entire plant. Process twins are used by plant managers to understand and analyse how all the units in a plant or process operate together. They are used to monitor the efficiency, timing and coordination of all units and to synchronize systems. For example, if a part of a factory produces its product at a high rate, this can lead to an overproduction of certain components, resulting in logistical issues such as storage and transport. With dual-process functionality, you can model the impact of adjustments such as raw material inputs, temperature, machine vibrations, etc. and see how those adjustments affect outputs without wasting resources on unsuccessful experiments or interrupting workflows. Process twins also enable users to monitor key business metrics supporting their decision-making and strategy. With this information, plant managers can optimize their workflows and keep their processes running at an optimal level (Broo & Schooling, 2021, pp. 78-99).

15.3 THE VALUE OF DT IN PROCESS MANUFACTURING

The benefits and advantages of a DT in process manufacturing depend on the level of adoption of the DT. According to Borangiu et al. (2019, p. 54), the higher the level of DT adoption, the more benefits and advantages your institution will have access to, including:

15.3.1 DECREASED DOWNTIME AND COST FOR MAINTENANCE, REPAIR, OR REPLACEMENT

Enhanced predictive maintenance with remote monitoring, simulations, and the ability to predict wear and tear, as well as various operational modes, on each part or process (Rani, S., Kataria, A., Kumar, S., & Tiwari, P., 2023).

15.3.2 IMMEDIATE INTERVENTION AT THE OPTIMAL DEGRADATION POINT

Reduced resource consumption, including reduced consumption of water, raw materials, and other resources, because all processes and components are optimized.

15.3.3 INCREASED PRODUCTIVITY THROUGH SYNCHRONIZATION AND FLOW OPTIMIZATION

DTs help identify bottlenecks more quickly, allowing for the resolution and removal of bottlenecks (Tanwar, R., Chhabra, Y., Rattan, P., & Rani, S., 2022, September).

15.3.4 DEVELOP PRODUCTS FASTER

Please provide a simulation of potential processes that can expedite the product development timeline while still maintaining a safe environment for experimentation and learning from failures. This approach to development, often referred to as "fail fast," is essential for achieving rapid iteration and innovation while minimizing risk. We request that you consider providing insights on how this can be achieved in a manner that is effective and efficient, while also ensuring that all applicable regulations and industry standards are met. Thank you for your expertise and assistance in this matter.

15.3.5 SIMULATE STRATEGIC PLANNING

To effectively plan and strategize, businesses can create models that simulate a variety of scenarios, including shifts in demand, changes in plant management, and other relevant factors. By analyzing the potential outcomes of each change, companies can enhance their position in the market, prepare for any shifts within the industry, and confirm their core values. This process involves utilizing diverse tools and methods to generate simulations that offer valuable insights and inform strategic decision-making. Employing this approach can prove to be a powerful way to maintain a competitive edge and ensure long-term success.

15.3.6 REMOTE TRAINING

In situations where employees are working remotely or in potentially hazardous conditions, they must receive training that is specifically tailored to their circumstances. Remote training is a great way for all employees to learn the skills they need to do their job safely and effectively, no matter where they are in the world. By offering remote training, companies can demonstrate their dedication to employee safety and health, while increasing productivity and reducing risk. Therefore, organizations must prioritize remote training for their workforce to maintain a safe and productive workplace.

15.3.7 REMOVE THE NEED

The implementation of DTs enables workers to conduct remote inspections of hazardous situations. By leveraging this technology, individuals can gain a comprehensive understanding of the situation at hand without physically being present. This approach offers a safe and effective means of assessing a hazardous situation, reducing the risk of injury or harm to workers. The use of DTs has become increasingly popular in various industries and has proven to be an invaluable tool for facilitating remote inspections.

15.3.8 INCREASE SAFETY

To promote a safer work environment, it is imperative to optimize the operation of machinery.

15.3.9 IMPROVE INNOVATION

Enhanced collaboration and knowledge sharing can effectively stimulate innovation and optimize operational efficiency in the realm of process manufacturing through the implementation of DTs. This, in turn, can lead to a more prominent competitive edge and greater profitability.

15.4 ENERGY EFFICIENCY AND SUSTAINABILITY

DTs are increasingly being used in the construction industry to improve energy efficiency and promote sustainability (Kumar, R., Rani, S., & Khangura, S. S. (Eds.), 2023). Real-time energy usage trends can be monitored and analyzed using DTs, allowing for virtual replicas of the construction and infrastructure projects to be developed. This allows for inefficiencies to be identified in real time and optimization opportunities to be realized. For instance, Tan et al., Seo et al., and others have developed DT models to optimize energy consumption related to lifts and university classroom lighting. DT models can also create Model Predictive Control by combining multiple variables (e.g., climate forecast, power statistics, current state of the environment) into one control algorithm. To do this, DTs act as parameterized models built into the overall control algorithm. The framework represents controlled environments in digital form. The system has a standardized information access interface that makes it easy to switch between simulation and real-life scenarios and allows for adaptation to different control environments.

Research has shown that DT can help in the generation of Mission Planning and Control Station (MPCS) which can be used to improve energy consumption and comfort of passengers. DT can use sophisticated modelling and statistical methods to plan scenarios, monitor design performance, and optimize building performance. Tang et al., for example, demonstrated the feasibility of DT technology in a study on the green alternative to outdated money making and inhabited building renovation in Guangzhou. The study showed that DT knowledge meaningfully contributed to the renovation of selected buildings.

In a framework that combines DT technology and the IoT, a method for dynamic sustainability assessment is proposed. This method focuses on user-centric perspectives and enables real-time assessment and management of multi-sustainability criteria.

Architects and engineers can utilize DT to model and enhance energy efficiency during the design process by creating a virtual replica of the structures. This virtual model provides an accurate prediction of energy consumption and highlights areas that require improvement. DT can simulate the energy efficiency of various building systems, including heating and ventilation systems, as well as the integration of renewable energy.

15.5 SUPPORTING KNOWLEDGE FOR DT EXECUTION IN INDUSTRY

The effectiveness of DTs depends on using a wide range of techniques. Previous studies suggest creating multilayer models that include various techniques to enhance DT's performance. For instance, Hu et al. created a six-layer model to monitor the health of complex devices in fields such as tunnelling, underground space engineering, and marine and wind engineering. Fuller et al. proposed a general model consisting of four technology levels to simplify DT implementation. Based on retrospective analysis, this study incorporates essential technologies into a five-layer model to implement DTs in the construction industry.

15.5.1 TECHNOLOGIES FOR MANIPULATING AND PERCEIVING THE PHYSICAL WORLD

Developing DTs requires the creation of a virtual environment that accurately replicates the physical world, including its entities, components, and relationships. This can be a complex process that demands a thorough understanding of the physical universe. The virtual representations of physical entities are not perfect and need to be adaptable over time in response to changes in the actual environment. To achieve accurate measurements of physical objects, techniques such as laser measurement, image recognition measurement, conversion measurement, and micro/nano-level precision measurement can be used.

The integration of DTs with the IoT allows for real-time data gathering from various sources within the physical environment. IoT acts as data sensors to record and transmit data about the condition, behaviour, and functionality of an asset or system. This integration supports asset management, optimisation, and decision-making across a variety of disciplines in the construction sector. By enabling DTs to deliver precise and current insights, the combination of DTs and constant data monitoring improves the virtual representation's fidelity and accuracy.

15.5.2 TECHNOLOGY THAT MAKES DATA MANAGEMENT POSSIBLE

When creating a high-fidelity DT model, it is important to securely store complex information such as geometry, physical properties, and condition data. Various technologies like bar codes, fast response codes, and radio frequency identification can be used to securely store data produced by DT systems. To efficiently store and manage large amounts of data, big data storage frameworks like MySQL, HBase, and NoSQL databases are utilized. MySQL arranges data in tables with columns representing specific data values and rows representing records, while HBase uses Hadoop MapReduce for high-speed processing and the Hadoop Distributed File System for storage. NoSQL databases are excellent at managing large amounts of data and have superior read-write performance. Data processing is a step in the data management process that produces useful and insightful insights from large and complicated datasets. Predictive analytics, data mining techniques, and analytical visualizations are all parts of big data analytics. Visualizations make use of graphical techniques to promote effective and transparent communication, while data mining algorithms make it possible to find hidden facts in huge databases. Advanced systems are used in predictive analytics to foresee future events and uncover real-time awareness utilizing past data. Data fusion is crucial for gathering, transferring, synthesizing, filtering, correlating, and extracting usable information from a variety of data sources.

Data integration techniques in construction are the gateway to groundbreaking innovation and revolutionizing the industry. They can be classified into three levels: signal-level fusion, feature-level fusion, and decision-level fusion. By utilizing a variety of techniques including Kalman filtering, image regression, principal component transform, K-T transform, and wavelet transform, effective data fusion can be achieved with ease. In the construction sector, artificial intelligence and machine learning technology play a pivotal role in processing and analyzing data produced by DTs. The powerful algorithms based on AI and ML are capable of deriving insightful patterns and hidden gems from data. With advanced data processing capabilities made possible by these technologies, correlations, trends, and anomalies within datasets can be found with ease.

The future of construction lies in embracing the potential of predictive modelling, optimization, and real-time monitoring capabilities through the use of AI and ML. Construction professionals can receive actionable information for well-informed decision-making and enhanced performance. AI and ML algorithms effectively create a holistic picture of construction projects by combining and integrating data from multiple sources. With the advent of edge computing, localized decision-making and autonomy for DTs can be achieved, enabling them to perform crucial analytics and make informed decisions without solely relying on cloud connectivity. This is particularly advantageous in situations where cloud connectivity is limited or degraded, paving the way for a brighter future in construction.

15.5.3 TECHNIQUES THAT MAKE DIGITAL PROTOTYPING PRACTICABLE

A rigorous, robust model should include essential elements including geometry, physical qualities, behavioural traits, and rule-based relationships, according to prior research. The geometry component requires using well-known computer-aided design software to visualize shape and location. Important specifics like tolerances and material qualities are included in physical information, which helps the virtual model be accurately represented. The way the virtual model interacts with the outside world and changes in its surroundings is captured in great detail by behavioural models. For performance analysis and optimization, associations and constraints must be defined using rule models. Several methods are used to extract rule information, such as data mining and semantic data analytics, which make it easier to find and extract pertinent rules.

15.5.4 SERVICES ARE ENABLED BY TECHNOLOGIES

With the use of DT technology, sophisticated monitoring, modelling, diagnosis, and prognosis are made possible. Technologies including computer graphics, image processing, virtual reality synchronization, and 3D rendering are used in monitoring. The simulation covers a wide range of topics, including process, structural, mechanical, electrical, and electronic simulation. Data analysis techniques like statistical theory, machine learning, neural networks, and fault tree analysis are used in diagnosis and prognosis. Services, which go through stages like service development, management, and on-demand utilization, can be created using hardware, software, and knowledge. An industrial IoT platform manages application services, resources, and knowledge services, and performs tasks such as service posting, searching, communication, and assessment.

15.5.5 TECHNOLOGIES FOR DATA TRANSFER AND CONNECTION

Establishing a trustworthy connection is crucial for real-time control and precise mapping between the virtual and physical states in DTs. There are numerous connection protocols for data flow between various pieces of software in cyberspace as well as between the physical world and the DT. Wired choices including twisted pair, coaxial cable, and optical fibre are also used for data transfer, as are wireless technologies like Zig-Bee, Bluetooth, Wi-Fi, ultra-wideband (UWB), and near-field communication (NFC). Technologies including GPRS/CDMA, digital ratio, spread spectrum microwave communication, wireless bridge, and satellite communication can be used for long-distance wireless transmission.

15.6 SUSTAINABILITY INDUSTRY

The European Green Deal agenda focuses on sustainable engineering. Its primary objective is to achieve eco-friendly goals and promote a cost-effective climate in the EU's circular economy. Sustainability and resource management (from production to installation, use, maintenance, disposal, or recycling) should be at the core of the digital and green transformation from an early stage. DTs are essential technologies in implementing Industry 4.0 and related fields. They can be used to model many inventions, matters, and construction processes. Another type of DT is a computer-generated workshop model that contains all the essentials, such as apparatuses, inventions, and the public, which can imitate invention actions for enhancements or executions. Moreover, the use of engineering information to create data services offers further innovations. Collected industrial information enables a sustainable industry that increases efficiency, elasticity, and resource efficiency by using big data for extrapolative conservation and speedy reconfiguration of the production system. The DT serves as a simulated model of the workshop, including all parts of the construction chain. This digital copy can be used in the purpose for disassembly, re-articulation, and reuse in engineering life cycle management. DT technologies can simulate sustainable and green management for resource efficiency in manufacturing life cycle supervision. Digital dual logistics related to supply chain management can be planned and evaluated using key circular economy metrics. Furthermore, the use of mechanized data to create data facilities offers further innovations. The sustainable industry is a crucial component of the European Green Deal project, which aims to appreciate the EU's efforts towards climate change mitigation and conservation goals.

15.7 CONCLUSION

Better delivery of post-operative medical care with a medical plan's DT Collaborating with a biotech organization and reproductive health hospital we will explore how the latest information technologies, medical advances and human factors interact to create a customized treatment plan to enhance patient quality of life and recovery (post-surgery treatment and simulation). In our proposed framework, each of these four DTs has specific characteristics for data handling, data management and data interpretation: Each transversal area of DT is applied based on cross-disciplinary research during the work to have a broad impact: presenting anti-DT protests in four different areas (construction projects, manufacturing, supply chain and healthcare), Communicate with real scenarios and specific companies, exchange methods, and design collaboration tools.

- Share news and expand your partnerships with nearby businesses and agencies
- Explore how the DT impacts health at work
- Organize the development and evaluation of DTs for patient treatment and recovery in collaboration with regional hospitals and public health teams

REFERENCES

Bali, V., Bali, S., Gaur, D., Rani, S., & Kumar, R. (2023). Commercial-off-the shelf vendor selection: A multi-criteria decision-making approach using intuitionistic fuzzy sets and TOPSIS. *Operational research in engineering sciences: Theory and applications.*

Bhambri, P., Rani, S., Gupta, G., & Khang, A. (Eds.). (2022). *Cloud and fog computing platforms for internet of things.* CRC Press.

Bilal, M., Kumari, B., & Rani, S. (2021, May). An artificial intelligence supported E-commerce model to improve the export of Indian handloom and handicraft products in the World. In *Proceedings of the International Conference on Innovative Computing & Communication (ICICC).*

Borangiu, T., Oltean, E., Răileanu, S., Anton, F., Anton, S., & Iacob, I. (2019). Embedded digital twin for ARTI-type control of semi-continuous production processes. *Service oriented, holonic and multi-agent manufacturing systems for industry of the future,* 113–133. 10.1007/978-3-030-27477-1_9

Broo, D. G., & Schooling, J. (2021). A framework for using data as an engineering tool for sustainable cyber-physical systems. *IEEE Access,* 9, 22876–22882. 10.1109/access.2021. 3055652

Dhanalakshmi, R., Vijayaraghavan, N., Sivaraman, A. K., & Rani, S. (2022). Epidemic awareness spreading in smart cities using the artificial neural network. In *AI-centric smart city ecosystems* (pp. 187–207). CRC Press.

Errandonea, I., Beltrán, S., & Arrizabalaga, S. (2020). Digital twin for maintenance: A literature review. *Computers in Industry,* 123, 103316. 10.1016/j.compind.2020.103316

Fathy, Y., Jaber, M., & Nadeem, Z. (2021). Digital twin-driven decision-making and planning for energy consumption. *Journal of Sensor and Actuator Networks,* 10(2), 37. 10.3390/jsan10020037

Franciosi, C., Voisin, A., Miranda, S., Riemma, S., & Iung, B. (2020). Measuring maintenance impacts on the sustainability of manufacturing industries: From a systematic literature review to a framework proposal. *Journal of Cleaner Production,* 260, 121065. 10.1016/j.jclepro.2020.121065

Franciosi, C., Miranda, S., Veneroso, C. R., &Riemma, S. (2021). A maintenance scheduling optimization model for a multi-component machine in a digitalized manufacturing context. *IFAC-PapersOnLine,* 54(1), 1254–1259. 10.1016/j.ifacol.2021.08.150

Glatt, M., Kölsch, P., Siedler, C., Langlotz, P., Ehmsen, S., & Aurich, J. C. (2021). Edge-based digital twin to trace and ensure sustainability in cross-company production networks. *Procedia CIRP,* 98, 276–281. 10.1016/j.procir.2021.01.103

Gupta, A., & Basu, B. (2019). Sustainable primary aluminium production: Technology status and future opportunities. *Transactions of the Indian Institute of Metals,* 72(8), 2135–2150. 10.1007/s12666-019-01699-9

Jain, S., & Narayanan, A. (2023). Digital twin–enabled machine learning for smart manufacturing. *Smart and Sustainable Manufacturing Systems*, 7(1), 20220035. 10.1520/ssms20220035

Jasiulewicz-Kaczmarek, M., Legutko, S., & Kluk, P. (2023). Maintenance 4.0 technologies—new opportunities for sustainability-driven maintenance. *Management and Production Engineering Review*. 10.24425/mper.2020.133730

Kaewunruen, S., & Lian, Q. (2019). Digital twin-aided sustainability-based lifecycle management for railway turnout systems. *Journal of Cleaner Production*, 228, 1537–1551. 10.1016/j.jclepro.2019.04.156

Kaewunruen, S., Sresakoolchai, J., Ma, W., & Phil-Ebosie, O. (2021). Digital twin-aided vulnerability assessment and risk-based maintenance planning of bridge infrastructures exposed to extreme conditions. *Sustainability*, 13(4), 2051. 10.3390/su13042051

Kataria, A., Agrawal, D., Rani, S., Karar, V., & Chauhan, M. (2022). Prediction of blood screening parameters for preliminary analysis using neural networks. In *Predictive modeling in biomedical data mining and analysis* (pp. 157–169). Academic Press.

Kataria, A., Puri, V., Pareek, P. K., & Rani, S. (2023, July). Human activity classification using G-XGB. In *2023 International Conference on Data Science and Network Security (ICDSNS)* (pp. 1–5). IEEE.

Kaur, D., Singh, B., & Rani, S. (2023). Cyber security in the metaverse. In *Handbook of research on AI-based technologies and applications in the era of the metaverse* (pp. 418–435). IGI Global.

Kumar, P., Banerjee, K., Singhal, N., Kumar, A., Rani, S., Kumar, R., & Lavinia, C. A. (2022). Verifiable, secure mobile agent migration in healthcare systems using a polynomial-based threshold secret sharing scheme with a Blowfish algorithm. *Sensors*, 22(22), 8620.

Kumar, R., Rani, S., & Khangura, S. S. (Eds.). (2023). *Machine learning for sustainable manufacturing in Industry 4.0: Concept, concerns and applications*. CRC Press.

Melesse, T. Y., Di Pasquale, V., & Riemma, S. (2021). Digital twin models in industrial operations: State-of-the-art and future research directions. *IET Collaborative Intelligent Manufacturing*, 3(1), 37–47. 10.1049/cim2.12010

Omrany, H., Al-Obaidi, K. M., Husain, A., & Ghaffarianhoseini, A. (2023). Digital twins in the construction industry: A comprehensive review of current implementations, enabling technologies, and future directions. *Sustainability*, 15(14), 10908. 10.3390/su151410908

Puri, V., Kataria, A., Solanki, V. K., & Rani, S. (2022, December). AI-based botnet attack classification and detection in IoT devices. In *2022 IEEE International Conference on Machine Learning and Applied Network Technologies (ICMLANT)* (pp. 1–5). IEEE.

Qi, Q., Zhao, D., Liao, T. W., & Tao, F. (2018). Modelling of cyber-physical systems and digital twins based on edge computing, fog computing and cloud computing towards smart manufacturing. *Volume 1: Additive manufacturing; bio and sustainable manufacturing*. 10.1115/msec2018-6435

Rachna, Chhabra, Y., & Bhambri, P. (2020). Comparison of clustering approaches for enhancing sustainability performance in WSNSL a study. TEQIP-III sponsored International Conference on Sustainable Development Through Engineering Innovations, (pp. 62–71), ISBN: 978-93-89947-14-4.

Rachna, Bhambri, P., & Chhabra, Y. (2022). Deployment of distributed clustering approach in WSNs and IoTs. *Cloud and Fog Computing Platforms for Internet of Things*, 85–98. 10.1201/9781003213888-7

Rachna, Chhabra, Y., & Bhambri, P. (2021). Various approaches and algorithms for monitoring the energy efficiency of wireless sensor networks. *Lecture Notes in Civil Engineering*, 761–770. 10.1007/978-981-15-9554-7_68

Rana, R. (2018, March). A Review of the evolution of Wireless sensor networks. International Journal of Advanced Research Trends in Engineering and Technology (IJARTET), vol. 5, Special issue, March 2018, ISSN2394-3777 (Print), ISSN2394-3785 (Online), Available online at www.ijartet.com

Rana, R., Chhabra, Y., & Bhambri, P. (2019). A review on development and challenges in Wireless Sensor Networks. International Multidisciplinary Academic Research Conference (IMARC, 2019), (pp. 184–188), ISBN: 978-81-942282-0-2.

Rana, R., Chhabra, Y., & Bhambri, P. (2021a). Comparison and evaluation of various QoS parameters in WSNs with the implementation of enhanced low energy adaptive efficient distributed clustering approach, Webology (ISSN: 1735-188X) Volume 18, Number 1, 2021.

Rana, R., Chhabra, Y., & Bhambri, P. (2021b). Design and development of distributed clustering approach in a wireless sensor network. Webology (ISSN: 1735-188X) Volume 18, Number 1, 2021.

Rani, S., Kataria, A., Kumar, S., & Tiwari, P. (2023). Federated learning for secure IoMT-applications in smart healthcare systems: A comprehensive review. *Knowledge-based systems*, 110658.

Rani, S., Bhambri, P., & Kataria, A. (2023). Integration of IoT, Big Data, and Cloud Computing technologies. *Big Data, Cloud Computing and IoT: Tools and applications*.

Rani, S., Pareek, P. K., Kaur, J., Chauhan, M., & Bhambri, P. (2023, February). Quantum machine learning in healthcare: Developments and challenges. In *2023 IEEE International Conference on Integrated Circuits and Communication Systems (ICICACS)* (pp. 1–7). IEEE.

Rani, S., Mishra, A. K., Kataria, A., Mallik, S., & Qin, H. (2023). Machine learning-based optimal crop selection system in smart agriculture. *Scientific Reports*, 13(1), 15997.

Rani, S., Kumar, S., Kataria, A., & Min, H. (2023). SmartHealth: An intelligent framework to secure IoMT service applications using machine learning. *ICT Express*.

Rani, S., Bhambri, P., Kataria, A., & Khang, A. (2023). Smart city ecosystem: Concept, sustainability, design principles, and technologies. In *AI-centric smart city ecosystems* (pp. 1–20). CRC Press.

Ritu, P., & Bhambri, P. (2023, February 17). Software effort estimation with machine learning – A systematic literature review. In Editor(s) (Ed.), *Agile software development: Trends, challenges and applications* (pp. 291–308). John Wiley & Sons, Inc.

Tanwar, R., Chhabra, Y., Rattan, P., & Rani, S. (2022, September). Blockchain in IoT networks for precision agriculture. In *International Conference on Innovative Computing and Communications: Proceedings of ICICC 2022, Volume 2* (pp. 137–147). Singapore: Springer Nature Singapore.

Vignesh, R., & Arunachalam, N. (2021). Design and development of the spiral grooved grinding wheel and their influence on the performance of the vertical surface grinding process. *Procedia Manufacturing*, 53, 251–259. 10.1016/j.promfg.2021.06.028

16 AI-Driven Digital Twin for Industrial Engineering Applications

Dileep Reddy Bolla, Ramesh Naidu, and Preethi Prerana

16.1 INTRODUCTION

The worldwide buildup of non-recyclable garbage in landfills and the exceptionally long duration it takes for the majority of its contents to decompose could have a significant influence on our way of life eventually, if we as a civilization do nothing to stop it from happening. The ability of waste accumulation to facilitate the transmission of disease by vectors like flies, mosquitoes, and other insects is another well-known worry for people. Inadequately handled garbage can contain hazardous substances that can poison soil and water (Bolla et al., 2019), in addition to harming the splendour of natural environments, cause deforestation, and land occupation to make way for landfills. In addition, pollution has the potential to change the food chain, which will undoubtedly result in an increase in illnesses and health problems for both people and the planet's natural ecosystems.

In the last 50 years, trash accumulation has become an increasingly serious issue for three main reasons. The first is the dearth of recyclable goods on the market, despite the fact that businesses have long been working to create more environmentally friendly and sustainable goods. The second factor is overcrowding, which is currently one of the most prominent issues. The number of products that could be recycled is rising, but instead they wind up in a landfill or even the ocean, posing a threat to the existence of thousands of marine species (Alharam et al., 2021). This is because dealing with waste generation poses a very difficult logistical task when supplying resources of all types to such a huge population. The lack of social engagement we exhibit about issues like climate change makes up the third and last argument.

It's crucial to recognize that between 7 and 9 billion tons of waste are produced globally each year, of which 70% are improperly disposed of and wind up in landfills, where they run the risk of harming the ecosystem and posing new health dangers like ocean microplastics (Kaur, D., Singh, B., & Rani, S., 2023). The amount of used, unwanted, and abandoned goods that people produce overall is covered by this data. The total amount of waste created differs from what is referred to as municipal solid waste (MSW), which solely includes garbage produced in metropolitan centres or their environs.

DOI: 10.1201/9781003395416-16

Annually, 2 billion tons of urban waste are produced, 33% of which are improperly managed, making MSW modest in contrast to other waste. It shows that each person produces, on average, between 0.1 and 4.5 kg of garbage every day. The fast-rising worldwide population and the requirement for the intensive use of natural resources for the expansion of industry and the upkeep of our civilization are also predicted to cause MSW to rise to 3.4 billion tonnes by 2050.

The full adoption of the circular economy model would be the ultimate response to the accumulation problem, as well as other problems like climate change and even supply shortages in some parts of the world. This is due to the fact that its three guiding principles - removal of trash and pollution, transportation of goods and materials, and environmental regeneration - lead to an efficient method of managing the natural resources that occasionally we don't appropriately appreciate. However, it is challenging to fully implement such a complex design due mainly to technological, engineering, and logistical limitations (Bali, V., Bali, S., Gaur, D., Rani, S., & Kumar, R., 2023).

16.1.1 MACHINE LEARNING IN ENVIRONMENT CARE

Despite these restrictions, several cutting-edge technologies are starting to alter the way we perceive and approach these issues. Machine learning, a subfield of artificial intelligence that enables computers to learn particular and difficult tasks like classification, prediction, decision-making, content generation, etc., is one of the most well-known in the modern world, by combining a large amount of data with state-of-the-art learning algorithms that are motivated by how humans learn (Thokrairak et al., 2021; Kaur et al., 2020). Due to its efficiency and scalability, machine learning can occasionally be quite helpful for humans when automating these jobs.

Wide-ranging jobs can be automated using machine learning, which is important given its connection to sustainability and the development of the circular economy. A few examples of how data trends can be used to enhance the quality of the air we breathe include locating rubbish in natural settings, categorizing different forms of garbage to enhance the efficiency of waste treatment facilities, and seeing trends in data to track the progression of global warming. In order to develop a sustainable circular economy model, recyclable materials must be properly identified and separated from other trash. However, more than we could have imagined, machine learning is now used in more environmental care-related tasks (Xiao et al., 2021). For instance, a model's accurate prediction of energy or product demand helps prevent environmental resource waste. Additionally, by experimenting with chemical structures, sufficiently complex models (Cui et al., 2021; Rana et al., 2020) can potentially create new materials, enhancing the efficiency and recyclable nature of commonplace goods.

16.2 LITERATURE REVIEW

This research work intends to further machine learning techniques for addressing environmental concerns like waste accumulation by developing a model that can distinguish between five different trash categories based on the production ingredients and therefore their recyclability. Additionally, discussing machine learning algorithms' fundamental workings and the advantages that can accrue to humanity as a result of them in the future can help society get a better knowledge of and confidence in such cutting-edge exponential technology. Focusing on innovative disruptive approaches to environmental challenges also raises our collective consciousness about protecting the environment, opening the door for the potential adoption of new sustainable behaviours in our daily lives (Kaur & Bhambri, 2020).

Our dataset will primarily consist of labelled images, which means that each image is labelled with the appropriate prediction (kind of waste material) (Khan et al., 2022) that the model must produce as an output (Fanca et al., 2022). As a result, we will require a convolutional neural network model architecture (Abela et al., 2021). The model will also require a fully linked network following the convolutional module in order to transform any answer. It offers a set of values with a predetermined structure that makes it possible for us to identify the class the model predicts (Devadutta et al., 2020). Convolutional networks are used to analyse the photographs with the objective of extracting certain patterns or qualities from photos that differ in their size, rotation, and location. Also along with the works carried out we have referred to the articles to understand the machine learning and AI-based models (Bolla et al., 2020; Xiao et al., 2021). Digital twins (DTs) power the structures, models, and real-world applications of the IIoT. Also being investigated for an intelligent and secure DT-IIoT are cutting-edge AI methodologies like transfer learning and federated learning as well as blockchain-based security solutions (H. Xu et al., 2022). With the help of DTs, you may assess performance, foresee the effects of network modifications, improve network management, and come to wise conclusions (M. Sanz Rodrigo et al., 2023). Due to its use in the manufacturing and space industries, the DT technology has recently attracted a lot of interest. In the DT environment, a replica of the real object is created in order to run simulations in the virtual world (G. Thakur et al., 2023). Edge computing and the Internet of Vehicles, which is powered by digital twinning, are integrated in order to improve the capabilities of intelligent mobility (X. Xu et al., 2022).

16.3   REQUIREMENT ANALYSIS/DESIGN

Our dataset will largely be made up of labelled images, where each image has a label. The simulation's output will need to accurately estimate the type of trash to be produced (Alawi et al., 2021). We will need a convolutional neural network model architecture because of this. The model will also need a fully connected network after the convolutional module to transform an arbitrary response it offers into a collection of values with a particular structure that will allow us to recognize the class the model predicts. Convolutional networks are used to analyse the images with the goal of extracting specific patterns or qualities from images with invariance in position, rotation, and scale. Labels like cardboard, metal, rubbish, etc., are placed in the image's pertinent region according to the class it belongs to. The method of drawing boundaries around the waste object in the photograph is part of this form of labelling (Schneider et al., 2021). In the entire dataset of garbage photos, 80% of the photographs for each category are used for training. The testing step will use the remaining 20% of the photographs (Kataria, A., Puri, V., Pareek, P. K., & Rani, S., 2023, July). This particular system's main goal is to teach the framework how to detect things. The CSV file can then be created from the XML file. Additionally, this CSV file includes the records of the information that is readily accessible, including the names of the recorded file, its height and width, as well as its labelled classes and acquired coordinate positions.

16.3.1 MODEL TRAINING

The XML files that include all the data for the train and test images are converted to CSV files to create TF-records, which are then used to create the training data. After the creation of the training data, a label map that alerts by characterizing a mapping of class ID numbers to class names, the system can determine what each object is. The object identification pipeline is eventually configured after the label map has been made, which helps define the kinds of parameters and models that will be utilized for training. After successfully setting up and configuring the training pipeline, TensorFlow began initializing the model training. Faster R-CNN requires a lot of processing power to train a large network. To prepare for our neural network training, we used a DELL laptop with an Intel i5 CPU and an NVIDIA GeForce GTX 1050 Ti graphics card (GPU). Additional requirements for the offered software were the installation of the CUDA® deep neural network Abela et al. (2021), Alawi et al. (2021) library CUDNN SDK and the use of the compute unified device architecture (CUDA) Toolkit on Windows 10 computers. For high-performance mathematical computations, TensorFlow GPU version 1.4.0 open-source software is employed along with Python version 3.5. Its customizable architecture as shown in Figure 16.1 makes it simple to deploy calculations across many stages.

16.3.2 MODEL TESTING

The approach is completed by testing the developed model. Once the training is complete, the frozen inference graph is exported. Using this, the elements in a real-time feed of camera, images, and videos may be recognized and categorized. In this stage, the developed model is evaluated using the test dataset. The framework processes the test dataset using the training dataset. After that, the framework determines the coefficient value and compares it to the value acquired through training. To test the newly trained object detection classifier on any webcam feed, image, or video, Python scripts are written using the OpenCV Python package. Finally, the framework categorises garbage into six groups (Cardboard, Plastic, Metal, Paper, Glass, and Trash).

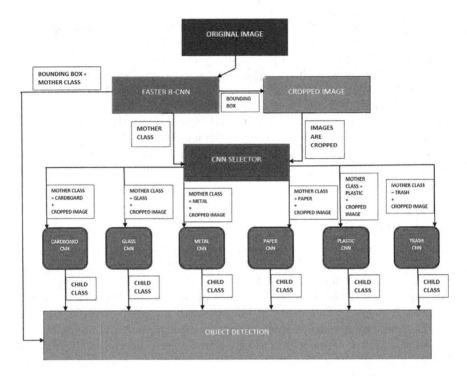

FIGURE 16.1 System architecture.

16.4 IMPLEMENTATION

We have used Python code running on the online platform Google Colab to construct the Convolutional Neural Network programmatically. Google Colab offers a quick, cosy, and stable cloud environment for building such sizable models. Additionally, a range of libraries geared toward building machine learning algorithms are available in the Python programming language, making training and evaluation much easier to use (Ramya et al., 2022). Tensorflow, Keras, Numpy, Matplotlib, etc., are examples of such libraries (Rani, S., Mishra, A. K., Kataria, A., Mallik, S., & Qin, H., 2023).

16.4.1 Data Collection and Processing

Before we can start designing, training, and testing our model, we need to gather a dataset of photographs that have been tagged with garbage (Rani, S., Kumar, S., Kataria, A., & Min, H., 2023). Let's begin creating the Colab Notebook with all the Python code once the data is prepared. However, we must first import the required libraries in order to utilize them. The following step is to segregate our data into two distinct datasets (train and test). Every single one of them is only used at the appropriate project phase (training and evaluation of the model). In order for the model to generalize from the provided data to any input that the user may use in production, this method is essential. The typical divisions for training and assessment are 70/30, 80/20, and 90/10, respectively. The dataset is preprocessed using the Keras API of the

Tensorflow library so that the data will be fed into the network during training in chunks of 128 images. This is accomplished by specifying a batch size of 128 and scaling each image to the normal business dimension of 256×256. Additionally, we can use tf. data to retrieve the number of classes from the train dataset object (in this case, nine classes) and save it in a variable. To improve the performance of training dataset objects and testing dataset objects, USE AUTOTUNE (Tanwar, R., Chhabra, Y., Rattan, P., & Rani, S., 2022, September).

16.4.2 Model Building and Training

It is practical to apply Transfer Learning, a standard strategy when training a model on such a huge amount of data because we are working with a sizable dataset (+5,000 images). This refers to using an already trained model to replace the convolutional portion of your model. So, owing to the learned convolutional component, your model will be able to extract valuable characteristics from the input photos before training. Additionally, it will just need to train the final few dense layers, requiring less time and computational power. There are many trained convolutional models available, but the ones that are used the most frequently are those that are part of the Keras API, which is what we are currently using for the project.

The model was built on top of the absence of the first and last Dense layers in the MobileNetV3Large pre-trained model. The 256 hidden neurons, a batch normalization layer to handle internal covariate shift, an ELU activation function, a layer that receives data from global average pooling, and a number of Dropouts are substituted for the original final Dense layers. The number of neurons in the final layer is equal to the number of output classes indicated by the 'numClasses' variable. Remember that overfitting, the primary cause of the lack of generality, must be avoided through L1 regularization. It is occasionally appropriate to unfreeze the final few convolutional layers of the pre-trained convolutional model in addition to transfer learning. This procedure, known as fine tuning, raises the performance of the model as a whole. Only the final six levels in this case are not frozen.

The Adam algorithm is used to optimize all of the network parameters after the model is generated, and the Sparse Categorical Cross entropy loss function is used to put the model together. The fit() function is then used to train the model over a period of 50 iterations (times that the entire dataset passes through the network).

16.4.3.1 Model Evaluation

The technology, model complexity, and dataset size all affect how long it takes to train an algorithm. Due to a Google Colab environment, a Tesla P100 GPU, a dataset of approximately 5,000 photos, and a model with over 4,500,000 parameters, only about a million and a half of them were trainabl; the training procedure in this case took around seven minutes (Kataria, A., Agrawal, D., Rani, S., Karar, V., & Chauhan, M., 2022).

Using the Matplotlib tool, we can create a graph of the loss and accuracy values over epochs as in Figure 16.2. when the training is complete to assess how the model performed. The accuracy increases regarding both the train and test values (one for each dataset) during the first epochs in a similar way, as shown on the

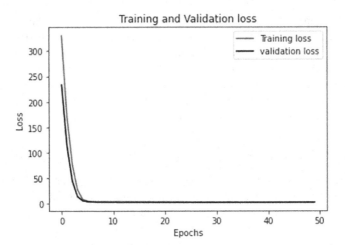

FIGURE 16.2   Training and validation loss.

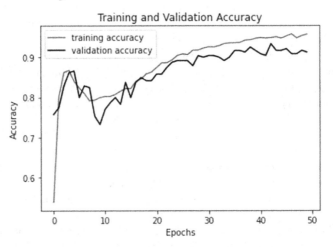

FIGURE 16.3   Training and validation accuracy.

chart, until a point where the test accuracy falls below the train accuracy (blue line) as in Figure 16.3. The greater the difference between the training and test values, the more overfitting there is and the less generalizable the model is. The change in this scenario, from 98.75% accuracy on training to 96.45% on testing, is less than 2%, which has no effect on the model's output despite the loss of generalization.

By creating a Confusion Matrix as in Figure 16.4 to analyse the model using information from the two datasets, we can see the final outcomes. The obtained accuracy is up to 98%, although the overfitting problem discussed earlier can bring this value down to 97% or even 96%. However, deploying the model to production and assessing its performance with a significant amount of "unseen" data is the ideal method to evaluate the model's performance. The primary application of this model is to make predictions over a single image. To do this, we may preprocess the input

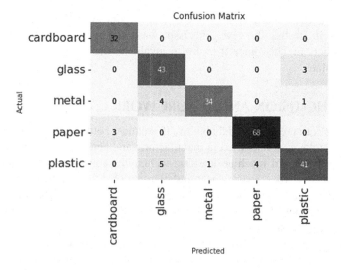

FIGURE 16.4 Confusion matrix.

image with the Keras API to turn it into an array of values, and then use the predict () function to obtain predictions from the model.

16.5 RESULT/OUTCOMES

On the test data, the developed model performs reasonably. Out of 507 photos, the model correctly predicted 461 of them, resulting in an accuracy rate of the model of roughly 91%. The model accurately classifies the various waste components by identifying the various categories of objects. Utilizing images of the testing data, the generated model's outcomes were assessed. The test data images have been meticulously incorporated into the testing code for the waste element detection. The model's overall detection time to identify a single object from an image is close to 8.05 seconds. In order to assess the model's actual correctness, the names of the images were actually provided so that it could be physically observed how well the model's functions had performed in those pictures as in Figure 16.5.

```
path = "plastic1.jpg"

img = tf.keras.preprocessing.image.load_img(path, target_size=(256, 256))
img_array = tf.keras.preprocessing.image.img_to_array(img)
img_array = tf.expand_dims(img_array, 0)

predictions = model.predict(img_array)
print(predictions)
print(classes)

[[0.03136026 0.19582006 0.04762305 0.11297981 0.6122168 ]]
['cardboard', 'glass', 'metal', 'paper', 'plastic']
```

FIGURE 16.5 Output showing plastic as the predicted class.

Multiple borders were initially seen being produced in the area of the object detection during testing; however, this issue was fixed by adjusting the threshold for picture prediction. This made it easier to invalidate the object's borders with low threshold values.

16.6 CONCLUSION AND FUTURE WORK

The purpose is to create a model able to differentiate between different waste kinds depending on the materials used in manufacture, and hence its recyclable nature, in order to push forward machine learning techniques aimed at addressing environmental concerns like waste accumulation, global warming, pollution, etc. Additionally, because it is open-source, professionals and subject matter experts will experiment with it. In the discipline of machine learning, experimentation is essential for enhancing model performance, along with the methods utilized for data collection and processing. Additionally, discussing machine learning algorithms' fundamental workings and the advantages that can arise for humanity as a result of them in the future can help society get a better knowledge of and confidence in such cutting-edge exponential technology. Focusing on innovative disruptive approaches to environmental challenges also raises our collective consciousness about protecting the environment, opening the door for the potential adoption of new sustainable behaviours in our daily lives. Future research will encompass a broader examination of AI-driven DT technologies in the application areas of healthcare, smart cities, and mobility. We believe that by rearranging and combining a number of extremely pertinent topics both horizontally and vertically, a synergistic effect will manifest, enabling the work in this study to contribute to additional AI-driven, DT-related research and assist various branches in developing new developments in their individual sustainable and smart fields.

In the upcoming future, in the digital era the AI and ML models are widely used with the aid of DT models and these techniques further help in analysis of the waste segregation and management in a global scenario. Further, the scope of work carried out is subject to extension based on a specific type of wastage and the needs of the end user/customer, which leads to an innovation in the coming future and can also lead to useful products in household, industry and medical fields.

REFERENCES

Abela, A., & Gatt, T. (2021). Using class activation maps on deep neural networks to localise waste classifications. *2021 IEEE 19th World Symposium on Applied Machine Intelligence and Informatics (SAMI)*. 10.1109/sami50585.2021.9378662.

Alawi, A. E. B., Saeed, A., Almashhor, F., Al-Shathely, R., & Hassan, A. E. (2021). Solid waste classification using deep learning techniques. *2021 International Congress of Advanced Technology and Engineering (ICOTEN)*. 10.1109/icoten52080.2021.9493430.

Alharam, A., Otrok, H., Elmedany, W., Bakht, A. B., & Alkaabi, N. (2021). AI-based anomaly and data posing classification in mobile crowd sensing. *2021 International Conference on Innovation and Intelligence for Informatics, Computing, and Technologies (3ICT)*. 10.1109/3ict53449.2021.9581443.

Bali, V., Bali, S., Gaur, D., Rani, S., & Kumar, R. (2023). Commercial-off-the shelf vendor selection: A multi-criteria decision-making approach using intuitionistic fuzzy sets and TOPSIS. *Operational Research in Engineering Sciences: Theory and Applications.*

Bolla, D. R., Shivashankar, Sandur, A., Bharath, M. L., Dharshan, G. B. G., & Mayur, A. S. (2019). Soil quality measurement using image processing and internet of things. *2019 4th International Conference on Recent Trends on Electronics, Information, Communication & Technology (RTEICT).* 10.1109/rteict46194.2019.9016971.

Bolla, D. R., Jijesh, J. J., Palle, S. S., Penna, M., Keshavamurthy, & Shivashankar. (2020). An IoT based smart E-fuel stations using ESP-32. *2020 International Conference on Recent Trends on Electronics, Information, Communication & Technology (RTEICT).* (pp. 333–336). Bangalore, India. doi: 10.1109/RTEICT49044.2020.9315676.

Cui, F., Cui, Q., & Song, Y. (2021). A survey on learning-based approaches for modeling and classification of human–machine dialog systems. *IEEE Transactions on Neural Networks and Learning Systems*, 32(4), 1418–1432. 10.1109/tnnls.2020.2985588.

Devadutta, K., Bhambri, P., Gountia, D., Mehta, V., Mangla, M., Patan, R., Kumar, A., Agarwal, P.K., Sharma, A., Singh, M., & Gadicha, A.B. (2020). Method for cyber security in email communication among networked computing devices [Patent application number 202031002649]. India.

Fanca, A., Puscasiu, A., Gota, D., Giurgiu, F. M., Santa, M. M., Valean, H., Domuta, C., & Miclea, L. (2022). Romanian coins recognition and sum counting system from image using TensorFlow and Keras. *2022 IEEE International Conference on Automation, Quality and Testing, Robotics (AQTR).* 10.1109/aqtr55203.2022.9802068.

Kataria, A., Agrawal, D., Rani, S., Karar, V., & Chauhan, M. (2022). Prediction of blood screening parameters for preliminary analysis using neural networks. In *Predictive modeling in biomedical data mining and analysis* (pp. 157–169). Academic Press.

Kataria, A., Puri, V., Pareek, P. K., & Rani, S. (2023, July). Human activity classification using G-XGB. In *2023 International Conference on Data Science and Network Security (ICDSNS)* (pp. 1–5). IEEE.

Kaur, D., Singh, B., & Rani, S. (2023). Cyber security in the metaverse. In *Handbook of research on AI-based technologies and applications in the era of the metaverse* (pp. 418–435). IGI Global.

Kaur, J., & Bhambri, P. (2020). *Hybrid classification model for the reverse code generation in software engineering.* Jalandhar: I.K. Gujral Punjab Technical University.

Kaur, K., Dhanoa, I.S., Bhambri, P., & Singh, G. (2020). Energy saving VM migration techniques. *Journal of Critical Reviews*, 7(9), 2359–2365.

Khan, S. Z., Hein, H., Alam, M. S., Moullec, Y. L., & Parand, S. (2022). NB-IoT based visual smart waste management system. *2022 18th Biennial Baltic Electronics Conference (BEC).* 10.1109/bec56180.2022.9935601.

Ramya, S., & Uma, M. (2022). Performance model evaluation of seizure classification using statistical features and random forest. *2022 International Conference on Electronic Systems and Intelligent Computing (ICESIC).* 10.1109/icesic53714.2022.9783473.

Rana, R., Chabbra, Y., & Bhambri, P. (2020). Comparison of clustering approaches for enhancing sustainability performance in WSNs: A study. In *Proceedings of the International Congress on Sustainable Development through Engineering Innovations* (pp. 62–71). ISBN 978-93-89947-14-4.

Rani, S., Kumar, S., Kataria, A., & Min, H. (2023). SmartHealth: An intelligent framework to secure IoMT service applications using machine learning. *ICT Express.*

Rani, S., Mishra, A. K., Kataria, A., Mallik, S., & Qin, H. (2023). Machine learning-based optimal crop selection system in smart agriculture. *Scientific Reports*, 13(1), 15997.

Sanz Rodrigo, M., Rivera, D., Moreno, J. I., Àlvarez-Campana, M., & López, D. R. (2023). Digital Twins for 5G networks: A modeling and deployment methodology. in *IEEE Access*, 11, 38112–38126, doi: 10.1109/ACCESS.2023.3267548.

Schneider, M., Amann, R., & Mitsantisuk, C. (2021). Waste object classification with AI on the edge accelerators. *International Conference on Mechatronics*. 10.1109/icm46511.2021.9385682.

Tanwar, R., Chhabra, Y., Rattan, P., & Rani, S. (2022, September). Blockchain in IoT networks for precision agriculture. In *International Conference on Innovative Computing and Communications: Proceedings of ICICC 2022, Volume 2* (pp. 137–147). Singapore: Springer Nature Singapore.

Thakur, G., Kumar, P., Deepika, Jangirala, S., Das, A. K., & Park, Y. (2023). An effective privacy-preserving blockchain-assisted security protocol for cloud-based digital twin environment. in *IEEE Access*, 11, 26877–26892, doi: 10.1109/ACCESS.2023.3249116.

Thokrairak, S., Thibuy, K., Fongsamut, C., & Jitngernmadan, P. (2021). Optimal object classification model for embedded systems based on pre-trained models. *2021 25th International Computer Science and Engineering Conference (ICSEC)*. 10.1109/icsec53205.2021.9684656.

Xiao, Q., Li, C., Tang, Y., & Chen, X. (2021). Energy efficiency modeling for configuration-dependent machining via machine learning: A comparative study. *IEEE Transactions on Automation Science and Engineering*, 18(2), 717–730. 10.1109/tase.2019.2961714.

Xu, H., Wu, J., Pan, Q., Guan, X., & Guizani, M. (2022). A Survey on digital twin for industrial internet of things: Applications, technologies and tools. In *IEEE Communications Surveys & Tutorials*, doi: 10.1109/COMST.2023.3297395.

Xu, X. et al. (Feb. 2022). Service offloading with deep Q-network for digital twinning-empowered internet of vehicles in edge computing. in *IEEE Transactions on Industrial Informatics*, 18(2), 1414–1423, doi: 10.1109/TII.2020.3040180.

17 Role of Digital Twin in the Design and Development of Smart Cities

Aman Kataria, Vikram Puri, and Sita Rani

17.1 INTRODUCTION

In an era characterized by rapid urbanization and technological advancements, the concept of Smart Cities has emerged as a transformative solution to address the complex challenges faced by urban areas. A Smart City is an urban environment that leverages cutting-edge technology, data-driven insights, and innovative infrastructure to improve the quality of life for its residents, enhance sustainability, and optimize resource utilization (Zamponi & Barbierato, 2022; Rani, Kataria, & Chauhan, 2022). The fundamental idea behind a smart city is to create a seamless and interconnected ecosystem where various elements, such as transportation, energy, communication, governance, and public services, work cohesively to meet the evolving needs of its inhabitants (Rani, S., & Gupta, O. P., 2017). The growth of Smart Cities is a response to the unprecedented urbanization trend witnessed worldwide. According to the United Nations, over half of the global population now resides in cities, and this number is expected to reach 68% by 2050. This rapid urban migration poses significant challenges, including increased pressure on resources, infrastructure, and public services (Rani, Bhambri, & Kataria, 2023) (Al Dakheel, Del Pero, Aste, & Leonforte, 2020; O'Dwyer, Pan, Acha, & Shah, 2019). In this context, the integration of technology and data-driven solutions becomes essential to build cities that are sustainable, efficient, and resilient. As shown in Figure 17.1, the key characteristics of Smart Cities include:

a. **Intelligent Infrastructure:** Smart Cities are equipped with advanced infrastructure embedded with sensors and connected devices. These technologies gather real-time data from various urban systems, allowing for intelligent and data-driven decision-making.

b. **Information and Communication Technology (ICT) Integration:** Smart Cities heavily rely on information and communication technologies to manage and coordinate various urban services. The integration of Internet of Things (IoT), big data analytics, artificial intelligence (AI), and

DOI: 10.1201/9781003395416-17

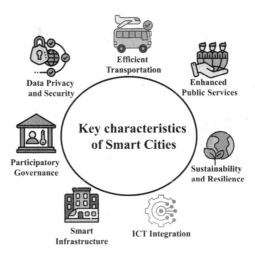

FIGURE 17.1   Key characteristics of smart cities.

cloud computing plays a pivotal role in transforming urban management and governance.

c. **Sustainability and Resilience:** A major focus of Smart Cities is to promote environmental sustainability and resilience. Technologies are used to optimize energy consumption, reduce carbon emissions, manage waste effectively, and protect natural resources.

d. **Efficient Transportation:** Smart Cities prioritize intelligent transportation systems to alleviate traffic congestion, improve public transportation, and promote sustainable mobility options, including electric vehicles and bike-sharing programs.

e. **Enhanced Public Services:** Digital solutions are employed to enhance public services, including smart healthcare, education, safety, and waste management. Citizen-centric platforms facilitate access to services and promote citizen engagement.

f. **Participatory Governance:** Smart Cities emphasize citizen participation and engagement in decision-making processes. E-governance platforms and digital channels enable residents to provide feedback, access information, and influence urban policies.

g. **Data Privacy and Security:** With the vast amounts of data generated and exchanged in a Smart City, ensuring data privacy and cybersecurity becomes paramount. Robust measures are implemented to protect sensitive information and safeguard against potential cyber threats.

The development of Smart Cities is a multi-dimensional process involving collaboration between various stakeholders, including government authorities, private companies, research institutions, and citizens (Ismail, Bagula, & Tuyishimire, 2018; Vattapparamban, Güvenç, Yurekli, Akkaya, & Uluağaç, 2016). Each city's unique characteristics, challenges, and goals shape its approach to becoming "smart," resulting in diverse solutions and implementations across different urban areas. The potential benefits of Smart Cities are vast, ranging from improved urban planning and resource management to increased economic opportunities and enhanced quality of life for residents. However, challenges related to data privacy, interoperability, funding, and citizen adoption must be addressed for the successful realization of the Smart City vision. As cities continue to evolve and embrace new technologies, the journey towards becoming truly smart is an ongoing process. The relentless pursuit of innovation, sustainability, and citizen-centricity will determine the success of Smart Cities in shaping a more connected, efficient, and inclusive urban future (F. Ullah & Al-Turjman, 2021; Z. Ullah, Al-Turjman, Mostarda, & Gagliardi, 2020).

17.1.1 Overview of Digital Twin Technology and Its Background

Digital twin technology is an innovative development that serves as a bridge between the physical and digital realms, providing a virtual duplicate of tangible objects, systems, or procedures. The utilization of this technology facilitates the ability to monitor, analyze, and simulate data in real time, hence enabling the acquisition of insights and the implementation of optimizations that were previously unachievable. The notion of digital twins has garnered considerable attention in diverse sectors such as manufacturing, healthcare, aerospace, and urban development, as they have a crucial impact on revolutionizing the processes of designing, operating, and maintaining intricate systems (Rani, S., Bhambri, P., & Chauhan, M., 2021, October).

17.1.2 Background

The phrase "digital twin" was introduced by Dr. Michael Grieves at the University of Michigan in 2002. Digital twins were originally developed in the manufacturing industry with the purpose of generating virtual representations of physical products (Singh, P., Gupta, O. P., & Saini, S., 2017). This technology allowed manufacturers to effectively monitor the performance of their products, identify and resolve any problems, and enhance the design of these products (Kataria & Puri, 2022). The uses of digital twins have expanded alongside the evolution of technology. In contemporary times, the concept of digital twins has beyond its initial application to singular items, and has now come to cover comprehensive systems, intricate processes, and even entire urban environments (Agostinelli, Cumo, Guidi, & Tomazzoli, 2021) (Sudevan, S., Barwani, B., Al Maani, E., Rani, S., & Sivaraman, A. K., 2021).

The fundamental principles underlying digital twin technology encompass the creation of a virtual replica of a tangible entity or complex system, wherein the virtual counterpart is consistently refreshed with up-to-date information obtained in real time. The digital duplicate in question is not merely a fixed representation, but rather a dynamic and interactive manifestation of the corresponding real object. Several important concepts can be identified, namely:

   a. **Virtual Representation:** It refers to the process of creating digital replicas of physical assets, which accurately capture their geometric properties, dynamic behavior, and other interactions. The breadth of digital representations can span from rudimentary three-dimensional models to intricate simulations that integrate data obtained from diverse sensors.

b. **Real-time Data Integration:** The process of real-time data integration involves the collection and incorporation of data from many sources such as sensors, IoT devices, and other relevant sources. This data is then utilized to create a digital twin, which accurately represents and reflects the current status and performance of the physical asset. The provided data facilitates the generation of precise and current insights.

c. **Simulation and Analysis:** The utilization of digital twins facilitates the process of scenario testing and modeling, so enabling the anticipation of potential impacts on the entire ecosystem resulting from alterations made to a specific component of the system. This approach holds significant value in the evaluation of prospective outcomes prior to implementing tangible modifications in the real world.

d. **Predictive Capabilities:** The predictive capabilities of digital twins are derived from the analysis of past data and present situations (Gupta, O. P., & Rani, S., 2013). Through this analysis, digital twins can anticipate and forecast probable failures, maintenance requirements, and performance concerns. Consequently, proactive actions can be taken to address these anticipated challenges (Kataria, Agrawal, Rani, Karar, & Chauhan, 2022).

Digital twin technology offers a wide range of applications, encompassing several domains and industries.

a. **Manufacturing:** The field of manufacturing encompasses various activities, including the optimization of production processes, the prediction of maintenance requirements, and the simulation of novel product designs.

b. **Healthcare:** The field of healthcare is currently exploring the development of digital replicas of patients as a means to facilitate individualized therapies and advance medical research.

c. **Aerospace:** The field of aerospace encompasses various activities, including the monitoring of aircraft performance, the prediction of maintenance requirements, and the simulation of flying situations.

d. **Energy:** The focus of this research revolves around the simulation and optimization of power plant operations, the prediction of energy consumption, and the improvement of grid management.

e. **Urban Development:** The concept of urban development entails the creation of digital replicas - known as digital twins - of cities with the aim of enhancing urban planning, infrastructure management, and disaster response capabilities.

17.2 FUNDAMENTALS OF DIGITAL TWIN TECHNOLOGY

17.2.1 DEFINITION OF SMART CITIES AND THEIR EVOLUTION

The concept of smart cities has evolved over time, driven by technological advancements and the need to address urbanization challenges. The evolution

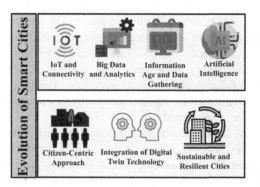

FIGURE 17.2 Evolution of smart cities.

of smart cities can be understood through the following stages as shown in Figure 17.2:

a. **Information Age and Data Gathering (1990s to early 2000s):** In this initial stage, cities began to collect data and leverage basic information technologies to manage certain urban aspects, such as traffic signals, waste management, and utility systems. The focus was on improving efficiency through data gathering and basic automation.

b. **IoT and Connectivity (mid-2000s to 2010s):** The proliferation of IoT technologies played a significant role in the advancement of smart cities. As more devices and sensors became connected, cities started gathering real-time data on various aspects, including traffic flow, air quality, and energy consumption. This connectivity enabled more informed decision-making and enhanced urban services.

c. **Big Data and Analytics (mid-2010s to present):** With the accumulation of massive amounts of data from diverse sources, cities began utilizing big data analytics to gain valuable insights. Data analytics helped identify patterns, optimize resource allocation, and predict urban trends. This stage saw the emergence of data-driven urban planning and management (Bali, V., Bali, S., Gaur, D., Rani, S., & Kumar, R., 2023).

d. **Sustainable and Resilient Cities (mid-2010s to present):** As environmental concerns and the impacts of climate change gained prominence, smart cities shifted focus towards sustainability and resilience. Technologies were employed to promote energy efficiency, reduce greenhouse gas emissions, and adapt to climate-related challenges. Concepts like green infrastructure and circular economy principles were incorporated into urban planning (Chauhan, M., & Rani, S., 2021).

e. **AI and Automation and Citizen-Centric Approach (present and future):** The integration of AI and machine learning (ML) into smart city systems marked the next phase in the evolution. AI-powered algorithms enabled cities to optimize resource management, automate processes, and enhance predictive capabilities. Smart cities began utilizing AI for autonomous vehicles, dynamic traffic management, and personalized urban services. The evolution of smart cities has also shifted the focus towards a citizen-centric approach. The involvement of residents in decision-making processes, participatory governance, and the use of citizen feedback in shaping urban policies became more prevalent. The idea is to ensure that technology is harnessed to improve the quality of life and meet the specific needs of the city's inhabitants.

f. **Integration of Digital Twin Technology (present and future):** Digital twin technology is gaining momentum in smart city development. Digital twins create virtual replicas of physical assets, infrastructure, and entire urban areas, enabling real-time monitoring, simulation, and predictive analysis. This integration allows cities to optimize operations, improve resilience, and enhance urban planning based on data-driven insights.

17.2.2 CONCEPTUAL FRAMEWORK OF DIGITAL TWINS

The establishment of a conceptual framework for digital twins in the context of smart cities is a crucial reference point that delineates the manner in which digital twin technology may be utilized to enhance the creation and administration of urban settings with more efficiency (Khang, A., Bhambri, P., Rani, S., & Kataria, A., 2022). Digital twins refer to virtual representations of real elements or systems. In the context of smart cities, these digital twins serve the purpose of modeling, monitoring, and optimizing different aspects of urban life, infrastructure, and services. Presented below is a conceptual framework aimed at comprehending the significance of digital twins within the context of smart city development (Kumar, R., Rani, S., & Awadh, M. A., 2022).

a. **Data Integration and Collection**
   1. **Physical Infrastructure Sensors:** In the context of a smart city, the urban environment is equipped with a diverse range of sensors to monitor and gather data on the physical infrastructure. The sensors are responsible for gathering data pertaining to various domains, including but not limited to traffic movement, air quality, energy usage, and trash management.
   2. **IoT Devices:** IoT devices and technologies have a substantial impact on the process of data collection. The devices encompassed within this category can vary, spanning from traffic cameras and weather stations to interconnected streetlights and waste bins.
b. **Data Processing and Analytics**
   1. **Data Ingestion:** The process of data ingestion involves the transfer and integration of data obtained from various sensors and IoT devices into a centralized data platform.
   2. **Big Data Analytics:** The field of big data analytics involves the utilization of advanced analytics techniques and ML algorithms to analyze large volumes of data. Through this process, important insights are extracted, trends are identified, and predictions are made.

3. **Real-time Monitoring:** The utilization of digital twins facilitates the continuous monitoring of critical systems within the urban environment, enabling prompt reactions to occurrences or irregularities.

c. **Digital Twin Creation**

1. **City Model:** The concept of a city model involves the creation of a digital twin that accurately represents either the entirety of an urban environment or certain elements within it, such as transportation networks, utilities, or buildings.

2. **3D Visualization:** The models are frequently displayed in a 3D visualization format, which provides a realistic depiction of the tangible environment.

d. **Simulation and Predictive Analysis:**

1. **What-If Scenarios:** The utilization of digital twins facilitates the simulation of diverse hypothetical situations. For example, urban planners have the ability to simulate the potential effects of planned alterations in transportation infrastructure or zoning restrictions.

2. **Predictive Analysis:** It entails utilizing past data and trends to enable digital twins to create prognostications regarding forthcoming metropolitan predicaments, encompassing but not limited to traffic congestion, energy demand, and environmental concerns.

17.3   KEY COMPONENTS OF A DIGITAL TWIN SYSTEM

The integration of these various components results in the establishment of a full Digital Twin system that accurately replicates the physical entity. This system offers significant benefits such as useful insights, predictive capabilities, and the capacity to manage and regulate real-world processes (Table 17.1).

TABLE 17.1
Key Components of a Digital Twin System

Component	Description
Physical Entity	The Digital Twin is a representation of a tangible entity, system, or procedure found in the physical world.
Sensors and Data	Sensors are responsible for gathering data from physical entities, encompassing various measurements, situations, and states.
Data Processing	Algorithms and data analytics technologies are utilized to effectively process and convert unprocessed data into actionable and meaningful information.
Communication	The bidirectional communication between the Digital Twin and the physical entity facilitates control and feedback.
IoT Connectivity	The establishment of a connection to the Internet of Things (IoT) enables the seamless interchange of real-time data between the digital twin and its corresponding physical object.

(Continued)

TABLE 17.1 *(Continued)*
Key Components of a Digital Twin System

Component	Description
Digital Model	A digital manifestation of a tangible object or entity, frequently employing three-dimensional models or simulation software.
Documentation	Comprehensive documentation and metadata pertaining to the configuration and operation of the Digital Twin.
Feedback Loop	The transmission of information from the Digital Twin to the corresponding physical entity for the purposes of control and optimization.
Maintenance Tools	The Digital Twin system is subject to health monitoring and undergoes regular upgrades, patches, and maintenance procedures.
Data Storage	The system securely retains historical and real-time data for the purposes of analysis, reference, and archive, ensuring data integrity and confidentiality.
Analytics Engine	The utilization of machine learning, artificial intelligence (AI), and various other methodologies to conduct data analysis and produce valuable insights.
Visualization	The Digital Twin and its associated data are presented in graphical formats to facilitate comprehension.
APIs and Integration	Enables seamless interface with diverse systems, applications, or platforms to augment functionality.
User Interface	The user interface serves as the primary means by which individuals engage with and oversee the operations of the Digital Twin system.
Security Measures	The organization implements cybersecurity rules and measures in order to safeguard sensitive data and maintain the integrity of the system.
Simulation Tools	This tool facilitates the examination of many scenarios, projections, and what-if assessments to support the process of decision-making.

17.4   TYPES OF DIGITAL TWINS AND THEIR APPLICATIONS

Digital twins refer to virtual representations of tangible objects, complex systems, or dynamic processes that exist in the physical world. Smart cities encompass a variety of classifications based on their focal points and applications (Arunachalam, P., Janakiraman, N., Sivaraman, A. K., Balasundaram, A., Vincent, R., Rani, S., ... & Rajesh, M., 2022). The many forms of digital twins each play an important part in the process of making smart cities more effective, resilient, and environmentally friendly. They make it possible to make decisions based on data, better resource management, improve infrastructure maintenance, and ultimately improve the quality of life for city residents while simultaneously lowering their impact on the environment (Kataria, Ghosh, & Karar, 2021; Puri, Kataria, & Sharma, 2021). The following discourse presents an overview of the primary classifications of Digital Twins and their respective utilization within the context of smart cities.

   a. **City-Level Digital Twins:** City-level digital twins are comprehensive virtual representations of a complete urban area or a substantial segment thereof, encompassing various elements such as infrastructure, buildings, transit systems, and utilities. The applications are as follows:

1. **Urban Planning:** Urban planning is a field of study and practice that focuses on the development and design of cities at a city-level scale. It involves the analysis, evaluation, and implementation of Digital twins to assist urban planners in simulating and optimizing urban layouts, infrastructure development, and land utilization.

2. **Traffic Management:** Traffic management systems enable the monitoring of traffic flow in real time, the prediction of congestion, and the implementation of optimal transportation routing strategies.

3. **Energy Management:** The focus of this study is energy management, namely the optimization of electricity and other utility distribution in order to enhance the energy efficiency of smart networks.

4. **Emergency Response:** Emergency response involves providing assistance in catastrophe preparedness, response, and recovery through the utilization of modeling techniques to simulate prospective scenarios (Banerjee, K., Bali, V., Nawaz, N., Bali, S., Mathur, S., Mishra, R. K., & Rani, S., 2022).

b. **Building Digital Twins:** The construction of digital twins entails a specific focus on individual buildings or complexes, wherein comprehensive data pertaining to their physical composition, operational systems, and occupancy is provided. Applications of Building Digital Twins are:

1. **Energy Efficiency:** The practice of energy efficiency involves the monitoring and optimization of various systems, such as HVAC and lighting, with the aim of minimizing energy use.

2. **Maintenance:** The implementation of predictive maintenance strategies to proactively detect and resolve issues in order to mitigate potential financial burdens.

3. **Occupant Comfort:** Occupant comfort refers to the practice of monitoring several parameters, such as indoor air quality and temperature, with the aim of improving the overall well-being of individuals residing in a particular space.

4. **Security:** The objective of this study is to explore the potential of real-time monitoring and threat identification in order to enhance building security.

c. **Infrastructure Digital Twins:** Infrastructure Digital Twins are virtual replicas that accurately simulate and model essential components of key infrastructure, including bridges, roadways, water treatment plants, and sewage systems. The utilization of Infrastructure Digital Twins encompasses various domains and sectors as follows:

1. **Maintenance:** The implementation of predictive maintenance strategies to maintain the safety and durability of infrastructure assets.

2. **Resilience Planning:** The topic of discussion pertains to resilience planning, namely the evaluation of the susceptibility of essential infrastructure to various natural calamities and other potential threats.

3. **Utilities Management:** The field of utilities management involves the optimization of the distribution and management of essential resources such as water, power, and gas.

4. **Environmental Monitoring:** The practice of environmental monitoring involves the systematic observation and assessment of various environmental factors, with the aim of identifying and addressing potential negative consequences on the environment. This involves monitoring and managing issues such as water pollution and air quality.

d. **Transportation Digital Twins:** It encompass the transportation network inside an urban area, comprising road infrastructure, public transit systems, and various types of automobiles. The utilization of Transportation Digital Twins encompasses the following domains:

1. **Traffic Management:** The subject of this study pertains to traffic management, specifically focusing on the real-time monitoring of traffic, forecast of congestion, and optimization of routes for commuters.

2. **Public Transit:** The objective of this study is to enhance the efficiency and accessibility of public transit timetables and routes.

3. **Fleet Management:** Fleet management involves the efficient management and optimization of municipal and commercial vehicle fleets.

4. **Transportation Planning:** Transportation planning involves providing support for the strategic development and enhancement of transportation infrastructure.

e. **Utility Digital Twins:** Utility Digital Twins are virtual replicas that simulate utility systems, including water delivery, wastewater treatment, and electricity grids. The utility digital twins possess a wide range of uses:

1. **Resource Management:** The field of resource management involves the strategic optimization of the distribution and allocation of essential resources, such as water and energy.

2. **Leak Detection:** Leak detection refers to the process of identifying and addressing leaks inside water or gas distribution networks in order to minimize their impact.

3. **Grid Resilience:** The objective of this study is to evaluate and improve the resilience of electrical networks in order to mitigate the occurrence of power outages.

4. **Sustainability:** The concept of sustainability involves the systematic monitoring and reduction of the use of resources in order to foster long-term environmental, social, and economic well-being.

17.5   REAL-TIME MONITORING AND DATA MANAGEMENT

17.5.1   IoT Integration in Digital Twin Systems

The integration of IoT technology within Digital Twin systems, aimed at facilitating real-time monitoring and efficient data handling, plays a pivotal role in the development of smart cities. Through the integration of physical infrastructure, devices, and sensors with Digital Twins, urban areas may effectively leverage the capabilities of the IoT to optimize efficiency, promote sustainability, and improve the general standard of living. Within this particular context, IoT devices are responsible for the collection of real-time data from a multitude of sources. These sources encompass traffic sensors, environmental monitors, energy meters, and other similar entities. The aforementioned data is subsequently included in the respective Digital Twin models, so generating a dynamic and precise depiction of the existing condition of the city. By means of this integration, smart cities have the capability to continuously observe and analyze several aspects such as traffic patterns, air quality, energy usage, and infrastructure performance in real time (Rani, Kataria, Chauhan, et al., 2022; Rani, Kataria, et al., 2021).

The advantages of this integration are significant. City planners and administrators are able to promptly get valuable knowledge on essential urban processes, which facilitates proactive decision-making and swift response to emergent difficulties such as traffic congestion, spikes in pollution, or failures in infrastructure. Through the examination of both historical and real-time data within the context of Digital Twins, smart cities have the potential to increase resource allocation, diminish energy consumption, bolster public safety, and elevate the overall quality of the urban environment. Furthermore, the integration of IoT technology facilitates the establishment of a basis for predictive analytics and ML (Rani, Kataria, Kumar, & Tiwari, 2023). This, in turn, empowers cities to proactively identify and address potential problems before they reach critical levels. Consequently, this integration promotes the development of urban environments that are more sustainable, resilient, and conducive to a high quality of life for their inhabitants.

17.5.2 Data Collection, Analysis, and Visualization Techniques

In the realm of smart cities, the efficient and cohesive handling of data is of utmost importance for the purposes of real-time monitoring and decision-making. This involves the gathering, processing, and visualization techniques employed to handle the data effectively. The process of data collection encompasses the utilization of an extensive range of sensors, IoT devices, and diverse data sources distributed across the urban environment. These instruments are employed to gather information pertaining to multiple dimensions, including but not limited to traffic patterns, air quality levels, energy usage, and other relevant factors. The aforementioned data is subsequently transmitted instantaneously to central repositories for the purpose of analysis. Sophisticated analytical methodologies, such as ML and AI, are utilized to extract significant insights, identify recurring patterns, and forecast forthcoming trends. The utilization of visualization is of utmost importance in effectively communicating intricate data in a comprehensible manner, frequently accomplished through the implementation of interactive dashboards, maps, and graphs. This facilitates the rapid comprehension of crucial information by municipal managers, inhabitants, and other relevant parties. Through the integration of these methodologies, smart cities have the potential to optimize the allocation of resources, improve public services, and promptly address emergent difficulties. This, in turn, can promote sustainability, efficiency, and the general welfare of their inhabitants (Rani, Mishra, et al., 2021; Wenjun, 2010).

17.5.3 Implementing Predictive Maintenance and Fault Detection

The use of predictive maintenance and defect detection in smart cities is a critical approach aimed at improving the effectiveness and long-term viability of urban infrastructure. This methodology utilizes cutting-edge technology, such as the IoT, AI, and data analytics, to actively detect and resolve challenges inside essential urban infrastructures such as transportation, utilities, and buildings. Smart cities have the capability to anticipate the failure or repair needs of equipment and infrastructure by employing sensors and data streams for continuous monitoring (Kataria, Ghosh, Karar, et al., 2020). This approach enables the implementation of planned and economically efficient repairs, hence reducing operational interruptions and mitigating the need for expensive unplanned repairs. Moreover, fault detection algorithms provide the capability to detect anomalies and deviations in real-time data, so facilitating prompt reactions to possible issues before they escalate. The implementation of predictive maintenance and defect detection has several benefits, including the reduction of maintenance costs and the extension of infrastructure lifespan. Additionally, it contributes to the improvement of overall quality of life for urban residents by maintaining the reliability and resilience of vital services in smart cities (Kataria, Ghosh, & Karar, 2018, 2020).

17.6 FUTURE TRENDS AND PROSPECTS

The future trends and prospects of smart cities are expected to be significantly influenced by the advancements in Digital Twin technology. These technological advancements provide significant potential to improve the quality of urban life, promote sustainability, and optimize efficiency. A notable trend in the field is the emergence of increasingly extensive and interconnected Digital Twins, which have the capacity to encompass entire urban areas or numerous systems inside them. The adoption of a holistic approach facilitates the integration of data from diverse sources, including transportation, energy, and environmental monitoring. This integration empowers city officials to develop a full view of their urban setting.

In addition, the field of AI and ML is witnessing notable advancements, leading to enhanced capabilities in predictive and prescriptive analytics within the context of Digital Twins (Kumar, Saini, Agrawal, Karar, & Kataria, 2023; Kumar, Saini, Agrawal, Kataria, & Karar, 2022). This implies that smart cities have the capability to predict and address potential problems in advance, hence enabling the implementation of proactive strategies in domains such as traffic control, energy usage, and infrastructure upkeep. Furthermore, the progress in sensor technology and the integration of IoT connectivity are enabling the collection of data in real time, thereby fostering a more dynamic and responsive ecosystem for Digital Twin.

The merging of augmented reality and virtual reality technologies with Digital Twins presents an additional promising opportunity. These immersive experiences will enable city planners, people, and enterprises to visually comprehend urban plans and simulations in novel and unparalleled manners, hence promoting enhanced participation and collaboration in the decision-making process. Furthermore, the heightened utilization of blockchain technology serves to enhance the safeguarding of data and the preservation of its accuracy within the context of Digital Twins, thereby cultivating a sense of confidence and reliance among various parties involved. The significance of this is paramount in sensitive domains such as healthcare and security within smart urban environments.

The progressions in Digital Twin technology have the potential to shape the trajectory of smart cities, providing comprehensive insights, predictive functionalities, and improved user experiences. These emerging trends not only have the potential for increased efficiency and sustainability but also facilitate the active engagement of individuals in defining the trajectory of their urban settings. Consequently, these developments have the capacity to enhance the livability and responsiveness of cities.

17.7 CONCLUSION

Digital Twins in smart city design and development will transform urban planning, administration, and sustainability. Digital Twins show infrastructure, buildings, transportation, and utilities in cities. They give city planners and decision-makers real-time data, predictive analytics, and scenario modeling to make better urban development decisions. To successfully utilize Digital Twins in smart cities, numerous critical elements must be considered. First, effective data governance frameworks and cybersecurity procedures are needed to protect sensitive data and assure data correctness and integrity. Data sharing and urban goals require collaboration between the government, the commercial sector, and community groups. To handle new technology expansion and integration, a scalable and interoperable digital infrastructure is essential. Digital Twins must also promote data-driven decision-making and digital literacy among city authorities and inhabitants. Finally, cities should monitor and evaluate their Digital Twin systems to ensure they meet urban demands and difficulties. Smart cities can achieve unparalleled efficiency, sustainability, and resilience in their creation and management by following these principles and embracing Digital Twins.

REFERENCES

Agostinelli, S., Cumo, F., Guidi, G., & Tomazzoli, C. (2021). Cyber-physical systems improving building energy management: Digital twin and artificial intelligence. *Energies, 14*(8), 2338.

Arunachalam, P., Janakiraman, N., Sivaraman, A. K., Balasundaram, A., Vincent, R., Rani, S., ... & Rajesh, M. (2022). Synovial sarcoma classification technique using support vector machine and structure features. *Intelligent Automation & Soft Computing, 32*(2), 43–55.

Al Dakheel, J., Del Pero, C., Aste, N., & Leonforte, F. (2020). Smart buildings features and key performance indicators: A review. *Sustainable Cities and Society, 61*, 102328.

Bali, V., Bali, S., Gaur, D., Rani, S., & Kumar, R. (2023). Commercial-off-the shelf vendor selection: A multi-criteria decision-making approach using intuitionistic fuzzy sets and TOPSIS. *Operational research in engineering sciences: Theory and applications.*

Banerjee, K., Bali, V., Nawaz, N., Bali, S., Mathur, S., Mishra, R. K., & Rani, S. (2022). A machine-learning approach for prediction of water contamination using latitude, longitude, and elevation. *Water, 14*(5), 728.

Chauhan, M., & Rani, S. (2021). Covid-19: A revolution in the field of education in India. *Learning how to learn using multimedia*, 23–42.

Gupta, O. P., & Rani, S. (2013). Accelerating molecular sequence analysis using distributed computing environment. *International Journal of Scientific & Engineering Research–IJSER, 4*(10), 262–265.

Ismail, A., Bagula, B., & Tuyishimire, E. (2018). Internet-of-things in motion: A uav coalition model for remote sensing in smart cities. *Sensors, 18*(7), 2184.

Kataria, A., Agrawal, D., Rani, S., Karar, V., & Chauhan, M. (2022). 9 - Prediction of blood screening parameters for preliminary analysis using neural networks. In S. Roy, L. M. Goyal, V. E. Balas, B. Agarwal & M. Mittal (Eds.), *Predictive modeling in biomedical data mining and analysis* (pp. 157–169): Academic Press.

Kataria, A., Ghosh, S., & Karar, V. (2018). Data prediction of optical head tracking using self healing neural model for head mounted display.

Kataria, A., Ghosh, S., & Karar, V. (2020). Data prediction of electromagnetic head tracking using self healing neural model for head-mounted display. *Science and Technology, 23*(4), 354–367.

Kataria, A., Ghosh, S., & Karar, V. (2021). Prediction analysis of optical tracker parameters using machine learning approaches for efficient head tracking. *arXiv preprint arXiv:2108.06606.*

Kataria, A., Ghosh, S., Karar, V., Gupta, T., Srinivasan, K., & Hu, Y.-C. (2020). Improved diver communication system by combining optical and electromagnetic trackers. *Sensors, 20*(18), 5084.

Kataria, A., & Puri, V. (2022). AI-and IoT-based hybrid model for air quality prediction in a smart city with network assistance. *IET Networks, 11*(6), 221–233.

Khang, A., Bhambri, P., Rani, S., & Kataria, A. (2022). Big data, cloud computing and internet of things.

Kumar, J., Saini, S. S., Agrawal, D., Karar, V., & Kataria, A. (2023). Human factors while using head-up-display in low visibility flying conditions. *Intelligent Automation & Soft Computing, 36*(2). doi: 10.32604/iasc.2023.034203

Kumar, J., Saini, S. S., Agrawal, D., Kataria, A., & Karar, V. (2022). *Effect of complexity and frequency of projected symbology of head-up display while flying in low visibility.* Paper presented at the 2022 IEEE International Conference on Machine Learning and Applied Network Technologies (ICMLANT).

Kumar, R., Rani, S., & Awadh, M. A. (2022). Exploring the application sphere of the internet of things in industry 4.0: A review, bibliometric and content analysis. *Sensors, 22*(11), 4276.

O'Dwyer, E., Pan, I., Acha, S., & Shah, N. (2019). Smart energy systems for sustainable smart cities: Current developments, trends and future directions. *Applied Energy, 237*, 581–597.

Puri, V., Kataria, A., & Sharma, V. (2021). Artificial intelligence-powered decentralized framework for Internet of Things in Healthcare 4.0. *Transactions on Emerging Telecommunications Technologies*, e4245.

Rani, S., Bhambri, P., & Kataria, A. (2023). Integration of IoT, Big Data, and Cloud Computing technologies. *Big Data, Cloud Computing and IoT: Tools and applications.*

Rani, S., Kataria, A., & Chauhan, M. (2022). Cyber security techniques, architectures, and design. *Holistic approach to quantum cryptography in cyber security* (pp. 41–66): CRC Press.

Rani, S., Kataria, A., Chauhan, M., Rattan, P., Kumar, R., & Sivaraman, A. K. (2022). Security and privacy challenges in the deployment of cyber-physical systems in smart city applications: State-of-art work. *Materials Today: Proceedings, 62*, 4671–4676.

Rani, S., & Gupta, O. P. (2017). CLUS_GPU-BLASTP: Accelerated protein sequence alignment using GPU-enabled cluster. *The Journal of Supercomputing, 73*, 4580–4595.

Rani, S., Kataria, A., Kumar, S., & Tiwari, P. (2023). Federated learning for secure IoMT-applications in smart healthcare systems: A comprehensive review. *Knowledge-based systems*, 110658.

Rani, S., Bhambri, P., & Chauhan, M. (2021, October). A machine learning model for kids' behavior analysis from facial emotions using principal component analysis. In *2021 5th Asian Conference on Artificial Intelligence Technology (ACAIT)* (pp. 522–525). IEEE.

Rani, S., Kataria, A., Sharma, V., Ghosh, S., Karar, V., Lee, K., & Choi, C. (2021). Threats and corrective measures for IoT security with observance of cybercrime: A survey. *Wireless communications and mobile computing, 2021*.

Rani, S., Mishra, R. K., Usman, M., Kataria, A., Kumar, P., Bhambri, P., & Mishra, A. K. (2021). Amalgamation of advanced technologies for sustainable development of smart city environment: A review. *IEEE Access, 9*, 150060–150087.

Singh, P., Gupta, O. P., & Saini, S. (2017). A brief research study of wireless sensor network. *Advances in Computational Sciences and Technology, 10*(5), 733–739.

Sudevan, S., Barwani, B., Al Maani, E., Rani, S., & Sivaraman, A. K. (2021). Impact of blended learning during Covid-19 in Sultanate of Oman. *Annals of the Romanian Society for Cell Biology*, 14978–14987.

Ullah, F., & Al-Turjman, F. (2021). A conceptual framework for blockchain smart contract adoption to manage real estate deals in smart cities. *Neural computing and applications*, 1–22.

Ullah, Z., Al-Turjman, F., Mostarda, L., & Gagliardi, R. (2020). Applications of artificial intelligence and machine learning in smart cities. *Computer Communications, 154*, 313–323.

Vattapparamban, E., Güvenç, İ., Yurekli, A. İ., Akkaya, K., & Uluağaç, S. (2016). *Drones for smart cities: Issues in cybersecurity, privacy, and public safety.* Paper presented at the Wireless Communications and Mobile computing Conference (IWCMC), 2016 International.

Wenjun, L. (2010). IoT makes the city smarter. *Scientific Culture, 10*, 12–13.

Zamponi, M. E., & Barbierato, E. (2022). The dual role of artificial intelligence in developing smart cities. *Smart Cities, 5*(2), 728–755.

18 Impact of Hybrid [CPU+GPU] HPC Infrastructure on AI/ML Techniques in Industry 4.0

B. N. Chandrashekhar, H. A. Sanjay, and V. Geetha

18.1 INTRODUCTION

The High Performance Computing (HPC) market will present new prospects (machine learning (ML)). It will proceed in this manner. HPC's computational capabilities will support the development of sophisticated algorithms that can handle massive amounts of data. It is necessary to gather and curate the data. This is the point at which artificial intelligence (AI) and ML will converge with HPC. To obtain an understanding of the data, a real-time AI-ML interface will be combined with HPC computing capability (Brayford et al., 2019; Michal et al., 2014).

This pairing occurs at a time when demand for data-based services is rising and HPC is the main route for data computing. As a result, HPC infrastructure is being used to build AI tools in order to fulfill the expanding demands of data-intensive services. It is possible to examine and distill large amounts of data to reveal profound insights and produce exact results (Lei et al., 2012).

New business models will emerge across verticals as a result of the AI-ML-HPC combination. Digital simulations will take place more quickly and more affordably than they did in the past (Kaur, D., Singh, B., & Rani, S., 2023). The logistics manufacturing can be optimized. Research on a mass scale can be conducted (The hybrid multicore consortium, 2010).

Applications in that discipline that have the potential to enhance each of our daily lives include personalized treatment and medical procedures for disease detection. Another application that makes it easy to identify credit card theft and other illicit activity is security (Sergeev & Balso, 2018).

It is difficult to enable data experts to use such architecture effectively since there is a dearth of packages that can meet both AI and HPC requirements, deep learning techniques are already being used by researchers in fields like high-energy physics to examine the enormous amounts of data produced by their experiments

 DOI: 10.1201/9781003395416-18

(Kumar et al., 2022). Traditional workstations cannot do this type of study, which calls for HPC resources and software that can handle large-scale data storage, data transfer, and computing (Chandrashekhar et al., 2021).

18.1.1 HPC INFRASTRUCTURE

Clusters, grids, and clouds have gained recognition as important emerging technologies for large-scale computing and enormous data processing over the past ten years. These innovations are frequently employed in modern computer systems to address both productions in commercial and industrial sectors as well as complex scientific challenges. UNIX and Linux are the two most often used operating systems for cluster construction. Adaptability, visibility, reconfigurability, availability, dependability, and high performance should all be features of clusters. Software tools are widely available to facilitate cluster computing (Lampropoulos, 2023).

Using a hybrid cluster, which has a computational architecture with multi-core central processing units (CPUs) and multicore graphics processing units (GPUs), is an innovative way to do parallel. The use of GPUs enables the completion of extremely parallel computations. GPU units have a wide range of natively supported operations that make the most efficient use of computational resources and maximum instruction throughput (Riasetiawan et al., 2023).

A brand-new paradigm for computing is emerging, and it delivers dynamic computing environments that are dependable, customizable, and QoS guaranteed. Clouds provide services for transparent access to hardware, software, and data Clouds provide services for transparent access to hardware, software, and data resources (Jha et al., 2022).

- Platform as a Service (PaaS)
- Software as a Service (SaaS)
- Infrastructure as a Service(IaaS)

Because it may offer expandable computational architecture, adaptive software features, and pay-as-you-use business models, cloud technology has enormous potential for processing vast volumes of data and tackling difficult computing problems (Kataria et al., 2020). Since it may provide flexible computational infrastructure, configurable software services, and pay-as-you-use business models, cloud computing promises to be very promising in processing large volumes of data and resolving complex computing difficulties.

18.1.2 HARDWARE INFRASTRUCTURES

18.1.2.1 CPU

Figure 18.1 illustrates the Multi-core CPU architecture with a cache hierarchy. The multi-core has two or more independent cores (computing units) on the same chip. The architecture of the *CPU core* consists of ALU (arithmetic logic unit) to perform arithmetic and logical operations, CU (control unit) to control and coordinate with

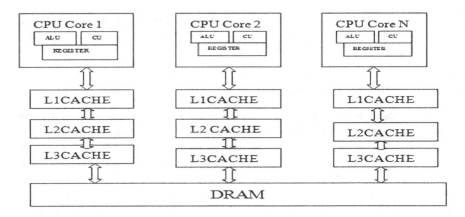

FIGURE 18.1 Multi-core CPU architecture with a cache hierarchy.

peripherals of the processors, RAM (random access memory) a high-speed temporary memory to access address directly in random order. Registers contain instructions sent to the hardware to fetch, store, and operate on data. Along with these parts, processor architecture also contains an important part which is the cache structure (Kaur et al., 2019). The cache is a high-speed buffer memory that assists fast access based on temporal locality (Kataria, A., Puri, V., Pareek, P. K., & Rani, S., 2023, July). The recent generation processors have three levels of cache that are L1, L2, and L3 (Mahajan, 2020). It is observed that after the creation of three-level caches, the performance of each core has been enhanced significantly because of their larger cache size, faster data transfer, and multithreaded nature.

18.1.2.2 GPU

In order to address the CPU architectural issues, the fast-growing video and gaming industry came up with lightweight many-core GPUs to achieve greater GFLOPS per video frame in high-end gaming applications (Bhambri et al., 2019). GPU architecture is shown in Figure 18.2. The architecture consists of an array of heavily threaded streaming multiprocessors (SMs). Each SM has numerous cores or streaming processors (SPs) that share common control logic and instruction cache. Individual SMs execute the instructions in SIMD (single instruction multiple data)

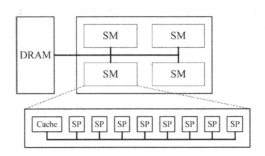

FIGURE 18.2 Many-core GPU architecture.

mode (Boesch, 2022). Each GPU has separate global memory DRAM (dynamic random access memory), which speeds up the rendering of graphics and computing of complex tasks. New-generation GPUs support both graphical and non-graphical applications (Rana et al., 2019). GPU supports thread-level parallelism based on its computing capability. GPU works with less memory and a small cache when compared with CPU.

Due to this extreme parallel architecture of GPU, it has been used in many fields such as machine learning, deep learning, artificial intelligence, medical imaging, and large-scale simulation. However, GPU has its disadvantages. In order to exploit the many-core GPU computing capability, the algorithms should be coded to reflect GPU architecture. Otherwise, high-performance computing applications will not effectively utilize all the available resources in a system (Tanwar, R., Chhabra, Y., Rattan, P., & Rani, S., 2022, September). This underutilization hurts the application's performance. The many-core GPU unit cannot run independently without the support of the CPU (Achar, 2022).

18.1.2.3 Hybrid

By combining CPU-GPU architecture (hybrid), performance can be further improved in massively parallel HPC applications. CPU and GPU have divergent design viewpoints, but merging their characteristics benefits healthier performance in numerous HPC applications (Rani, S., & Gupta, O. P., 2017; Rani, S., & Gupta, O. P., 2016). Figure 18.3 depicts CPU-GPU heterogeneous architecture with two CPUs and two GPUs. CPU-GPU communication happens via the I/O chipset, and they are connected to the I/O Hub by a Quick Path Interconnect Link (QPI) and PCIE. CPUs and GPUs have separate memory (DRAM) (Chandrashekhar & Sanjay, 2018).

Application control, workload distribution among the CPU and GPUs, starting the GPU processing, receiving the output from the GPUs, and some processing workloads themselves are all done by the CPU. The GPUs are in charge of carrying out extremely parallel computing (Bhambri et al., 2020).

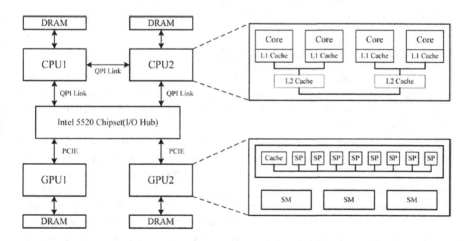

FIGURE 18.3 Multi-many core CPU-GPU hybrid architecture.

Many scientific and commercial innovations are built on HPC. Research facilities, the entertainment sector, financial services, artificial intelligence, and the oil and gas industry are just a few of the major advantages of HPC (Kataria, Ghosh and Karar, 2020). HPC applications, as their name suggests, handle vast amounts of data very quickly; hence, they demand a lot of processing power. One of the elements influencing the advancement of computer hardware is the desire for such HPC power (Chandrashekhar and Sanjay, 2019a). One example is the hybrid system, which combines GPUs and CPUs. One such technology that makes it possible to run HPC workloads effectively is the hybrid system, which combines CPUs and GPUs. Even though the CPU and GPU have different architectural styles, a hybrid design combines them to improve performance when running HPC workloads (Sharma et al., 2020).

A cluster that has multiple CPU-GPU nodes can be either homogeneous or heterogeneous. In homogeneous clusters, the architectures of the CPUs and GPUs are the same in each node, and so are the computing capabilities (Rossum, 1995). On the other hand, the architectures of the CPUs and GPUs will be different in each node in the case of heterogeneous clusters. Inter-node and intra-node communication, effective workload scheduling while taking into account the various CPU and GPU architectures, and efficient workload allocation across the nodes are the major obstacles to improving performance in a heterogeneous cluster (Chandrashekhar & Sanjay, 2019b).

18.1.3 SCOPE OF THE CHAPTER

This chapter's goal is to present a method for quickly moving common AI workloads from the AI that makes use of the system's hardware and optimized libraries to those workloads that make use of the HPC architecture (Rani, S., Mishra, A. K., Kataria, A., Mallik, S., & Qin, H., 2023).

To achieve this goal, we test the different AI/ML techniques such as Fully Connected Neural Networks, Convolution Neural Networks, and Recurrent Neural Networks, using Operators and Network parallelization techniques. Then, we develop workload partitioning algorithms to improve the performance of AI/ML techniques based on applications on hybrid HPC infrastructure.

18.2 AI/ML TECHNIQUES FOR HPC

By enabling innovative scientific detections, personalized medical analysis, and treatment, accurate weather prediction, state-of-the-art spam detection, automated cars, and much more, AI/ML technology has the potential to drastically impact our lives (Cui et al., 2013).

Because HPC and AI are linked, their convergence will spur business and innovation across many industry sectors. High-Performance Computing boosts AI, making it not only faster and smarter but also more precise in its output (Kataria & Puri, 2022). This demonstrates unequivocally that the interaction between AI and HPC is simple. For instance, machine learning, deep learning, and AI workloads are assisting businesses in training systems that use data to gain insights. In addition, HPC clusters assist in making connections between these data at a much faster rate (Shamoto et al., 2016).

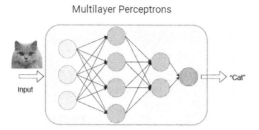

Multilayer Perceptrons

FIGURE 18.4   Fully connected neural networks.

18.2.1   Impact of Fully Connected Neural Networks on HPC

In a fully connected neural network, every neuron in every layer communicates with every neuron in the layer below it as shown in Figure 18.4. The main advantage of fully linked networks is that they are "structure agnostic," which implies that no specific input assumptions are needed. Fully linked networks can be utilized in a range of scenarios since they are structure-indifferent, although they usually perform worse than networks specifically built to handle the structure of a particular issue space.

Each additional layer is composed of a group of nonlinear functions that represent the weighted sum of all the outputs from the preceding layer.

18.2.2   Impact of Convolutional Neural Networks on Hybrid [CPU+GPU] HPC

Inspiration for our work is employing GPUs. For both training and testing, we suggest a GPU implementation of convolutional neural networks. GPUs have a fundamental advantage over CPUs. This is true even for matrices with thousands of rows and columns. The second benefit of GPUs is their substantial parallel pipelines, each of which has an ALU that may greatly accelerate computations (Rani, S., Kumar, S., Kataria, A., & Min, H., 2023).

GPUs do not, however, have a memory cache and cannot perform basic looping and branching operations. Without explicit loops or conditionals, SIMD instructions are challenging to implement. Convolutional neural networks are another variety of fully neural networks (CNN, or ConvNet). Convolutional neural networks are used most frequently in processer vision. Given a succession of real-world pictures or videotapes and utilizing CNN, Inevitably, an AI system will take the characteristics of these inputs and use them to accomplish a predetermined task, such as object recognition, facial detection, or scene understanding. One or more convolution layers in CNN models use convolution operations to extract the basic properties from input, in contrast to completely linked layers in Master Limited Partnerships (MLPs) as shown in Figure 18.5.

The mathematical functions that make up each level compute weighted sums of neighboring subsets of the results from the layer above at various points. GPUs, however, lack a memory cache and support.

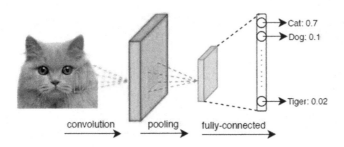

FIGURE 18.5 Convolutional neural networks.

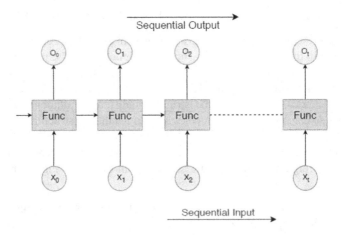

FIGURE 18.6 Recurrent neural network (RNN).

CNN machine learning models can capture the high-level representation of the input data by applying several convolutional filters, making CNN techniques very common in computer vision tasks.

18.2.3 Impact Recurrent Neural Network (RNN) on HPC

RNNs are a different type of artificial neural network that uses incremental data feeding. In order to report the problem with time series caused by sequential data input, recurrent neural networks have been developed as shown in Figure 18.6. The current input and the prior samples make up the RNN's work. A directed graph is created by the connections made among the nodes along a temporal sequence. Each RNN neuron's internal memory also stores the computation from the prior samples.

18.3 CONVERGENCE OF HYBRID [CPU+GPU] HPC SYSTEM WITH AI

HPC systems typically have 16-64 nodes, each one containing two or more Processor cores. When compared to conventional systems, this provides significantly too much processing power. Furthermore, every node in an HPC system offers efficient processing and memory, as well as assets, providing a degree of ability and faster performance than existing systems.

Many HPC systems include graphical processing units (GPUs) to increase processing power even further. A GPU is a committed processor that works in conjunction with the CPU as a co-processor. Hybrid computing refers to the combination of CPU and GPU.

Computing hybridization [CPU+GPU] HPC services will help AI in a variety of ways:

- GPUs are used to process AI-related algorithms such as neural network models more efficiently.
- Concurrency and co-processing accelerate computations, allowing large data sets and massive-scale experiments to be processed in less time.
- More space and memory allow for larger data volumes to be processed, improving the accuracy of AI modeling techniques.
- AI Tasks can be scattered between many resources, enabling individuals to make the most of what they have.
- When compared to conventional approaches, High-performance computing frameworks can get more expensive supercomputing. You could also obtain HPC as a cloud-based service, preventing overhead expenses and incurring only for what you use.
- The High-performance computing industry is enthusiastic about integrating AI and HPC, thereby improving performance.

The succeeding advancements will promote the future convergence of AI and HPC:

- Improving computational systems for acquiring AI infrastructures and heuristic strategies that will work best with HPC systems.
- Gaining the ability to specialize in areas such as information technologies, Artificial intelligence-based methodologies, statistics, and system startup.
  Ability to analyze the interactions between artificial intelligence methodologies, and to use as well as develop software solutions that can be applied across diverse disciplines instances.
- Expanding the use of open-source software and platforms. This could boost AI adoption on HPC and improve support for standardized tooling.

18.3.1 Proposed HPC Architecture for AI HPC Applications

A heterogeneous cluster with one CPU and two GPUs with various computational capabilities is depicted in Figure 18.7. The PCI-E 2.0 bus slot received the GPUs. CUDA IPC (inter-process communication) establishes a direct connection between the two GPU chips to better utilize the processing power of CPUs and GPUs for practical applications (Kataria et al., 2022).

Both the CPU and the GPU have their own memory, and they interact through the PCI-E bus. Each CPU has numerous cores and a separate cache. Application

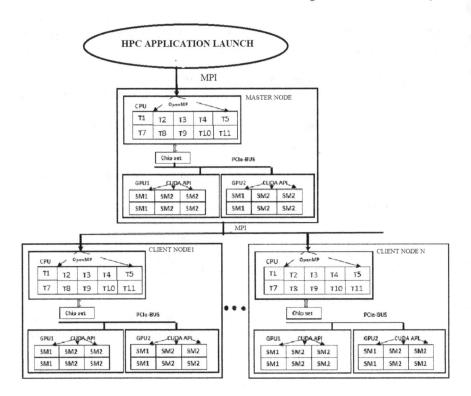

FIGURE 18.7 Heterogenous HPC cluster.

control, task distribution in between multi-core-CPU and many cores- GPU, commencing the GPU processing, and reading the many cores GPU result are all responsibilities of the multi-core-CPU. The GPU supports extremely parallel processing because of its numerous SMs.

MPI is an obvious solution for data interchange across nodes in a heterogeneous cluster. Due to its high latency and lack of usage of share-memory communications, MPI may not be the optimal option for CPU-GPU information exchange. Therefore, the pinned memory approach is used in this study with several OpenMP threads running in a unique MPI process on each node.

The pinned memory technology minimizes data transfers, which lowers the overhead of inter-node communication and boosts memory bandwidth. Before distributing the HPC workload to the cluster's client nodes, the master node splits it effectively using our analytical model. The computed workload is initially moved by the MPI process from the master node to the appropriate nodes on a heterogeneous cluster. Based on their computing power and hardware requirements, the CPU and GPUs will receive a dynamic workload distribution from the node-level master process.

One OpenMP thread will serve as the master thread among several others. The other threads run relevant computations in parallel, but only the master thread communicates with the GPU. The CUDA kernel is called by the master thread, and it is then executed concurrently by all of the GPU threads. Results are obtained by the OpenMP master thread from GPUs. The result is transferred from each slave node to the master node in the last step of the MPI process.

18.3.2 PARALLELIZATION METHODS ON HPC

Most HPC software is created in Fortran, C, or C++. Legacy extensions, libraries, and interfaces created in these languages are used to support HPC processes. AI, however, relies mainly on programs such as Julia and Python.

Both the interface and software must work together successfully for both to leverage the same infrastructure. This typically means that existing applications will be supplemented with AI frameworks and languages while still functioning as before. This enables programmers for AI and HPC to keep using their preferred tools without switching to another language.

18.3.2.1 Python

In the fields of artificial intelligence, machine learning, and data pre- and post-processing, Python is a popular high-level, interpreted programming environment. The language is frequently viewed as being approachable for prototyping algorithms in contrast to conventional programming languages like C++. Additionally, because Python is an interpreted programming language rather than C++, it does not need to be recompiled for a variety of CPU architectures.

Scientists can benefit from Python's productivity and the ever-improving performance of contemporary hardware by downloading the free Intel® distribution for Python* package. Implementing. Additionally, multi-user, multi-framework applications should not employ a single Python instance.

18.3.2.2 Hybrid [OpenMP+ MPI+PYCUDA] Architecture for Parallel Computing

On an HPC cluster, combining MPI, OpenMP, and PYCUDA's three parallel programming paradigms makes a lot of sense. To effectively tackle issues involving vast amounts of data is a frequent motivation. Due to the limited memory size of a GPU, CUDA alone will take longer to process a high data size problem. Utilizing the CPU to conduct meaningful computations helps to increase performance when employing the hybrid programming approach. A CPU can do valuable computations by using OpenMP, which is utilized for intra-node communication. Data communication between nodes is done using MPI. CUDA is used to allow GPUs to perform massively parallel computations.

Figure 18.8. depicts the Hybrid [OpenMP+MPI+PYCUDA] Framework. It is feasible to share a tiny piece of the computation task with the CPU by combining OpenMP with CUDA+MPI. This makes it easier to employ the CPU's processing capability for practical purposes. If not, data transfer will be the only task the CPU performs.

To reduce MPI send/receive overhead, the OpenMP+MPI+PYCUDA hybrid programming model leverages the *cudaMemcpyAsync* function to shift workloads from CPU to GPU and vice versa. The pinned memory technique is another tool the

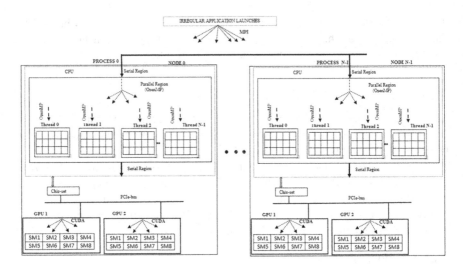

FIGURE 18.8   Hybrid [OpenMP+MPI+PYCUDA] framework.

framework uses to cut down on CPU and GPU data transfer latency. Kernels are the computational components of a PYCUDA-written application. The kernel has several threads to carry out tasks concurrently. GPUs can only read and write to host-attached memory. The PYCUDA API cudaMallocHost allows the GPU to acquire a block of main memory (). Results must be transported back to the main memory after execution, this challenge.

18.3.3   Proposed AI Workload Division Strategy on Hybrid [CPU+GPU]

This section describes the workload distribution strategy to allocate the AIML task between these nodes of a homogeneous CPU/GPU cluster. The CPU cannot be adequately kept occupied during the launch of the GPU kernel and memory transfer if the CPU is given less work, and the delay could be effectively concealed. The GPU kernel must wait for the CPU to complete the tasks if the workload is greater before producing the results. The workload should be proportional to the CPU and GPU's processing power.

Let W be the overall workload for each cluster, and let $Nnode$ represent the total amount of homogeneous nodes on the CPU-GPU homogenous cluster. Then work load per node [$Lnode$] is given by equation 18.1.

$$Lnode = \frac{W}{Nnode} \qquad (18.1)$$

Effective workload division can be achieved by considering the computation speed of the CPU and GPU.

$$Lcp = Lnode \times \frac{CP_{flops}}{(Node_{flops})} \tag{18.2}$$

Where

$$Lcp - Load \ on \ CPU$$

$$CP_{flops} - CPU_{flops}$$

$Node_{flops}$ is nothing but the sum of CPU_{flops} and GPU_{flops} present in that node, considering this equation 18.2 can be rewritten as shown in equation 18.3

$$Lcp = Lnode \times \frac{CP_{flops}}{(CP_{flops} + GP_{flops})} \tag{18.3}$$

where

$$GP_{flops} - GPU_{flops}$$

By dividing the load on CPU by the number cores the load per core is calculated as shown in equation 18.4.

$$LCP_{core} = \frac{LCP}{Nc} \tag{18.4}$$

where

$$LCP_{core} - Load \ per \ core,$$

Nc - Number of cores

To find out the load on GPU equation 18.3 can be modified as follows

$$LGp = Lnode \times \frac{GP_{flops}}{(CP_{flops} + GP_{flops})} \tag{18.5}$$

By using the above equation, we compute the GPU workload and CPU workload.

18.4 EXPERIMENT AND OUTCOMES

AIML Feature Extraction HPC applications workload experiments were demonstrated in order to validate the effects of hybrid HPC infrastructures.

18.4.1 EXPERIMENTAL SETUP

The trials are carried out on a private cluster. There are eight homogenous nodes in the cluster. The cluster's nodes each has a 6-core/socket Intel Xeon(R) E5-2620 processor, a 447-core GPU (NVIDIA Tesla M2075), and 32 GB of extendable, up to 500 GB, RAM. The MPI library is set up on the nodes with MPICH2-1.2. The operating system is Fedora 24, and the compilers used are GCC version 4.4.7 and NVIDIA nvcc version 5.0.

18.4.2 RESULTS AND ANALYSIS

This section describes the experimental results of the workload division strategy with hybrid programming approaches using popular Feature Extraction AIML benchmarks.

Based on the colors, feature extraction is taken into account. Let's use a few examples of photographs of Homer and Bart to tell them apart solely by their colors. It should be noted that the features are only extracted based on colors and not on any other characteristics like shape, size, etc. (Figure 18.9).

We take the intensity of each channel and contrast it with a predetermined set of colors that let us tell Homer from Bart. In order to visualize the outcome, we have used the colors of Homer's mouth, clothes, and shoes as the features and colored them yellow. Similarly to this, in order to see the outcome, we used the color green to highlight Bart's footwear, shorts, and T-shirt as characteristics.

Normalize the feature area by adding all of the pixels together. For instance, if an image has 100×200 pixels and 2,000 of those pixels have been detected as having a mouth feature, then $(2,000 / 20,000) \times 100 = 10$ or 10% of the image has pixels to be used to detect the mouth feature.

Table 18.1 demonstrates the test data accuracy on various HPC cluster platforms using various AIML neural network algorithms using test data with 10,000 photos. In comparison to FCNN and RNN, CNNs on hybrid [CPUs+GPUs] HPC cluster [OpenMP+MPI+PYCUDA] are considered to be superior.

From Table 18.2 it can be seen that on test data with 10,000 images, Training time on different HPC cluster platforms with different AIML neural networks techniques, CNNs are given the best performance on Hybrid [CPUs+GPUs] HPC Cluster [OpenMP+MPI+PYCUDA]compared to FCNN and RNN.

Fully linked networks don't make any assumptions about the input, which makes them less efficient and bad for feature extraction (see Figure 18.10). Additionally, they must train a greater number of weights, which increases training time. In

FIGURE 18.9 Feature extraction.

TABLE 18.1

Accuracy of Test Data on HPC Clusters

Implementation/ Factors	Accuracy of Test Data On CPU HPC Cluster [OpenMP+MPI]	Accuracy of Test Data On GPU HPC Cluster [PYCUDA]	Accuracy of Test Data Hybrid [CPUs+GPUs] HPC Cluster [OpenMP +MPI+PYCUDA]
CNN	87.32098742	90.32478463	98.59259259
FCNN	75.12803712	89.32492374	96.67466747
RNN	67.98364709	76.83264283	87.03703704

TABLE 18.2

Execution Time of Training Data on HPC Clusters

Implementation/ Factors	Execution Time (µs) for Training Data On CPU HPC Cluster [OpenMP+MPI]	Execution Time (µs) for Training data On GPU HPC Cluster [PYCUDA]	Execution Time (µs) for Training Data on Hybrid [CPUs+GPUs] HPC Cluster [OpenMP+MPI+PYCUDA]
CNN	68732923792	22910974597	9818989113
FCNN	8.74365E+12	2.91455E+12	1.24909E+12
RNN	9.0605E+11	3.02017E+11	1.29436E+11

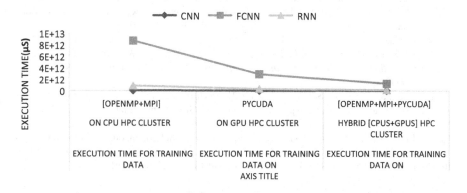

FIGURE 18.10   Execution time of CNN, FCNN, and RNN on a different HPC cluster.

contrast, CNNs only need to train a small number of parameters to learn how to recognize and extract the best characteristics from the images for the given task.

18.5   CONCLUSION

We provided a brief review of the various HPC cluster computing systems that integrate CPU and GPU technology in this chapter. We concentrated on three AIML

Technique variations that combine computational devices with various architectures into a single transparent system. For massively parallel computation, the proposed hybrid [CPU+GPUs] HPC cluster has already shown to be very beneficial. Its efficiency and scalability are shown by the experimental findings reported in the chapter. Final thought: CNN methods are obvious choices for feature extraction AIML benchmark applications for massively parallel computing on computational platforms merging CPU and GPU units. We intend to use a hybrid [CPU+GPUs] HPC cluster with a parallel programming paradigm [OpenMP+MPI+PYCUDA] for a variety of AIML research in the future.

REFERENCES

Achar, S. (2022). Adopting artificial intelligence and deep learning techniques in cloud computing for operational efficiency. *International Journal of Information and Communication Engineering*, 16(12), 567–572.

Bhambri, P., Sinha, V. K., & Jaiswal, M. (2019). Change in iris dimensions as a potential human consciousness level indicator. In *Proceedings of the International Conference on Innovations in Communication, Computing and Sciences* (pp. 182–186). IEEE.

Bhambri, P., Sinha, V. K., & Dhanoa, I. S. (2020). Development of cost effective PMS with efficient utilization of resources. *Journal of Critical Reviews*, 7(19), 781–786.

Boesch, Gaudenz (2022). Deep neural network: The 3 popular types (MLP, CNN and RNN) read more at: https://viso.ai/deep-learning/deep-neural-network-three-popular-types/.

Brayford, David, Vallecorsa, Sofia, & Atanasov, Atanas. (2019). Deploying AI frameworks on secure HPC systems with containers 978-1-7281-5020-8/19/$31.00 ©2019 IEEE.

Chandrashekhar B. N., & Sanjay, H. A. (2018) Dynamic workload balancing for computing-intensive application using parallel and hybrid programming models on cpu-gpu cluster. *Journal of Computational and Theoretical Nanoscience*, 15, 2836–2840.

Chandrashekhar, B. N., & Sanjay, H. A. (2019a) Performance framework for HPC applications on the homogeneous computing platform. 11, 28–39, 2019. 10.5815ijigsp.2019.08.03.

Chandrashekhar B. N., & Sanjay H. A.(2019b) Performance study of OpenMP and hybrid programming models on CPU-GPU cluster. *In Emerging Research in Computing, Information, Communication, and Applications(ERICICA)*, 906 https://ISBN: 978-981-13-6000-8.

Chandrashekhar, B. N., & Sanjay, H. A. (2021) Performance Driven Framework for High-Performance Computing Applications on CPU-GPU Hybrid Platform, thesis VTU.

Cui, Y., Zhou, J., Poyraz, E., Choi, D. J., & Guest, C. C. (2013) Multi-GPU implementation of a 3d finite difference time domain earthquake code on heterogeneous supercomputers. In *Proceedings of the International Conference on Computational Science*, p. 1255–1264.

Jha, Shantenu, Vincent, R. Pascuzzi, & Matteo, Turilli. (2022) AI-coupled HPC Workflows. arXiv preprint arXiv:2208.11745.

Kataria, A., & Puri, V. (2022). AI-and IoT-based hybrid model for air quality prediction in a smart city with network assistance. *IET Networks*, 11(6), 221–233.

Kataria, A., Ghosh, S., Karar, V., Gupta, T., Srinivasan, K., & Hu, Y. C. (2020). Improved diver communication system by combining optical and electromagnetic trackers. *Sensors*, 20(18), 5084.

Kataria, A., Ghosh, S., & Karar, V. (2020). Data prediction of electromagnetic head tracking using self healing neural model for head-mounted display. *Science and Technology*, 23(4), 354–367.

Kataria, A., Agrawal, D., Rani, S., Karar, V., & Chauhan, M. (2022). Prediction of blood screening parameters for preliminary analysis using neural networks. In *Predictive modeling in biomedical data mining and analysis* (pp. 157–169). Academic Press.

Kataria, A., Puri, V., Pareek, P. K., & Rani, S. (2023, July). Human Activity Classification using G-XGB. In *2023 International Conference on Data Science and Network Security (ICDSNS)* (pp. 1–5). IEEE.

Kaur, D., Singh, B., & Rani, S. (2023). Cyber security in the metaverse. In *Handbook of research on ai-based technologies and applications in the era of the metaverse* (pp. 418–435). IGI Global.

Kaur, J., Bhambri, P., & Kaur, S. (2019). SVM classifier based method for software defect prediction. *International Journal of Analytical and Experimental Model Analysis*, 11(10), 2772–2776.

Kumar, J., Saini, S. S., Agrawal, D., Kataria, A., & Karar, V. (2022, December). Effect of complexity and frequency of projected symbology of head-up display while flying in low visibility. In *2022 IEEE International Conference on Machine Learning and Applied Network Technologies (ICMLANT)* (pp. 1–4). IEEE.

Lampropoulos, G. (2023). Artificial intelligence, big data, and machine learning in Industry 4.0. *In Encyclopedia of data science and machine learning 2023* (pp. 2101–2109). IGI Global.

Lei, Guoqing, Dou, Yong, Wan, Wen, Xia, Fei, Li, Rongchun, Ma, Meng, & Zou, Dan (2012). CPU-GPU hybrid accelerating the zuker algorithm for RNA secondary structure prediction applications. *BMC Genomics*, 13, 2012.

Mahajan, Pooja (2020) Fully connected vs convolutional neural networks. Fully connected vs convolutional neural networks | by Pooja Mahajan | The Startup | Medium.

Michal, Marks, & Ewa, Niewiadomska-Szynkiewicz. (2014). Hybrid CPU/GPU platform for high-performance computing. In *Proceedings - 28th European Conference on Modelling and Simulation, ECMS 2014* (pp. 508–514). 10.7148/2014-0508.

Rana, R., Chhabra, Y., & Bhambri, P. (2019). A review on development and challenges in wireless sensor network. In *International Multidisciplinary Academic Research Conference* (pp. 184–188).

Rani, S., & Gupta, O. P. (2016). Empirical analysis and performance evaluation of various GPU implementations of protein BLAST. *International Journal of Computer Applications*, 151(7), 22–27.

Rani, S., & Gupta, O. P. (2017). CLUS_GPU-BLASTP: Accelerated protein sequence alignment using GPU-enabled cluster. *The Journal of Supercomputing*, 73, 4580–4595.

Rani, S., Mishra, A. K., Kataria, A., Mallik, S., & Qin, H. (2023). Machine learning-based optimal crop selection system in smart agriculture. *Scientific Reports*, 13(1), 15997.

Rani, S., Kumar, S., Kataria, A., & Min, H. (2023). SmartHealth: An intelligent framework to secure IoMT service applications using machine learning. *ICT Express*.

Riasetiawan, Mardhani, et al. (2023). GamaBox-One: A proposed architecture for cloud-based big data management platform for multipurpose computation using hybrid architecture.

Rossum, G. (1995) *Python reference manual*, CWI (Centre for Mathematics and Computer Science).

Sergeev, A., & Balso, M. Del. (2018) Horovod: Fast and easy distributed deep learning in TensorFlow," 2018.

Shamoto, H., Drozd, A., Shirahata, K., Sato, H., & Matsuoka, S. (2016). GPU accelerated large-scale distributed sorting coping with device memory capacity. *IEEE Transactions on Big Data*, 2, 57–69, 10.1109/TBDATA.2015.2511001.

Sharma, R., Bhambri, P., & Sohal, A.K. (2020). Energy bio-inspired for MANET. *International Journal of Recent Technology and Engineering*, 8(6), 5580–5585.

The hybrid multicore consortium, (July 2010). https://computing.ornl.gov/HMC/index.html.

Tanwar, R., Chhabra, Y., Rattan, P., & Rani, S. (2022, September). Blockchain in IoT networks for precision agriculture. In *International Conference on Innovative Computing and Communications: Proceedings of ICICC 2022, Volume 2* (pp. 137–147). Singapore: Springer Nature Singapore.

19 Image Sensing for Industry 4.0 Using Auto Resonance Networks
A Case Study

Shilpa Mayannavar and Uday Wali

19.1 INTRODUCTION

One of the key elements of a new industrial revolution, Industry 4.0 is Internet of Things. It poses many opportunities for optimization and improving performance. Currently, Artificial Intelligence and Machine Learning techniques are being used to enable significant advances to improve the image sensing, which is an essential part of Internet of Things [1,2]. Deep Learning (DL) systems have been very successful in solving complex problems like image recognition, robotic motion control and natural language processing. Some of the popular DL systems include Convolutional Neural Networks (CNNs) [3,4] for image recognition, Long Short-Term Memory [5] for robotic control and time series prediction, Generative Adversarial Networks [6] for image synthesis, etc.

DL systems are computationally intensive. Graphics Processing Units (GPUs) have shouldered most of this burden [7] till now. Several software tools and platforms like Caffe [8], Theano [9] and TensorFlow [10] have been developed around GPUs. However, several new platform specific hardware designs have been available to implement DL applications. Cambricon [11], IBM TrueNorth [12] and Google TPU [13] are some examples of such hardware accelerators for DL systems. Multi-layer Artificial Neural Networks (ANNs) are at the core of all DL systems. Complexity of DL systems arises from the large number of inputs and inter-dependency of system parameters, generally called as the curse of dimensionality [14]. ANNs implementing such DL systems, therefore, tend to be very sparse: A significant part of the computation may not contribute to final outcome of the DL system. Most of the neural networks do not clearly demarcate the neuronal paths or their dependencies in any particular recognition. So, pruning the networks becomes difficult. It should be possible to increase the overall performance of ANN by increasing the density of the network.

Neural networks in biological systems consist of various kinds of neurons, each performing a specific function. Role of specific neurons depends on various factors like their structure, position in the network, connectivity, dendrite density, length of

DOI: 10.1201/9781003395416-19

axon, neurotransmitters and inhibitors used, chemical receptors and gateways, type of input and output, timing response and a plethora of other factors. It is therefore important to explore various neural architectures to move toward realization of anything closer to Artificial General Intelligence. Further evolution in ANNs has to see several new types of neural architectures evolving, generalizing as well as specializing in the functionality of a neuronal type. The necessity of refining existing DL neural models is being reported in recent literature, e.g., capsule networks [15] and spiking networks [16].

Auto Resonance Networks (ARN) proposed by Aparanji et al. [17], for use in robotic path planning using graphs, has some interesting properties in this direction. Each node in ARN is analogous to a biological neuron capable of specific recognition function. ARN has two distinct learning mechanisms: (a) The nodes learn by tuning their resonance characteristics in response to variations in input and (b) layers of ARN learn by identifying spatial and temporal associations between neuronal outputs in lower layers or input data. Output of every node in ARN is limited to an adjustable but finite upper bound. This alleviates the stability problems typically seen in Hebbian-like associative learning systems. As the output is constrained to an upper bound, long strands of patterns may be identified by multi layer ARN. Both learning modes impart an ability to dynamically morph the solution space in response to variations in input. Further, activation paths established by the network corresponding to specific input-output relations can be traced and explained. Therefore, it is easy to find how and why ARN performed a particular task. This makes it easy to prioritize nodes and paths that significantly contribute to overall functioning of the network. In turn, this allows pruning of the network to increase computational efficiency of the recognition system. Temporal behavior of ARN and its application has also been discussed in [17]. However, no implementation details were presented. Use of ARN in other applications has not been well documented. In this chapter, we have reported implementation details of an image identification/classification system based on hierarchical ARN. One of the standard benchmarks used in image classification is the hand written character dataset in MNIST library [18,19], which has been used in this work. Implementation details, elaborations and results are presented in this chapter.

Section 19.2 of this chapter presents an overview of ARN and its adaptation for image identification/classification. Section 19.3 discusses implementation details. Results are presented in Section 19.4. Discussion on other applications that may benefit from hierarchical ARN are presented in Section 19.5.

19.2 AUTO RESONANCE NETWORK

Basic neuronal structure in ARN is different than that used in other ANN. Therefore, an overview of the model is made here. A typical biological neuron has several dendrites that receive inputs from sensor neurons or intra neurons in its vicinity. The strength of the dendrite connection presents a scaled version of its input to the neuron. These scaled inputs are added to generate an internal state of excitation. When the level of excitation exceeds a threshold, the neuron fires output. The output is related to the level of excitation but the physical transport mechanism puts an upper limit on the output. Therefore, the output is a saturating non linear function of the sum of scaled inputs. This also implies that there is a certain noise tolerance built into this neuronal excitation: Variations in inputs can still result in the same level of excitation. Connection strength of individual inputs to the neuron varies with repeated use, which forms the basis of constrained Hebbian learning. Level of excitation is indicated by the time through which the excited state is held.

19.2.1 CONSTRAINED HEBBIAN LEARNING

Hebbian rule states that the strength of a dendritic connection improves as a particular input is applied more frequently or reduces if not used. The rule is somewhat partial as it does not clearly state how the output of a neuron is limited to a saturation level or the length of time the neuron stays in excited state. Most of the current interpretations of Hebbian rule use it without any constraint on the strength of the connection. This leads to the classical weakness of Hebbian learning, i.e., continued use of a connection will scale the input so much that the node becomes unstable. In a biological system, this never happens as the physical limits on transport will limit the strength of connection and hence the Hebbian rule must be subjected to an upper limit. ARN implements such a constrained Hebbian learning mechanism that limits the output of a node to a threshold. Characteristics of ARN nodes are discussed in the following sections.

19.2.2 THE RESONATOR

Consider a simple resonator like

$$y = x * (k - x) \tag{19.1}$$

It has a resonance (peak) value of $y_m = k^2/4$ occurring at $x_m = k/2$. Both y_m and x_m are independent of x. Therefore, this peak value remains unaffected by translation, scaling or other monotonic transformations of x like sigmoid or hyperbolic tangent. It is possible to shift the point of resonance by translating the input to required value by translation or scaling.

For translation, $X \Leftarrow x - p$, peak occurs at

$$x_m = (k/2) + p \tag{19.2}$$

For scaled input, $X \Leftarrow xp$, peak occurs at

$$x_m = k/(2p) \tag{19.3}$$

In either case, peak value is bound by

$$y_m = k^2/4 \tag{19.4}$$

This is an important feature as the output is bound irrespective of how x is scaled by the strength of connection. Though k may be used for gain control, using fixed value per layer or network yields stable systems. We have used k = 1 giving a peak value of 1/4. Thus, output may be multiplied by 4 to yield a peak value of 1. It is also possible to use k = 2 for peak value of 1.

Several envelop function to transform input are discussed in [20]. One of these interesting input transformations is the sigmoid:

$$X = \frac{1}{1 + e^{-\rho(x-x_m)}} \tag{19.5}$$

where ρ, called the resonance control parameter, is a positive real number and x_m is the resonant input. For now, we will assume k = 1. Note that $(1 - X)$ has form similar to equation (19.5) and is given by

$$(1 - X) = \frac{1}{1 + e^{\rho(x-x_m)}} \tag{19.6}$$

Substituting (5) and (6) in (1), we get

$$y = X(1 - X) = \frac{1}{(1 + e^{-\rho(x-x_m)})} \frac{1}{(1 + e^{\rho(x-x_m)})} \tag{19.7}$$

The output of a resonator expressed by equation (19.7) attains a peak value of $y_m = 1/4$ at $X_m = 1/2$ as expected. Incidentally, equation (19.7) is also the derivative of equation (19.5) which has a well-known bell shaped curve.

Figure 19.1 shows some node outputs for k = 1. Figure 19.1(a) and Figure 19.1(b) show shifting resonance by input translation and input scaling given

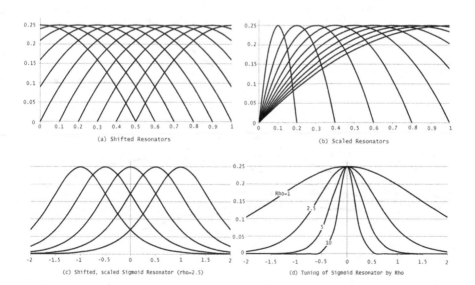

FIGURE 19.1   Resonating curves of ARN nodes (k = 1).

by equations (19.2) and (19.3), respectively. Figure 19.1(c) shows the output curves for sigmoid transform for different values of x_m. Resonance of each shifted sigmoid in Figure 19.1(c) can be altered by using resonance control parameter ρ, as shown in Figure 19.1(d). These equations allow constrained Hebbian learning to be incorporated into ANNs without the associated instability problems. It must be emphasized that our usage of the term constrained Hebbian learning is only a holistic description of the ARN's learning algorithm. Actual learning algorithm may be a variation of Hebbian learning, suitable for specific use case.

19.2.3 SELECTING THE RESONANCE PARAMETERS

The location of the peak and the maximum value for equation (19.1) are controlled by the only parameter k. In case the input is transformed, the effect of k on the resonance should be studied. For example, equation (19.5) transforms real input x to X. Corresponding ARN in equation (19.7) has a peak of 1/4 occurring at $X_m = k/2 = 1/2$ or equivalently $x = x_m$. In order to scale the peak to 1, we may use $k = 2$. However, X_m shifts to 1 and X does not cross 1 for any x. Therefore, the resonator can only implement left side of the resonance function. This suggests that choice of k must ensure that the reverse transformation $x = f^{-1}(X)$ will yield x on either side of $X_m = k/2$. Conversely, k should be selected such that x is distributed on either side of x_m. It is not necessary that the transformation is symmetric about X_m but must have values spread on either side. For example, Figure 19.2 shows the effect of transformation given in equation (19.5). As k shifts, X_m and x_m also shift.

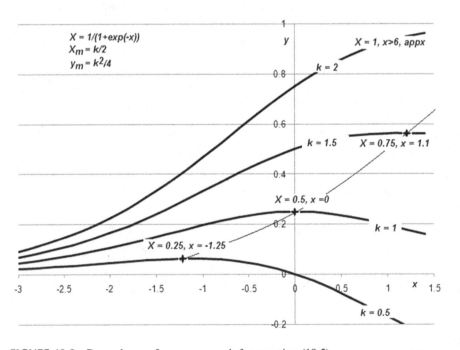

FIGURE 19.2 Dependence of resonance on k for equation (19.5).

There may be other parameters like ρ in equation (19.7) that are specific to the chosen transformation which also need to be checked for validity of the input range.

19.2.4 THRESHOLD, COVERAGE AND LABEL OF A NODE

A node is said to be triggered if the output is above a pre-selected threshold T. Several input points in the neighborhood of the peak will cause the node to be triggered. The set of input values to which the node is triggered is called the coverage of the node. As mentioned earlier, node learns by adjusting the coverage in response to the input. No two nodes will have same coverage. Coverage of two or more nodes may overlap only partially, which can cause several nodes to be triggered for some inputs. If only one node fires, network has identified the input and hence can classify it. If the input is covered by more than one node, one of the nodes may adjust its coverage to produce stronger output. If no node produces an output above threshold T, then a new node is created. Clearly, the number of nodes in ARN varies depending on the type of inputs, training sequence, resonance control parameter (ρ) and threshold (T).

The output of a node is a constrained real value, which may be input to the nodes in higher layers. Nodes may also be labeled with a class which reflects the type of primary input. Many nodes may be tagged with the same label. Therefore, a label may indicate an arbitrary collection of nodes. This allows input space to be continuous or disconnected, convex or concave, linear or non-linear, etc. This feature of ARN layers gives them an ability to learn from any input set.

19.2.5 THE AGGREGATOR

A node in ARN can have several inputs, each with its own resonator and a distinct coverage. Assuming that suitable transformation has been applied, output of the node with N inputs is given by, say

$$y = \frac{4}{Nk^2} \sum_{i=1}^{N} X_i\,(k - X_i) \qquad (19.8)$$

with a peak value of 1. The term $4/Nk^2$ is used to normalize the output to 1. If this output is above a threshold, the node gets triggered and therefore identifies the input.

19.2.6 CONSTRUCTING AN ARN

In a biological system, neurons develop during early childhood but the connections are made on learning. It is possible to start an ARN with randomized weights but a computationally efficient ARN may be implemented as a dynamic network which grows with variations in applied input: The connections are simultaneously the cause and effect of learning. As an illustration, consider Figure 19.3. On initialization, only inputs 1 and 2 are present, representing the axonal receptacles

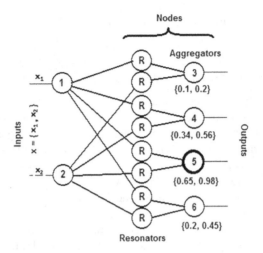

FIGURE 19.3 A layer of ARN structure.

from the primary sensor or outputs of other layers. The ARN layer is empty on initialization. Nodes get appended to the layer as the inputs are applied. For illustration, consider the first input {0.1, 0.2} applied to input nodes 1 and 2 shown in Figure 19.3. There will be no output from the network as there are no output nodes, implying no recognition. This causes node 3 to be created as first node in the layer. The second input {0.34, 0.56} is outside the coverage of node 3 and hence the network does not produce any output again. Another node, node 4 is created to resonate at this input and appended to the layer. The process continues on arrival of unmatched input. An input of {0.55, 0.86} is within the coverage of node 5 and hence, it fires. The winner node is highlighted with thicker lines. The two- and three-dimensional views of coverage of each output node are shown in Figure 19.4.

The rectangles in Figure 19.4(a) represent the coverage of each output node. There are four rectangles corresponding to four output nodes of ARN shown in Figure 19.3. Each node is tuned to one unique input and has its own coverage. For example, the rectangle in thicker line representing the node 5 has the coverage area bound by the range $0.5 < x_1 < 0.8$ and $0.79 < x_2 < 1.2$. The test input {0.55, 0.86} shown as black dot (see Figure 19.4(a)) is within the coverage area of node 5 and therefore it fires.

19.2.7 INPUT RANGE, COVERAGE AND TUNING

When a new node is created, default coverage is assigned to the node. Under certain transforms, coverage depends on point of resonance, as in Figure 19.4. In order to better control the learning in ARN, it is necessary to relate the statistical parameters of the input to the resonance control parameter and selection threshold of ARN nodes. It is possible to assume some reasonable values when a node is created but it would be more interesting if there is a basis for the estimate. Typical procedure to

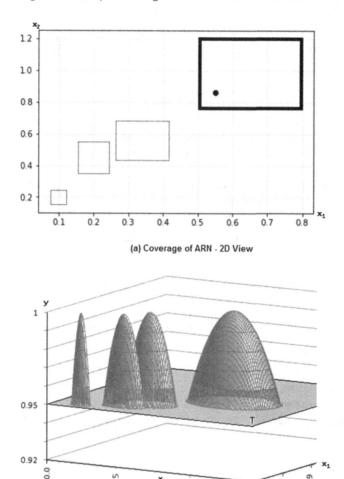

(a) Coverage of ARN - 2D View

(b) Coverage of ARN - 3D view

FIGURE 19.4 Coverage of sample ARN: (a) 2D view and (b) 3D view.

calculate initial coverage for a node is given below. The method may be suitably modified for other transformations.

One reasonably good threshold point is half power point, i.e.,

$$T = \text{half power point} = \sqrt{\frac{0.25^2}{2}} = 0.176 \qquad (19.9)$$

Assuming $k = 1$ and the output of a node to be equal to threshold (T), we can equate equation (1) to T and write

$$X(1 - X) = T = 0.176 \qquad (19.10)$$

Let us use scaled input model of Figure 19.1(b) as an example, i.e., X = xp. By solving for x we get two points x_c indicating bounds of coverage points:

$$x_c = \frac{1 \pm \sqrt{(1 - 4T)}}{2p} \tag{19.11}$$

Both x_c points are symmetrically placed around the resonant point, which is given by equation (19.3) to be $x_m = 1/(2p)$. This is also evident from Figure 19.1(b).

Similar evaluation can be done for sigmoid transform. From equation (19.7), assuming $x_m = 0$, we can write

$$0.176 = \frac{1}{(1 + e^{-px})} \frac{1}{(1 + e^{px})} \tag{19.12}$$

Simplifying, and substituting $(e^{px} + e^{-px})/2 = \cosh(px)$, we get

$$x_c = \frac{\pm\cosh^{-1}(1.8409)}{p} = \frac{\pm 1.2198}{p} \tag{19.13}$$

Therefore, as the value of p increases, coverage reduces and vice versa. The graph of p Vs. x_c is shown in Figure 19.5.

Input range between the two x_c is the coverage. Coverage for each of the inputs, i.e., x_1, x_2 needs to be computed. The coverage and resonance control

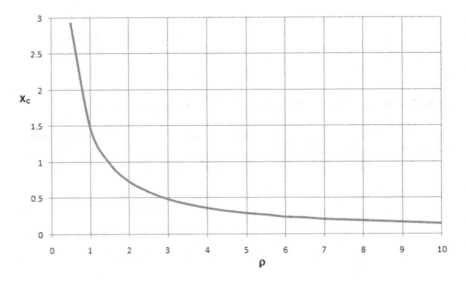

FIGURE 19.5 x_c as a function of resonance control parameter, p from equation (19.13).

parameter depend on the transform used. Reduced coverage indicates focused learning. It is also helpful in resolving ambiguities in learning: In case of multiple winners, one of the nodes can relax control parameters to increase the coverage and enhance the output.

19.2.8 DATA VARIANCE AND NODE COVERAGE (ρ)

As coverage is a data dependent parameter, we may try to relate it to the statistical distribution of values arriving at a node. Assuming that the incoming data has a Gaussian distribution, we can derive a relation between the statistical variance of the data and coverage of ARN node. The Gaussian distribution is given by equation (19.14).

$$y = \frac{1}{\sqrt{2\pi\sigma^2}}e^{\frac{-(x-x_m)^2}{2\sigma^2}} \tag{19.14}$$

Where, x_m indicates resonant input and σ^2 is variance. At $x = x_m$, we get the maximum value of y as

$$y_{peak} = \frac{1}{\sqrt{2\pi\sigma^2}} \tag{19.15}$$

Value of Gaussian distribution function at half power point can be written as

$$y_c = \sqrt{\frac{(y_{peak})^2}{2}} = \frac{1}{2\sqrt{\pi\sigma^2}} \tag{19.16}$$

Equating equations (19.14) and (19.16) and substituting $x_m = 0$, which is similar to the condition for equation (19.13), we get,

$$x_c = \pm 0.8325\sigma \tag{19.17}$$

In equation (19.17), x_c represents the range of inputs (coverage of a node) and σ represents standard deviation. From equations (19.13) and (19.17) we can get the relation between ρ and σ;

$$\rho = \frac{\pm 1.4652}{\sigma} \tag{19.18}$$

When the mean and standard deviation are known, we can compute the corresponding values of x_c and ρ. This in turn yields the coverage of the node. Graph in Figure 19.6 describes the coverage of node in range {0, 1} at $x_m = 0.5$.

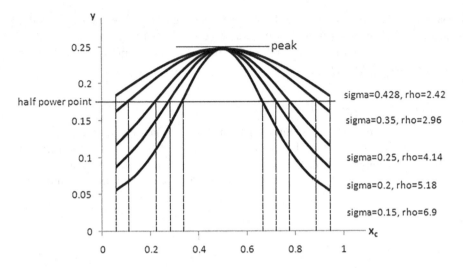

FIGURE 19.6 Tuning ARN nodes.

For other values of x_m the coverage in terms of standard deviation can be expressed as

$$x_c = x_m \pm \alpha\sigma \qquad (19.19)$$

where α indicates a scaling factor, similar to the constant in equation (19.17).

19.3 ARN-BASED IMAGE RECOGNITION

Image recognition and classification has become a routine task using CNNs. However, there is still room for improvement. Capsule networks suggested by Hinton et al. [15] incorporate a spatial relation among the features recognized by CNNs. Sensitivity of CNN to quantization has been explored in [21]. Computational complexity of CNNs is very large, requiring support of large servers with special purpose accelerators. High performance implementations suitable for mobile devices are also being explored [22]. This situation hints at the necessity to explore alternate architectures to address the image recognition and classification problems. In this section, we will demonstrate the capability of ARN for Image Recognition.

For a quick proof of concept implementation, the network is trained using public MNIST database of handwritten digits [18]. It has a collection of 60,000 training samples and 10,000 test samples. As ARNs are noise tolerant, small number of training samples is sufficient. Set of 50 randomly chosen samples of each digit, making a total of 500 samples were used for training. The performance of ARN was evaluated using 150 test samples, representing about 30% of training set size. An accuracy of about 93% was observed. Details of this implementation are presented below. Larger datasets were used after the algorithm was validated.

19.3.1 ARCHITECTURE

Essentially there are two layers of ARN marked as L1 and L2. L1 receives parts of image as input and converts them in a feature index. These recognized indices are temporarily stored in a spatially ordered list. This list is applied to L2, which will recognize the digit. Nodes in L2 are labeled with the class of image identified by the layer. During supervised training, the nodes are marked with specific class labels. For MNIST database, the labels are the values of digits, viz., zero to nine.

Tiling may be used to break the image into parts, to be input to L1, which recognizes them by identifying a matching part index. The sequence of recognized features represents a spatial relation between the features of input image. If the order of tiles is changed, the spatial relation between the features is altered and hence the output from the classifier may differ. For example the tiles may be numbered 1 to 16 from top left to bottom right. Presenting them to L2 in reverse order rotates the image by 180 degrees. Similarly, spatial reordered lists can be interpreted as mirror, shift, rotate, etc. These operators are not significant for digit recognition but may improve recognition in several other use cases. Effectively, reordering of the feature list can serve as an internal synthesizer. Layer L2 can be trained with these altered lists to improve recognition accuracy.

We have trained the network for different training sample sizes, viz., 50, 100, 200, 300, and 500. As the number of training samples increases, the accuracy of recognition also increases. Tunability of ARN nodes makes it possible to achieve an accuracy of up to 93% with very few training samples as 50×10. Both ρ and T have effect on learning, as shown in Figure 19.7 and Figure 19.8: for the given dataset, $\rho = 2.42$ and $T = 0.9$ gave better overall results. These observations are discussed later in Section 19.3.4.

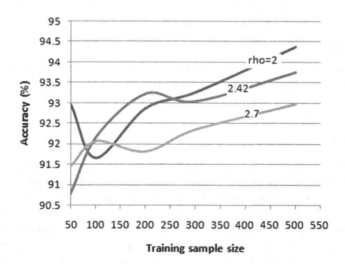

FIGURE 19.7 Training sample size vs recognition accuracy.

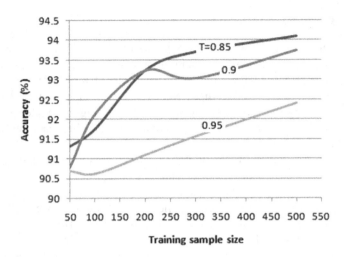

FIGURE 19.8   Effect of threshold T on learning.

19.3.2   EFFECT OF PERTURBATION

Perturbation refers to introduction of small changes to the system. In a network with large number of nodes, appending new nodes that are related but different from existing nodes is equivalent to a learning step. Perturbed nodes may require validation during later stages of learning but it provides an opportunity to respond well to an unknown input. Recognition accuracy of ARN can be improved by adding perturbed nodes to the network, albeit at the cost of increased computation. Perturbation can occur in input, output or network parameters. Perturbation may be random but limited to small variations such that the estimated response is not wrong but within a limited range of acceptability. In some cases, it may even be possible to use locally correct analytical equations to synthesize perturbed nodes. Adding a perturbation layer to ARN, will also reduce the number of images required to train the network. Some of the samples after rotating the image by small angles are shown in Figure 19.9.

Aparanji et al., in a paper on generation of path for robotic motion using ARN [23], have reported that results may be improved by perturbing output and system parameters.

19.3.3   EFFECT OF INPUT MASKING

The number of resonators can be reduced if we can use sparse connections instead of complete image tile. For MNIST images, it was reasonable to avoid resonators which were tuned to black pixels and keep only those with pixel values greater than some predefined limit. This could result in reduced number of resonators. As the bulk of computation happens in resonators, it could reduce the time to compute. However, experiments indicated significant loss of accuracy. Possible reason for this is that filtering the pixels reduces the information content and hence it takes longer for ARN to learn. This results in reduced accuracy. To further illustrate the effect, consider two

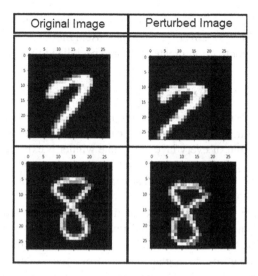

FIGURE 19.9   Example of perturbed images.

numbers 3 and 8. Presence of low value pixels on the left side is as critical to recognition of 3 as high valued pixels on the right side. Absence of the resonators identifying low value on left side of image will make it harder for ARN to distinguish 3 from 8.

19.3.4   EFFECT OF TUNING ON LEARNING

Learning in ARN varies depending on the value of ρ, T and training size. As mentioned earlier, increase in value of ρ, reduces the coverage and vice-versa. However, for $\rho < 2$ the resonance curve shown in Figure 19.6 is almost flat. It means that there would be very few nodes created and coverage of one node may overlap with another, leading to multiple recognitions. This scenario reflects early stages of learning when the image is identified but not properly classified. As more learning occurs, resonance gets sharper and more images will get identified. For $\rho > 3$, the resonance curve gets very narrow. Lower coverage means more failures during test. Therefore, the network starts adding large number of nodes with small coverage to attain a reasonable overall result. Recognition accuracy for these values of ρ will be smaller (~85%). Threshold also has a similar effect on learning. When the threshold is low, the coverage is large and hence most of the images are recognized but because of overlap of coverage, they will not be correctly identified. Increasing the threshold will reduce the coverage and increase the number of nodes in the ARN layers. Half power point is a reasonable threshold to start with (see Sections 19.2.6 and 19.2.7). For improved performance, the threshold has to be increased slowly. Very high threshold reduces the coverage and thereby increases the number of nodes. Threshold of around 0.9 (when peak is normalized to 1) yields good results.

As indicated in earlier sections, choice of resonance control parameter is data dependent and therefore needs experimentation with any given dataset. However, the results presented here give reasonable values for good learning (see Figure 19.7

and Figure 19.8). Learning within a node happens by improving the coverage. Both dilation and contraction of coverage have their use. Dilation of coverage generalizes recognition, while contraction creates a more specialized recognition.

19.3.5 AMBIGUITY RESOLUTION

There are three possible cases of recognition, viz., Correct recognition, Wrong recognition and Multiple recognition. The case of multiple recognition needs some attention. At the output of every layer, only one winner is expected. However, there will be cases when two or more nodes produce the same output at times because of learning and numerical inaccuracies. There are two possible approaches to resolve such ambiguities.

If the incoming input shifts the statistical mean toward the new input, resonance of such node may be shifted toward new input either by supervisory action of trainer or by reinforcement. This will reduce the distance between the peak and input, resulting in higher output from the node. Alternately, if the standard deviation of input is increasing, one of the nodes can relax the resonance control parameter to produce a slightly higher output. Relaxing the resonance will increase the coverage.

Resolving the ambiguity in recognition is best implemented as a wrapper around every layer. The wrapper provides local feedback and ensures that only one winner is presented at all times. Functionality of such wrapper is best implemented as a small function that suggests local corrective action. In the current implementation, it is completely supervised.

19.3.6 EXPLAINABLE PATHS IN ARN

In a multi layer ARN, each layer represents a level of abstraction. Each layer is independent and implements a partial recognition function. There is only one winner at every layer for any input (see Section 19.3.5). Output from a layer may be accumulated over several iterations over input space, reshaped and applied as input to next layer. Therefore, a relation between the sequentially firing neurons is input to the nodes in higher layer. This relation can be causal, temporal, spatial or a combination, depending on the function of the layer. The interface between two layers essentially records delays in the output from a lower layer and presents it as input to next layer(s). As the input to higher layers is a firing sequence, learning in ARN is similar to Hebbian learning that occurs in biological systems.

Further, output of a multi layer ARN can be traced across the layers up to the primary input layer, through a specific set of nodes and a temporal sequence. A node in every layer identifies a specific part of the whole recognition. An interface detects a relation. Therefore, every recognition event is caused by a specific path from primary input up to the output layer, with as many segments as the number of layers in ARN. This segmented path is unique to every recognition event. Therefore, input to the output can be easily interpreted in terms of partial recognitions at every layer. The path also provides a justification for the output.

19.4   RESULTS AND DISCUSSIONS

A network may be considered as robust if following conditions are met: (a) Output is range bound and does not drift, oscillate, overshoot or vanish and (b) Network recognizes the input in the presence of noise. ARN is inherently robust because (a) output of a node or layer is always range bound and (b) resonance characteristics give noise tolerance. It is possible to add any number of feed forward layers without affecting the network stability. Further, the path taken for any specific recognition is always uniquely identifiable. This leads to a better understanding of the network and helps in performance improvement.

Three possible cases of recognition are shown in Figure 19.10. The first two rows show the images with correct recognition. Though the matched images are fairly different from the input, ARN matches the image correctly, demonstrating the ability of ARN to select visually similar images. Images in third and fourth rows are different digits but the large part of the images is very similar, emphasizing the ability of ARN to perform visual comparison. Methods to resolve ambiguities in recognition are discussed in Section 19.3.5.

As discussed in earlier sections, the performance of ARN depends on ρ, T and sample size. It is noticed that, for a sample size of 50 per digit, the recognition is about 93% at $\rho = 2$, defined by half power point. Also at T = 0.85, accuracy of 91% is noted. As we increase the sample size, the recognition rate also increases. The learning curves of two-layer ARN for MNIST image recognition are shown in Figure 19.7 and Figure 19.8.

The confusion matrix for training sample size = 200 × 10, $\rho = 2.42$ and T = 0.9 is given in Figure 19.11 as an illustration. Notice that digit 1 has highest true positive and 3 has lowest true positive, indicating that a higher layer is required to resolve issues with recognition of digit 3.

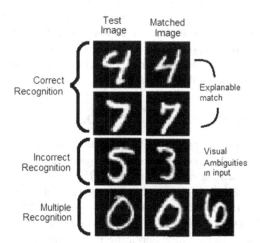

FIGURE 19.10   Capability of ARN to identify visually similar digits.

	0	1	2	3	4	5	6	7	8	9	Total
0	**41.75**	1.00	2.50	2.75	0.00	3.75	2.00	0.00	6.25	0.00	60
1	0.00	**59.00**	0.00	0.00	0.00	0.00	0.00	1.00	0.00	0.00	60
2	1.31	4.14	**35.97**	8.03	1.61	2.11	1.11	2.61	1.98	1.11	60
3	0.00	6.17	3.33	**25.83**	0.333	13.33	1.17	5.00	4.50	0.33	60
4	2.00	5.92	1.42	0.00	**37.58**	0.17	0.16	2.17	0.48	10.16	60
5	3.25	1.70	0.70	3.25	1.67	**37.95**	3.50	0.20	4.78	3.00	60
6	3.19	1.36	2.20	0.00	4.69	2.36	**44.30**	0.11	1.61	0.11	60
7	0.00	4.03	0.00	1.33	3.20	0.00	0.00	**40.03**	0.70	10.70	60
8	5.37	2.50	5.20	2.70	1.58	4.37	1.20	1.58	**32.41**	3.08	60
9	0.25	1.00	0.00	1.25	8.67	0.25	0.00	2.83	2.58	**43.16**	60

FIGURE 19.11 Confusion matrix for $\rho = 2.42$, T = 0.9, training sample size = 200 × 10 and test sample size = 60 × 10.

19.5 COMPARATIVE PERFORMANCE OF DIFFERENT NETWORKS ON MNIST IMAGE RECOGNITION

One of the main advantages of ARN based models is the small size of training dataset to achieve reasonable accuracies. In comparison, most of the existing Deep Neural Network (DNN) models require large dataset to achieve similar performance. Smaller dataset also reduces the size of network, which in turn reduces the computational time and resource requirements.

A comparison of several DNNs for image recognition with MNIST dataset is available in literature [19]. The paper lists accuracies of various DNNs for 25, 50, 75 and 100% of MNIST dataset of 60,000 images, corresponding to 15, 30, 45 and 60 thousand training images. As expected, the recognition accuracy increases as the size of training dataset increases. At 25% of full dataset, the reported accuracies for all DNNs reported in [19] are below 88%. All the tests reported in [19] used GPU support.

As mentioned in earlier sections, we have used a maximum of 5,000 samples (at 500 samples per digit), i.e., only 9% of MNIST images to achieve accuracies above 93%. All our computations were done on an entry level Pentium Xeon server with 4GB RAM and no GPU support. Therefore, the performance of the new structure exceeds that of others in terms of accuracy of recognition as well as the number of samples required to achieve that accuracy.

19.6 CONCLUSION AND FUTURE SCOPE

ARN looks like a promising solution to some problems in modern Artificial Intelligence. It has been used successfully in robotic path planning. This work shows its ability to perform visual comparison. The network is also being used for other biomedical applications that need image processing.

It is also possible to implement temporal relations into ARN. One such method is described in [17]. These networks can be useful for time series prediction and natural language processing. These applications are currently under development.

Fast parallel implementations of ARN with partitioned input space are possible. The problem of how features are shared among multiple partitions needs to be explored. It appears that intelligent selection of input dataset can yield better performance. Effect of adding feature neighborhoods in a multi-dimensional output of ARN needs to be explored.

Essentially, ARN is an approximating network. Therefore, use of low precision arithmetic for ARN is natural to its implementations. A 16-bit fixed point representation is being explored [24] for use in ARN. Use of low precision arithmetic in other structures like spiking neural networks [25] has also been reported in literature. Coverage of ARN node intrinsically supports quantization of input space and hence use of lower precision in number representation has little effect on accuracy but greatly reduces the computational time.

ACKNOWLEDGMENT

Part of this work was reported by the authors in a recent conference [26]. The authors would like to thank C-Quad Research, Desur IT Park, Belagavi, India, KLE Technological University, Hubballi India, NMIT Bengaluru, India and University of Sydney Australia for all the facilities and support provided.

REFERENCES

1. Thakur Ritica Manekar et al. "Artificial Intelligence-Based Image Classification Techniques for Hydrologic Applications," 36(1), Applied Artificial Intelligence, Taylor & Francis, 2022
2. Zixuan Zhang, et al. "Artificial Intelligence-Enabled Sensing Technologies in the 5G/ Internet of Things Era: From Virtual Reality/Augmented Reality to the Digital Twin," Wiley Online Library, March 2022.
3. Alex Krizhevsky, Ilya Sutskever and Geoffrey E Hinton. "ImageNet Classification with Deep Convolutional Neural networks," *Advances in Neural Information Processing Systems*, 25, 1097–1105, 2012.
4. Alexander Waibel, Toshiyuki Hanazawa, Geoffrey Hinton, Kiyohiro Shikane and Kevin J Lang. "Phoneme Recognition using Time-Delay Neural Networks," *IEEE Transactions on Acoustics, Speech and Signal Processing*, 37(3) 328–339, 1989.
5. Sepp Hochreiter and Jurgen Schmidhuber. "Long Short-Term Memory," *Neural Computation*, 9(8):1735–1780, 1997.
6. Ian J. Goodfellow, Jean Pouget-Abadie, Hendi Mirza, Bing Xu, et al. "Generative Adversarial Nets," arXiv:1406.2661v1 [stat.ML], 2014.
7. "NVidia GeForce 1080," White paper, NVidia https://international.download.nvidia. com/geforce-com/international/pdfs/GeForce_GTX_1080_Whitepaper_FINAL.pdf (Last accessed 25-05-2019), 2016.
8. Yangqing Jia, Evan Shelhammer, Jeff Donahue, Sergey Karayev, Jonathan Long, Ross Girshick, Sergio Guadarrama, Trevor Darrell, "Caffe, convolutional architecture for fast feature embedding," Cornell University archives, arXiv: 1408.5093v1 [cs.CV], 20 June 2014.
9. James Bergstra, Olivier Breuleux, Frederic Bastien, Pascal Lamblin, Razvan Pascanu, Guillaume Deshardians, Joseph Turian, David Warde-Farley and Yousha Bengio, "Theano: a CPU and GPU math compiler in Python," Proceedings of the 9th Python in Science Conference, SCIPY, 2010.
10. Martin Abadi, Ashish Agardwal, Paul Barham, Eugene Brevdo, Zhifeng Chen, Craig Citro, Greg S Corrado, Andy Davis, Jeffrey Dean, Matthieu Devin et al., "TensorFlow:

Large-Scale Machine Learning on Heterogeneous Distributed Systems," Preliminary White Paper, Nov. 2015.

11. Shaoli Liu, Zidong Du, Jinhua Tao, Dong Han, Tao Luo, Yuan Xie, et al. "Cambricon: An Instruction Set Architecture for neural networks," in ACM/IEEE 43rd Annual International Symposium on Computer Architecture, pp. 393–405, 2016.

12. Filipp Akopyan, Jun Sawada, Andrew Cassidy, Rodrigo Alvarez-Icaza, John Arthur, Paul Merolla et al. "TrueNorth: Design and tool flow of a 65mW 1 million neuron programmable neurosynaptic chip," *IEEE Transactions on Comp. Aided Design of Integrated Circuits and Systems*, 34(10), 1537–1557, 2015.

13. Norman P. Jouppi, Cliff Young, Nishant Patil, David Patterson, Gaurav Agarwal, Raminder Bajwa et al. "In-Datacenter performance analysis of a Tensor Processing Unit," in 44th International Symposium on Computer Architecture (ISCA), pp. 1–12, ACM, Toronto, ON, Canada, 2017.

14. R.B. Marimont and M.B. Shapiro, "Nearest Neighbour Searches and the Curse of Dimensionality," *IMA Journal of Applied Mathematics*, 24(1): 59–70, 1979.

15. Sara Sabour, Nicholas Frosst and Geoffrey E Hinton. "Dynamic Routing Between Capsules," in 31st conference on Neural Information Processing Systems (NIPS 2017), Long Beach, CA, USA, 2017.

16. Maxence Bouvier, Alexandre Valentian, Thomas Mesquida, Francois Rummens, Marina Reyboz, Elisa Vianello and Edith Beigne, "Spiking Neural Networks hardware implementations and challenges: A survey," *ACM Journal on Emerging Technologies in Computing Systems*, 15(2), April 2019.

17. V M Aparanji, Uday V Wali and R Aparna. "Pathnet: A Neuronal Model for Robotic Motion Planning," Proceedings of International Conference on Cognitive Computing and Information Processing, Bangalore, pp 386–394, Springer, 2017.

18. Yann LeCun, Corinna Cortes, Christopher J C Burges, "The MNIST Database of hand written digits," http://yann.lecun.com/exdb/mnist, 1998.

19. Feiyang Chen and Nan Chen, Hanyang Mao, Hanlin Hu, "Assessing Four Neural Networks on Handwritten Digit Recognition Dataset (MNIST)," arXiv:1811.08278v2 [cs.CV] 20 July 2018.

20. V M Aparnaji, Uday Wali, "Tunability of Auto Resonance Networks," in Proceedings of the International Conference on ISMAC in Computational Vision and Bio-Engineering (ISMAC-CVB) 2018.

21. Wu Jiaxiang, Cong Leng, Yuhang Wang, Qinghao Hu and Jian Cheng. "Quantized Convolutional Neural Networks for Mobile Devices," arXiv:1512.06473v3 [cs.CV], 2016.

22. Niu Wei, Ma, Xiaolong, Wang, Yetang and Ren, Bin. "26ms Inference Time for ResNet-50: Towards Real-Time Execution of all DNNs on Smartphone," arXiv:1905.00571vl [cs.LG], 2019.

23. V. M. Aparanji, Uday V Wali and R Aparna. "Robotic Motion Control Using Machine Learning Techniques," International Conference on Communications and Signal Processing, Melmarvattur, India, pp. 1241–1245, IEEE April 6-8 2017.

24. Shilpa Mayannavar and Uday Wali, "Hardware Accelerators for Neural Processing," *International Journal of Computer Information Systems and Industrial Management Applications (IJCISIM)*, ISSN 2150-7988, 11, 046–054, May 2019.

25. Mike Davies, Narayan Srinivasa, Tsung-Han Lin, Gautham Chinya, Yonqiang Cao, Sri Harsha Choday, et al., "Loihi, A Neuromorphic ManyCore Processor with on-chip learning," *IEEE Micro*, 38(1), 82–99, 2018.

26. Shilpa Mayannavar and Uday Wali. "A Noise Tolerant Auto Resonance Network for Image Recognition," in 4th International Conference on Information, Communication and Computing Technology, New Delhi, pp. 156–166, Springer, Singapore, May 11 2019.

Index

Printed in the United States
by Baker & Taylor Publisher Services